Several other places chapters – Seville, Córdoba, Ronda and the Costa del Sol – were updated by **Norman Renouf**, who spends part of his time in the USA and the rest in the hinterland of the Costa Tropical south of Granada. As well as writing on Spain for Insight, Renouf has written Insight Pocket guides to Washington D.C. and Helsinki.

Tourism in the western area of Southern Spain has changed considerably in recent years. Direct flights to Jerez de la Frontera, fabulous Atlantic beaches, the dramatic *pueblos blancos* of Cádiz province, and a glut of new bijou hotels are attracting visitors looking for a quieter experience than that offered by the Costa del Sol. To reflect such developments **Michelle Taylor**, the winner of Insight's 2005 Travel Writing Competition, run in conjunction with *Red* magazine, went off to Cádiz and Huelva to write brand-new chapters on the provinces. Lastly, Málaga-based **Josephine Quintero** updated the Travel Tips.

Contributors to the first edition of this book, whose work is still evident in this edition, include **David Baird**, **Thomas Hinde**, **Alastair Boyd**, **Jane Mendel**, **Nigel Bowden**, **Vicky Hayward** and **Philip Sweeney**.

Most of the photographs in this edition are the work of Insight regulars **Gregory Wrona**, **Jerry Dennis** and **Mark Read**.

Neil Titman proofread the guide, and the index was compiled by **Penny Phenix**.

The contributors

This new edition of *Insight Guide: Southern Spain*, based on an earlier version by **Andrew Eames**, has been reshaped by Insight editor **Dorothy Stannard**, who has travelled extensively in the region as well as neighbouring Morocco, with which Andalucía shares so much of its past.

Stannard enlisted the skills of several writers and updaters with homes in Andalucía. Chief among them is **Nicholas Inman**, a travel writer and editor who divides his time between France and Spain. As well as revising and expanding the chapters on Granada, the Alpujarras, Almería and Jaén, Inman contributed a new feature on the Andalusians, a new places chapter on Antequera and La Axarquia, and new boxes on hiking and Almería's booming agriculture.

CONTACTING THE EDITORS

We would appreciate it if readers would alert us to errors or outdated information by writing to:

Insight Guides, P.O. Box 7910, London SE1 1WE, England.
Fax: (44) 20 7403-0290.
insight@apaguide.co.uk

www.insightguides.com
In North America:
www.insighttravelguides.com

Contents

Map Legend

	Autopista with Juction
	Autopista (under construction)
	Dual Carriageway
	Main Road
	Secondary Road
	Minor road
	Track
	Footpath
	International Boundary
	Regional Boundary
	Province Boundary
	National Park/Reserve
	Ferry Route
✈✈	Airport
✝✝	Church (ruins)
✝	Monastery
	Castle (ruins)
⁂	Archaeological Site
∩	Cave
★	Place of Interest
⌂	Mansion/Stately Home
※	Viewpoint
	Beach
	Autopista
	Dual Carriageway
	Main Roads
	Minor Roads
	Footpath
	Railway
	Pedestrian Area
	Important Building
	Park
❶	Numbered Sight
	Bus Station
❶	Tourist Information
✉	Post Office
	Cathedral/Church
☪	Mosque
✡	Synagogue
⚑	Statue/Monument

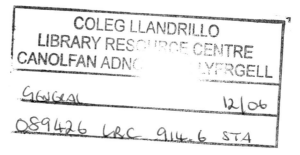

SOUTHERN SPAIN
COSTA DEL SOL ✦ ANDALUCIA

Discovery
CHANNEL

APA PUBLICATIONS
Part of the Langenscheidt Publishing Group

✶ INSIGHT GUIDE

SOUTHERN SPAIN

Editor
Dorothy Stannard
Art Director
Klaus Geisler
Picture Editor
Hilary Genin
Production
Kenneth Chan
Cartography Editor
Zoë Goodwin
Editorial Director
Brian Bell

Distribution

UK & Ireland
GeoCenter International Ltd
The Viables Centre, Harrow Way
Basingstoke, Hants RG22 4BJ
Fax: (44) 1256-817988

United States
Langenscheidt Publishers, Inc.
36–36 33rd Street 4th Floor
Long Island City, New York 11106
Fax: (1) 718 784-0640

Australia
Universal Publishers
1 Waterloo Road
Macquarie Park, NSW 2113
Fax: (61) 2 9888 9074

New Zealand
Hema Maps New Zealand Ltd (HNZ)
Unit D, 24 Ra ORA Drive
East Tamaki, Auckland
Fax: (64) 9 273 6479

Worldwide
**Apa Publications GmbH & Co.
Verlag KG (Singapore branch)**
38 Joo Koon Road, Singapore 628990
Tel: (65) 6865-1600. Fax: (65) 6861-6438

Printing

Insight Print Services (Pte) Ltd
38 Joo Koon Road, Singapore 628990
Tel: (65) 6865-1600. Fax: (65) 6861-6438

©2006 Apa Publications GmbH & Co.
Verlag KG (Singapore branch)
All Rights Reserved

First Edition 1990
Fourth Edition 2006

ABOUT THIS BOOK

The first Insight Guide pioneered the use of creative full-colour photography in guidebooks in 1970. Since then, we have expanded our range to cater for our readers' need not only for reliable information about their chosen destination but also for a real understanding of that destination. Now, when the internet can supply inexhaustible (but not always reliable) facts, our books marry text and pictures to provide that much more elusive quality: knowledge. To achieve this, they rely heavily on the authority of locally based writers and photographers.

How to use this book

The book is structured to convey an understanding of Andalucía:

◆ To understand the region today, you need to know something of its past. The first section covers its people, history and culture in lively essays written by specialists.

◆ The Places section provides a full run-down of all the attractions worth seeing. The main places of interest are coordinated by number with full-colour maps.

◆ Photographic features illuminate aspects of the region's festivals, art and gardens.

◆ Photographs are chosen not only to illustrate landscapes and buildings but also to convey the moods of Andalucía and the life of its people.

◆ The Travel Tips listings section provides a point of reference for information on travel, hotels, shops and festivals. Information may be located quickly by using the index printed on the back cover flap – and the flaps are designed to serve as bookmarks.

THE BEST OF ANDALUCÍA

Setting priorities, saving money, unique attractions…
here, at a glance, are our recommendations, plus some
tips and tricks even Andalusians won't always know

ANDALUCIA FOR FAMILIES

These attractions are popular with children,
though not all will suit every age group.

Spain is ultra-child
friendly and even
boisterous toddlers
can be taken any-
where that grown-ups
go at any time of day
or night without rais-
ing an eyebrow.
● **Waterparks**. Open
May/June to Septem-
ber, they can be found
at Mijas, Granada,
Torremolinos, Cór-
doba, Seville, Puerto
de Santa María
(Cádiz), Torre del
Mar, Almuñécar, Car-
taya (Huelva) and at
Vera (Almería) *(see
page 265).*

● **Theme parks**.
Visit Seville's Isla
Mágica *(see page 86)*
and Tivoli World *(see
page 141)* on the
Costa del Sol.
● **Zoos and Aquariums**.
Three of the best are
on the Costa del Sol:
Selwo Aventura at Es-
tepona *(see page145)*
and Selwo Marina and
Sea Life, both in
Benalmádena *(see
page 141).*
● **Cable cars**. Take the
Teleférico at
Benalmádena. *See
page 141.*
● **Shows**. The Real
Escuela Andaluza del
Arte Ecuestre at Jerez
is famous for its danc-
ing horses *(see page
105)*. Mini-Hollywood
(see page 218) in
Almería exploits a
wild west theme.
● **Fun and educational**.
For hands-on learning
visit the Parque de las
Ciencias (Science
Park) in Granada
(see page 195).

BEST BUILDINGS

● **The Alhambra**,
Granada.
See page 187.
● **The Mosque**, Cór-
doba. See page 160.
● **Reales Alcázares**,
the Cathedral and the
Maestranza bullring,
Seville. S*ee pages
72–8 and 80.*
● **Arab baths** in Ronda
(see page 131), Jaén
(see page 179) and

Granada *(see page
186).*
● **Castles** of Málaga
(see page 138) and
Almeria *(see page
217).*
● **Menga and Romeral
dolmens, Antequera**
(see page 152).
● **Ruins** of Itálica
(see page 87) and
Medina Azahara
(see page 167).

Left: larger than life in the
Isla Mágica, Seville.
ABOVE RIGHT: inside La
Mezquita.

THE BEST PLACES FOR ART

- **Seville's Museo de Bellas Artes**
Housed in a 17th-century convent with a magnificent baroque chapel, Seville's Fine Arts Museum is well worth visiting. The collection, second in national importance after the Prado, includes works by El Greco, Goya, Murillo, Zurbarán and Velázquez (*see page 83*).

- **Seville's Hospital de la Caridad**
The chapel of this 17th-century charity hospital is known for the outstanding artworks in its chapel, including the ghoulish works by Valdés Leal depicting the transitory nature of life (*see page 79 and photograph right*).

- **Museo Picasso, Málaga**
Picasso was born in Málaga. This collection of 155 paintings, drawings, sculptures and ceramics spans his career (*see page 137*).

- **Julio Romero de Torres Museum, Córdoba**
This artist specialised in paintings of sultry Andalusian women (*see page 166*). Next door is Córdoba's Museo de Bellas Artes (*see page 165*).

Also see the photo feature on Andalucía's artists, page 92–3.

ABOVE: *In Ictu Oculi* (In the Blink of an Eye), by Valdés Leal, in Seville's Hospital de la Caridad.
BELOW LEFT: the tiled rooftops of Zahara de la Sierra.

PICTURESQUE PUEBLOS

- **Arcos de la Frontera**
See page 121.
- **Benahavís**
See page 144.
- **Capileira**
See page 208.
- **Casares**
See page 118.
- **Cómpeta, Comares, Frigiliana, Salares.**
See pages 155–56.
- **Grazalema**
see page 123.
- **Guadix**
See page 196.
- **Montefrio**
See page 196.
- **Ohanes**
See page 211.
- **Priego de Córdoba**
See page 170.
- **Ronda**
See page 127.
- **Salobreña**
See page 198.
- **Zahara de la Sierra**
See page 123.
- **Zuheros**
See page 170.

BEST BEACHES

- **Costa de la Luz**
In Cádiz, the best are Caños de Meca (Barbate), Bolonia, Zahara de los Atunes and Cabo de la Plata. In Huelva, head for Punta Umbría, La Casita Azul (El Hoyo), El Asperillo, Torre del Oro, El Alcor.

- **Costa del Sol**
There are still a few nice beaches between the resorts: Costa Natura (Estepona), Lindavista (San Pedro de Alcántara), Tajo de la Soga (Benalmádena), Almayate-Bajamar (near Torre del Mar); Cala del Cañuelo, Cala del Pino, Las Alberquillas and Molino de Papel (all near Nerja).

- **Costa Tropical**
Try Ensenada de los Berengueles (Marina del Este, La Herradura), Cabria (Almuñécar), La Rijana (near Calahonda).

- **Almería**
Recommendations include Cala de En Medio (near las Negras), Cala del Bergantín (Rodalquilar), Cala de las Hermanicas and La Negrita (near San José), Los Genoveses, Cala Chica Cala del Barronal and Monsul.

GREATEST GOLF COURSES

Andalucía has more than 60 golf courses, most of them 18-hole. Half of them are on or near the Costa del Sol, the so called "Costa del Golf".

The list below picks out some of the choicest courses. For more recommendations, *see page 260.*

● **Desert Springs**
Cuevas de Almanzora, Almería. This is Europe's first "desert golf course", a splash of green on Almería's east coast.

● **Granada Club de Golf**.
Has lovely views of the Sierra Nevada.

● **Dunas de Doñana**
Matalascañas, Huelva. Between the beach and the Doñana National Park.

● **Montecastillo**
Jerez de la Frontera (Cádiz). Designed by Jack Nicklaus and used for the Volvo Masters and other championships.

● **Club de Campo de Córdoba**
A demanding course of dog-legs and slopes in the hills north of Córdoba.

● **La Quinta**
Located near Puerto Banús.

● **Guadalmina**
San Pedro de Alcantara. Made up of two parts, north and south, the latter being only for experts because of its thick vegetation.

● **Los Naranjos**
A demanding course of dog-legs and slopes in the hills north of Marbella.

● **Antequera Golf**
Set at an altitude of 650 metres (over 2,000 ft) and surrounded by mountains. The fairways are separated by 200-year-old olive trees and numerous lakes act as both obstacles and reservoirs.

A TASTE OF SPAIN

● **Fish and seafood**
Order fish fried or *a la plancha* – cooked on a griddle and therefore much less oily. Málaga *(see page 139)* has some of the best fish restaurants in the region, as does El Puerto de Santa Maria near Jerez on the Costa de la Luz *(see page 107).*

● **Sherry**
The world famous fortified wines are made in Jerez de la Frontera *(see page 107).* The less well known Montilla-Moriles *denominación de origen (see page 169)* makes similar, equally good wines but without fortifying them with grape spirit.

● **Gazpacho**
This tasty cold soup of pulped tomatoes and garlic, is served all over Andalucía, but some regions have their own versions, such as *salmorejo* in Córdoba and *porra* in Antequera. Another good cold soup is *ajo blanco*, made with garlic and almonds

● **Olives and Olive oil**
These are the specialities of Jaén province *(see page 176).* Be sure to try the traditional Andalusian breakfast of toast dribbled with olive oil rather than spread with butter.

● *Jamón serrano*
Dry-cured ham needs clean mountain air for its preparation and the best in Andalucía comes from Trevélez in the Alpujarras *(see page 208)* and Jabugo in the Sierra de Aracena *(see page 102).*

● **Tropical fruits**
Grown on the coast of Granada *(see page 198).* Depending on the season, they include avocados, mangoes and *chirimoyas* (custard apples).

ABOVE: carving *jamón serrano*, cured mountain ham. **LEFT:** a familiar sign in Jerez de la Frontera, the home of sherry.

FAVOURITE FIESTAS

● **Carnival**, Cádiz (Feb/March). This is mainland Spain's biggest carnival celebration where the local speciality is the singing of humorous songs.

● **Easter Week** (Semana Santa). Celebrated everywhere but at its most sensual in Seville; *pasos* (religious sculptures) are pushed or carried through the streets during some 50 processions.

● **April fair**, Seville (second or third week after Easter). This is virtually a semi-private party with lots of flamenco dancing, groomed horses and sherry. Córdoba, Granada and Almería have smaller summer fairs, which are more accessible to visitors.

● **Romería de la Virgen de la Cabeza,** northern Jaén (last Sun in April). The biggest of Andalucía's many *romerías* – mass pilgrimages to country shines.

● **Festival de los Patios**, Córdoba (May). Many of the pretty patios that are normally concealed behind wrought iron gates are opened to the public for a week.

● **Fería del Caballo**, Jerez (May). A horse fair with equestrian competitions, decorated carriages, sherry in abundance and flamenco dancing.

● **El Rocío** (Whitsun: May/June). A colourful and exuberant mass pilgrimage to the town of El Rocío on the edge of Doñana National Park.

● **Virgen del Carmen**, (16 July). On this day Andalucía's various coastal communities parade a statue of the patroness of sailors on a flower-decked boat in order to bless the local waters for the coming year.

ABOVE: young party-goers at the annual *romería* in El Rocío, Huelva province.

For more information about Andalucía's numerous festivals, see page 257 of Travel Tips and the photo feature on pages 44–45.

MONEY-SAVING TIPS

Menú del día and tapas The cheapest eating option is always the set meal *(menú del día)*, which the majority of restaurants – even expensive ones – offer on weekday lunchtimes and sometimes in the evenings and at weekends. It can be a good idea to eat well at lunchtime and have a lighter meal or snacks in the evening, but note that even if tapas seem cheap individually, the cost of a succession of them soon adds up. In Granada and Almería, however, tapas are still served free with drinks, and the more wine or beer you consume, the more elaborate they get.

Rural hotels City hotels are considerably more expensive than their country counterparts and it may pay to commute to the sights. Spain has a glut of idyllic rural hotels that offer very cheap rates outside peak seasons. Always ask about special offers for stays of more than one night.

Shopping Street markets are the cheapest places to shop for food, clothes and everyday items. On the Costa del Sol there are numerous car boot sales where you may pick up unusual bargains. In the countryside, look out for roadside farms selling fruits and other produce direct.

Local transport Walking is the best and cheapest way to get around Andalucía's city centres but if you are going to use buses, get a *bonobus* from an *estanco* (tobacconist) which will give you 10 journeys costing up to 50 per cent less than the price of individual tickets. In Seville a *Tarjeta Turística* gives you 1 to 3 days unlimited use of public transport.

Bono Turístico Granada For concentrated sightseeing in Granada it may be worth buying a *bono turístico* (tourist pass) which gives a 30 percent reduction on admission prices to sights, including the Alhambra, and free use of buses.

EU passport holders receive free admission to some sights and museums, so they should keep their passport to hand (though it isn't always necessary to show it). Senior citizens are usually required to show proof of their age in order to receive concessionary rates.

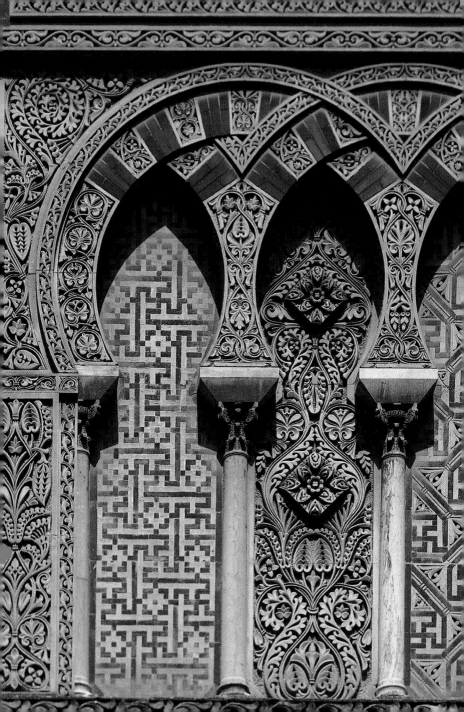

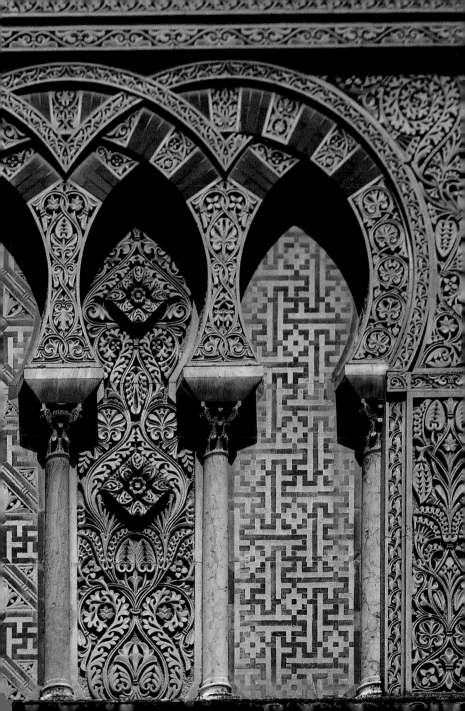

THE SOUL OF SPAIN

**Andalucía is the source of many Spanish clichés,
from sherry, flamenco and *machismo* to cheap
and cheerful package-holiday resorts.
But this vast region has a wealth of less
obvious attractions to entice visitors**

Andalucía is the largest region in Spain, covering around 17 percent of its total area. As such it is scenically diverse and culturally rich, offering a vast array of attractions for visitors. For many package holidaymakers, it is synonymous with the Costa del Sol, the ultimate Spanish *costa*, a 180-km (110-mile) long chain of marinas, golf clubs and white urbanisations. For cultural visitors, however, the highlights of the region are the cities of Seville, Córdoba and Granada, with their glorious Moorish monuments – the Giralda, Mezquita and Alhambra – and the *pueblos blancos* (white towns), the perched villages of the sierras. For lovers of wild, open spaces, Andalucía offers some of the highest mountains in Europe, crossed by hiking trails (and ski slopes near Granada), and the watery marshes of the Parque Nacional de Doñana, a haven for migrating birds.

Moorish domination for more than 700 years left a permanent imprint on the region and its people. The year Granada fell, 1492, heralded a new era for Spain. Christopher Columbus's historic voyage across the Atlantic turned Seville into a flourishing city, enriched by the wealth of the New World, though this did not filter through the surrounding region.

Centuries of stagnation followed, and the poverty and lack of opportunity forced large numbers of Andalusians (*Andaluces* in Spanish) to emigrate. Many helped populate the Americas, while in the 1950s and 1960s thousands went to work in the factories of northern Spain and other European countries. On the edge of Europe, between the Third World and the First, Andalucía continued to drift in a cultural and economic limbo. Change was slow, at first confined to the Costa del Sol, where the package-holiday industry was taking off. But, following Generalísimo Franco's death, the advent of democratic government and membership of the European Union, Andalucía was booming – a trend stimulated by the colossal spending on infrastructure that preceded Expo '92 in Seville.

Away from the raucous Costa and the cities, life is also changing in the mountain *pueblos* and the agricultural hinterland. Today, Andalucía is a prosperous region. These pages are a testament to its evolution, recalling the past, portraying the present and predicting the future. ❏

PRECEDING PAGES: La Mezquita, Córdoba; the white town of Alcalá de los Gazules.
LEFT: flamenco school, Granada.

EARLY DAYS

Andalucía was conquered by most of the warlike peoples of the Mediterranean over the centuries, but time and again the Andalusians won a more subtle victory over their invaders by influencing their lifestyle and culture

The south of Spain was originally settled by the Iberians, a Mediterranean race of uncertain origin. However, the first inhabitants for whom there is firm historical evidence were the Tartessians of the Bronze Age in the 2nd millennium BC.

The lost city of Tartessos has never been found. Nevertheless, quite by accident in 1957, Mata Carriazo, a professor of archaeology at the University of Seville, picked up a bronze of a fertility goddess in a Seville junk shop and identified it as being of Tartessian origin. This was followed by the discovery of a sculpture, the "Mask of Tharsis", by a mining company near Huelva; and in 1961, during construction work in the hills across the river from Seville, a workman's pick struck a metallic object, the first in a hoard of Tartessian plates, bracelets and necklaces, which came to be known as the Carambolo Treasure.

During recent years archaeologists have unearthed thousands of other artefacts, testifying to a knowledge of mining, industry and agriculture in Andalucía at a very early date, bearing out the Greeks' description of Tartessos as a veritable eldorado.

Trading places

The Tartessians ventured far afield, fishing along the Atlantic coast and around the

Canaries. Their sailors are reliably said to have sailed the "tin route" to Galicia and possibly as far as Cornwall. It was largely because of the abundance of tuna and the availability of tin, used in making bronze, and of other metals from the mines of Huelva that the Tartessians' trading partners and allies, the Phoenicians, established a factory at Gadir around 1100 BC.

There was peaceful competition from the Phocaean Greeks, who founded a trading post at Mainake near Málaga, and Tartessos was at its most prosperous in the 6th century BC. But it suffered an abrupt change of fortune after the battle of Alalia around 535 BC, and from

LEFT: 8th-century BC statuette of the Phoenician goddess Astarte, found among a hoard of ancient artefacts at El Carambolo near Seville in 1961.
RIGHT: a Tartessian mask.

then on Carthage, founded as a North African colony of Tyre, had a free hand in Spain and supplanted the Phoenicians. The Kingdom of Tartessos disintegrated, and in the 3rd century BC, in spite of defeat by Rome during the First Punic War, Carthaginian forces unified most of greater Andalucía and proceeded up the Valencian coast.

The Romans watched events in Spain with growing anxiety. The Carthaginian general Hannibal's attack on the city of Saguntum, which was under Roman protection, led to the outbreak of the Second Punic War (218–201 BC), in which Hannibal famously crossed the Alps on elephants and invaded Italy itself. Slowly the Romans fought back. A new Roman commander, Publius Cornelius Scipio, was sent to Spain in 209 BC. He seized the Carthaginian base of Carthago Nova (Cartagena) by a surprise attack, and by 201 BC had driven out the last of the Carthaginians.

Roman rule

The Roman occupation of Spain was to last for some seven centuries, during which agriculture was reorganised, bridges, roads and aqueducts were built, and the Roman legal system was introduced. The country was divided into three provinces, of which the most southerly, Baetica, corresponded roughly to present-day Andalucía. Hispania, and especially Baetica with its flourishing agriculture and mineral resources, was to become one of the Empire's richest provinces.

Roman cities the length and breadth of the Empire were built to a pattern, and many of those in Andalucía preserve the remains of temples, forums, aqueducts, bridges and theatres. Bridges survive at Córdoba (Roman name Corduba) and Espejo (Ucubi); aqueducts at Seville (Hispalis) and Almuñécar (Sexi); theatres at Málaga (Malaca) and Casas de la Reina (Regina); an amphitheatre at Écija (Astigi); a temple and baths at Santiponce (Itálica); while at Bolonia in Cádiz province the ruins of Baelo include a fortified precinct, streets lined with columns, and the remains of a forum, temples, an amphitheatre and houses.

The Visigoths

With the decline of the Roman Empire the first "barbarians" entered Spain via the Pyrenees in AD 407–9, but left little mark on the south. They were shortly followed by the Visigoths, a Germanic people, theoretically auxiliaries of the tottering Roman Empire until the Visigothic king, Euric, broke with Rome in 468. The Visigoths passed quickly down through the peninsula, meeting little resistance in the south. The Hispano-Roman nobility, dependent on a slave society, quickly came to terms with the new rulers. After the conversion of Visigothic King Reccared to Christianity in 568, the Church played a central role in unifying the country.

However, the lack of a law of succession resulted in instability. Of the 33 Visigothic kings who ruled Hispania from 414 to 711, three were deposed, 11 assassinated and only 19 died a natural death.

The Muslims march in

In 711 Tariq ibn-Ziyad, Governor of Tangier, an outpost of the Damascus Caliphate, crossed the Straits of Gibraltar with some 7,000 men at his side and established himself

COSTLY CONVERSIONS

The levying of tribute from converts to Islam was not permissible, so had there been conversions to Islam on a large scale the invaders would have suffered severe loss of income.

ly turned tail. Roderick was either killed or took flight, never to reappear.

The advance into Spain was the tip of an Arab thrust along the North African coast. It had begun in 642 with the annexation of Egypt by the second of the Umayyad caliphs of Damascus, and was to be halted only in France at the battle of Tours in 732. During

on the flanks of Mount Calpe (subsequently known as Gibraltar, from the Arabic Jebel Tarik, "the mountain of Tariq"). King Roderick, the last Visigothic king, massed a large army and launched a frontal attack on the Muslims, now reinforced and in a strong position near the present-day city of Algeciras. The king fought bravely, but the flanks of his army, commanded by renegades, treacherous-

LEFT: the Carthaginian general Hannibal crossing the Alps with elephants in 218 BC, in an epic instalment of the Second Punic War between Carthage and Rome.
ABOVE: annihilation of the Visigoths by the Arabs under Tariq ibn-Ziyad in AD 711.

the 30 years after the first incursion, Muslim governors of al-Andalus followed thick and fast, pressing northwards until al-Andalus, as the Muslim-occupied part of Spain was known, covered virtually all of modern Spain and Portugal.

The invaders were, however, split into different factions, the Qaysites and Kalbites of pure Arabian descent, and the North African Berbers, on whom Tariq and his successors largely relied in the conquest of the country. Al-Andalus was eventually united by the establishment of the Umayyad dynasty of Córdoba, which was to control its destiny for some 300 years.

The new regime

It has been argued that the Muslim invasion of Spain was a jihad (holy war). In truth, the victorious Muslims did not display much enthusiasm for converting the indigenous Christians and Jews, let alone putting them to death for refusing. But in granting a large degree of religious freedom, the invaders were not as disinterested as might appear at first sight. Some were desert nomads with no bent for cultivating the lands they had seized, men who preferred to move on to fresh conquests and quick booty. Others settled in the cities, leaving agriculture to the original owners. Providing that they were People of the Book (i.e. Christians or Jews and not polytheists), the conquered people enjoyed local autonomy and freedom to pursue their own religion, subject to the payment of taxes.

In all probability, no more than 40,000 Arabs crossed into Spain with the invading armies. As time went on they married the local women, and as a result the later Umayyads were more Spanish than Arab. However, the lustre of their royal origin survived, and they remained fiercely proud of their Arab descent. This was to prove a two-edged sword, since in the eyes of both Christians and Berbers they remained a foreign dynasty.

A PALACE FIT FOR A CALIPH

The construction in 936 of Abd-al-Rahman III's Madinat al-Zahra (now known as Medina Azahara), near Córdoba, was a massive project. According to Henri Terrasse in *Islam d'Espagne*, it involved "10,000 to 12,000 workmen; 15,000 mules and 4,000 camels... each day called for 6,000 items of dressed stone and 11,000 loads of lime and sand, without counting bricks and gravel".

The centrepiece of the great pillared reception hall was a pool of quicksilver, reflecting a quivering light over the whole interior and giving an exhilarating overall impression of constant movement.

Glorious era

Al-Andalus reached its zenith under Abd-al-Rahman III (912–61). On his accession he found it in a disturbed and rebellious state, but he worked quickly to pacify the kingdom and secure its border. He settled accounts with dissidents within al-Andalus and then directed equally forceful operations against the Christians of the Marches to the north. In 929 he took the important step of declaring himself Caliph, thus asserting his rights as sovereign. As a symbol of his new status, in 936 he embarked upon the Medina Azahara, a magnificent palace 8 km (5 miles) west of Córdoba. It lay on three levels, with a mosque below, gardens in the middle and the palace above. Unfortunately it was destroyed by Berbers just 70 years after its completion.

The overflowing wealth of al-Andalus was rooted in agriculture and the exploitation of mineral resources, rather than on foreign trade. The most important crops, as in Roman times, were cereals, beans, peas, olives and vines, though many new crops, herbs and fruits were introduced, notably bitter oranges and lemons, almonds, saffron, nutmeg and black pepper. The Arabs also planted semi-tropical crops that depended on efficient irrigation, and greatly extended irrigation systems instituted by the Romans. Gold, silver, copper, mercury, lead and iron had also been worked by the Romans, but the mines had fallen into disuse during the Visigothic period. They were reopened by the Moors, who also mined cinnabar (a source of mercury) at Almadén near Córdoba.

For all its brilliance, the Caliphate suffered from an infrastructure that was to lead to disintegration and downfall. The sharp division of social classes into the monied and influential and an amorphous proletariat subject to the least whim of the Caliph and his deputies resulted in a passivity and lack of initiative amongst the mass of the population – a state of affairs that the Arabs had themselves exploited when overrunning the earlier Visigothic kingdom. As went went on, the inhabitants of al-Andalus, enjoying ever-increasing prosperity, preferred a life of peace and plenty, and paid mercenaries to fight the belligerent Christians of the north.

Christian resurgence

By the end of the Caliphate in 1013, al-Andalus had disintegrated into some 30 small principalities governed by so-called *reyes de taifas* or "party kings". In the east the Slavs (mercenaries from northern Europe) and the eunuchs of the palace guard carved out kingdoms for themselves in Valencia and the Balearics; Granada and Málaga were taken over by Berbers; while in the western heartland of Seville and Córdoba, Muslims of both Arab and Spanish descent held sway.

LEFT AND RIGHT: life in Moorish Spain. The Moors were industrious agriculturalists, but also lovers of poetry and song.

DRINKING LAW

Wine was openly drunk even by the emirs and caliphs, though in deference to the Koranic prohibition of the consumption of alcohol it was made and sold by Christians.

Meanwhile, the Christians of the north, inspired by a new religious zeal, began making inroads into al-Andalus under leaders such as Fernando I of León-Castile, his son Alfonso VI of León-Castile and, scourge of the Moors, the freebooting El Cid. The most brilliant soldier of his generation, El Cid, having quarrelled with his liege lord Alfonso VI, began

SUPREME VICTORY

Perhaps the greatest conquest of the Muslims was the great expedition of 997 undertaken by the general and statesman al-Mansur (938–1002), which, striking at the heart of Christian Spain, destroyed Santiago de Compostela. The city and its cathedral were razed to the ground, with only the tomb of St James left intact (at the express command of al-Mansur). The army marched back to Córdoba with an enormous booty, including the bells and doors of the cathedral, carried by Christian captives and used to embellish the Great Mosque. Later, when Córdoba fell to the Christians, the bells were carried back to Santiago, this time by Moorish prisoners.

his private campaign against the Moors, culminating in the capture of Valencia in 1094. In a sudden reversal of roles as the Reconquest got under way, it was increasingly the Muslims who became tributaries of the Christian kings. Impoverished as they were, these kings were, to begin with, only too pleased to accept this arrangement. The adjustment seems to have been made without much difficulty, since Muslims and Christians had been used to living side by side and pursuing their different religions.

Of all the *taífas*, the Abbasid Kingdom of Seville most nearly approached the fallen Caliphate in the extent of its territories and the splendours of its court. Its founder, al-Mutadid (1042–69), extended his realm as far as southern Portugal. Ruthless, cruel and sensual, he planted flowers in the skulls of his decapitated enemies, using them to decorate the palace gardens, and had his first son put to death on suspicion of plotting against him.

He was succeeded by the gifted and intellectual al-Mutamid, under whom 11th-century Seville saw a remarkable flowering of culture. But the initial idyll was not to last. Al-Mutamid might be as a lion to the rulers of the other *taífas*, but was no match for Alfonso VI of León-Castile. Alfonso captured Toledo in 1085, declared himself Emperor of Spain and issued a peremptory demand for the surrender of Córdoba. The writing was on the wall, and after much heart-searching al-Mutamid took the momentous step of summoning aid from the fanatical Yusuf ibn-Tashufin, the leader of the Almoravids in North Africa.

The Almoravids fight back

The Almoravids, a warlike and puritanical sect devoted to a return to the original purity of the Koran, had swept across half of North Africa. Their leader, Ibn-Tashufin, already 70 years old, dressed in wool, partook only of barley bread, milk and the flesh of the camel, and viewed with repugnance the wine-imbibing, the music and culture of al-Andalus.

Caught unawares by the landing of the Almoravids in June 1086, Alfonso marched to meet the invading army, which was swelled by the forces of al-Mutamid and other party kings, at Sagrajas near Badajoz. Here, for the first time, the Christians faced the tactic of compact and well-ordered bodies of infantry, supported by lines of Turkish archers and manoeuvring as a unit to the command of thunderous rolls from the massed tambours of the Moors.

Used, as they were, to single combat, where personal valour counted above all, the Christians broke and fell into confusion. Only 500 horsemen, most of them wounded, survived, among them Alfonso.

The battle of Sagrajas set back the cause of Reconquest in al-Andalus for some 60 years, but the rulers of the *taífas*, soon to be expelled from their kingdoms, were equal losers. All al-Mutamid's misgivings about Ibn-Tashufin were justified. In September 1091, after heroic

RODERICS DEVIVAR

RULE OF IRON

Under the zealous and puritanical regime of the Almoravids, Seville was shorn of its former glories. The common people initially welcomed their new rulers, but quickly found that they had exchanged the flamboyant liberalism of the Arabo-Andalusian aristocrats of the *taífas* for the uncompromising rules of Muslim theologians, the fanatical *faqihs*. It was now the Christian kingdoms of the north that tolerated a symbiosis of religions and cultures; and although the Christians and Jews suffered most under the Almoravids, Muslim poets, philosophers and scientists also soon experienced the full force of a religious Inquisition.

resistance and a desperate plea for help to the erstwhile enemy Alfonso VI, Seville was overrun by the Almoravids. Al-Mutamid and his queen were exiled to Aghmat in the Atlas Mountains, where he lived in penury until the end of his life.

In spite of a publicly proclaimed austerity, even the Almoravids fell victims to the easy lifestyle of al-Andalus. A new Christian champion had meanwhile arisen in the shape of Alfonso El Batallador ("The Fighter") of Aragón, who in 1125 struck deep into the south, reaching the Mediterranean near Málaga.

By now the power of the Almoravids was spent. Once more al-Andalus seemed ripe for

tion of *reyes de taífas*, who had filled the vacuum left by the downfall of the Almoravids, trimmed their sails to the wind and swore allegiance to the new Almohad Caliph, one of whose achievements was the building of the Great Mosque of Seville.

The Reconquest

Al-Andalus, extended by the conquest of most of present-day Portugal, remained firmly in Almohad hands for the rest of the century. In 1195 at Alarcos the Christians suffered one of their worst defeats in the history of the Reconquest. Undaunted, Alfonso VIII, the lion-hearted King of Castile,

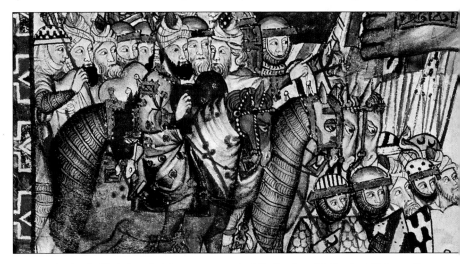

reoccupation by the Christians, but they were to be thwarted for another century.

The Almoravid Empire in North Africa was overturned in 1145 by that of the Almohads, also religious in inspiration but with a broader interpretation of Islam and bitterly opposed to the narrow doctrines of the Almoravids. In 1171 Abu-Yaqub Yusuf embarked on the systematic subjugation of al-Andalus. The rulers of a second genera-

LEFT: El Cid, campaigner against the Moors.
ABOVE: Alfonso X (the Wise) referred to the conflicts between Muslims and the Christians in his famous work of poetry, *Cantigas de Santa Maria.*

worked tirelessly with the Archbishop of Toledo to cement a grand alliance, and his efforts were recognised by Pope Innocent III, who in 1211 declared a crusade against the Moors. By May of that year Alfonso VIII had assembled a huge army, swelled by some 60,000 crusaders from beyond the Pyrenees, and in July he faced the Moors at Las Navas de Tolosa in the Sierra Morena.

It was a fiercely fought battle. According to one account, the Caliph had a premonition of disaster and his negro guard was hemmed around him with iron chains. At the end of the day the Moors were routed, the plucky Archbishop Arnold of Narbonne who took part

FLAMES OF INTOLERANCE

Two thousand heretics were burned in Seville in the year 1481. The Jews were suspect both because of their religion and their wealth, which provoked jealousy.

putting their dead at 60,000, against the loss of 40,000 Christians.

During the 13th century, Moorish resistance in al-Andalus crumbled under the hammer blows of James the Conqueror of Aragón, of Fernando III of Castile and of his son Alfonso X (The Wise). Baeza and Ubeda in the east were taken in 1233, Córdoba in 1236, Jaén in

1245 and Seville in 1248.

The lands retaken from the Moors were made over to the knights and barons who had fought beside the kings. Many land grants were small or medium-sized, but vast tracts of land were also ceded to families such as the Guzmáns, forebears of the dukes of Medina Sidonia. Initially, the new Christian rulers reverted to the tolerant policies of the earlier Moorish regimes, Muslims and Jews remaining free to practise their religions, subject to a capitation tax. Mudéjars (Muslims living in the reconquered Christian areas, as distinct from *Moriscos,* Christian converts from Islam) formed most of the agricultural work-

ers, and estates were taken over by their new Christian owners without changing the pattern of country life.

Granada, the last bastion

By the time the Catholic Monarchs, Isabel and Fernando, became joint rulers of Spain in 1479, the sole remaining Moorish enclave was the Kingdom of Granada, which also comprised Málaga and Ronda. At its peak it extended only 180 km (112 miles) from east to west and 80 km (50 miles) from the sea to its inland border. Towards the end of Moorish rule, as many as 100,000 people crowded into this small area.

That Granada lasted so long was because Ibn-al-Ahmar, the founder of its Nasrid dynasty, had become a vassal of Fernando III of Castile and had assisted in the capture of Seville in 1248. Ibn-al-Ahmar further helped Fernando's successor, Alfonso X, to overthrow the remaining emirates in the south.

Thereafter the Nasrids cleverly played off their North African allies against the Castilians and, by keeping a low profile and by the payment of tribute, staved off a frontal attack. Ibn-al-Ahmar nevertheless took the precaution of constructing a chain of watchtowers along the mountainous borders of his kingdom. Remains of these defences can still be seen in the village of Alhama de Granada on a small road between Granada and Málaga (C340).

The Inquisition

The fall of Granada in 1492 cannot be explained simply by internal weaknesses or by the feud between its leaders leaving it prey to the advancing Christians. By the beginning of the 14th century, signs of religious and racial conflict began to appear, which grew increasingly bitter during the reign of the Catholic Monarchs.

The Christians in the reoccupied territories were aware of the abilities of the Mudéjars as workmen and artisans, and of the Jews as administrators, doctors and merchants. From this, it was a short step to postulate that such employment was unworthy of a Christian, and any attempt by the Jew or Mudéjar to better his status was fiercely resented.

Once the doctrine of *limpieza de sangre* (purity of blood) had been declared, it became a disgrace for any convert to Christianity to be remotely tainted by Jewish blood. Only those who could claim purity of blood were admitted to positions of public authority.

Starting with the setting up of the Inquisition and the first *auto de fe* – the pronouncement of sentence on heretics and their burning at the stake – in Seville in 1481, the Catholic Monarchs issued a decree in March 1492, giving Jews a choice between baptism or expulsion, and allowing unbaptised Jews four months to liquidate their property and possessions.

When it became apparent that the Jews were emigrating en masse, even the harsh conditions of the decree were dishonoured and many of the *emigrados* were stripped of their possessions and forced to leave the country destitute. The *Moriscos* were soon to suffer the same fate as the Jews. Spain was thus deprived of the services of its best doctors, administrators and financiers, large numbers of skilled *Morisco* artisans and a sizeable part of its agrarian labour force.

By 1482 the Catholic Monarchs began to make plans for the overthrow of Granada, and another crusade was declared by the Pope.

Meanwhile, a family feud had broken out in Granada. The Amir, Abu'l-Hasan, returned from a military expedition to find that the Alhambra's garrison had declared in favour of his son, Muhammad Abu-Abd-Allah, known as Boabdil. Abu'l-Hasan was forced to take refuge with his brother, al-Zaghal, the only member of his family still loyal.

The campaign against Granada began disastrously for the Christians. So confident were they of success that their army was accompanied by a train of merchants anxious to profit in the anticipated spoils. In the event, the invading force was routed in March 1483, and the merchants spent their gold in buying their own freedom.

Unlucky king

Boabdil's reign began as disastrously as it was to end – not for nothing was he named "the Unlucky" by his subjects. Overreaching himself in an attack on the Christians, he was taken captive and released by King Fernando on condition that he acknowledged vassalage to Castile and took the part of the Christians against his father and his uncle, al-Zaghal.

During the next 10 years, Fernando's forces moved in on Granada. Málaga fell after an epic resistance in 1487, and Fernando decided to make an example of it. The town's citizens were deported en masse to other parts of Spain and those unable to pay crippling ransoms were sold into slavery. Boabdil had been living under the delusion that he would be left in possession of Granada, but after the final defeat of al-Zaghal was bidden to deliver up the city. This caused an immediate public outcry, and Boabdil belatedly decided to fight.

In 1491 a Christian army of 40,000 foot-

soldiers and 10,000 cavalry invaded the lush *vega* below the city. They were beaten off by the Moorish general Musa ibn-Abu'l-Ghazan, and Fernando then decided to sit it out and set up a huge tented encampment outside the city. It was only a matter of time before the besieged town was starved into submission. After prolonged negotiations the capitulation was signed on 25 November 1491. So, in a minor key, almost 800 years of Moorish rule in the Peninsula came to an end. Boabdil had surrendered the last outpost without a fight to the end, and the bitter reproach of his mother, Aisha, rings down the centuries: "Weep like a woman for what you could not defend like a man." ❑

LEFT: the Moors are driven back to Africa.
RIGHT: the Moors admit defeat.

THE MAKING OF MODERN ANDALUCÍA

Columbus's discovery of the Americas transformed Seville into a glittering centre of world trade. But reversals of fortune followed, and the road to modern prosperity in Andalucía was marked by poverty, hunger and war

In January 1492, with the surrender of Granada signed and the Christian army about to enter the city, Christopher Columbus, a lonely and Quixotic-looking figure on a mule, rode into the encampment of Santa Fe. It had been six years since he had first petitioned Queen Isabel for support in his project of reaching the Indies by sailing to the west. The project had been ridiculed and rejected by a commission of inquiry; Columbus was in despair and staying at the monastery of La Rábida near Huelva before sailing for France.

While there, he discussed his hopes with one of the friars, Juan Pérez, who had previously served as the Queen's confessor. Pérez wrote to Isabel; as a result, Columbus was recalled to court, and seven months later his three ships set forth on their epic voyage of discovery.

Andalucía was thus associated from the outset with the discovery of the New World. The three ships were crewed with sailors from Palos, Moguer and Huelva; many of the conquistadors and most of the first colonists were from Andalucía or neighbouring Extremadura. By 1503 Seville was playing such a central role in trade with America that Queen Isabel established a Casa de Contratación in the city to regulate all trade with the New World.

Gateway to a new world

Seville (and from 1717 Cádiz) thus acquired a virtual monopoly of the trade with America.

LEFT: Seville prospered during the 16th century, thanks to the New World riches introduced by Christopher Columbus (**RIGHT**).

The ships of the time were limited in range, and depended on the trade winds and a staging post in the Canaries to make the voyage at all; the Andalusian ports were therefore much better-placed than those of the north or the Mediterranean.

Another compelling reason for routing ships through Seville or Cádiz was to organise convoys. To begin with, ships sailed singly or in groups unguarded; but as buccaneers and pirates began preying on the treasure ships off the Spanish mainland, fleets were assembled at Seville, Cádiz or Sanlúcar de Barrameda, and sailed under the protection of heavily armed galleons.

The practice survived until the mid-18th century, when even eight or 10 galleons could no longer protect the fleets against the depredations of the British Navy. The attacks on Spanish shipping by Sir John Hawkins and Sir Francis Drake during the 1570s and 1580s contributed to Felipe II of Spain's decision to embark on the ill-fated invasion of England with his massive Armada.

Rivers of gold

During the early years of trade with the Americas, "rivers of gold" poured into Seville, and there was lavish spending on public works, palatial houses and churches. Perhaps the most grandiose project was the construction in the late 16th and early 17th centuries of the Lonja de Mercaderes, or Exchange, now the Archivo de Indias, which was financed with just one-quarter of one percent of the silver arriving from the Americas.

Another source of wealth was the export to the colonies of olive oil and wine; in return, Andalucía received new plants and foodstuffs, such as maize, tobacco, peppers and chocolate.

That said, historians believe Seville failed to take advantage of the enormous opportunities afforded by its near trading monopoly during the early period. This has been put down to its lack of industry, except on a small artisan

GIBRALTAR: THE ROCK AND A HARD PLACE

The issue of Gibraltar has soured relationships between Spain and Britain for three centuries. The dispute dates from the War of the Spanish Succession (1701–13), when Carlos II of Spain died without an heir, and the choice of a successor lay between Archduke Charles of Austria and Philip of Anjou. After Philip was crowned with the support of Louis XIV, war broke out between Spain and France on the one side and Austria on the other, supported by Britain, Holland and Portugal.

In 1704 the allies decided to open a new front by seizing Gibraltar. The Spanish garrison was hopelessly outnumbered and outgunned by an Anglo-Dutch fleet, and after a siege of only three days the governor surrendered. Gibraltar was ceded to Britain in 1713 as part of the Treaty of Utrecht, by which the war was brought to an end. The Spanish were soon to question Britain's right to its possession. During 1779–83 Gibraltar underwent one of the most famous sieges in history, when it was beset both by sea and land by the armies and fleets of Spain and France. It was, however, well prepared, with storage galleries cut into the rock and the latest types of artillery capable of raking the attackers at low angle.

The argument over Gibraltar rumbles on, with Spaniards resenting the presence of a foreign enclave on Spanish soil.

scale, such as the manufacture of textiles and tiles. The textile industry could not compete with that of northern Europe, and most of the textiles exported to the Americas through Seville were not made in Spain but came from England and the Low Countries.

By the time of Felipe IV (1621–65), inflation was rampant, not least because of a decision of Count Duke of Olivares to squander American silver and human resources on a fruitless war in Flanders. By this time the Atlantic trade had declined considerably, and Andalucía's most valuable export was its own people.

Emigration from Andalucía and neighbouring Extremadura was 40 percent from 1493 to

1600. The result is a prevalence of Andalusian customs in South America and the close resemblance of Latin American Spanish to that of Andalucía.

The Napoleonic Wars

European history through much of the 18th and beginning of the 19th century was dominated by the British–French struggle for supremacy, and Spain allied itself according to its best interests. Disastrously, it allied itself with France at the battle of Trafalgar, fought

ABOVE: *The* Victory *being towed into Gibraltar with the body of Nelson* by Clarkson Stanfield.

off the Cádiz coast in 1805 and resulting in a masterful British victory, albeit at the cost of Nelson's life. But Napoleon's attempts to occupy the whole of Spain and Portugal in the 1807–14 Peninsular War saw the British and Spanish for once on the same side. The French assault on Andalucía began in January 1810 after a series of Spanish defeats. Marshal Soult and Joseph Bonaparte, with 40,000 men, were faced by 23,000 Spanish along a front of 240 km (150 miles).

Córdoba fell without a fight on 24 January. The junta which had been ruling the country from Seville decamped for Cádiz on the 23rd, followed by the military commander, the Duke of Albuquerque, with his troops. The city fell into the hands of an excited mob; nothing was done to destroy the arsenals, the largest in Spain; and vast quantities of munitions, as well as tobacco to the value of £1 million, were lost to the invaders when they took over on 29 January.

Soult lost no time in despatching General Victor to take Cádiz, but he arrived too late to intercept Albuquerque's 12,000 troops, who had entered the city two days before, blowing up the bridge over the channel between the mainland and the Isla de León on which Cádiz is built.

Despite a French blockade lasting for years, Cádiz was under no serious threat thanks to the presence of gunboats in its harbour and larger units of the Spanish and British navies further out. In the hour of their peril the Spanish forgot earlier fears about the landing of British troops, and in February 1810, 3,500 men under General William Stewart landed to reinforce the garrison. Meanwhile, the rest of Andalucía lay open to the ravages of Marshal Soult, a connoisseur of paintings, and of General Sebastiani, a plunderer of churches.

Sweeping as the French victory had been, their hold on Andalucía was tenuous and confined to the larger towns and cities. The French were never safe from the activities of the guerrillas, which tied down huge numbers of troops.

Fernando VII's repudiation of the liberal constitution of Cádiz was far from being the end of the matter. A first fruit of his autocratic policies was the revolt and loss of the American colonies between 1810 and 1824; and the

HUNGRY FOR WORK

During the terrible depression of the post-war years, hundreds of thousands of Andalusians emigrated to factory jobs in France and Germany.

struggles between liberals and absolutists rumbled on through the 19th century. The Liberal-inspired disentailments of 1836 and 1855 stripped the Church of much of its land and property (resulting in the further loss of artworks). In 1873 a Liberal government proclaimed Spain a republic, though it lasted only 11 months before the monarchy was restored by the army.

Spanish military. The Spanish king was forced into calling municipal elections, which were won overwhelmingly by proponents of a Spanish republic. Taking the hint, the chagrined king headed for exile, and Spain's Second Republic was born.

It was a short-lived exercise, as confrontation between left- and right-wing supporters gathered steam. In 1936, the Spanish army posted in Morocco rose up against the government, under their commander General Francisco Franco. The word was sent out to military commanders all over Spain, many of whom joined the revolt. Andalucía was split in two. The sanguine Queipo de Llano seized control

The road to Europe

Spain entered the 20th century minus most of its remaining overseas possessions, lost in the Spanish-American War of 1898. Alfonso XIII, at the head of a shaky constitutional monarchy, was king of a country plagued by increasing civil unrest. In 1923, the Jerez-born General Miguel Primo de Rivera seized power, although the king retained the throne. Primo de Rivera was a more or less benign dictator who counted on considerable popular support, but he was an incurable optimist and hopeless at economics. He drove Spain to the brink of bankruptcy, and was ultimately deposed by more constitutionally correct

of Seville, and Granada fell shortly afterwards, leading to reprisals in which thousands of Republican supporters were executed, including the Granada-born poet Federico García Lorca. Málaga was captured in 1937 after bombardment from navy ships and the arrival of Italian troops seasoned by the wars in Abyssinia. The support of Italy and Nazi Germany, and Franco's superior firepower, were decisive in the insurgents' final victory in 1939.

Franco, who was ruthless and incorruptible in equal measure, was to decide the destiny of Spain for the next three-and-a-half decades. Although officially neutral, Spain was sympathetic to the Axis during Word War II, and afterwards Spain was an outcast from the community of nations. Franco's government preached an extreme form of isolationism, hoping against hope to rely on the country's own resources. The devastation of war was followed by a prolonged drought which led to the "Years of Hunger". Andalucía was especially hard hit. Things were to change in 1953 when Spain agreed to cooperate with US efforts in the Cold War, and allowed four American bases to be built, including an enormous naval base at Rota, near Cádiz.

Fuelled by a fresh inflow of cash, Spain edged its way into the 20th century. Franco still held the country in his iron grip, but a

Hotels sprouted along the Andalusian coast, farmers abandoned their land to become waiters. More importantly, Spaniards came into contact with foreign ways and ideas, and they were perfectly prepared when Franco died in 1975 and the newly proclaimed King Juan Carlos led Spain into democracy. The first democratic elections were held only two years after Franco's death, and Spain was welcomed back into Europe, joining the European Community (now the European Union) in 1986.

From 1982–96, the country was governed by the nominally socialist PSOE party, headed by the charismatic (and corrupt) Felipe González. Before world recession enforced a

number of the more repressive rules were relaxed, and Spaniards began to enjoy a measure of middle-class comfort.

The first tourists

But the true revolution was triggered by the arrival of curious foreign visitors. The first were artists and writers seeking an inexpensive life in the sun. Next came the hippies. Finally, the first planeload of package holidaymakers landed at Málaga airport in the late 1960s, and there was no stopping the flood.

LEFT: 1960s sun-worshippers in Marbella.
ABOVE: Expo '92 celebrating Sevile's rebirth.

spell of belt-tightening, the government was profligate with public spending, and Spain lived through a boom period. Andalucía was a main beneficiary of new roads and cash, much of it European funds.

The whole world was invited to a party to witness the Andalusian miracle: Expo '92 in Seville, when Spain celebrated the 500th anniversary of Columbus's voyage to the New World. Since this time, the property boom, particularly in Málaga province, has rocketed. Work on the Córdoba–Málaga leg of the high-speed AVE rail track is due for completion in 2007. This will reduce the train journey from Málaga to Madrid to just over two hours. ❏

Decisive Dates

800,000 BC Earliest evidence of human habitation on the Iberian Peninsula dates from this time.

30,000 BC Last of the Neanderthals live in Gibraltar.

2500–2000 BC Megalithic civilisation flourishes in southern Iberia.

1100 BC Phoenician traders settle in Cádiz.

800–550 BC The Tartessos civilisation thrives near Huelva and Cádiz, then vanishes.

237–228 BC Carthaginians expand their territory in southern Iberia.

218–201 BC Romans occupy Iberia after defeating Carthaginians in Second Punic War; in 206 BC city of Itálica is founded near Seville.

61–60 BC Julius Caesar is governor of present-day Andalucía.

55 BC Seneca the Elder is born in Córdoba.

45 BC Julius Caesar defeats army led by Pompey's sons at the battle of Munda, near present-day Osuna, ending the Roman civil war.

99 AD Itálica-born Trajan becomes Emperor of Rome.

407–415 Germanic tribes, including the Vandals, occupy Spain; Visigoths take over most of the Peninsula at the behest of the crumbling Roman Empire.

568 Visigoths convert from Arianism to Catholicism.

711 Tariq ibn-Ziyad, a Berber commander, lands at Gibraltar and launches the Islamic conquest of the Iberian Peninsula.

720 Christians defeat Muslims at Covadonga in northernmost Spain, initiating the "Reconquest" of Iberia, which was to take 772 years.

756 Abd al-Rahman I establishes an independent Emirate in Córdoba, ruling most of the Iberian Peninsula.

785 Construction begins on Córdoba Mosque.

929 Abd al-Rahman III proclaims the Caliphate of Córdoba. Al-Andalus reaches its zenith.

1010–13 The city-palace of Medinat al-Zahra is destroyed by rebellious Berbers; the Caliphate of Córdoba breaks up into petty kingdoms.

1086 Almoravids from North Africa reunite Islamic Spain.

1126 Birth of the Moorish philosopher Averroes in Córdoba.

1135 Maimonides, the Jewish philosopher, is born in Córdoba.

1147 Almohads invade Spain from North Africa.

1211 Christian armies cross Despeñaperros Pass into Andalucía and defeat Moors at Las Navas de Tolosa.

1236 Córdoba conquered by Fernando III.

1238 Castle built on site of the Alhambra.

1248 Fernando III conquers Seville.

1340 Islamic forces are defeated at the battle of Río Salado near Seville, ending all efforts of invasion from northern Africa.

1348 Black Death sweeps through Spain.

1364 King Pedro the Cruel orders construction of royal palace within Seville's Alcázar.

1391 Widespread pogroms against Jews.

1401 Construction begins on Seville's Cathedral.

1474 Isabel becomes Queen of Castile.

1481 Inquisition instituted in Spain.

1485 Columbus arrives in Spain.

1492 Fernando and Isabel conquer Granada, last Moorish kingdom in Spain; Columbus sails from Palos de la Frontera (Huelva) in search of the Indies; Jews who refuse to convert to Christianity are expelled.

1502 Last Muslims living in Spain ordered to convert to Christianity or leave; all save a few hundred convert; they are known as *Moriscos*.

1519 Magellan sets sail from Sanlúcar de Barrameda to circumnavigate the world.

1559 First cultivation of tobacco in Spain.

1568 The *Moriscos*, converted Moors, revolt against Castilian overlords in the Alpujarra Mountains south of Granada.

1587 Sir Francis Drake attacks Cádiz and sets fire to the Spanish fleet.

1596 Lord Essex emulates Drake's feat and ransacks the port of Cádiz.

1597 Cervantes is jailed in Seville accused of fiddling accounts while a tax collector; in prison he conceives his masterpiece, *Don Quixote*.

1599 Diego de Velázquez is born in Seville.

1608 Publication of *Don Quixote*.

1617 Bartolomé Murillo is born in Seville.

1701–13 Spanish King Carlos II dies childless, sparking War of Spanish Succession; Treaty of Utrecht grants throne to the Bourbon pretender; Gibraltar is ceded to Great Britain.

1768 Spain's first census shows the country has 10.2 million inhabitants.

1779–83 Great Siege of Gibraltar by Spanish and French.

1780 Last victim of the Inquisition is burned at the stake in Seville.

1785 Inauguration of the bullring in Ronda.

1805 Admiral Nelson defeats combined Spanish–French fleet off Cape Trafalgar in Cádiz.

1808 Napoleon replaces Spanish king with his brother, Joseph Bonaparte; Spaniards revolt against occupying French army.

1812 Spain's first constitution is drafted in Cádiz.

1832 Publication of Washington Irving's *Tales of the Alhambra*.

1835 Church property in Spain is confiscated and auctioned off.

1878 A plague of phylloxera (vine-root louse) decimates vineyards in Andalucía.

1881 Pablo Picasso is born in Málaga.

1883 Members of the Black Hand, an anarchist organisation, are executed by garrotte in Cádiz.

1885 Devastating earthquake kills hundreds and destroys thousands of homes in the provinces of Granada and Málaga.

1898 Spain loses Cuba and Philippines in Spanish-American War.

1923 Primo de Rivera seizes control as dictator, with Alfonso XIII remaining as king.

1929 Ibero-American Exposition in Seville.

1931 Spain becomes a republic.

1936 Spanish army revolts, led by General Franco, and three-year Spanish Civil War begins; the poet Federico García Lorca is shot in Granada.

1939 Spanish Civil War ends with Franco's victory.

1953 Spain agrees to US military bases on Spanish soil, ending 15 years of isolation.

1955 Spain joins the United Nations.

1966 US Air Force plane accidentally drops four non-activated atom bombs in Almería.

1969 Spain closes border with Gibraltar.

1975 Franco dies, and Spain becomes constitutional monarchy under King Juan Carlos.

1977 First free elections in Spain following restoration of monarchy.

1982 Andalucía becomes an autonomous region.

1985 Gibraltar border reopens.

1986 Spain joins European Community.

1992 Seville hosts Expo '92.

2002 The euro replaces the peseta.

2007 Scheduled completion of the final leg in the AVE rail link from Málaga to Madrid. ❑

LEFT: the Megalithic caves of Antequera.
RIGHT: the crown of Isabel, one of the Catholic Monarchs, now in the Capilla Real, Granada.

THE ANDALUSIANS

Andalucía has always been seen by outsiders as a place of romance and wish-fulfilment rather than a complex society worth taking the trouble to understand. But the apparent nonchalance of its people's live-for-today *informalidad* belies their deep appreciation of life

The Andalusians *(Andaluces)* have much to live up to – or live down. In the imagination of the world, theirs is a region of all things typically, desirably Spanish: flamenco music strummed on guitars accompanied by rattling castanets; brave bulls and even braver bullfighters; inscrutable, twinkle-eyed gypsies; philandering Don Juans beguiling sultry, fiery-eyed Carmens behind their filigree black grilles; stunning white hill towns under intense blue skies; minaretted palaces straight from *The Thousand and One Nights*; wild sierras inhabited by bandits with a picaresque sense of honesty – in short, a place of vivacity, sensuality and life-or-death passion, the antidote to the mediocre and banal.

Since at least the 17th century, foreign travellers have been descending on southern Spain in search of all these things, and returning home to add to the picture of Andalucía as an animated Elysian Fields where the sun always shines, nature is generous and people dedicated to living life to its fullest. Only a few admitted to disappointment – like Hans Christian Andersen, who was dismayed when his party was not held up by *bandoleros*, picaresque or otherwise, while crossing the mountains into Andalucía.

Modern tourists still expect to find here the time-old ingredients of a good holiday: tapas, paella, sangria and the rest, all served up in resorts where anything goes day or night in the eyes of its hedonistic, *mañana*-shunning, siesta-sleeping, ever-partying people.

Every Spanish stereotype, cliché and hyperbole comes to roost here, and, whether through a secret pride in their reputation or a sense of canny commercial self-promotion, Andalusians don't do much to dispel the misconceptions. Andalucía may be the best-known part of Spain – the monuments of Seville, Granada and Córdoba and the excesses of the Costa del Sol are world-famous – but in a more important sense, most visitors don't get to know it at all.

Territory and identity

Although geographically Andalucía is the most clearly defined *comunidad autónoma*, or

---

PRECEDING PAGES: café on Málaga's Calle Marqués de Larios. **LEFT:** embracing well-loved stereotypes. **RIGHT:** modern Andalusians, informal but elegant.

autonomous region, of Spain, it has a suprisingly poor sense of its own identity. Its territory begins in the west on the banks of the Río Guadiana, the natural frontier between Spain and Portugal, and stretches across the rest of the Iberian Peninsula, all the while incontestably defined to the north by the broad mountains of the Sierra Morena, separating it from La Mancha and the rest of Spain. On three sides there is sea: it is lapped by the Mediterranean in the east and pounded by the breakers of the Atlantic in the west. Only in its northeast corner is Andalucía's frontier at all fuzzy, falling rather arbitrarily somewhere between Vélez Rubio and Puerto Lumbreras in Murcia.

place where outsiders have come to from other parts of Spain or abroad to plunder resources – and also because of the lack of a unifying culture. Whereas the other two regions have their own indigenous languages, Andalusians speak Spanish, a language imported from Castile, albeit with a distinctive accent which clips off the final "s" of words.

Andalusians identify more with their provinces than their region, and are much more interested in the differences that divide them than the common causes that could unite them. It doesn't take much to get a group of Andalusians laughing about the characteristics attributed to the people of

Yet the notion of Andalucía is a relatively recent one. It was only with the move towards devolution on the death of Franco that the eight traditional provinces of the south were rounded up as the country's second-biggest region under the Junta de Andalucía in Seville – an uncentred capital if ever there was one. Within the heavily devolved country that is modern Spain, Andalucía, holding 7.5 million people or 17 percent of the population, is one of the least cohesive, least nationalistic of regions – far less vociferous in its demands for autonomy than the much smaller Basque Country and Catalonia. This is largely because of economic underdevelopment – Andalucía has always been a

each province: *Sevillanos*, for instance, are often regarded as showy and hedonistic, whereas *Granadinos* have a reputation for their sour tempers.

Highs and lows

Andalucía manages to fit in a bit of everything into its territory, from desert to subtropical valleys. Its central zone is made up of the fertile basin of the Río Guadalquivir, but to all sides there are mountains. Indeed, a third of the region is over 600 metres (2,000 ft), which inhibits communications and historically has engendered communities little interested in the world beyond the horizon.

Oldcomers and newcomers

The population is as multifarious as the landscape. Andalucía has always been and continues to be a melting pot of races. A few of its inhabitants may be distantly related to the original tribes of southern Spain, but most are of mixed ancestry. In particular, many people almost certainly descend from the Moors who dominated Andalucía's history for so long.

When the Muslims were forced to leave Spain, there was an influx of migrants from central and northern Spain as the abandoned countryside was repopulated. Later, when Spain was an empire, settlers from Central Europe were brought in to create new towns

Most cross the Straits of Gibraltar however they can, landing on the beaches of Cádiz and making a run for it. Some do not complete the crossing but are apprehended by the police or, sadly, drowned at sea. Those that do fan out through Spain and Europe, but inevitably many stay in Andalucía to take what work is available and legalise their situation when they can.

While wanting to be seen to defend Europe's borders, Andalusians have a vague sense of sympathy and solidarity towards these new arrivals – and accept them as a cheap source of labour to fill jobs in agriculture and construction that many locals no longer want to do.

in northern Jaén, adding a starkly different strain to the gene pool. It is not uncommon to meet Andalusians – according to stereotype full-blooded Latins – who have blond hair and piercing blue eyes.

Gateway to Africa

Now that Andalucía is part of the free internal market of the EU, uncounted immigrants from the Maghreb countries and black Africa have been entering southern Spain illegally.

LEFT: a cool glass of beer in the sherry capital, Jerez.
ABOVE: upmarket stores reflect a new affluence.
ABOVE RIGHT: no shortage of reading matter.

Foreigners with means

If poor, powerless workers make up one part of the quarter of a million foreign residents of Andalucía, an even bigger chunk is composed of individuals from the other end of the economic scale. These are the rich and relatively rich – mostly from the countries of northern Europe, but also from the USA and, more recently, former Soviet countries – who have chosen to settle in or near the Costa del Sol. Some of them live ordinary humdrum lives gardening in the sunshine, but the coast is also a magnet for celebrities, people evading the tax authorities and officialdom in general, even criminals on the run. Not many of the coast's residents learn fluent Spanish or integrate in any meaningful sense; rather, they are content to live in a multilingual sub-community with its own newspapers and radio stations, a community that overlaps mainstream Andalusian society but barely touches it, like some phantom fourth dimension. Some of them, however, earnestly embrace the country they have chosen to live in; the more discerning are to be found doing up old farmhouses inland or writing books about their adopted region.

The young ones

Almost a more important determinant than racial provenance in 21st-century Andalucía

is age. Conditions of life have changed dramatically within living memory, so much so that the old and young can barely understand each other's experiences. Those generations formed after the Civil War and under Franco were born into a world at worst of dire hardship and at best of little choice. Conformity to social and religious mores was the norm, and no one expected to live like the pampered foreign tourists who were beginning to litter the beaches of the Costa del Sol. Many people migrated to the industrialised Basque Country or Barcelona, or even France or Germany, in search of work – with or without their families.

ROMANCE OF THE RING

Nowhere in Spain, with the possible exception of Madrid, is bullfighting as exalted as in Andalucía. To be a *figura de torero* earns huge respect and status. Indeed, for some bullfighting goes to the heart of the Andalusian character, epitomising courage, artistry and refinement.

The region has about 70 bullrings altogether. Seville's is the most important, while Ronda's, which is one of the oldest in Spain, hosts the much-esteemed Goyesca bullfight in September, when the matadors are dressed in elaborate costumes from the Goya era. Top *toreros* perform in up to 70, 80 or even 90 corridas a year, for wages varying according to the size and category of the

ring, from €9,000 in a small town to more than €30,000 for the major San Isidro Fair in Madrid. These apparently impressive fees are reduced considerably after the salaries of a minimum of eight employees are deducted, along with all their hotel, food and travel expenses, the manager's commissions, taxes and the cost of publicity, sequinned suits, capes, swords and other paraphernalia.

In the summertime the schedule is extremely pressing, and bullfighters criss-cross the country with barely enough time to rest before the corrida. To learn more about this fascinating but controversial aspect of the culture, visit the bullfighting museums in Seville, Córdoba or Ronda.

But young people who have come of age in democratic Spain have grown up not only used to political freedom but expecting comfortable lives with unlimited choices. Whereas for their parents a formal education was a luxury not all families could afford and job satisfaction not even a consideration, they take it for granted that a range of university courses will be available to them and expect à la carte careers of their choosing. Forty years ago a trip to a big city was a major excursion; now new motorways and EU-funded roads criss-cross Andalucía, affording a mobility no one could have dreamed of then.

A return to tradition

Significantly, not many Andalusians choose to leave their native region, except for a brief spell or unless compelled to for their work. Even a greatly boosted salary will not necessarily compensate them for the loss of an enviable climate and a friendly lifestyle. And interestingly, some young people opt for the traditional ways rather than the glamour of modern life. Two signs of this are the number of charming small hotels being opened in the Andalusian countryside by young entrepreneurs wanting to stay close to their roots, and the number of inhabited caves that have been restored with pride by new owners as more desirable places to live than modern flats.

Within two or three generations, Andalucía has gone from being an essentially rural society to one in which most of the population live in cities. The economy has correspondingly shifted from a dependence on agriculture to a dependence on the service sector, as if the age of industrialisation had passed the region by completely. One of the main motors of change has been tourism, which has transformed Andalucía's coast from a poor strip of wasteland into a playground for the affluent.

Family and Church

Surprisingly, perhaps, two principal institutions of Andalusian society – the family and

the Church – have so far survived the changes. Even the footloose young feel strong links to their families, and often they keep their attachments to the *pueblo* – the country town the family originally hails from. But there may be a crisis around the corner, as the average Andalusian family is shrinking fast. In common with the rest of Spain, the birth rate in Andalucía has plummeted from an average of over three babies per woman in the 1970s to less than one-and-a-half today – an effect attributed to the consumer society and improved opportunities for women.

The Catholic Church, meanwhile, has seen congregations slump in the face of the

GYPSY MINORITY

Andalucía's 300,000 gypsies *(gitanos)* comprise the region's largest ethnic minority. Gypsies often proudly reject the values of *payo* (non-gypsy) society and as a result are often marginalised, with high rates of illiteracy and other forms of social deprivation. But many seamlessly integrate into society, running businesses and holding down jobs like any other citizens. It is impossible to overestimate the impact they have had on the region, and sometimes – as seen in flamenco music and dance and all its derivatives – it is impossible to differentiate between gypsy and Andalusian culture.

LEFT: matadors enjoy enormous respect and status.
RIGHT: a window on the world.

same consumer society, but it still manages to insinuate itself into all corners of life. Most children still carry Christian forenames (María and Jesús are perennially popular); the shrines of saints everywhere are maintained and visited on key days of the year; and annual fiestas, for all the fun they seem to be, are essentially sober religious feast days at heart.

Living in the present

In this rich and complex mosaic it is not easy to say exactly how Andalusians differ from other Spaniards. As communications quicken and customs become more nationalised and

globalised, it could well be argued that Andalusians are merely the extrapolation of general Spanish traits – the southern end, as it were, of a continuum of national characteristics. But taken together, these traits still constitute an unmistakable Andalusian identity.

Chief among them are sociability and gregariousness. Andalusians like to be in the street, to see and be seen – and they have the climate for it. They have no reservation about making noise and have no shame in showing their emotions, as can be seen in any of their many exuberant fiestas.

They are, with exceptions, a generous, hospitable and straightforward people who do not play mind games or keep a score of social debts and obligations. Theirs is a world of unspoken and unenforced honour, in which it is assumed that anyone they are introduced to by a friend, relation or business partner is to be trusted to uphold their own sense of honour. It can be hard to pay for a round of drinks when out with a group of Andalusians – especially men; even when entertaining a visitor clearly wealthier than themselves, they would never ask or expect him to reach into his pocket.

Above all, Andalusians are zealous about living life in the present – which can be either charming or frustrating to the outsider depending on the circumstances, especially when trying to get something done. This comes across mainly in the Andalusian habit of *informalidad*. It is hard to define this term exactly, but it reduces to an understanding that everyone does what they feel like doing when they feel like doing it, and no one has the right to tell them otherwise.

A typical aspect of *informalidad* is unpunctuality – as when a friend turns up for an appointment an hour or two late, without apology or excuse, assuming that those he has arranged to meet will have felt free to behave in the same way. Another common example of *informalidad* is when a tradesman promises to come on a certain day but doesn't show up. He might have meant to come at the time but his plans then changed; more probably, he knew full well he couldn't come at the time of asking, but simply felt it would be bad manners to refuse.

Rather than considering *informalidad* something to be ashamed of, a vice to be rectified, Andalusians are adamant that it is the only sane way to live, especially in a world in which stress and overwork are regarded as the inevitable price to pay for material gain. Take away the urgency and obligation, they will point out, and everything still gets done, just in a more enjoyable way than elsewhere. The concept of *mañana* has always been misunderstood beyond the Sierra Morena. All it means is that life is to be lived in full, today. ❏

LEFT: watching the boys on the beach.

Flamenco

The earliest origins of flamenco, a synthesis of music and dance which has come to be identified with the essence of Spain, are unclear. Flamenco crystallised in the gypsy communities of southern Andalucía in the mid-18th century (its historic heartland is the delta between Seville, Jerez and Cádiz), and features in common with Indian and Arab song attest to this migratory heritage. There are traces, too, of Jewish and Byzantine Christian religious music, as well as regional folk styles.

The rise of flamenco to an art appreciated by the educated and moneyed fits the pattern familiar from forms like the Blues, which started as rough but vital lower-class entertainment. The word "flamenco", both an adjective and a noun, denotes a way of life, and a person who is unsettled, emotional, unpredictable, in every sense anti-bourgeois. In a way, today's flamenco-rockers are truer to the music's origins than some established concert performers.

The flamenco repertoire is based on songs with specific contexts – songs about work or religion, dance tunes, expressions of life's joys and sorrows. The oldest are sung unaccompanied, or with basic percussion; some are still recorded with the clang of a simulated hammer and anvil, after the blacksmiths' forges where they originated.

The numerous styles of flamenco are sometimes divided into *cante grande* (great song), *cante intermedio* and *cante chico* (little), the last brighter, lighter and often accompanied by dances such as the *bulería*, *alegría* or *tango*. The pinnacle of the flamenco singer's art is the body of great songs – often called *cante hondo* (deep song) – which are expressive of the profoundest emotion and are most difficult to perform. It is here that the quality known as *duende*, literally spirit or demon, is crucial: a form of involuntary inspiration that takes over a performer, provoking a murmur – or roar – of *"olé!"* from the audience.

The development of flamenco into a public entertainment started in the 1850s, with the growth of *cafés cantantes* featuring gypsy artistes such as El Planeta and El Fillo. By the 1920s, the so-called Golden Age of flamenco had become a tinsel age, with its popularity leading to increasingly gaudy spectacle. Associations with Franco alienated large numbers of youthful, progressive Spaniards in the 1960s and 1970s, until a number of developments finally heralded flamenco's return to form. The first was the emergence of the Cano Roto sound, a fast blend of guitars, bass and drums based on the rhumba rhythm and expounded by young gypsy-dominated

groups such as Los Chorbos and Los Grecas. Also establishing themselves were the brilliant guitarist, Paco de Lucía, and a charismatic singer from Cádiz, El Camarón de la Isla, who would influence a generation.

Today, state-funded festivals provide abundant audiences for custodians of the *cante*, such as Pepe de la Matrona, as well as younger stars like the Habichuela family, Tomatito, Enrique Morente and Vicente Soto. Experiments combining flamenco singers with Moroccan groups – El Lebrijano with the Orchestra of Tangier, José Heredia Maya with the Orchestra of Tétouan – look set to be repeated with increasing popularity. ❑

RIGHT: a typically spirited display.

FIESTAS FOR ALL SEASONS

The Andalusian character shines brightest at the region's fiestas, which are some of the best in Spain

Andalusian fiestas come in seasonal cycles, and many trace their roots to pagan times. Even the deeply solemn Semana Santa procession has pagan roots, as a celebration of spring. Other celebrations are unabashedly pagan, such as the Eve of San Juan (23 June), when bonfires are lit, effigies are burned, and participants leap through the flames and then cleanse the spirit by bathing in the sea.

Every town holds an annual *feria*, usually in summer, though the most famous is Seville's April Feria. In the harvest season, wine-growing areas host a Fiesta de la Vendimia. Other crops, from oranges to olives, are similarly honoured.

Solstice celebration

The winter solstice has been celebrated for thousands of years, although we now know it as Christmas. In Spain, Christmas lasts for two weeks, starting with Nochebuena ("the good night"), on Christmas Eve. People greet Nochevieja ("the old night"), New Year's Eve, in front of the clock in the main square, where they eat 12 grapes of good luck, one for each chime. Finally comes the Epiphany, or Feast of Three Kings, when Spanish children receive their presents.

The cycle ends with Carnival, the final fling before the abstemious Lent period leading up to Holy Week and a new round of fiestas.

ABOVE: carriage at Jerez de la Frontera's annual Horse Fair in May. No town takes its horses as seriously as the sherry town, the birthplace of the Carthusian breed.

ABOVE: troubadours sing satirical verses during Carnival. Such songs were banned under Primo de Rivera and also under Franco – apart from in Cádiz.

RIGHT: traditionally an agricultural region, Andalucía has numerous and various harvest festivals. In the September Fiesta de la Vendimia in Jerez de la Frontera, grapes are trodden in front of the main church, recalling wine-making methods of days gone by.

ABOVE: Seville's April Feria, El Rocío's *romería* and the annual Horse Fair in Jerez de la Frontera are all opportunities for parading in traditional Andalusian costume.

VIRGIN WORSHIP

The story is repeated in countless villages throughout Andalucía: a hunter, a shepherd or a farmer stumbles across an image of the Virgin Mary, hidden in a grotto or in the hollow trunk of an ancient tree, reputedly to conceal it from the heathen Moors. The countryman tries to take it back to his village, but falls asleep and, on waking, finds the Virgin has miraculously returned to her original hiding place. Word of the miracle spreads, a shrine is erected, and it becomes a place of pilgrimage.

Some of these pilgrimages, called *romerías*, after the custom of gathering wild rosemary *(romero)* along the route, have become mass events, such as the pilgrimage of the Virgen de la Cabeza in Andújar (Jaén), the pilgrimage of the gypsies in Cabra (Córdoba), the seaborne processions to honour the Virgen del Carmen *(photo below)* or, the biggest of all, the Romería del Rocío, on the edge of the Parque Nacional de Doñana, which attracts around one million people every Whitsuntide *(see page 97).*

ABOVE: Christ's Passion and death are re-enacted in outdoor plays in many towns, such as Riogordo (Málaga), whose *Paso* (passion play) spans two days.

RIGHT: a hooded penitent in one of Málaga's Holy Week processions, an image harking back to the Middle Ages. He is a member of a *cofradía*, the brotherhoods that organise such processions, which can last 8, 10 or even 12 hours.

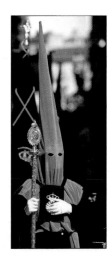

RIGHT: in fishing communities the image of the Virgen del Carmen, patroness of fishermen, is taken out in seaborne processions in July.

THE ANDALUSIAN KITCHEN

Sardines grilled on an open fire; home-cured olives, oozing flavour; a bowl of garlicky gazpacho; almond biscuits that dissolve on the tongue... Today's restaurant menus reflect the region's remarkable range of fresh produce

From its jagged mountains to the golden beaches of the Mediterranean, from dry, scrubby hillsides to lush river valleys, Andalucía covers a vast and diverse landscape. The region's food and drink reflects this diversity. Not only does each province have its own culinary character and signature dishes, but the experience of eating out offers endless variety: it can be as subtle and refined as a cool sherry sipped in the dappled shade of a grape arbour, as brash as a noisy tapas bar; or as simple as the aroma of bread baking in wood-fired ovens.

Taster session

The best introduction to authentic Andalusian food – in fact, to the southern Spanish way of life in general – is the tapas bar. Here wine, sometimes served from the barrel, is dispensed along with small saucers of snacks, both hot and cold, which are usually consumed while standing at the bar.

Tapas themselves may be the simplest of delicacies: a plate of fat, herb-scented olives; toasted almonds; paper-thin slices of salt-cured *serrano* ham; prawns in their shells; or sliced sausages like paprika-red *chorizo*, peppery *salchichón* or smoky *longaniza*.

Then come *tapas de cocina*, cooked dishes such as croquettes, battered prawns, ham rolls stuffed with cheese (*flamenquines*), bite-sized pieces of crisp-fried fish or vegetables. Salads include roasted peppers or tomato and onion

(*pipirrana*); *campera*, made with sliced potatoes, onions and olives in a lemon-flavoured dressing; *remojón*, an exotic combination of oranges, onions and cod; and *pulpo*, diced octopus with tomatoes, garlic and parsley.

Seafood selections might include *gambas al pil pil*, prawns sizzled with garlic; clams or mussels *a la marinera* and *boquerones al natural*, fresh anchovies dressed with garlic and vinegar. Other favourites are meatballs, rabbit, chicken in garlic, tiny pork cutlets, stewed tripe with *garbanzos* (chickpeas), kidneys in sherry, and *tortilla*, a thick potato omelette.

Some tapas bars specialise in just a few dishes, others may have up to 40 different

---

LEFT: a simple salad with wine and bread.
RIGHT: a waiter with his hands full in Málaga.

choices, sometimes listed on a blackboard. A tapa really is just a nibble – in some bars, served free with a *copa* of wine. Those wanting a larger serving should ask for a *media* (half) or *ración* (full serving).

The drink of choice is dry fino, either sherry or Montilla, both of which are fortified wines made in Andalucía.

Mealtimes are late in Andalucía: 2–3pm for the *comida*, or midday meal, which for Spaniards is the main meal of the day, and 9–10pm for the *cena*, evening meal. So tapas bars are places to pass a pleasant few hours snacking before dinner.

Other popular eating places are *ventas*, grown locally, which is mostly exported to northern Europe. Dried beans and lentils, usually cooked with locally made sausages and vegetables, are also daily fare. It is simple food, without pretensions, but the subtlety of flavourings and the freshness of the ingredients make it special.

The simplicity is hardly surprising, given the intense poverty the region witnessed in previous centuries. People learned to exist on the barest essentials and still make them palatable. Gazpacho, the classic cold soup, originated in Andalucía and is little more than bread, oil, garlic and a few vegetables. Equally uncomplicated is *cocido*, also called *puchero*

country restaurants serving rustic fare, and *chiringuitos*, shanty restaurants set up on the beach. Here you should try *espetones*, a simple speciality of fresh sardines speared on sticks and grilled on an open fire.

Fresh ingredients

The basics of Andalusian cooking are olive oil, tomatoes and peppers (both from the New World), garlic and onions, together with fish on the coast and pork products inland. Potatoes are a staple, either fried as a side dish, or cooked in a casserole with other ingredients. Rice features in all sorts of recipes, including paella – but not the long-grained variety

FRUITS OF THE EAST

The Arabs brought the first orange trees to Spain. These were bitter oranges, sour as lemons, but wonderful in marmalade. These are still used ornamentally in southern Spain, where their blossoms perfume courtyards and their juice is used in cooking, but the fruit is not eaten.

These invaders from the East also contributed rice and spices such as saffron, cinnamon and nutmeg, as well as aubergines and many other fruits and vegetables, which thrive in this temperate zone. For the wealthy with access to new, exotic ingredients, cooking evolved into a high art, and Andalusian cuisine was soon enjoying a reputation as the most refined in Europe.

or *olla*, in which chicken, hambone, pulses and vegetables are all cooked together. The broth is served with rice or noodles as a first course, followed by the meat and vegetables.

Essential eating

Gazpacho is just one of the specialities to savour on a visit to Andalucía. *Serrano* or mountain ham is another. Salt-cured and aged from seven months to several years, it is served raw as an appetiser. The most sought-after hams are those that specify their village of origin, such as de Jabugo (from Huelva), de Pedroches (Córdoba) and de Trevélez (Granada), and, most expensive of all, those

bones and baked for All Souls' Day. *Borra-chuelos* and *pestiños* are fried pastries, dipped in honey or sugar syrup; *polvorones*, *mante-cados* and *perrunas* are crumbly biscuits shared at Christmastime, as are *roscos*, ring-shaped biscuits either fried or baked.

from *pata negra*, a breed of black-footed, brown Iberian pigs which roam semi-wild and feed on acorns.

Even more irresistible are the sweets of Andalucía, richly flavoured with aniseed, cin-namon and sesame, and drenched in honey – a lavish celebration of the Moorish influence on the region's cuisine. Biscuits, too, cram every bakery shelf. Try *tortas*, round, flat cakes studded with aniseed, often eaten for breakfast; *soplillos,* almond macaroons, and *huesos de santo* ("saint's bones"), shaped like

You will find these delicacies throughout Andalucía. But each province also has its own local specialities, and it can be fun to track them down.

Seville: city of tapas

Seville, cosmopolitan heart of Andalucía, is famous for its olives, generally served with sherry, but also cooked with meat, chicken and duck. Keep an eye out, too, for home-cured olives, which have been cracked open and cured in brine with garlic, thyme and fennel. This is the city where tapas originated, and you'll probably eat better in tapas bars than in most restaurants. Try *menudo* (tripe);

LEFT: almonds are used extensively in sweets and pastries. **ABOVE:** Tarifa's bars are great for seafood.

huevos a la flamenca, a fancy version of baked eggs with ham, peas, asparagus and *chorizo* sausage; and authentic *yemas de San Leandro*, from the convent of the same name.

Huelva's Iberian pigs supply delectable pork loin *(lomo de cerdo)*, while its famous *pata negra* hams can be purchased straight from the producers in Jabugo, Cortegana and Cumbres Mayores. The province also has excellent game and lamb, and much-prized wild mushrooms and white truffles, not to overlook plentiful fish and seafood. Dishes to ask for are *chocos*, tiny cuttlefish stewed with beans, and *mojama* ("ham of the sea"), salt-cured dried tuna, served in slivers as an appe-

cones to eat as you stroll. Prawns from nearby Sanlúcar de Barrameda are incomparably sweet, and the fried sole tastes as if it had jumped straight from the sea into the pan.

Restaurants and tapas bars here and in Cádiz offer a number of interesting variations on fish stew, including *abajá de pescado* and *urta a la roteña* (with bream). "Dog" soup, *caldillo de perro*, is nothing more sinister than fish flavoured with sour oranges; "cat" soup is laced with garlic. The essential dessert to order in Cádiz is *tocino del cielo*, a rich caramel custard which is truly divine.

Not far from Cádiz is Jerez de la Frontera, home of sherry wine and the now fashionable

tiser. Many of the strawberries imported into northern Europe come from the beds of Huelva, which also has its own wine region, Condado, producing light white table wines.

Seafood in Cádiz

Cádiz is a wonderful place to eat fish and seafood, both in the city and the coastal environs. Here you'll find prawns, lobsters, crabs and oysters at their freshest. For a real treat, take a ferry across the bay to Puerto Santa María; on the promenade facing the port are various *cocederos* and *freidurias* where you can buy 20 or more different kinds of freshly cooked shellfish and fish, wrapped in paper

sherry vinegar. The wine is much used in cooking throughout Andalucía: try it in *riñones al jerez*, kidneys braised in sherry; mushrooms stewed in sherry or sweetbreads with oloroso.

Along the *costa*

With more than 150 km (93 miles) of coast, the province of Málaga is unsurprisingly famous for its seafood. Try *fritura malagueña*, a mixed-fish fry of fresh anchovies, so crisp you can eat them bones and all, rings of tender squid, prawns, and a piece of a larger fish such as hake. Other local dishes are *pescado al horno*, fish baked with layers of potatoes, tomatoes, onions and peppers, *rape a la marinera*, monkfish with tomato and garlic; and *lubina a la sal*, a whole sea bass baked in a case of coarse salt.

Besides gazpacho, Málaga has a delightful summer soup of its own, *ajo blanco con uvas*, a tangy white concoction of crushed almonds, garlic and grapes. *Cazuela de fideos* is a variation on *paella* – seafood, peas and peppers cooked with saffron and spaghetti.

On the Costa del Sol, you can eat French, Italian, Danish, Thai, Moroccan, Chinese, Indian and many other world cuisines. In fact, you might have a hard job finding any authentic Spanish food.

DISH OF THE DAY

Menú in Spanish always refers to the fixed-price meal of the day. If you want the à la carte menu, you should ask to see *la carta*.

Lovers of game should head for the northern reaches of Jaén and Córdoba, and the Sierra Morena, where venison, wild boar, partridge and hare feature heavily on the menu. *Andrajos*, which literally means "rags", is a game casserole with pasta squares; *perdiz en escabeche* is marinated partridge. Lamb, excellent in both these provinces, is usually served braised.

Inland bounty

Inland, the almond groves around Granada have inspired a delicious soup, *sopa de almendras*. Ground almonds are also used as seasoning for rabbit, chicken and fish dishes.

From the Alpujarras Mountains come *serrano* hams. Try broad beans fried with chunks of ham or fresh trout sautéed with ham. Other favourites include *tortilla sacromonte*, an omelette made with sweetbreads, kidneys, red pepper and peas, and *choto al ajillo*, young goat or lamb laced with garlic.

Córdoba is known for its vegetable dishes, especially artichokes, cardoons (similar to artichokes), wild asparagus and aubergine. Summer specialities include *salmorejo*, like a very thick gazpacho, topped with hard-boiled egg, and white gazpacho, made with almonds and spiked with apples or melon.

Pastel cordobés is a dessert of flaky pastry filled with "angel's hair" – candied threads of apple. Those with a sweet tooth can bring home a jar of *dulce de membrillo*, a quince jelly that originates from the town of Puente Genil. Córdoba also makes world-class wines, in particular those of Montilla and Moriles. ❑

LEFT: a busy bar in Priego de Córdoba.
ABOVE: cured and salted mountain hams.

The Story of Sherry

There was a wine-maker in Jerez de la Frontera in the mid-19th century named Manuel González who did a healthy trade exporting the dark, sweet, nutty wine of the region to England. He had an uncle, José Angel de la Peña – Pepe for short – who was fond of a type of wine which, unlike the popular sweet sherry, was crystal clear in appearance and bone-dry to the palate. There was a section in the wine cellar where Uncle Pepe kept a few barrels of the stuff, for

his personal enjoyment and for sharing with friends.

One day, one of Pepe's barrels was included in a shipment to England. Word soon got back from the importers. Could they have some more of that rare, clear stuff, please? So the winery started making more of this style of wine, naming it after the vintner's uncle: Tío Pepe. Thus was a Jerez legend born, and today Tío Pepe is one of the top-selling wines.

The land of sherry abounds in such anecdotes. Few tipples have the mystique surrounding those from this corner of the province of Cádiz, where a unique combi-

nation of soil, grape, climate and ageing methods gives rise to the world's most popular aperitif wine.

Reposing in the cellars of Jerez are around half a million wood barrels – the large sherry *botas*, or butts, each containing 500 litres (110 gallons) of liquid gold. These veritable cathedrals of wine are the best places to learn about the different types of sherry and how they are made. The wineries welcome curious travellers and have become the town's major attraction.

Sherry country

Sherry is born in what has been called the "Golden Triangle", a wedge of gently rolling country in western Cádiz. At one corner is Jerez itself. At the two other corners are El Puerto de Santa María, the port from which sherry was traditionally shipped, and Sanlúcar de Barrameda, at the mouth of the Guadalquivir. Each has a distinct character: where Jerez is aristocratic and proud, El Puerto is a workaday port and Sanlúcar a relaxed fishing town. Between them lie the expanses of white, chalky soil, carpeted with the vines.

Most sherry is made with the Palomino grape. It is a high-yielding white grape, but aside from that there is nothing much to be said for it: white wines made from Palomino are thin and prone to oxidation (darkening). Yet in Jerez it reaches new heights, thanks to a combination of circumstances.

First, there is the soil, the chalky *albariza*, which has the characteristic of soaking up the water from the torrential winter rains and storing it so that the deep-rooted vines can survive the long, hot summer months. Then there is the prevailing humidity, due to the area's proximity to the Atlantic and the wetlands of the Doñana park.

When the wine is put into barrel, a coating of yeast – called the *flor* – forms on the surface, thanks to this humidity, and this seals the wine, protecting it from the air, feeding on the sugars and giving the wines their exceptional dryness. In Sanlúcar, the most humid part of the region, the layer of *flor* is thicker and the resulting wine, called manzanilla, even drier.

Every detail of the wine cellar is designed to keep the vital *flor* happy. High vaulted ceilings keep summer temperatures down; windows, covered with esparto mats which can be raised or lowered to control ventilation, are oriented to trap the damp westerly winds. The cellar floors are compacted sand, which is watered down regularly. Even the gardens surrounding the wineries are for a purpose: they help maintain a cool, humid microclimate around the cellars.

After the grapes are pressed and fermented, the wine is aged for a year or two, then it enters the *criaderas*, rows of barrels that hold blends of different vintages. A portion of wine is drawn off from the casks, called the *soleras*, which contain the oldest blend for bottling. These casks are topped off with wine from casks containing the second-oldest blend, which in turn is replenished from another row of casks, right on up to those containing the youngest blend, which are topped off with the most recent vintage. The system evolved from the need to keep stocks fresh and consistent in flavour. Therefore, with one or two exceptions, there is no vintage sherry; practically all are blends.

Sherries are fortified wines, which means extra alcohol is added just before bottling for fino sherries or before they age for olorosos. They should be drunk within a year or two of bottling.

Fundador brandy

Just as important to the local economy is Jerez brandy, also produced by the sherry wineries, which make 90 percent of Spain's brandy. Sweeter than French brandy, it acquires its distinctive character when the basic wine spirits (for which grapes from other Spanish regions are used) are left to age in casks that have previously held sherry wine. Its discovery came about quite by accident. In 1860, the Domecq winery received an order for 500 barrels of *"holandas"* (as clear wine spirits were called, Holland being the main customer), but payment was not forthcoming, and the shipment never left the cellar. Instead, it sat forgotten in old sherry casks for five years, until it occurred to the foreman to sample it. He found it had turned a golden colour, with a good flavour and aroma. Thus was another Jerez legend born: Fundador brandy.

Today more than 80 million litres (over 17 million gallons) of sherry are produced a year. With around 80 percent of that sold abroad, it continues to be Spain's most exported wine, but in a competitive market

the trade needed modernising. The wineries underwent restructuring, with the number of workers plummeting from 10,000 to 2,000 in 15 years.

Yet when you attend the *feria*, where men and women in traditional costume proudly ride their horses, you know that Jerez will always have some of that old spirit. In a reversal of history, in 1998 members of the González Byass family bought back the 30 percent share of the bodega which they had sold to a British multinational in 1992, the winery thus becoming family-owned once again. Tío Pepe would have approved. ❑

LEFT AND RIGHT: from the vine to the glass in Jerez de la Frontera.

WILD ANDALUCÍA

Almost one-fifth of Andalucía is protected, as
Andalusians – and increasing numbers of visitors – come to
appreciate the rugged wilderness that houses some of
Europe's rarest birds, mammals and plant life

In a special enclosure high in the Sierra de Cazorla of southern Jaén, five lammergeier vultures were slowly adapted to the mountainous conditions. Found injured in other parts of Spain and carefully nursed back to health, the birds would never fly again; instead, they formed the basis of an ambitious breeding programme to reintroduce the species to the national park.

With a wingspan up to 3 metres (10 ft), the lammergeier is the biggest bird in Europe, and one of the rarest. In Spain, its last major refuge, it is known as *quebrantahuesos*, or "bone-buster", for its habit of dropping bones from a great height to get at the nutritious marrow.

Similar conservation programmes are under way all over Andalucía, as plant and animal species are monitored to ensure their survival, and unspoilt areas earmarked for official protection. It is a reflection of a new awareness among Andalusians that wildlife is something to be treasured.

Waking up to nature

A total of 17 percent of the region is afforded official protection as natural wilderness, more than triple the national average. In all, there are more than 80 different locations classified as nature park *(parque natural)*, nature reserve *(reserva natural)* or nature enclave *(paraje natural)* – from small, inaccessible lagoons that are crucial to migrating birds, to vast forested tracts, such as the Cazorla nature park.

The Doñana National Park

The jewel in the crown of wild Andalucía is Doñana National Park, spreading 500 sq. km (195 sq. miles) at the mouth of the Guadalquivir river. About two-thirds of the park consists of marsh and wetlands, the most valuable in Europe, for they provide a breeding ground for more than 100 species of birds, and are a wintering ground or stopover on the migration route for many others. The extremely rare imperial eagle soars in the skies here, while scattered trees provide convenient perches for spoonbills, storks, egrets and herons.

Two thousand years ago, this was a vast brackish estuary, peppered with islands, but

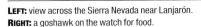

LEFT: view across the Sierra Nevada near Lanjarón.
RIGHT: a goshawk on the watch for food.

gradual silting up of the Guadalquivir river created the marshes. Hunting was the main activity here for centuries, but in the 1960s intensive farming threatened its very existence: water drawn off for irrigation reduced the wetlands from more than 1,800 sq. km (700 sq. miles) to 310 sq. km (120 sq. miles), and only the area's designation as a nature park in 1969 saved it from disappearing altogether.

Europe's desert

At the opposite end of the region, Almería's landscape provides a sharp contrast to the wetlands of Huelva. Tabernas is the only true desert in Europe, with less than 20 cm (8 inches) of

rainfall a year, and its landscape of parched, eroded hills has served as a backdrop for countless Western movies.

The equally arid landscape stretching from the Cabo de Gata, the southeastern tip of Andalucía, up the coast to Carboneras is now also protected as a nature park, with volcanic cliffs, isolated coves of black sand and hillsides covered in prickly pear cactus (a species introduced from the Americas). Even this moonscape supports wildlife, including types of snapdragon and lily unique to this area.

Not long ago, the coast of Cabo de Gata was accessible only to millionaires on private yachts or via a long trek over goat trails, but

roads have opened up the area to travellers, and campsites, hotels and restaurants have sprung up to serve them. The same is happening all over Andalucía, where "rural tourism" is the latest trend – leading to debates over the compatibility of tourism and conservation.

Primeval forests

To get an idea of what the primeval forests that covered much of Andalucía looked like before the arrival of man, head for the mountains that straddle the provinces of Cádiz and Málaga. Near the coast is the Parque de los Alcornocales, 1,700 sq. km (655 sq. miles) of cork oak, holm oak and Lusitanian oak. As you

Friends and foes

Tourists aside, the 20th century brought new perils to Andalucía's wildlife: agricultural pesticides and artificial fertilisers; irrigation systems that depleted underground water sources; reforestation with fast-growing, non-native pine trees and eucalyptus which crowded

ascend towards Ronda, following the old tobacco smugglers' route from Gibraltar, this gives way to the heights of the Sierra de Grazalema, home to peregrine falcons, eagle owls and one of Europe's largest colonies of griffon vultures. Among the trees found here is the *Abies pinsapo*, a fir which grows nowhere else in Europe. It requires shaded valleys at high altitude and constant humidity, which it finds here in what is the wettest spot in Spain (an average of 225 cm/88½ inches of rain a year).

native species, as did the introduction of alien animal species for hunting or breeding purposes – everything from mouflons to rainbow trout and Louisiana crayfish.

Fortunately, wild Andalucía has had several things going for it: the sheer size of the region, the fact that much of it consists of inaccessible mountains and, sadly, the social injustices of the past. When Andalucía was conquered by the Christians, and the *Morisco* farmers were ultimately expelled, most of the territory fell into the hands of absentee landowners, who were more interested in counting gold from the New World or hunting for wild boar than in turning their properties into working

LEFT: the Parque Nacional de Doñana.
ABOVE: desert landscape, Almería. **ABOVE RIGHT:** limestone fromations at El Torcal, near Antequera.

agricultural concerns. Emigration, uninterrupted for centuries, left much of rural Andalucía under-populated, so nature was allowed to go its own way more or less unhindered.

The lynx under threat

Some of the wildest terrain is to be found in the Sierra de Aracena, at the western extreme of the Sierra Morena, the mountain range that separates Andalucía from Castile. A string of protected nature areas – the Sierra del Norte in Seville, Sierra de Hornachuelos and Sierra de Cardeña–Montoro in Córdoba, Sierra de Andújar and Despeñaperros in Jaén – form a wild corridor nearly 320 km (200 miles) long.

The further east you go, the more rugged and mysterious is the scenery.

These mountains are the home of one of the rarest mammals in Europe, the Iberian lynx. The lynx is the animal that best embodies Andalucía's struggle to protect its wildlife. Only around 150 are left in the whole of Spain, in the national parks of Andújar in Jaén and Doñana in Huelva, after a myxomatosis plague all but wiped out their main diet of rabbits. In 2002 the World Conservation Union listed the Iberian lynx as a Category One Critical Endangered Species, which meant that money was made available for a rescue project. Doñana now has an active

breeding programme; the only problem is finding a suitable breeding male.

For other species, the future is more promising. White storks have returned to nest in Ronda after an absence of 20 years. The white-headed duck, not long ago on the verge of extinction, is finding new breeding grounds in the lagoons of southern Spain. The chameleon, which for decades had been fighting a losing battle with real-estate developers, is on the increase again, with colonies detected in Almería and Granada.

Some of the most striking examples of Andalusian wildlife are among the smallest. Southern Spain is a botanist's paradise, with

over 4,000 different plant species, more than 150 of which are endemic (not found anywhere else in the world). They have evolved in unique microclimates such as those of Cazorla, where the Cazorla violet grows, or Sierra Nevada. Contemplating the windswept heights around the ski resort, where no trees will grow, you might think the landscape barren following the spring thaw. But look closely, and you might spot the rare Nevada daffodil *(Narcissus nevadensis)* or Nevada saxifrage *(Saxifraga nevadensis)*, just two of 70 catalogued. ❏

LEFT: nesting stork, a symbol of luck and nativity.
ABOVE: a lynx, one of the rarest mammals in Europe.

Hiking in Andalucía

Southern Spain's countryside is extraordinarily varied, and while parts are suitable only for hurrying through to get from one place to another, others make perfect walking country. Find the right patch of hillside strewn with wild flowers beneath high-altitude crags overflown by eagles and vultures, or wooded valley alive with birdsong and the trickle of water, and there is no better place to be out of doors.

There are two national parks and 20 *parques naturales* (nature parks) in the region, all of them geared up for hikers, with signposted routes of various length and usually a good choice of rural hotels, bars and restaurants and other services.

The two most popular areas for walking holidays are the Alpujarras *(see page 207)* south of Granada (together with the rest of the Sierra Nevada National Park) and the Sierra de Grazalema *(see page 122)* near Ronda. Other good areas are the forested sierras and valleys of Cazorla *(see page 180)* and the chestnut, cork and holm-oak woods of the Sierra de Aracena in Huelva *(see page 102)*. Beauty spots for short walks include Doñana National Park *(see page 97)*, El Torcal near Antequera *(see page 153)*, the cliffs and coves of Cabo de Gata *(see page 219)* in Almería and, close to the Costa del Sol, around the town of Istán *(see page 144)*.

For serious walkers there are nine long-distance (GR) footpaths crossing Andalucía in two or more daily stages, most famous among them being the 1,280-km long GR7 (E4), or "Mediterranean Arc" which connects the Aegean Sea with the Atlantic Ocean. Shorter walks, normally between 1 km (½ mile) and 10 km (6 miles) long and often circular, are designated PR–A. They are graded according to their difficulty *(dificultad)* from *baja* (easy) to *muy alta* (for experienced walkers only). Tourist offices and visitors' centres will be able to advise on walks.

Spring and early summer are the best times to go walking in Andalucia, when the landscape is smothered in wild flowers but

the days are not too hot. The Mediterranean vegetation burns dry in the heat of July and August, although these are good months to go walking at higher, normally snowcapped altitudes. Autumn and winter are good for exploring the countryside near the coasts when the access roads aren't clogged with tourist traffic.

Whenever and wherever you go walking, common-sense advice applies: stick to walks on marked paths within your ability; never walk alone; take the best map you can find; and make sure someone knows where you have gone and when you expect to be back. Wear proper walking shoes

(boots are best), a hat and something warm if you are going to any altitude. Always carry plenty of drinking water.

Good walking maps are available locally, but it is wise to buy them beforehand. The best are in the 1:25,000 series published by Centro Nacional de Información Geográfica (CNIG, www.cnig.es). The Spanish army (Servicio Geográfico del Ejército) produces 1:50,000 maps suitable for walking, as does the regional government, the Junta de Andalucía, and several specialist publishers. The best place to shop for maps is Librería Índice, Calle Panaderos, 2 (on the corner with Puerta del Mar), Málaga. ❑

RIGHT: a pause for thought.

PLACES

A detailed guide to the region with
the principal sites clearly cross-referenced
by number to the accompanying maps

The autonomous region of Andalucía is Spain's most populous, with over 7 million inhabitants in its eight southernmost provinces. It covers an area of some 87,000 sq km (33,600 sq miles), an expanse the size of Portugal and twice the size of the Netherlands.

Within these confines the variety of landscape is tremendous. To the north is the long ridge of the Sierra Morena, a mountain range that effectively seals the region off from the rest of Spain, where the rich *sevillanos* go hunting; to the south is the Costa del Sol, playground of foreigners, where Europe's working classes rub shoulders with aristocrats and the famous. In the centre lies the flat agricultural plain of the Guadalquivir. To the east are the arid desert lands of Almería and the mountains of Granada, and to the west the marshlands of the Coto Doñana nature reserve. On the horizon from almost anywhere is North Africa, whose influence is felt in the history and the towns of this southernmost region of Spain and of Europe.

Each of Andalucía's old cities, Seville, Córdoba and Granada, have major Moorish monuments of international significance. But others have their claims to fame: Cádiz, the home of the Armada and the signing of the first Spanish constitution: Ronda, the birthplace of bullfighting; Huelva, from where Columbus sailed for the New World. Parts of the province of Almería are so desolate that it's a popular location for shooting westerns; nearby Jaén is the undulating heartland of the olive growing industry, which financed the city's many Renaissance and baroque buildings.

Distances between provinces and cities are not enormous, but travel times may well be longer than expected, either because of the winding mountain roads, or because of the weight of traffic, particularly in the coastal areas (though new toll motorways offer faster if less interesting alternatives to the old main roads). Places of interest are numbered in the text and can be cross-referenced with the maps. Map locations are shown by the map icon in the top right corner of every right-hand page. ❑

PRECEDING PAGES: the Plaza de Toros, Málaga; the sierra village of Grazalema.
LEFT: flying the flag in Puerto Banús on the Costa del Sol.

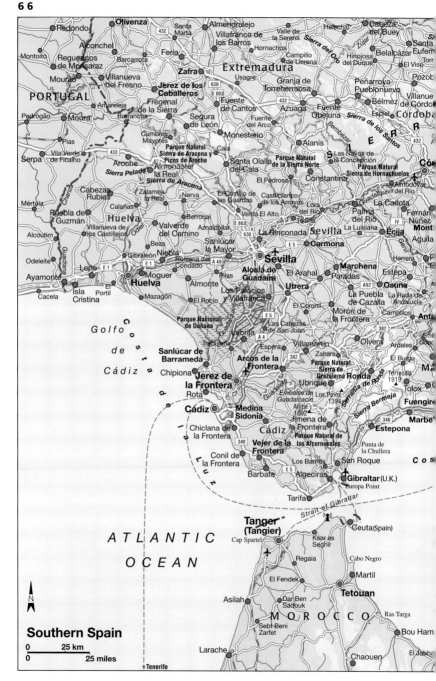

Southern Spain

0 — 25 km

0 — 25 miles

SEVILLE

Seville is undeniably romantic, with its gracious
architecture, horse-drawn carriages and avenues
of shady orange trees. But it is also an
exhilarating modern city with good shops,
great bars and a lively arts scene

I f Andalucía is the embodiment of
the Spanish clichés of flamenco,
gypsies, fiestas and bullfights,
then **Seville ❶** (Sevilla), its capital,
is its heart. This is the home of the
sultry temptress Carmen, of the lover
Don Juan, and of Figaro, the Barber
of Seville.

At one time this was Spain's
largest city, through which all the
riches of the New World poured.
Today, with a population of around
800,000, it is a prosperous hub of
commercial and industrial enterprise,
but you wouldn't immediately realise
it. Such is the *Sevillanos'* laid-back
attitude to life and devotion to fun and
fiestas, late nights and sluggish morning starts, that visitors may wonder
how they ever accomplish any work.

Seville is a city of undeniable
beauty. For *Sevillanos*, it's almost as
if no other place existed. In fact,
when you suggest to a *Sevillano* that
his or her city is the most beautiful in
Spain, you'll most probably get the
following response: *"No, en el todo
mundo"*, "No, in the whole world".

Glory and decay

Hispalis, the forerunner of Seville,
was founded by the Phoenicians in
around 500 BC, although native
Iberians populated the area from
around 700–600 BC. The Romans re-
developed Hispalis and also founded

nearby Itálica, the birthplace of
emperors Trajan and Hadrian. When
the Moors invaded Spain in AD 711,
it took them just a year to conquer
Seville and make it their cultural centre. They named it Ishbillya, and by
the 10th century it was one of the
most important cities in the caliphate
of Córdoba.

By the early 11th century the
Caliphate had split into some 30
taíffas. Ishbillya was the most powerful of these, and it prospered under
the reign of al-Mutadid (1042–69)

Maps:
City 70
Area 89

LEFT: La Giralda and
the Plaza de los Reyes.
BELOW: a ride in a
coche de caballo.

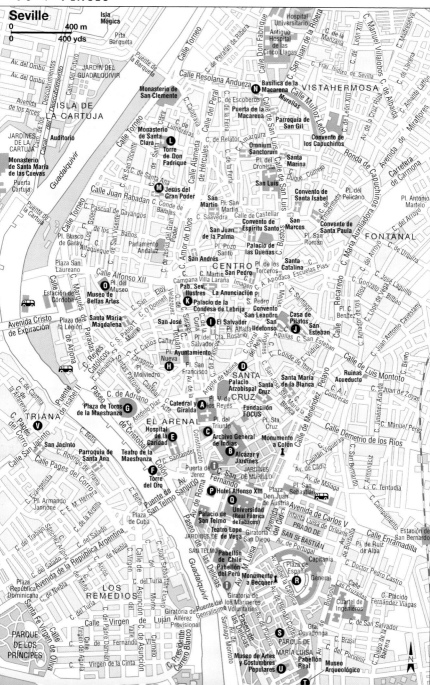

Seville

0 _____ 400 m
0 _____ 400 yds

and his son al-Mutamid (1068–91). In 1091 it was taken over by the Almoravids, who reunited al-Andalus, and then by the Almohads, who made Seville the capital of Muslim Spain. La Giralda, the ornate minaret that later became the bell-tower of the cathedral, dates from the Almohad era, as does the Torre del Oro.

After a 15-month siege by Fernando III in 1248, Seville was recaptured by the Christians. Seville then entered a golden age, and in 1401 construction began on the massive new Cathedral, which was to replace the mosque. The city was the home port for Christopher Columbus returning from his voyage of discovery in 1492. In 1503 Seville's Casa de Contratación was awarded the monopoly on Spanish trade with the Americas, ushering in a period of unprecedented prosperity that lasted nearly two centuries.

By the early 1600s Seville, with a population of 85,000, which included 7,000 slaves, was probably the fourth largest city in the world, after Naples, Paris and Venice. The ships departed and returned in convoys (in 1608 alone there were 283 sailings from Seville to the New World), creating periods of great activity and, inevitably, great inactivity. Seville had a vicious underworld whose gangs were always at each other's throats. And with the gold on the ships came disease. During the most serious epidemics up to 600 people died in the city every day.

By the late 17th century Seville was in decline. A combination of larger ships, an accumulation of silt in the Guadalquivir, improved facilities at Cádiz and a decreasing flow of desirable goods from America resulted in a downturn in trade. In 1680 the Admiralty was transferred to Cádiz, followed by the Casa de Contratación in 1717. In 1810, during the Wars of Independence, French troops occupied Seville, remaining for two years until expelled with the help of the Duke of Wellington (considered a hero in Spain to this day). Subsequently, Seville lapsed into a quiet, almost provincial town.

Nonetheless, 1848 was the inaugural year of the world-famous Feria de Sevilla, and the Ibero-American Exposition was held in 1929. During the Spanish Civil War, Seville was one of the first cities to fall to Franco's Nationalist rebels, who used the captured Radio Sevilla to spread their propaganda. To this day the Guadalquivir forms the basis of the city's prosperity, as it has through the centuries. Indeed, Seville is the only river port in Spain.

Orientation

The most important sights in Seville are clustered around the southern edge of the old city, sandwiched between the Avenida de la Constitución, San Fernando and Menéndez Pelayo. Next to Constitución is the Cathedral and the Archivo de Indias, with the Alcázar, a stone's throw to the south, its walls the

Map on page 70

He who has not at Seville been Has not, I trow, a wonder seen.
– RICHARD FORD
A Handbook for Travellers in Spain, 1855

BELOW:
the 13th-century Torre del Oro, built by the Almohads on the east bank of the Guadalquivir river.

The April Feria is an exhilarating time to be in Seville, but also crowded and expensive. Hotels must be booked a year in advance.

BELOW RIGHT:
making an impact at
the April Feria.

eastern border of the labyrinthine Barrio de Santa Cruz, the former Jewish quarter.

Between Constitución and the river are the Hospital de la Caridad, the Torre del Oro and the Plaza de Toros. The Museo de Bellas Artes, the Casa de Pilatos, the Alameda de Hércules and the main shopping area centring on Calle Sierpes lie to the north.

To the south, and still east of the river, the land is more open and the architecture grander; here you will find the old Tobacco Factory, now the University, and the exotic relics the 1929 Ibero-American Exhibition, including Hotel Alfonso XIII, the Plaza de España, San Telmo Palace and the Parque de María Luisa.

West of the river, opposite the Torre del Oro and the Plaza de Toros is the old Barrio de Triana, home to Seville's gypsies until they moved to high-rise apartments on the edge of town, allowing for the slow gentrification of the area. A little further north is the Isla Cartuja, the site of the 1992 World Fair, now the site of the Isla Mágica theme park.

The Cathedral

The **Cathedral** (Catedral y Giralda; Mon–Sat 11am–5pm, Sun and holidays 2.30–6pm; admission charge; audioguides available) is listed in the *Guinness Book of Records* simply for being big, but the close-packed streets that cluster around this vast edifice make this hard to appreciate from the outside.

A mosque was built on this site in 1172, and 12 years later a minaret was added. The huge Almohad mosque was consecrated for Christian use immediately after the Reconquest, but it was not until the beginning of the 15th century that work began on raising a cathedral.

The bulk of the Cathedral was built between 1401 and 1507; thus the principal structure is Gothic, with later additions, such as the choir, altar and Sacristía de los Cálices, which are late Gothic (1496– 1537); the Capilla Real (1530–69) at the eastern end, which is plateresque (intricately ornamented, from *platero*, meaning silversmith) and additions to the southern end, which are baroque.

City Celebrations

I n spring, before the heat becomes intolerable, Seville hosts two important and exhilarating fiestas in swift succession: Semana Santa and the Feria. The Feria (mid-April) started as a livestock market but has developed into a week-long celebration of spring, with dancing, drinking, displays of horsemanship, fireworks, bullfighting competitions and much more. A large area of the Los Remedios district on the west side of the Guadalquivir is transformed into a kaleidoscope of fairground attractions, where *Sevillana* ladies and their escorts, dressed to the nines, parade in their carriages.

Semana Santa (Easter) features more than 100 floats carried by 57 hooded brotherhoods who each have their own image of Christ or the Virgin; from the crowd come passionate songs of devotion, called *saetas* (literally arrows).

Both celebrations attract large numbers of people, which pushes up prices and makes accommodation almost impossible to find unless you reserve well in advance. If you can be in Seville for either or both, it is likely to be an experience you won't forget *(for more information on festivals, see pages 44–45).*

Independent visitors enter the cathedral by the **Puerta de San Cristóbal** (groups enter via the Puerta del Lagarto). A reception area leads through a small museum containing paintings (including work by Zurbarán and Murillo), church plate and other items of interest.

A faded photocopy of the *Guinness Book of Records* certificate sits in a glass information case alongside the Cathedral's floor plan: 126 metres (413 ft) long by 83 metres (272 ft) wide by 30 metres (100 ft) high, the Cathedral has the largest interior in the world, and is the third-largest cathedral in Christendom, after St Peter's in Rome and St Paul's Cathedral in London.

Inside, the Cathedral's immensity is not instantly apparent, as the centre of the building is filled by the **Capilla Mayor** (Main Chapel). The altarpiece of gilded hardwood contains 36 tableaux of the Old and New Testaments, comprising more

than 1,000 figures. Reaching 20 metres (66 ft) in height, almost to the roof, it was begun in 1482 by the Flemish sculptor Pieter Dancart and not finished for another 82 years.

In 1995 it was the dazzling focus for the marriage of King Juan Carlos's daughter Elena and Jaime de Marichalar y Sáenz.

Near by is the Gothic-Mudéjar Choir *(coro)*. Examine the detail in the carving, including the beautifully carved misericords.

On the south side, close to the entrance, is the grand but rather comic monument to Christopher Columbus, the great man's tomb carried by four figures representing the kingdoms that made up the Spanish crown at the time of his voyage – Castile, Navarre, Aragón and León. Many of Columbus's voyages were planned in Seville, as is documented by the Archivo General de Indias *(see page 78)*. It is not certain that the elaborate sarcophagus contains

Map on page 70

TIP

Although the Cathedral doesn't open to tourists until 11am, worshippers can attend Mass at 8.30am and 10am. The prayer chapel is open from 8am.

BELOW: Seville's Cathedral is the last and largest of the Gothic cathedrals in Spain.

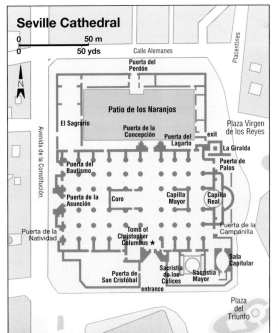

Seville Cathedral

0 ___ 50 m
0 ___ 50 yds

Calle Alemanes

Puerta del Perdón

Placentines

Patio de los Naranjos

El Sagrario

Puerta de la Concepción

Puerta del Lagarto

exit

Plaza Virgen de los Reyes

La Giralda

Avenida de la Constitución

Puerta del Bautismo

Puerta de Palos

Puerta de la Asunción

Coro

Capilla Mayor

Capilla Real

Puerta de la Natividad

Tomb of Christopher Columbus ★

Puerta de la Campanilla

Sala Capitular

Puerta de San Cristóbal

Sacristía de los Cálices

Sacristía Mayor

entrance

Plaza del Triunfo

N

The Patio de los Naranjos, courtyard of the original mosque.

BELOW: La Giralda's belfry. **BELOW RIGHT:** the Virgen de la Estrella is one of several precious icons in the Cathedral.

the remains of the great discoverer, as Columbus's widow had these taken to Santo Domingo in the Dominican Republic, from where they were later moved to Havana's cathedral and then back to Spain, a confusing journey that was poorly documented. Attempts to test the DNA of the bone fragments have so far proved inconclusive.

Before climbing La Giralda, the minaret of the original mosque, it is worth exploring the numerous side chapels and anterooms (especially on the south side), many of which are adorned with important paintings and statues. The treasury (**Sacristía Mayor**), contains a wealth of silverware, as well as the keys given to Fernando III by the Muslim and Jewish citizens following the reconquest of Seville in 1248.

Next door, the **Sacristía de los Cálices**, which has a fine vaulted ceiling, is hung with paintings by Goya, Valdés Leal and Zurbarán, among others. Look out for Goya's anachronistic painting of Justa and Rufina, Sevillian saints martyred during Diocletian's persecution of the Christians.

Behind the 3rd-century saints is the 12th-century Giralda tower.

In the eastern corner of the Cathedral is the 16th-century **Sala Capitular** (Chapter House). Built in elliptical shape with leather seats and marble floor, it was specifically designed for convocations of the Cathedral Council. Poised above the archbishop's throne is Murillo's fine *Imaculada*, dominant in a series of Murillos incorporated in the dome.

At the eastern end of the Cathedral is the **Capilla Real** (Royal Chapel), the most used and ornate of the side chapels, containing the royal tomb of Fernando III. Fittingly, his remains lie at the feet of the Virgen de los Reyes, the patron saint of Seville. Also here is the tomb of Fernando's queen, Beatriz, and his son Alfonso X (the Wise). On the north side of the Cathedral, don't miss the **Capilla de San Antonio** containing Murillo's *Vision of St Antony of Padua*.

La Giralda

Literally and figuratively, the high spot of the cathedral is the tower, the

much-photographed 94-metre (308-ft) minaret, which has been admired ever since its inception on the orders of Moorish ruler Abu-Yaqub Yusuf in 1184. The exterior, adorned with typical *sebka* decoration, is in direct contrast to the bland interior, where a series of 35 gently elevated ramps (designed so that horsemen could ride up them) lead visitors to an observation platform at a height of 70 metres (230 ft). Archaeological finds and other interesting items are displayed on the landings; they include a pair of 14th-century Mudéjar doors combining Gothic motifs and verses from the Koran.

From the top there are panoramic views of the city, the many patios invisible from street level unveiled in the patchwork below. You can also appreciate the immense scale of the cathedral from here, its soaring pinnacles and flying buttresses.

La Giralda is said to be the finest relic of the Almohad dynasty (although two similar minarets exist in Rabat and Marrakesh). Its beauty reputedly saved it from destruction following the Reconquest in 1248.

When negotiating the terms of their surrender, Muslim rulers, tormented by the prospect of the mosque and minaret falling under Christian control, wanted them destroyed. But Alfonso the Wise is said to have refused their plea, threatening to put to death anyone who attempted it.

An earthquake destroyed the tower's original ornamental top in 1356, and it was not until 1558 that it was replaced by the bells and weather vane (*giralda* in Spanish) – a goddess representing Faith by Hernán Ruiz.

Off the north side of the Cathedral, near the access to La Giralda, is the **Patio de los Naranjos**, the courtyard of the original mosque, from where you exit the Cathedral. The nearby **Puerta del Legarto** (Gate of the Lizard) is named after a life-size wooden alligator hanging from the ceiling, purportedly a replica of a live alligator given to Alfonso X by the Sultan of Egypt.

The Alcázar

The second architectural jewel in Seville is a short hop from La

Map on page 70

A pot in the extensive garden of the Alcázar, the former palace of Muslim and Christian rulers.

BELOW: the tomb of Christopher Columbus in the Cathedral.

Handle on the door of the main entrance to the Alcázar.

BELOW: looking into the Ambassador's Hall.

Giralda. Hidden behind battlemented ochre walls on the Plaza del Triunfo is the **Alcázar** (Alcázar y Jardines; Tues–Sat 9.30am–7pm, Sun and winter 9.30am–5pm, closed Mon; admission charge; audioguide available; www. patronato-alcazar-sevilla.es), the fortress-palace of both Muslim and Christian rulers.

The Moroccan invaders built the first fortress on this site in 712. In the 9th century a palace, walls of which are still standing, was added by Amir Abdal-Rahman II. The Moors built additional palaces, though these were still in the fortress style, and added to the gardens during the 11th and 12th centuries.

Following the reconquest, the Christian monarchs established a court here, and King Don Pedro (known as Pedro the Cruel) built a luxurious Mudéjar style palace on this site in 1364. It was renovated in the 16th century by Carlos V.

The juxtaposition of the contrasting styles has created a particularly intriguing complex. The examples of Moorish architecture are surpassed only by those found in the Alhambra.

Visiting the Alcázar

The entrance to the complex is through the **Puerta del León**, marked by a heraldic lion, in the original 11th-century walls. Beyond the ticket office are the gardens of the **Patio del León**, a former assembly ground, at the far end of which three arches lead into the Patio de la Montería, the inner courtyard. Before proceeding through here, take the passage in the far-left corner to reach the **Sala de Justicia**, considered to be the first example of Mudéjar-style architecture, built by Alfonso XI, and beyond that the lovely **Patio del Yeso** (Courtyard of Plasterwork), which formed part of the 12th-century Almohad palace.

Regaining the Patio del Lón, proceed through the arches to the **Patio de la Montería**, faced by the ornate facade of Don Pedro's Palace. On the right-hand side is the **Sala del Almirante** (Admiral's Hall), containing historical memorabilia and 18th-century paintings depicting the overthrow of the Moors. It was here that the Catholic Monarchs founded the Casa de la Contratación, for the organisation of expeditions to the New World. Its functions included the furnishing of embarkation permits; the inspection of ships; the supply of mercury for refining silver; the registration of merchandise and the handling of the gold, silver and pearls destined for the royal exchequer. It also administered justice, saw to the despatch of missionaries, and served as a centre for navigational studies.

In the adjacent **Chapel** (which has a fine 16th-century coffered ceiling), the altar painting has a nautical theme appropriate to the rooms, which were specifically built for the planning of naval expeditions. A figure hidden in the Virgen de los Navegantes' skirts is supposed to be Christopher Columbus.

The main entrance to the palace is surmounted by an inscription to

Pedro the Cruel. Inside, turn left. The dog-leg vestibule (typical of Arab architecture but here also used to confuse would-be assasins) leads into the **Patio de las Doncellas** (Maids Courtyard). It has a compact grace and quiet beauty. Koranic inscriptions ("None but Allah Conquers") combine with Mudéjar motifs.

Notable in the apartments is the magnificent **Ambassador's Hall** (Salón de los Embajadores), effectively the throne room, dating from the 11th-century palace. It has an intricately carved and gilded dome (15th-century), resting on a frieze of alternating castles and lions, and exquisite geometric and floral carvings on the walls. Beyond is the small **Patio de las Muñecas** (Courtyard of the Dolls), a private family chamber, named after two tiny faces, eroded but still visible, in the decoration on the columns, and the **Cuarto del Príncipe** (Prince's Suite), named after the son of the Catholic Monarchs, who was born here in 1478.

The Christian royal inhabitants also left their mark on the Alcázar in a more predictable manner, notably in the **Gothic Palace**, containing the **Salones de Carlos V** (Charles V's Apartments). The banquet room was the setting for the marriage of Carlos V and Doña Isabel of Portugal; its windows were added by his son, Felipe II, who introduced Renaissance trends. Charles's military campaigns in Tunisia are depicted in faded tapestries by the Dutch artist Juan de Vermayen, who included a self-portrait in his upside-down map of the Mediterranean.

The Alcázar's gardens

The Salones de Carlos V lead into the **Gardens**, a complex of patios, pools and pavilions. Nearest to the Salones de Carlos V is the Garden of El Estanque (The Pool), Renaissance in style but set around a rectangular pool that once irrigated the Moors' orchards. From here the **Gallery of El Etrusco** (1612–21), with views over the Garden of Las Damas (The Ladies), follows the course of the **Almohad Wall**.

Before leaving the Alcázar look out for the **Baños de María de Padilla**, the Moorish baths of Pedro

Map on page 70

The bronze statue of Mercury in the central pool of the Alcázar's Garden of El Estanque.

BELOW: in the Alcázar's gardens.

La Gitana (The Gypsy), just one of the many lively bars in the Barrio de Santa Cruz.

the Cruel's mistress, who was said to have had several lovers. Men of the court lined up for the strangely erotic act of drinking her bathwater – all except one who, it is said, excused himself on the grounds that "having tasted the sauce, he might covet the partridge".

Archivo General de Indias

Between the Alcázar and the Cathedral is a square, rather austere Renaissance-style building, once the Lonja (Stock Exchange) and now housing the **Archivo General de Indias** Ⓒ (Mon–Fri 10am–1pm; free admission). Constructed between 1583 and 1596 by Juan de Herrera, the architect of El Escorial near Madrid, its central patio, main marble staircase, and unusual Cuban wood shelves are of intrinsic interest. The collection comprises some 80 million pages relating to the discovery and colonisation of the New World. A small exhibition of historic and highly colourful documents, including extracts from Columbus's letters and diary, is maintained in one of the long galleries up the stairs.

Santa Cruz

The northeastern wall of the Alcázar borders on the **Barrio de Santa Cruz** Ⓓ, the former Judería (Jewish quarter), which is entered by an archway in one corner of the Patio Banderas (from which you exit the Alcázar). This corner of Seville unashamedly celebrates a fair few clichés about the city: the Seville patio is here in super-abundance, with *azulejo*-decorated courtyards glimpsed through wrought-iron gates, and young men playing flamenco in the squares. The Plaza de Santa Cruz is the site of Los Gallos, one of the best-known of the traditional flamenco venues in town.

Calle Justino de Neve or Pimienta will lead you to the Plaza Venerables at the centre of the barrio and the **Hospital Venerables**, founded in 1675 by Justino de Neve. This lovely two-level structure, with its slightly sunken central patio, is considered one of the best examples of baroque architecture in the city. Since 1991 it has served as home to the **Foundation FOCUS** (Fondo de Cultura de Sevilla).

Santa Cruz is sometimes criticised for being overly prettified and not much better than a tourist trap, but, with its many bars, restaurants and interesting little shops, it remains an appealing place to wander on a summer evening.

Between the Cathedral and the Guadalquivir river

Running south of the Cathedral, parallel to the river, is the Avenida de la Constitución. Between here and the river lies an old and characterful area of Seville known as El Arenal, the old port area. It has good traditional bars and restaurants, and includes the Torre del Oro, the Plaza de Toros and the Hospital de la Caridad, a 17th-century charitable hospital with a richly endowed baroque chapel.

From the Avenida de la Constitución, walk towards the river down Calle Almirantazgo, perhaps stopping in the **Plaza del Cabildo**, the scene of a coin-collectors' market on Sunday and the location of **El Torno**, a shop selling biscuits and knitted babywear made by nuns from the convents in Seville. Alternatively, take Calle Santander from Consticución, passing the former **Real Casa de Moneda** (Royal Mint), a fine building earmarked for restoration.

The **Hospital de la Caridad** Ⓔ (Mon–Sat 9am–1.30pm and 3.30–6.30pm, Sun 9am–1pm; admission charge; www.santa-caridad.org), on Calle Temprado, was founded in 1674 as a charity hospital for the homeless and the sick, a function it still serves to this day. It is best-known for the outstanding artworks in its chapel, which exemplifies such institutions' great patronage of the arts during Seville's Golden Age. In addition to the highly ornate *Holy Interment* altarpiece by Pedro Roldán, considered one of the finest baroque altarpieces in Spain, the walls are hung with remarkable paintings. There are works by

Murillo and, above and opposite the entrance, two spine-tingling works by Valdés Leal showing the transitory nature of life, which passes *In Ictu Oculi* (In the Blink of an Eye – *see the picture on page 7*).

Leaving the hospital you will see in the small garden opposite a statue of Don Miguel de Mañara, a dissolute Calatrava Knight who reputedly established the charitable hospital after experiencing a vision of his own funeral procession. Don Miguel is considered by some to be the role model for the legendary Don Juan, the cynical lover with 1,003 Spanish mistresses. Decide for yourself if this man looks like a reformed seducer or the eponymous hero of Mozart's *Don Giovanni*, who is eventually dragged down to hell by demons. The hospital became a port of call for romantic visitors who believed Seville to be the hot bed of the lascivious south. Byron explained why in his own *Don Juan*:

What men call gallantry, and gods adultery,
Is much more common where the climate is sultry.

Map
on page
70

TIP

For a modern and luxurious version of the Arab *hammam* (bathhouse) visit Aire de Sevilla, Calle Aire, 15 (www.airedesevilla.com; tel: 955-010 025/26) in the Barrio de Santa Cruz.

BELOW: the Hospital de la Caridad, a rich repository of art.

The 13th-century Torre del Oro on the east bank of the Guadalquivir is the starting point for hour-long river cruises, which operate throughout the day and until 10pm.

BELOW:
La Maestranza.

Just a block away on the riverbank, the **Torre del Oro** ❻ (once covered with golden tiles) stands like a chess piece on the bank of the river. Dating from 1220, it was built outside the city walls as a watchtower. It also served a defensive purpose by anchoring a chain that stretched across the river. At other times it was used to store gold brought back from the Americas, and as a prison. The round top and spire were added in the 18th century. Today the tower houses a **Maritime Museum** (Tues–Fri 10am–2pm, Sat and Sun 11am–2pm; small admission charge) filled with fascinating odds and ends, from a shark's jaws to paintings of the famous navigators. Murals here show how Seville in the 1700s was a great maritime port.

As well as being the starting point for river cruises, the tower marks the start of hop-on, hop-off bus tours.

A little upstream to the north is the modern **Teatro de la Maestranza** opera house (Calle Núñez de Balboa), built in 1991, and beyond it the **Plaza de Toros** and **La Maestranza** ❼, the bullring

(9.30am–7pm; admission charge; www.realmaestranza.com), one of the oldest rings in the country. Guided 20-minute tours in English and Spanish take in the bullring itself, the museum, matadors' chapel, operating theatre, stables, etc. Owned by the Knighthood of Real Maestranza, the bullring was begun in 1761 but not completed in its present form until the 1880s.

Look out for the small covered bridge linking the plaza with the social club for members of the Real Maestranza. The museum is quite interesting, though not as good as some of its genre.

North of the Cathedral

Directly north of the cathedral, the Avenida de la Constitución leads up to the **Plaza Nueva** ❽, on which stands the old, plateresque **Ayuntamiento** (Town Hall), dating from 1572. Behind and east of it is the **Plaza San Francisco**, once used for tournaments. Narrow streets from the top right of the Plaza San Francisco lead to the 17th-century church of **El Salvador** ❾, at a nexus of shops

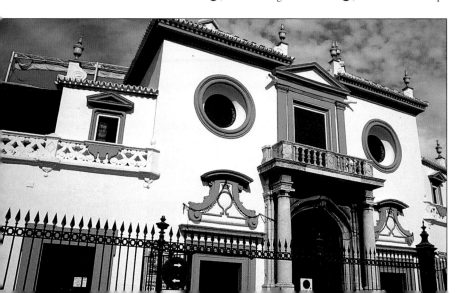

selling wedding dresses. This church, ramshackle from the outside but with spectacular gold *retablos* (altarpieces), was built on the site of earlier places of worship, including the city's first mosque. Archaeological excavations have also uncovered finds from a Roman Temple and early Christian, Visigoth and Mozarbic churches. Notice the Arabic inscriptions above the side door. On **Plaza del Salvador**, Bar Alicantina is famous for its seafood tapas.

From here it is a short hop to the **Plaza Alfalfa**, a busy little square with an excellent patisserie (Horno San Buenaventura), and the site of a pet market on Sunday mornings. A little further east is the 16th-century **Casa de Pilatos** ❶ (Plaza de Pilatos; daily 9am–7pm; admission charge for ground floor plus an additional charge for the upstairs rooms; audioguide available). Said to have been modelled on Pontius Pilate's house in Jerusalem, a place of pilgrimage for its original owner (hence its name), the house was built in Mudéjar and Renaissance styles. The central patio beyond the *apeadero*

(carriage yard) is enclosed by a two-storey arcade of Moorish (bottom) and Gothic (top) arches.

This courtyard contains dazzling *azulejos* in puzzle-book patterns. To the right is the chapel and Pilate's study. A monumental staircase leads up to a late Mudéjar cupola dating from 1537. There are brief guided tours (in English) of the furnished upper apartments every 30 minutes.

Opposite the Casa de Pilatos is the **Convento San Leandro**, a closed-order convent, whose contact with the outside world is via the sale of its famous *yemas* (candied egg yolks).

Directly north from the Plaza Nueva is the pedestrianised **Calle Sierpes**, lined with stylish shops. This is the heart of the shopping area.

At Calle de la Cuna, 8 (parallel with Sierpes), **Palacio de la Condesa de Lebrija** ❶ (Mon–Fri 10.30am–1.30pm, 4.30–7pm, Sat 10am–1pm; admission charge for ground floor plus an additional charge for the upstairs rooms; guided tours available; www.palaciodelebrija.com), is an outstanding palace built in the 16th century and

Map on page 70

Shop until you drop on Calle Sierpes, the main shopping artery, then stop off at La Campana (No. 1), for delicious cakes and coffee.

BELOW: the main courtyard of the Casa de Pilatos.

Looking for Carmen

When it was built between 1728 and 1766, the Real Fábrica de Tabacos (Royal Tobacco Factory), now part of Seville University, was the second-largest building in Spain after the Escorial palace near Madrid.

Here, thousands of women, known as *cigarreras,* worked to produce cigars and powdered snuff. The place was surrounded by tight security, for the Spanish State enjoyed a lucrative monopoly on the tobacco trade.

The tobacco factory, which functioned as such until the 1960s, is known as the home of Carmen, one of the most memorable literary stereotypes Spain has inspired. In the story, by the French dramatist Prosper Mérimée, published in 1845, the brigadier José Navarro becomes smitten with passion for a gypsy *cigarrera* whom he must accompany to prison. He risks all by allowing her to escape, then deserts the army and becomes a smuggler and bandit for her sake.

But Carmen isn't faithful to her brigadier, and José stabs her to death outside the Maestranza bullring after he finds her flirting with a *toreador* (bullfighter).

Most people remember Carmen from Bizet's beloved opera, premiered 30 years after Mérimée's story was published. It marked a turning point in the genre, and continues to be the most popular opera in the world. The character Carmen came to represent the classic Andalusian temptress – demure yet defiant, feminine and independent at the same time, capable of turning men mad with desire.

Did Mérimée base his heroine on a real person? To find out, one should to cross the river to the Los Remedios district, where a modern building houses Seville's new tobacco factory. On the third floor are the archives from the old tobacco factory – thousands of ledgers, each containing lists of the women who worked at the factory, with specific descriptions of each one.

The books list quite a few women named Carmen or María del Carmen, any one of whom could have served as a model for Mérimée. One of them, for instance, is "María del Carmen García, from Seville, unmarried, aged 15, small, light-coloured, black eyes, who was dismissed for having spoken insulting and scandalous words to her companions, and for throwing a pair of scissors at Concepción Vegue". In fact, the custodian of this peculiar archive believes Merimée's Carmen was most likely a composite of the women who worked there when the author visited in 1840.

The Seville factory, in which up to 3,500 *cigarreras* would be working at one time, was Spain's biggest employer, and provided the first opportunity for women to gain financial independence from their menfolk. These *cigarreras* were the breadwinners in many a household, while their husbands loitered on street corners, smoking the cheroots that their womenfolk had smuggled out of the factory. The women organised themselves well, working in teams, with one member appointed to look after her colleagues' children. Their spirit of camaraderie and their self-confidence must have made a strong and lasting impression on Merimée. ❏

LEFT: Gonzalo Bilbao's *Las Cigarreras* (1915) in the Museo de Bellas Artes.

remodelled in the 19th with a Renaissance-Mudéjar patio and mosaics from Itálica on the walls and floors, brought here by the late Countess of Lebrija, who was an archaeologist.

A few blocks further north is the **Alameda de Hércules**, a broad avenue marked at one end by two pillars topped by statues of Julius Caesar and Hercules. It hosts a Sunday flea market *(rastro)* and forms the hub of a lingering red-light district. Many of the houses have been transformed into bars and clubs, some catering to the gay community.

One or two buildings are worth visiting in this quarter, notably the **Monasterio de Santa Clara**  (Convent of Santa Clara), and, near the river, the ancient **Torre de Don Fadrique** (1252).

Several churches in the northern part of the old city have interesting Mudéjar details, including **Santa Catalina** and **San Marcos**. Other churches are important for the icons they contain. The church of **Jesús del Gran Poder** (the Powerful Jesus), on Plaza San Lorenzo, has an unusual image of Christ carrying the cross; worshippers kiss or touch the image's heel to help speed their prayers.

At the northern end of the old city, near Puerta Macarena, is the **Basílica de la Macarena**, built (1949) to house the Virgen de la Esperanza (La Macarena), Seville's best-loved icon. She leaves her pedestal once a year during Semana Santa. A small museum contains her many costumes for the journey and the *paso* (bearer) on which she is carried.

The Museo de Bellas Artes

Northwest of the Plaza Nueva is the **Museo de Bellas Artes** (Fine Arts Museum; Plaza del Museo, Tues 3–8pm, Wed–Sat 9am–8pm, Sun 9am–2pm; admission charge for non-EU visitors), housed in the 17th-century Convento de la Merced Calzada, which was closed following the disentailment of many convents and monasteries in 1835. Its architectural highlight is the magnificent baroque chapel with frescoed vaulting and dome. Considered second in national importance after the Prado, its collection is well worth seeing. There are works by El Greco, Goya, Murillo, Zurbarán, Velázquez and Valdés Leal, among others, many expropriated from religious properties. Don't miss the carved Christs, Virgins and saints in gilded and polychrome wood. Developed from a folk-art tradition, image-carving had its own school in Andalucía, exemplified in Seville by Juan Martínez Montañes.

South of the Cathedral

South of the Cathedral, the Avenida de la Constitución leads past the Archivo de Indias *(see page 78)* to the Puerta Jerez roundabout, marking the site of one of the old city gates.

Just off the roundabout is the palatial **Hotel Alfonso XIII** , built in imitation of the Seville patio style specifically for the 1929 Ibero-American Exhibition. The bar in the central patio is a great place to enjoy

Map on page 70

Stained-glass panel in the vestibule of the Hotel Alfonso XIII.

BELOW: Hotel Alfonso XIII, Puerta Jerez.

Figure on the top of the Real Fábrica de Tabacos, now the University's faculties of science and law.

BELOW: the moat of the Plaza de España.
RIGHT: feeding the park's many doves.

an early-evening cocktail while listening to the resident pianist.

Alongside the hotel is one of the biggest buildings in the Western world, erected in 1750 to house the **Real Fábrica de Tabacos** (Royal Tobacco Factory), in which the mythical Carmen immortalised by Bizet in his opera of the same name supposedly worked with thousands of other *cigarreras (see page 82)*. Now this handsome, if austere, building is part of the University (open to the public weekdays). For a rather idealised picture of life in the factory in its heyday, visit the Museo de Bellas Artes *(see page 83)*, where there are several paintings showing the factory women at work.

Beyond the University are the beginnings of the Parque de María Luisa and the site of Seville's Ibero-American Exhibition of 1929. Some of the pavilions have been put to new uses, such as the biological research station for the Coto Doñana Nature Reserve (Avenida de Chile), which has a striking courtyard in pink marble decorated with animal carvings. The most eye-catching

legacy of the exhibition is the semi-circular **Plaza de España** . The extraordinary moated building surrounding it took 15 years to build and functioned as the Spanish pavilion. Its towers were inspired by the cathedral at Santiago de Compostela, and the elaborately tiled panels below the colonnade depict the Spanish provinces, running in alphabetical order from left to right. The moat, with its little *azulejo*-decorated bridges and rowing boats for hire, is currently being restored.

Across from the plaza is the **Parque de María Luisa** , a successful mixture of formal landscaping and wilderness areas, where familiar European plants and flowers are found next to exotic species from Africa and the Americas. Its shady paths are wonderfully cool on a stiflingly hot summer's day and lovely to tour by carriage or bicycle in the early evening (bikes and tricycles can be hired near the gates). It is full of life and surprises: *azulejo*-covered benches; ceramic frogs spouting water; walled patios with frescos; duck sanctuaries full of white doves.

The park once belonged to the **Palacio de San Telmo**, now the headquarters of the Andalusian regional government, which stands at its northern end. St Telmo is the patron saint of sailors, and this building, which has an elaborately carved baroque main archway, was built in the 17th century as a university for seafarers. In the 18th century it became a naval academy, and was later expanded into the residence of the dukes of Montpensier. Duchess Marie Louise of Orléans donated the grounds to the city in 1893.

Two museums

The **Plaza de América** at the southern end of the park is the location for two museums. The **Museo Arqueológico 🅣** (Archaeological Museum; Tues 3–8pm, Wed–Sat 9am–8pm, Sun 9am–3pm; admission charge for non-EU visitors) covers local excavation sites, with representative material from Neolithic through to Tartessian, Roman and Moorish times. Pottery, silver and gold work include items originating from the countries of Andalucía's trading

partners at the time, such as painted ceramics from Phoenicia. The Roman collection is typical of the significant Roman cities that once surrounded Seville, a map of which is on the wall.

In particular, seek out the replica Carambolo Treasure (the original items are kept in a bank vault), a cache of 21 beautifully worked gold pieces (jewellery and statuettes) found during construction work in Seville in 1961. Dating from around the 5th century BC, the treasure is possible evidence of the mysterious Tartessian civilisation.

Opposite, the sleepy **Museo de Artes y Costumbres Populares 🅤** (Arts and Folklore Museum; open Tues 2.30–8.30pm, Wed–Sat 9am–8.30 pm, Sun 9am–2.30pm; admission charge for non-EU visitors) celebrates some familiar aspects of Andalusian culture – famous bullfighters, the Seville Feria, Semana Santa traditions and traditional costumes (with excellent background classical music). More surprising is a massive ploughing exhibition and a series of domestic interiors.

Map on page 70

Azulejo *detail on the colonnade of the Plaza de España. The word* azulejo *is thought to derive from* alzulayj*, the Arabic for "little stone".*

BELOW: the Museo de Artes y Costumbres Populares.

The finishing straight on the Anaconda rollercoaster at the Isla Mágica theme park.

BELOW: the Expo area.

Triana

A little west of the Plaza de Toros, the lovely **Puente de Isabel II**, with a statue of the famous bullfighter Manolete (1917–47) at its end, crosses the Guadalquivir to the **Triana** district, once known as the gypsy quarter but now a lively working-class area visited during the day for the ceramic factories and at night for its restaurants and bars (expensive along the riverside **Calle Betis**, which has wonderful views over to the Torre del Oro on the east bank; cheaper along **Calle Castilla** and nearby side streets). A favourite for local specialities is **Casa Cuesta**, officially called the Cervecería Ruiz, on the corner of Castilla and San Jorge. Opposite, a dark alleyway, appropriately named the **Callejón de la Inquisición** (Seville witnessed some of the Spanish Inquisition's greatest purges) leads down to the river.

Expo site

To the north of Triana, the **Isla de la Cartuja** used to be a swampy wasteland, but was transformed for the Expo '92 Universal Exposition, commemorating the 500th anniversary of Columbus's discovery of the Americas. The area was landscaped and a new outdoor auditorium built, while two new suspension bridges were constructed to connect the "island" to the rest of Seville, the elegant, wishbone-shaped **Alamillo**, designed by the well-known Spanish architect Santiago Calatrava, and the **Barqueta** bridge, the main link to the Isla Mágica theme park (*see below*). Afterwards part of La Cartuja was transformed into a technological park.

Isla Mágica, the largest theme park in southern Spain (open Apr–Oct: daily mid-Jul–mid-Sept, Tues–Sun Apr–mid-July, Fri–Sun Oct; admission charge, with reduced prices in the afternoons and evening; www.islamagica.es). This 35-hectare (86-acre) fantasy land has a rollercoaster and other rides, all with a South American theme, plus live shows with actors in period costume. New attractions are added regularly. Recent additions include *La Mágica del Caballo* horse show, the Ciklón and Don Quixote adventure rides.

The island is named after the 15th-century **Carthusian Monastery**, Santa María de las Cuevas, at its centre. Columbus was a regular visitor, and was temporarily buried here when he died. In the 19th century, the monastery had a ceramics factory, where the prized Cartuja china was made until 1982. Part of the building houses the **Centro Andaluz de Arte Contemporáneo** (Tues–Fri 10am–8pm, Sat 11am–9pm, Sun 10am–3pm; admission charge; www.caac.es), showing temporary international exhibitions and a permanent exhibition of modern Andalusian art.

Seville province

The industrial and residential influence of Seville extends some way into the countryside, but there are no other towns of any real size in the province. To the north lies the Sierra Morena, a vast belt of hills covered with rough woodland; to the south lie agricultural flatlands dominated by the Guadalquivir; to the west is the province of Huelva; and to the east soft rolling agricultural land,

the Campiña, has a chain of ancient settlements.

Visitors heading due south in the winter months may find minor roads frustrating; a combination of heavy rain and high tides can mean many a route is cut by swollen streams. The central town to these flatlands is **Los Palacios**, a quiet, rural place and the site of an agricultural research station.

West of Seville

Once across the Guadalquivir, roads west of Seville swiftly leave the city behind. Up the far bank of the river to the north, near Santiponce, is the Roman site of **Itálica ❷** (Tues–Sun; admission charge for non-EU visitors), built as a resort facility for Roman troops in 206 BC. Later, two Roman emperors, Hadrian and Trajan, were born there.

Excavations have revealed a huge amphitheatre (thought to be the third-largest in the Roman Empire) and an extensive grid-plan of streets, still under excavation. Several fine mosaics have also been revealed: indeed, Itálica was the source of

Maps:
City 70
Area 89

Column from Itálica, the principal Roman city of the region. To get to Itálica from Seville, take a bus from Plaza de Armas. A service runs through the day.

BELOW:
the Alamillo bridge, built for Expo '92.

Map on page 89

Carmona has the largest Roman necropolis outside Rome.

LEFT AND RIGHT: the amphitheatre and residential area of Itálica.

many of the stunning mosaics in the Palacio de la Contesa de Lebrija in Seville *(see page 81).*

North of Seville

Roads north from Seville cross the flat river valley and ascend into the **Sierra Morena**, a thinly populated belt of hills which provides the plain with its water. The Sierra's main attraction is its refreshing coolness after the heat of the lowlands; in the winter it is a hunting centre, and the towns of **Cazalla** and **Constantina** ❸ (the latter surprisingly prosperous, with a dramatic figure of Christ on the hillside above) are filled with well-dressed young men from Seville swapping hunting stories in the bars. The area is protected as the **Parque Natural de la Sierra del Norte**, www.sierranortedesevilla.com, a wonderful place for walking and trout fishing.

East of Seville

Three important historical towns lie east of Seville. **Carmona** ❹, the closest, most interesting and most atmospheric, was an important Roman centre. A Roman amphitheatre and necropolis and museum lie on the Seville side of town; the necropolis (Tues–Sun; closed pm Sat–Sun and in summer; admission charge for non-EU visitors), the largest Roman burial ground outside Rome, is well laid out, complete with a crematorium with walls that are still discoloured by the fire, a large numbers of small paupers' tombs as well as a couple of much grander edifices.

The town itself commands an extensive view over the plain. The ancient **Córdoba Gate**, well corroded but remarkably intact considering its age (originally 2nd-century, with Moorish and baroque additions). The other gate, the **Puerta de Sevilla** (on the Seville side of town), is gigantic and features a protective double entranceway. The building incorporates another Alcázar and the tourist office. In front, in the newer town, the church of **San Pedro** has one of many imitation Giraldas found around the province, this one dating from 1704.

Écija ⑤, some 56 km (34 miles) east of Seville, has many such towers. Unlike most Andalusian towns, it is built in a valley bowl rather than on a hill, and consequently has no summer breeze to relieve the heat. The town hall promotes Écija as "the city of sun and towers"; however, it is better known as "the frying pan of Spain" on account of its relentless summer heat.

The church of **Santa María** (southwest of Plaza Major) has a Mudéjar patio filled with archaeological artefacts. The covered market is worth dipping into, and Calle Caballeros (north of the main square) has several rambling and ornate merchants' houses, including the **Palacio de Peñaflor**, which has an unusual curved balcony. The town is littered with crumbling church towers, all of which echo Seville's Giralda in some way.

South of Écija is **Osuna ⑥**, again with a large collection of merchants' houses, reflecting its prosperous history as the seat of the dukes of Osuna. Here the Giralda imitation is built into a grand facade on the Calle San Pedro, next door to which is the grandly baroque **Palacio del Marqués de La Gomera**. The Arab tower on the hill has a small archaeological museum (Tues–Sun; closed 1.30–3.30pm; admission charge) documenting the town's period as the Roman town of Urso.

Also on the hill is the 16th-century turreted **Universidad de Orsuna** (visits by guided tour only), and the **Collegiate Church of Santa María** (Tues–Sun; closed 1.30–4pm and Sun pm; admission charge), which is big and bare inside. Below the church is the **Convent of La Encarnación** (same hours as Santa María; admission charge), which houses a museum of religious art.

From Osuna a good road makes for the heights of the Sierra Nevada and the city of Granada.   ❑

Map below

BELOW: Plaza de España, Écija.

RESTAURANTS & BARS

Best Areas

As befits the regional capital, Seville has the best choice of restaurants in Andalucía. For the most part these are fairly traditional in character (unlike, say, the fashionable establishments in Madrid or Barcelona), with tiled interiors and mountain hams suspended from the ceilings. Good areas for eating are **El Arenal,** between the Cathedral

PRICE CATEGORIES

Prices for three-course meal per person with a half-bottle of house wine:
€= under €20
€€ = €20–€40
€€€ = €40–€60
€€€€= over €60

and the river and **Santa Cruz**. Triana's riverside **Calle Betis** is packed with restaurant-cum bars with outside terraces and fine views over the sights on the east bank.

Restaurants

Casablanca
Calle Zaragoza, 50
Tel: 954-224 698
L & D. Closed Sun. €€€
You have to fight your way through the tiny bar to reach the small dining room to sample this restaurant's famous seafood dishes. There is no menu, so just point at what you want.

Casa Robles
Alvarez Quintero, 58
Tel: 954-560 637
L & D. €€

A classic Seville restaurant serving regional specialities, some with a modern twist. Typical Seville decor. The bar is famous for its tapas.

Corral del Agua
Callejón de Agua, 6
Tel: 954-224 841
L & D. Closed Sun and Jan.
€€€
Situated on the edge of the Barrio Santa, this elegant restaurant occupies a restored 18th-century house, centred on a pleasant patio with plenty of potted plants and a fountain. Traditional Andalusian dishes.

Don Raimundo
Argote de Molina, 26
Tel: 954-223 355
L & D. Closed Sun evening.
€€
Near the cathedral, this large restaurant occupying a 14th-century monastery, offers a classic *sevillano* experience. The house specialities are meat and game; large portions.

Egaña–Oriza
San Fernando, 41
Tel: 954-227 211
L & D. Closed Sat L, Sun and Aug. €€€
The Basque-inspired cuisine of this elegant, modern restaurant near the Murillo gardens is among the best in Andalucía. Best to reserve.

El Buzo
Calle Antonio Diaz, 5
Tel: 954-210 231
L & D. €€
Famous for its much-photographed blue tile facade. Inside, a marine theme prevails, both in the menu and decor.

El Cairo
Calle Reyes Católicos, 13
Tel: 954-213 089
L & D. €€
Plenty of pavement tables for outdoor dining. Meat dishes are on offer, but the speciality is grilled sea bream or sea bass. Reliably good.

Enrique Becerra
Gamazo, 2
Tel: 954-213 049
L & D. Closed Sun. €€€
Small restaurant in an old Seville house in the El Arenal area. Serves high quality Andalusian fare. Has a popular tapas bar as well.

El Giraldillo
Plaza Virgen de los Reyes
Tel: 954-214 525
L & D. €€€
A favourite with tourists on account of its position next to the Cathedral with a view of the Giralda. But rest assured, the food is as good as the setting.

Hostería del Laurel
Plaza de los Venerables, 5
Tel: 954-220 295
L & D. €
www.hosteriadellaurel.com

LEFT: Seville claims to have invented tapas, and there is no shortage of tapas bars.

On a small square in the Barrio de Santa Cruz, Hostería del Laurel is enormously popular, both as a good-value dining spot and a tapas venue. Traditional Andalusian cuisine.

La Albahaca
Plaza Santa Cruz, 12
Tel: 954-220 714
L & D. Closed Sun. €€€
A pretty restaurant located in the heart of Seville's Barrio Santa Cruz, in an old townhouse. The accent is on the decor as well as on the food – an imaginative mixture of Andalusian, French and Basque influences. Best to reserve.

La Alicantina
Plaza del Salvador, 2–3
Tel: 954-226 1122
L & D. €€
A long-established and very popular seafood restaurant on an atmospheric square. Great tapas; always packed.

La Isla
Arfe 25
Tel: 954-215 376
L & D. Closed Aug.€€
Excellent seafood restaurant, also serving simple meat dishes. Try the Catalan seafood stew for a real tastebud treat.

La Taberna del Alabardero
Zaragoza, 20
Tel: 954-502 721
L & D. Closed Aug. €€€
One of a well-known chain of restaurants, with Spanish/international cuisine in a typical setting. An adjoining cafeteria is a good option for budget travellers.

Las Piletas
Marqués de Paradas, 28
Tel: 954 220 404
L & D. €€
Bullfighting themed bar-restaurant popular among locals, with a busy bar and an old-fashioned restaurant. The meat and fish are good, but ask the waiters for their recommendations.

Ox's
Calle Betis, 61
Tel: 954-276 275
L & D. Closed Mon and Sun evening. €€€
Ox's is reputed to serve the best steak in Seville (and it serves good charcoal-grilled fish, too), in a small dining room decorated with understated elegance.

Salvador Rojo
Calle San Fernando, 23
Tel: 954 229 725
L & D. Closed Sun. €€€
If you tire of traditional Andalusian fare and the ambience that tends to go with it try this modern restaurant serving innovative food made with seasonal produce.

San Fernando
Hotel Alfonso XIII
Calle San Fernando, 2
Tel: 954 917 000
B, L & D. €€€
The restaurant of Seville's top hotel is worth investigating, as it often has good value promotional menus.

San Marco
Calle Mesón del Moro
Tel: 954 564 390
L & D. €€
One in a chain of three pizza-pasta restaurants which are notable for their locations. This branch is housed in 12th-century Arab baths.

Bars and Cafés

Seville claims to have invented tapas and can even tell you the bar where this national custom originated: **El Rinconcillo**, Calle Gerona, 40 (near the Santa Catalina church) claims to have been serving tapas since 1670. If you're a serious tapas addict head for **Modesto** (Calle Cano y Cueto, 13), **Hostelería del Laurel** (see restaurants) or the hugely popular **La Antigua Bodeguita**, Plaza del Salvador, 6. Another tapas institution is **Cala Manolo** (Calle San Jorge, 16) in Triana on the west bank of the Guadalquivir.

For a tapas lunch just a stone's throw from the Cathedral, try **Cervecería Giralda**, Plaza Virgen del los Reyes. It is also good for breakfast while waiting for the Cathedral or Alcázar to open.

For atmospheric bars, visit **Calle García de Vinuesa** in the Arenal near the bullring. It is lined with old-fashioned bodegas.

Seville also has some great *pastelerías* (cake shops-cum-cafés), which do a roaring trade in the late afternoon. Two of the best in the central area are **Horno San Benaventura**, on Plaza Alfalfa, and **La Campana**, (Calle Sierpes, 1), a fine resting place for shoppers.

RIGHT: preparing for the day's trade. Note that, like most Spaniards, *sevillanos* lunch and dine late.

FROM LA PILETA TO PICASSO

Artistic treasures abound in Andalucía's museums and churches. In the 17th century Seville was the centre of a Golden Age of Art

ABOVE: *St Hugo of Grenoble in the Carthusian Refectory* (1633) by Francisco Zurbarán (1598–1664), in the Museo de Bellas Artes, Seville. Zurbarán worked extensively in Seville.

BELOW: *Mater Dolorosa* (1665) by Bartolomé Esteban Murillo (1617–82), in Seville's Museo de Bellas Artes. The foremost exponent of baroque religious art in his day, Murillo is known for his ethereal virgins wreathed in clouds and cherubs.

Pablo Picasso was born in Málaga in 1881 and, although his family moved north when he was only 10, throughout his life he considered himself first and foremost an Andalusian. He was heir to a formidable artistic legacy, stretching back 25,000 years to the time when prehistoric man decorated the walls of caves such as La Pileta.

The Moors leaned more towards decorative arts, which adorned their palaces and ceramics. Under the Christians, Andalucía experienced a flourishing in the arts, and in the 17th century Seville was the cradle of Spain's Siglo de Oro ("Golden Age") of art, with masters such as Francisco de Zurbarán, Bartolomé Murillo and Diego de Velázquez all working around the same time. The Church, profiting from the activities of the Inquisition, grew rich during this period and commissioned grand altarpieces and religious paintings. Recognised artists would gravitate to the court in Madrid, but Seville was always decisive in their careers.

In the 19th century, the age of Romanticism, Andalusian art tended to historical themes and *costumbrista* portrayals of everyday life. One of the most popular artists of the day was Julio Romero de Torres, famous for his paintings of Andalusian women, demure and provocative at the same time *(see above)*.

ABOVE: *Naranjas y Limones* (Oranges and Lemons), a classic work by Julio Romero de Torres (1874–1930), who specialised in Andalusian beauties. Córdoba has a museum dedicated to the artist.

ANDALUCÍA'S ICONS

One of the most typical manifestations of Andalusian art are the polychrome wood sculptures of the 17th century, an art form that developed from a folk-art tradition. Unlike northern European carving, the general theme was religious, and churches were filled with fine images and carved altarpieces, often used in the Semana Santa processions. The genre was extremely popular because the expressive statues of virgins and martyred saints appealed to the Andalusian sense of drama and pathos.

Two main schools were established around the central figures of Juan Martínez Montañes in Seville and Alonso Cano in Granada. Both artists had numerous followers, such as Juan Gómez and Pedro Roldán in the case of Montañes and Pedro de Mena and José de Mora in the case of Cano, whose work developed increasingly exaggerated, baroque expressiveness.

Many of these priceless images were destroyed in the course of various wars (including the Napoleonic invasion and the Spanish Civil War), but others still survive in the churches of Andalucía and are well worth seeking out.

TOP: *Purísima Concepción* by Alonso Cano (1601–67), an architect and painter, but best-known for carvings.
ABOVE: *Cristo de la Clemencia* by Juan Martínez Montañes.

BELOW: *Composición* by Rafael Zabaleta (1907–60). Popular rural scenes were a theme for this artist from the village of Quesada, near the Sierra de Cazorla. There is a museum of Zabaleta's work in Jaén.

LEFT: *Homage to Picasso* (1976) by Miguel Berrocal which is situated outside the Museo de Picasso in Málaga. Like Picasso, Berrocal was born in Málaga (1933). He is known for his puzzle sculptures.

HUELVA AND THE PARQUE NACIONAL DE DOÑANA

Huelva's sleepy towns and marshy estuaries create an ethereal beauty. Its attractions for visitors include the Parque Nacional de Doñana, Europe's most important wetland area, and sweeping Atlantic beaches

Seville
Huelva

Stretching to the Portuguese border, Huelva is one of the less visited provinces of Andalucía. Although quickly and easily reached from Seville, the region has an air of peripheral isolation that can be felt in its remote mountain villages, gloriously empty beaches and the vast, wild Doñana National Park – all of which makes for pure, undisturbed escapism.

Meanwhile, evidence of a more significant past emanates from Huelva's two historical sources of wealth and reputation: the first lying many hundred feet below ground, the second linked to a "new world" several thousand miles across the sea.

Rich natural deposits of minerals and precious metals (still mined and exported) were reputedly traded by the 6th-century BC kingdom of Tartessos. Akin to Atlantis, this advanced ancient civilisation vanished without trace, leaving a small number of impressive archaeological relics and a belief that its foundations lie somewhere under Doñana's marshy floodplains.

The same copper and iron on which Tartessos prospered are responsible for the coloured waters of the Río Tinto – a river that has played a pivotal role in world history. From its estuary banks in 1492, Christopher Columbus, with royal sponsorship, set sail on his first epic expedition, to seek a westerly route to the Orient. Instead, of course, he stumbled upon the Americas

Orientation

Huelva is sparsely populated, with most development clustered either side of the A49 highway, which bisects the province from Seville to Portugal. To its north, the best and most attractive route into the Sierra de Aracena is the N435. South of the east–west axis is the strictly pro-

Map on page 96

LEFT: beach in the Parque Nacional de Doñana.
BELOW: messing about on the beach at Punta Umbria.

The Iglesia de San Martín in Niebla incorporates evidence of a Visigothic church and a mosque, reflecting the town's long history.

BELOW: festive transport at the Romería del Rocío.

tected Parque Nacional de Doñana, which, along with the River Guadalquivir, creates an impassable boundary with Cádiz province, forcing any southbound traffic via Seville. Points of interest for visitors lie in a cross shape, so a degree of backtracking is inevitable.

Wine country

On entering the province from Seville, the first stop is **La Palma del Condado ❶**. Many of the taller buildings within easy flying distance of the Doñana mudflats have been occupied by nesting storks, and La Palma's attractive 18th-century church, San Juan Bautista, is no exception. A tangle of twigs tops its ornate blue baroque tower like a chimney brush.

This is Huelva's wine-growing region, and it has been planted with vines for centuries. Of the three main Condado (county) towns – **La Palma**, **Rociana** and **Bollullos**, the

last offers cavernous, high-ceilinged bodegas with trestle tables to accommodate noisy wine-tastings. Typically the region's wines, derived from the local Zalema grape, are amber-coloured, nutty olorosos, similar to dark sherry. However, in recent years, wine-makers have been switching to fruity young whites which go well with the local seafood.

Historic Niebla

The red oxides that tinge the soil and waters of Río Tinto can be seen in the crimson walls of ancient **Niebla ❷**. Approached from the A472 via a restored Roman bridge over the river, the town has been important in the downstream movement of extracted metals since perhaps the 9th century BC. Completely enclosed by fortifications incorporating a magnificent *alcázar* dating from 1402, the town is virtually sound-proof. At its centre are the attractive **Plaza Santa Maria**

Huelva Province

0   20 km
0   20 miles

and church of the same name: 10th-century, with a minaret, intricate gates and mihrab testifying to its 13th-century conversion from a mosque.

The town has several other ancient churches. The **Iglesia de San Martín** incorporates evidence of Visigothic origins, Muslim conversion and Mudéjar remodelling, reflecting the history of Niebla itself.

El Rocío

Heading south, the A483 enters an extraordinary time warp at **El Rocío ❸**. Tarmac gives way to wide open sandy thoroughfares, and white-washed stone is replaced by large timber ranches – built to house the large number of pilgrims who come for the annual *romería (see below)*. Under a midday sun, shade is hard to come by, and the town is eerily quiet, adding to its Spaghetti Western character. Despite this film-set appearance, shops are selling cowboy hats for local farmers, not visitors. El Rocío was the place from which many Spanish pioneers emigrated for America, and they faithfully exported the look and feel of their home town.

The village is dominated by the bell-tower facade of **Ermita del Rocío**, the focus for one of Spain's largest and most ecstatic annual pilgrimages, the Romería del Rocío. At Pentecost, this sleepy backwater is transformed by festivity, overrun with up to a million costumed, singing revellers, riding in flower-filled carriages. Excitement centres on a tiny wooden effigy of the Virgin Mary above the church altar, Nuestra Senora del Rocío, revered for a miraculous legend about her discovery *(see Virgin Worship, page 45)*.

Overlooking the beginnings of the protected coastal *marismas* (wetlands), El Rocío is a good spot for watching birds, including flocks of flamingos. There is an ornithological observatory (closed Mon) near the water and, just south of town, an information centre, from which tracks lead to hides near a lagoon at the edge of the reserve.

Parque Nacional de Doñana

El Rocío is a springboard for the **Parque Nacional de Doñana ❹**. An alternative base, less interesting

Map on page 96

TIP

If you fancy exploring the periphery of the park on horseback, take an equestrian tour organised by Doñana Ecuestre (tel: 959 442 474) or Turismo a Caballo (tel: 959 442 084), both based in El Rocío.

BELOW: even the lay birder, armed with binoculars and a decent field book for identification, is bound to spot a few rarities.

Visiting the Cota de Doñana National Park

To protect its fragile environment, access to the interior of the Coto de Doñana is restricted to organised tours, though you can access the beaches independently. A popular four-hour 4x4 trip can be arranged (twice daily except Mondays) with Doñana National Park Tours (www.donanavisitas.com; tel: 959-430432). It is a good idea to book at least a couple of days in advance. Trips depart from the visitors' centre in El Acebuche, just north of the resort of Matacasalañas but also easily reached from El Rocío. The tour begins on the coast then weaves through the pines and scrub along the river Guadalquivir to the seasonal wetlands and then back to the sand dunes along the coast.

Serious nature enthusiasts might like to investigate Discovering Doñana (tel: 959-442 466; www.discoveringdonana.com), which operates a variety of 4X4 excusions (six-hour or 12-hour trips) into the park from their base in El Rocío. Expert guides accompany the tours, which take in a variety of flora and fauna, but place special emphasis on ornithology. They operate in winter and summer and can supply binoculars, field guides, etc.

Eagles are a watchful presence in the Parque Nacional de Doñana.

BELOW: La Rábida Monastery, a haunt of Christopher Columbus.

but slightly closer to the access point at El Acebuche, is **Matalascañas** – a built-up 1960s resort in stark contrast to the 1,000 sq. km (400 sq. miles) of wilderness it serves.

The park is a World Heritage Site, Spain's largest reserve and a refuge for endangered species. A flooding and retreating delta, which creates seasonal wetlands and cyclically shifting and evolving dunes, forms an unusual combination of ecosystems supporting a precious habitat for a huge diversity of birds and mammals.

The coast is home to oystercatchers, dunlins, sanderlings and low-swooping sandwich terns and gulls. Along the Guadalquivir, pine woods and scrub are the habitat of lynx, mongoose and the rare Spanish imperial eagle, though all these are elusive. Inland, vast seasonal wetlands flood in winter, attracting huge numbers of waterbirds. In summer, as the lake shrinks to a cracked, clay plain, flamingos, storks, herons and spoonbills arrive to feast on trapped fish.

Large mammals such as red deer and boar are drawn to a strip of lush vegetation on the edge of the marsh.

Mazagón

If concrete Matalascañas doesn't appeal as a seaside base for Doñana, a more authentic alternative 20 km (12 miles) further along the coast is **Mazagón**. It is an easy going town with an attractive marina, lively restaurants and a long stretch of clean, golden sand and clear water (good for swimming), which truly earns the right to the name Costa de la Luz. To the east of the centre, stretching for 10 km (6 miles), the beach is backed by pine-topped sandstone cliffs.

Columbus was here

After Mazagón, the coastline is interrupted by the mouths of the rivers Odiel and Tinto. At the point where they meet, against a background of heavy industry on the outskirts of Huelva, rises a giant statue (sculpted in 1929) of Christopher Columbus staring out to the Atlantic. The A494 bends inland to reach the sites associated with the great discoverer.

Hidden by the forests of the surrounding oil refineries, the Franciscan monastery of **La Rábida** ❺ is a tranquil sanctuary (Tues–Sun 10am–1pm and 4–6.15pm; admission charge; www.monasteriodelarabida.com). It was at La Rábida that Columbus met Friar Juan Pérez, the former priest of Queen Isabel, who intervened on Columbus's behalf and persuaded the Spanish monarchy to back his expedition. Murals depicting the events of 1492 and headset commentary in English vividly bring to life Columbus's time at the monastery.

The visit includes the cloister, set around a Moorish courtyard, the early 15th-century church (where one of Columbus's locally recruited captains, Martín Alonso Pinzón, is buried, and the chapel where the explorer is thought to have prayed before departure.

From the upstairs chapter house,

in which much of the voyage was planned, there is a view of the river and a reproduction of the 15th-century harbour, **Muelle de las Carabelas**. Here, fully accessible to visitors, there are life-size replicas of the maiden flotilla. The surprisingly small dimensions of the wooden vessels and the confined living quarters highlight the remarkable bravery and achievement of the crew.

The tiny fleet set sail in August 1492 from **Palos de la Frontera**, 4 km (2½ miles) from La Rábida and once a sizeable port. It has since clogged up with silt from the Tinto estuary, so Columbus's precise departure point is hidden under clay. A great source of local pride is that the town was home to the Pinzón brothers, who captained caravels *Nina* and *Pinta*, both constructed in Palos, while Columbus captained his ship the *Santa María*. There is a museum at the Pinzón family home (on Calle Cristóbal Colón) and a monument to Martín Alonso Pinzón in the central square, marking the spot where the royal order for the "Enterprise of the Indies" was declared.

Upstream from Palos, **Moguer** ❻ also claims a connection with Columbus, as it was the recruiting ground for much of the crew. It is also home to the 14th-century **Monasterio de Santa Clara** (Tues–Fri 11am–1pm and 5–7pm; admission charge; guided tours), where Columbus prayed through the night in thanks for his safe return.

The town retains a distinctly Moorish feel with its whitewashed walls and dead ends. Buildings of interest include the graceful 18th-century **Ayuntamiento** (Mon–Fri), which has a fine patio, on Plaza del Cabildo. Opposite is a statue of local poet Juan Ramón Jiménez, winner of the 1956 Nobel Prize for Literature. The poet is celebrated in the **Casa Museo Zenobia y Juan Ramón** (Tues–Sat 10am–1pm and 5–7pm; Sun 10am–1pm; admission charge).

Provincial capital

Across the Tinto is **Huelva** ❼, the provincial capital. Beyond its smoky suburbs, parts of the city's historic centre that withstood the 1755 Lisbon earthquake stand elegant and

Map on page 96

Frescos depicting Columbus's life at La Rábida Monastery.

BELOW: visiting La Rábida Monastery.

Detail on the facade of Huelva's Catedral de la Merced.

RIGHT: the rusty hues of the Río Tinto.

proud. The baroque **Catedral de la Merced** dominates a shady plaza (off Paseo Buenos Aires) which has the grand but slightly edgy feel of a South American plaza – a reminder of Huelva's inter-continental influence. Trade with the New World brought wealth, though in time most of this was absorbed by Seville.

Conjuring up these affluent times, lofty palms are evenly spaced along wide avenues, casting shadows on the tiled facades of five-storey mansion blocks. A smart pedestrianised shopping district runs south of the central **Plaza de las Monjas**, parallel to Gran Vía. At the eastern end of this main thoroughfare, the **Museo Provincial** (Tues 2.30–8.30pm, Wed–Sat 9am–8.30pm, Sun 9am–2.30pm; free admission) sheds light on the enigmatic Tartessos civilisation, which is thought to have centred on Huelva.

Another prosperous period for the city was the late 19th century, when the British-owned Río Tinto Mining Company brought the industrial revolution to the region. The huge iron Río Tinto Pier, designed by British engineer George Barclay Bruce, is now redundant, but it still arcs out into the estuary like a long broken roller-coaster. The British also built Barrio Reina Victoria, a quintessentially English-style suburb, with neat lawns and tended rose bushes.

Best beaches

In search of a seaside escape, Victorian expatriates travelled by paddle steamer to **Punta Umbria**, the first of the beach resorts dotted along the coast towards Ayamonte on the border with Portugal. It is still a popular, low-key resort, with a long stretch of clean, gently sloping sand backed by holiday homes, a few guesthouses and the occasional *chiringuito*. Today Punta Umbria is reached along the A497, which skirts the **Paraje Natural Marismas del Odiel** (Visitor's Centre, tel: 959-500 236), a wetland reserve attracting similar bird species to Doñana.

Continuing east, a spectacular unspoilt beach runs pas **El Portil,** hidden by dense pine thickets and bumpy, tufted dunes. The shore looks out onto a flat sandy spit which has accumulated at the

Precious Waters – the Río Tinto

Writing in the 4th century, the chronicler Avienus in his *Ora Maritima* noted a Mount Argentario whose "slopes glint and shine in the light when the sun's rays ward the earth's surface. The river Tartessos is laden with nuggets of ore and washed the precious metal to the very doors of the city". The Greeks and Phoenicians sailed the length of the Mediterranean to get the ore, and the local tribesmen founded the Tartessos civilisation on the profits. But it was the Romans who developed the potential of the Río Tinto's resources. Roman miners – first slaves, then free men – worked in galleries 1 metre (3ft) in diameter, lit by tiny oil lamps. The problem of flooding was solved by waterwheels that lifted the water from one level to another.

The mines survived the fall of Rome, and Niebla grew into a powerful Moorish enclave through its control of the Río Tinto. Later, the easy pickings that were to be had in the Americas almost put an end to the mines. They were finally bought in 1873 by a consortium of British and German bankers. Today, the mines are the property of the miners themselves, who continue to extract copper, as well as small amounts of gold and silver.

mouth of the Río Piedras, forcing the road to detour inland. Where the river meets the ocean, fresh water attracts line-fishermen, and a blustery wind trap makes it a popular spot for kite-surfing. The long beach peters out near the original river mouth at **El Rompido**, an attractive fishing village.

Regaining the coast necessitates a dog-leg through row upon row of strawberry bushes and the town of **Lepe**, Spain's foremost producer of the fruit. In Spanish, to be "from Lepe" means to be from the proverbial back of beyond. In the chronicles of Columbus's voyage of discovery the first person to see landfall was "a man from Lepe".

Turning back towards the sea, **El Terrón**, on the west bank of the Río Piedras is little more than a fishing quay carpeted with colourful nets. Unfortunately this is the last traditional village before modern overdevelopment engulfs the coast at **La Antilla** and **La Islantilla**.

Sharing a degree of this development, but for the time being retaining genuine character, is **Isla Cristina ❸**. As its name suggests, the area was once an island. Today the town is joined to the mainland, lapped by a tidal estuary which serves as an effective base for a commercial fishing fleet that supplies Seville. The *puerto pesquero* (fishing port), a pungent tangle of nets and busy vessels, is a wonderfully animated place to dine on the very freshest seafood. Plaza de las Flores in the town centre is another lively evening spot.

From the harbour, the beach extends east, across crab-burrowed mudflats and past unsightly apartment blocks. It quickly becomes brilliant-white sand crossed by a boardwalk and backed by hotels shaded by a eucalyptus grove. Beachfront action is limited.

Within sight of Portugal is the border town of **Ayamonte**. The pretty palm-lined marina lined by restaurants makes it worth a pause before crossing the Río Guadiana (by bridge or ferry) to the Algarve. The town's outlying resort of **Isla Canela** has a good beach, but development has been rapid and contrived, resulting in an expanse of tarmac, modern blocks and box-like hotels.

Mining country

Leaving the coast, the N435 climbs steadily up-country towards some of Huelva's best but least known sights. Just northwest of Zalamea la Real on the A461 are the **Minas de Río Tinto ❾**. Carved out like an amphitheatre, open-cast Corta Atalya mine (one of the largest in the world) is a miniature Grand Canyon of exposed earth: sunset-coloured bands of rusty red, orange and yellow contrasts with the deep-blue waters and green pines of the Gossan reservoir. Now owned by Spanish miners, rather than the British, it is still an operational site of tracks and trucks, but has also been developed for visitors. Attractions, open daily, include a Corta Atalya tour, a

Map on page 96

Strawberries are a springtime speciality of Lepe.

BELOW:
a quiet afternoon as usual in Jabugo.

Map on page 96

Pata negra, a *speciality of Jabugo, is derived from a breed of black-footed Iberian pigs which roam semi-wild and feed on acorns.*

BELOW: view from the castle, Aracena.

20-km (12- mile) restored-steam-train ride along the old miners' railway and a mining museum. All tickets are purchased at the museum.

The Sierra Morena

The road lifts and twists into the cool air of the western **Sierra Morena**, a landscape of green woodlands, streams and mountains. Just inside the **Parque Natural Sierra de Aracena**, the Portugal–Seville N433 and quieter A470 cut west to east, taking in a handful of villages.

Jabugo is a tiny place renowned for Spain's finest *jamón ibérico*. A line of bars just outside the centre offers the prized (and pricey) cured ham as tapas. Aside from its pork business, Jabugo is an isolated settlement, centring on the crumbling **Iglesia de San Miguel**. Nearby **Galaroza** is prettier, wrapped in greenery, refreshed by streams and dominated by a baroque church.

The furthest west of Huelva's sierra towns is **Aroche ⑩**. Unselfconscious in its remoteness, it has a strong identity and sense of camaraderie that make for interest- ing people-watching in the central square. The town receives few tourists, but its cobbled streets are worth exploring, not least for the medieval *castillo*, converted into an unconventional bullring.

East of here is **Almonaster la Real ⑪**, which rises to the crest of a hill where a 10th-century mosque is a perfect miniature of Córdoba's renowned Mezquita, but without the crowds. Its Islamic features, including brick-pillar horseshoe arches, fountain and minaret tower (that offers a free view of the next-door corrida) are impeccably preserved.

Further along the A470, watched over by a tiny hilltop church, **Pena de Arias Montano**, are **Alajar** and **Linares de la Sierra**: attractive but depopulated hamlets that are not much more than farms.

Aracena ⑫ is the largest market town in the area. There is a good vantage point from Cerro del Castillo, a hill (reached via a steep trail from the cobbled Plaza Alta), topped by a Gothic-Mudéjar church built by the Knights Templar in the 13th century.

Aracena's main attraction lies under the castle. **Gruta de las Maravillas** (guided visits in Spanish, 10am– 1.30pm and 3–6pm; admission charge) is a labyrinth of grottoes. An hourly tour investigates chilly chambers where pools have collected among fantastic mineral formations. The circuit concludes at Sala de los Culos (Chamber of the Buttocks), named for reasons that are obvious.

Heading back towards Seville on the N433, a final detour is warranted by spectacularly sited **Zufre**. Clinging to a slim crag above cliffs of several hundred metres, the isolated village seems bemused by visitors. Horses negotiate uneven steps to drink from troughs outside a 16th-century Mudéjar church, while daily life centres on the Paseo, a garden square with magnificent panoramic views of the natural park.   ❑

RESTAURANTS & BARS

Restaurants

Like neighbouring Cádiz, Huelva is one of the best places in the south to eat inexpensive fish and seafood. Some restaurants close in winter.

Alajar

Mesón Restaurante El Corcho
Plaza de Espana, 3
Tel: 959-125 779
L & D daily. €€
A traditional bar with a long restaurant, decked out in cork. The cluttered decor adds to the quirky atmosphere, while the hearty, typical sierra menu is tasty and the hospitality warm.

Almonaster la Real

El Rincón de Curro
Calle Carretera, 3
Tel: 959-143 149
L & D daily. €€–€€€
A well-presented, popular restaurant where service is very welcoming. The local menu offers more meat than fish and the speciality is pork sirloin.

Aracena

José Vicente
Avenida Andaucia, 53
Tel: 959-128 455
L & D daily. €€
On the outskirts of Aracena, this is great value and a real find. Offers superb sierra cuisine, including excellent *jamón iberico*, pork and wild mushrooms.

Doñana

La Cantina de Los Mimbrales
Cortijo de Los Mimbrales Hotel, Ctra Rocio – Matalascanas A483.
Tel: 959-442 237
L & D. Dec–Jan weekends only. €€€
www.cortijomimbrales.com
This is a gastronomic destination where locally inspired dishes are expertly prepared and presented by chef Mañuel Espinosa. House specialities include asparagus in almond sauce, Jabugo ham in saffron sauce, and rice stews with game and Sanlucar prawns.

El Portil

El Paraíso
Ctra Huelva – El Portil.
Tel: 959-312 756
L & D daily. €€
Set among pine trees near the beach, this large restaurant has a deserved reputation for good value, fresh seafood, especially the clams and white prawns.

Restaurante El Bosque
Ctra El Rompido–El Portil
Tel: 959-504 099
L & D daily. €€–€€€
In a quiet grove between El Rompido and El Portil, this restaurant commands a dramatic cliff-top location with fine views across the estuary. Traditional menu.

Isla Cristina

Hermanos Moreno
Avenida Padre Mirabent, 39
Tel: 959-343 571
L & D daily. €€
A quality restaurant above a small, informal tapas bar, where the fish (priced by the kilo) is as fresh as it gets. Service can be slow at busy times, so relax and savour the harbour atmosphere.

Casa Rufino
Avenida de la Playa Central
Tel: 959-308 10
L & D daily. €€–€€€
Renowned for its *tonteo* (tasting menu) of eight fish dishes, this is a sociable option available for a minimum of four diners. Also good for tuna, shellfish and rice.

Chiringuito del Brizo
Playa de Isla Cristina (near Taray campsite, east of town)
Tel: 646-064 618
L & D. Closed Jan–Feb. €
An isolated hut on a stretch of beach between Isla Cristina and La Islantilla, this *chiringuito* is reached via a boardwalk through the pines.

Jabugo

Restaurante Xauco
Ctra S Juan el Puerto.
Tel: 959-121 498
L & D daily. €
This is a no-frills local on a street crowded with bars and restaurants, where the local speciality, Jabugo ham, tops the tapas bill.

Mazagón

Restaurante El Remo
Avenida Conquistadores 123. Tel: 959-536 138
L & D daily. €€
With its great beach-front location, this is the place in Mazagón for fish and sea-food. Specials include a fine local pâté.

Moguer

La Parrala
Plaza de las Monjas, 22.
Tel: 959-370 452
L & D daily. €–€€
A friendly, unpretentious place serving traditional tapas, good fish and meat. There are wooden tables outside on Plaza de Las Monjas, opposite Monasterio Santa Clara.

Punta Umbria

Chiringuito Camaron
Avenida del Oceano
Tel. 959-659 038
L & D. Closed Nov–Feb. €€
This is a stilted wooden bar on the beach with ocean views from a sandy veranda. Good choice of fresh fish and seafood – sizzling garlic prawns are a speciality.

PRICE CATEGORIES

Prices for three-course meal per person with a half-bottle of house wine:
€= under €20
€€ = €20–€40
€€€ = €40–€60
€€€€= more than €60

JEREZ, CÁDIZ AND THE COSTA DE LA LUZ

Thanks to the international airport at Jerez de la Frontera, more and more people are discovering Cadíz province. It has an illustrious seafaring history, a centuries-old wine and sherry industry and a truly stunning coastline, the aptly named Costa de la Luz

Occupying a coastal right-angle to the point of Andalucía's most southerly tip, Cádiz province is influenced in character by its proximity to Morocco and elemental exposure to the vast Atlantic. Clues to a confrontational history abound in the names of hill towns carrying the suffix "de la Frontera", many of which are defensively and dramatically perched atop striking crags of the inland sierra.

The region lived as a frontier for centuries: at the frontline of Moorish invasion and Christian re-conquest; violently harassed by Drake and Nelson; its New World riches ransacked by pirates. The strategically located provincial capital, Cádiz city, was once an island gateway to the entire Phoenician trading empire, then named Gadir, meaning "the defended place".

Today, the Cádiz coast is affronted merely by incessant ocean winds and the threat, so far repulsed, of an architectural fate similar to that of the neighbouring province of Málaga. It remains resolutely underdeveloped, facing west to inspirational sunsets and offering its visitors a feast of fresh fish and crisp local sherry, while quietly delighting in the miles of brilliant white sand that earned it the name, Costa de la Luz – Coast of Light.

Gateway to the province

Improved flight connections to the provincial airport at Jerez have made this appealing corner of Andalucía increasingly accessible.

More affluent and sophisticated than the provincial capital Cádiz, **Jerez de la Frontera ❶** is gracefully typified by La Real Escuela Andaluza del Arte Ecuestre (Royal Andalucian School of Equestrian Art; tel: 956 318008; www.realescuela.org), where dressage training to a soundtrack of Spanish guitar

Map on page 106

LEFT: Palacio Domecq, Jerez de la Frontera.
BELOW: Calle Larga, Jerez.

Practice makes perfect at the Royal Andalusian School of Equestrian Art. Watch the horses train every day from 11am–2pm.

music can be watched daily (11am–2pm; admission charge), with a stables tour (in English at 11.30) and entry to the museum. The horses give a polished performance in the arena on Thursdays at 1pm.

In the old city, to the west of the lively Calle Larga, sophistication is manifest in stylish plazas (notably de Arenal, Plateros and de la Asunción) and a grand Gothic-Baroque cathedral. Nearby, surrounded by orange blossom, the original Islamic **Alcázar** (10am–6pm; admission charge) incorporates an exquisite mosque, attractive gardens and Arab baths lit by starry skylights. An 18th-century palace has been built within the medieval walls.

There are two good excuses for staying overnight in Jerez. Firstly, there is no better neighbourhood in which to kick off a tour of Cádiz province than the **Barrio de Santiago**. Here, a well-integrated Roma gypsy community keep alive deep-rooted flamenco traditions, dancing a distinctive style of flamenco known as the Buleria. Secondly, a bodega visit *(see box, page 107)*, culminating in some sherry tasting, is a must do, and a good reason for abandoning the hire car.

Jerez has grown rich on its bodegas, the largest of which is Gonzalez Byass (tel: 956-357 000), the producer and exporter of Tio Pepe, whose advertising you will see everywhere. One of its cellars, La Concha, located near the cathedral and Alcázar, was designed by Gustave Eiffel, who also built the Tour Eiffel in Paris.

Alternatively, near to the equestrian school is **Bodegas Sandeman** (tel: 956-151 711), where the guides wear the black cape and *caballero* hat of the trademark Don. Other familiar bodega names are Domecq and Harveys. For any visit, it is a good idea to book ahead: there are fewer tours on Sundays.

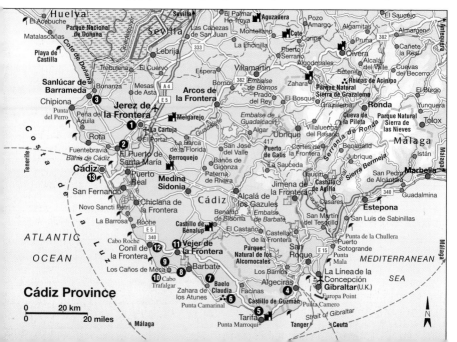

The coast

West of Jerez, **El Puerto de Santa Maria ❷** is a thriving port near the mouth of the River Guadalete. On summer evenings locals and visitors tend to converge on the Ribera del Mariscso, to enjoy the sociable atmosphere and first-rate seafood.

The town is ringed by wineries, including the vast Bodegas Osborne (tel: 956-869 100), the brand advertised by the iconic black bull, whose silhouette is a familiar feature on roadside hills throughout Andalucía. El Puerto's good beaches are a few kilometres west of town, becoming less crowded the further they are from the centre – the best is **Playa Santa Catalina**.

The coast road northwest of El Puerto detours around a naval base and the small fishing port at **Rota**, then curves round to a jolly holiday-home resort at **Chipiona**.

On the wide estuary of the Rio Guadalquivir, **Sanlucar de Barrameda ❸** once acted as Seville's port and shared in its New World spoils. Historical wealth accounts for some elegant architecture, focusing on the palm-lined Plaza del Cabildo. The sizeable town includes a laid-back fishing district around Bajo de Guia, which has a nationwide reputation for shellfish. Excellent restaurants front a fine beach, near the departure point for organised 4x4 tours to the Coto Doñana National Park (Viages Doñana; tel: 956-362 540) on the opposite bank.

A festival at the end of May toasts Sanlucar's local *manzanilla* wine, considered to be more delicate than sherry. It derives its distinct flavour from the salty, humid conditions that prevail here. Friendly rivalry persists with nearby Jerez.

East of Jerez

Heading east, the plains that carry the road inland from chalky vineyard country lead to Arcos de la Frontera, a springboard for the so-called "white towns" *(pueblos blancos)*, which straddle the provinces of Cádiz and Málaga *(see separate chapter on the White Towns, pages 120–123)*. To the southeast lies **Medina Sidonia** and **La Ruta del Toro**, so called because nearby lowland

Map on page 106

It is well worth spending a day in Jerez de la Frontera, an elegant city, with graceful architecture and attractive plazas.

BELOW: famous name in Jerez.

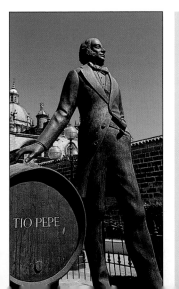

Visiting A Sherry Bodega

The palomino white grape thrives in the chalky soil and humid, windy climate of northwest Cádiz, a combination of environmental factors that are ideal for sherry production.

A bodega tour through sweetly aromatic, high-vaulted buildings offers a fascinating insight into the biological process that transforms *vino* into *jerez*. Pressed grapes are allowed partially to ferment, creating a skin of yeast called *flor*. Inside 500-litre (100-gallon) oak barrels, this layer forms a natural barrier against oxidisation. The sherry's colour and sweetness depend on how this film is preserved: if it collapses, like an apple left without peel, the result is a sweet, dark oloroso, but when it survives, the sherry is a dry, white fino.

The bodega is kept cool and damp to promote the *solera* aging process. Cathedral-height ceilings accommodate huge barrels stacked at least three-high and maturing sherry is filtered downwards. The bottom casks are never entirely drained and, because every drop is a blend of harvests, there is no such thing as a "bad year" – good news when the tour concludes with a generous tasting.

The Straits of Gibraltar offer year-round winds. Playa los Lances, north of Tarifa, is the European capital of windsurfing.

BELOW: Moorish Tarifa.

pastures are home to herds of fighting bulls bred for the *corrida*.

Southeast of **Alcalá de los Gazules**, another white town *(see page 121)*, the A381 skirts the Barbate reservoir and, leaving behind clear mountain air, descends into the urbanised bay of Gibraltar. In **Algeciras ❹**, a polluted, sprawling port, there is a magnetic seaward pull and a transitory atmosphere. Ferries for Tangier and Ceuta (a Spanish enclave on the North African coast) leave throughout the day *(see box on Going to Morocco, opposite)*.

You might also consider visiting **Gibraltar**: the 5-km by 1-km (3-mile by ⅜-mile) Rock is clearly visible on the far side of the bay. To do this, simply follow signs to La Línea – Spain's border with Gibraltar. You can leave your car in the guarded car park, cross the border on foot and pick up a bus or taxi to take you to the centre.

Laid-back Tarifa

A Moorish flavour pervades the town of **Tarifa ❺**, 20km (12 miles) further west. After dark, the streets inside its medieval walls buzz with an eclectic mix of dimly-lit bars, cushion-strewn cafés, aromatic restaurants and art galleries. Laid-back and a touch bohemian, Tarifa relishes its reputation as "a piece of washed up Africa" and is determined not to go the same way as resorts on the nearby Costa del Sol. From here Tangier is a mere 35 minutes away by hydrofoil *(see box, page 109)*; the distant Rif mountains are visible from the waterfront.

On the ramparts of the restored **Castillo de Guzman** (Tues–Sat 11am–2pm and 6–8pm or 4–6pm in winter; admission charge), originally a Moorish Alcázar, a huge catapult is displayed, seemingly aimed across the Straits of Gibraltar, a reminder that living on Morocco's doorstep has brought friction as well as fusion. Tarifa takes its name from Tarif ibn Malik, who led a reconnaissance mission to Spain preceding the North African invasion in 711.

The earliest surviving part of Tarifa's castle is 10th-century. In 1292 it fell to Christian forces, but as the closest point to Africa it remained a point of conflict. Alsonso de Guzman's heroic defence of the town

Map
on page
106

two years later earned him the epithet "El Bueno", the Good. Guzman had sacrificed his own son rather than surrender the castle to the Muslims. Guzman was subsequently ennobled and became the Duke of Medina Sidonia. Some 300 years later, a descendant of Guzman led the Spanish Armada.

On the wild side

For all its exotic heritage, Tarifa is also a busy resort, offering surf boutiques, shipwreck dives and organised whale-watching trips. The latter (book a day in advance) are organised by several commercial companies as well as the Foundation for Information and Research on Marine Mammals (tel: 956-627 008; www.firmm.org). Dolphins and pilot whales can be spotted year-round (they are often also seen on the ferry crossing to Morocco). Another natural phenomenon worth catching is the migration of birds between Europe and Africa. Birds migrate south from February to June and return between September and October. Good spots to watch the passage

are the lookout points over the Strait of Gibraltar, just east of Tarifa.

Windsurfers' paradise

The growth in tourism is mainly due to the town's reputation as mainland Europe's windsurfing capital, best appreciated by walking between the town's two beaches, the sheltered **Playa Chica**, on the Mediterranean to **Playa de los Lances**, on the Atlantic and usually lashed by a sand-blasting gale.

Further up the coast at **Playa la Plata** the wind, a little more bearable here, gathers dunes under the bluff at **Punta Valdevaqueros**, the venue for international kite-surfing championships (for more information, contact KiteSurfing (tel: 956-681668; www.kitesurfingtarifa.com) based in Tarifa. On the hills to the east, the climate is put to environmental use by an army of giant wind turbines.

Roman outpost

North of Tarifa, a stunning coastline unfolds. **Bolonia** is protected from the wind by headlands and the sea is calm. Cattle and cockerels wander

Looking out to sea at Baelo Claudia (Bolonia), the ancient Roman town on the edge of the Atlantic.

BELOW: Morocco is visible in the distance.

Going to Morocco

A short hop across the Straits of Gibraltar, Morocco makes an interesting overnight or even day excursion from Southern Spain. Ferries leave throughout the day from Algeciras to Tangier (no need to book), though this is a fairly long voyage at up to 2½ hours, depending on the type of ferry and the prevailing wind (there is also a 1½-hour crossing to Ceuta, an uninteresting Spanish enclave on the North African coast). It is preferable to take the less frequent but much quicker hydrofoil crossing (35 minutes) from Tarifa to Tangier, but this is only available to EU passport holders. Be aware that very windy weather can delay crossings, or even bring the service to a halt.

No visas are required for EU or US visitors to Morocco, but you must fill in an arrivals form and get your passport stamped on board the boat. Tangier's port lies immediately below the medina, the heart of the old town, so it isn't that difficult to find your own way around. That said, you may be badgered by would-be guides offering their services and they can be a good option when time is short. If you go down this route, point out that you want to see the sights (medina, kasbah, Grand Socco), not the shops, and agree a fee beforehand.

Thousands of wind turbines punctuate the hillsides overlooking the coast, testifying to the windy conditions.

BELOW:
fun in the sun and surf.

aimlessly in front of a handful of *chiringuitos* (beach bars) on the grass behind a curved bay. It is appealingly rustic and unspoilt.

Also at Bolonia are the substantial Roman ruins of **Baelo Claudia** ⑥ (Tues–Sat 10am–7pm, until 8pm in summer; admission charge for non-EU passport-holders), including the remains of an amphitheatre, paved forum and temples. Having prospered on its production of garum, a salted fish paste that was popular across the Roman Empire, the settlement is believed to have fallen into decline following an earthquake in the 2nd century.

The beaches

Next along the coast (reached via an inland dog-leg via the N340) is **Zahara de los Atunes** ⑦, an easy-going fishing village, which is a popular summer escape for Sevillian families. It feels a little rough and ready, partly thanks to unfinished beachfront construction that hints at an increase in low-key, development. Zahara's straight, broad beach is somewhat exposed

and weather-beaten, making inroads into the friendly and unpretentious town, where you will find several low-key tapas bars.

Zahara blends into **Atlanterra**, where a string of characterless apartments have sprung up. Keep driving for several kilometres to the dead end at **Punta Camarinal**, to discover a powdery white cove, reached on foot along overgrown footpaths, hidden from the road.

Continuing northwest from Zahara, the road hugs the coastline, crossing marshy wetlands that soak up the estuary of the Rio Barbate, before arriving at the town of **Barbate** ⑧. A hard-working fishing port with canning factories, it is renowned for locally caught blue fin tuna. Seafood eateries dot the otherwise unremarkable Paseo Maritimo.

Rising from the harbour, a pretty drive (or rewarding 5-hour cliff-top walk) leads up through the umbrella pines of the **Parque Natural de la Brena y Marismas de Barbate** and down into to the coastal village of Los Caños.

Los Caños de Meca ⑨, tucked

under pine-clad hills, was once a hippie resort and an uninhibited mood encourages discreet naturists, who swim from the smaller southern bay. A few hotels and restaurants are scattered along a ridge of sandstone cliffs, with hidden caves and two stunning golden beaches nestled beneath. This spot is captivating at sunset, when the sun sinks into the ocean behind the nearby Cape.

The Battle of Trafalgar

Cabo Trafalgar ⑩ was the scene of Admiral Nelson's famous obliteration of the combined fleets of France and Spain on 21 October 1805. Despite being vastly outnumbered, the British fleet won the day through their skill and experience, though Nelson himself was fatally wounded in the battle. The battle was decisive in ensuring Britain's supremacy at sea for the next 100 years. Without reference to the historical significance of the site, a lighthouse topping a breezy, dune-smothered spit marks the spot. North of the cape, **Zahora** offers a secluded swish of soft, toe-wriggling sand.

A detour inland, passing through fields of sunflowers, leads to **Vejer de la Frontera ⑪**, a *pueblo blanco* with the ultimate sea view. Vejer's elevated isolation is impressive, like a suspended white-iced wedding cake, looming above the road. Behind Moorish gates a maze of steep and twisting alleyways lead to the Castillo, 16th-century church of Divino Salvador, built around the minaret of a mosque, and vertiginous vistas. The town is a tangible collision of Moorish and Andalusian character. The central Plaza España is reminiscent of Seville, with its orange trees and *azulejo*-decorated fountains.

Back at the coast, a bumpy road runs beside a sweep of clean, bright sand at **El Palmar**, a cluster of casual beach-facing developments in elemental surroundings. The stretch peters out at the mouth of the Rio Salado, facing the town of Conil on the opposite side.

Conil de la Frontera ⑫, a down-to-earth fishing community, has managed to embrace tourism while remaining true to itself.

Map on page 106

The lighthouse at Cabo Trafalgar.

BELOW: seafood feast on the Playa de Santa Maria.

The entrance to the Bay of Cadíz, just beyond the fortified island of San Sebastián, is where the Bucentaure, the flaghip of the French fleet at the Battle of Trafalgar (1805), commanded by Admiral Villeneuve, went down. In fact this area of ocean is littered with shipwrecks, including others from the Battle of Trafalgar, as well as merchant vessels that have fallen foul of treacherous weather.

BELOW: the Puerta de Tierra, Plaza de la Constitución.

Behind its wide concrete promenade and family-friendly beach (Playa de Los Bateles), the village climbs up to an attractive old quarter with an upbeat atmosphere. A kilometre (½ mile) to the north is the quieter cliff-bound **Playa de la Fontanilla**, with its own al-fresco restaurants.

As the road approaches the southern suburbs of Cádiz, old seaside towns are replaced by unimaginative blocks of flats. But what **Novo Sancti Petri** lacks in a sense of identity, it makes up for in golf courses.

Cádiz

Cádiz ⓭ still has the feel of a fortified outpost, almost entirely surrounded by sea, anchored to its province by a finger of land and a high bridge carrying traffic across the bay. The imposing **Puerta de Tierra**, divides the old town from more modern development along the deep Atlantic beaches. **Playa de la Victoria** offers a relaxed, breezy

base as an alternative to the old town. From the lively *chiringuito* bars there is a beguiling view of the city, 30 minutes' walk away – the golden (in reality, yellow-tiled) dome of the cathedral glinting hazily in the sun, flanked by high turreted towers, protected by a bastion of sea defences.

Approaching from Victoria, a stroll around the narrow peninsula serves as useful orientation. On the western side is **Barrio de la Vina**, a fisherman's quarter whose leathery-looking inhabitants can often be seen collecting crabs by the causeway to the military islet of **Castillo de San Sebastián**. They moor their boats in the small **Playa de la Caleta**.

Further on are the **Castillo de Santa Catalina** and two shady parks, **Parque Genovés** and the **Alameda de Apodaca**. The largest, leafiest square is the **Plaza de España ⓐ**, from where streets delve into a warren of atmospheric, slightly seedy nooks and crannies.

Cádiz

0 ——————— 300 m
0 ——————— 300 yds

Despite the confusing jumble of back streets, it is impossible to get lost in Cádiz. The city is no more than 2 km (1½ miles) wide in any direction, so whichever way you walk the ocean soon reappears. It rewards inquisitive zig-zag wandering.

Cádiz entered a golden era in the 18th century, when it overtook Seville as the centre for transatlantic trade. It is from this period that the city's most impressive architecture dates, including watchtowers, the highest being **Torre Tavira ❸** (daily 10am–5.30pm, until 7.30pm in summer; admission charge), and some of the grander avenues such as **Calle Ancha** ("Broad Street").

The city's prosperous heyday produced a discursive middle class, who earned the city a liberal reputation. The **Museo de las Cortes de Cádiz ❸** (Tues–Fri 9am–1pm and 5–7pm, Sat 9am– 1pm; admission free) records the short-lived democratic constitution of 1812, declared at the Oratorio San Felipe Neri next door. Liberal attitudes prevail today, displayed most expressively at the city's carnival in February.

The vast **Catedral Nueva ❹**, (Tues–Fri 10am–1.30pm and 4.30–7pm, Sat 10am–1pm; admission charge) fronted by a wide, open, pedestrianised plaza, is one of the largest cathedrals in Spain and took 122 years to complete (1716–1838), hence the mix of baroque and neo-classical design. Entered separately from the Plaza de la Catedral, a spiral climb inside one of the bell towers, Torre de Poniente, offers a 360° panorama.

In the shadow of the "new" cathedral, **Barrio del Populo** (the heart of 13th-century Cádiz, with three surviving medieval gates) is home to the old one. The **Iglesia Santa Cruz ❺** was virtually demolished by the British in 1596 and later rebuilt. A short walk across **Plaza de San Juan de Dios** leads to the harbour. To this day Cádiz is a significant port for cruise liners and commercial vessels. The docks are also the departure point for a trip across the bay back to El Puerto de Santa María, to conclude a circuit of the region with a seafood supper, and perhaps one last sherry. ❑

Maps:
City 112
Area 106

Spain's best known composer, Manuel de Falla was born in Cádiz. This portrait of him hangs near his tomb in Cádiz's Cathedral.

BELOW: the Mirador Torre de Poniente, Cádiz's Cathedral.

RESTAURANTS & BARS

Barbate

El Campero
Avenida de la Constitucion
Tel: 956-432 300
L & D daily. €€
Bright, cheerful and
simple, with a popular-
ity based on food
quality rather than
fashion, serving up tuna
from the Almadraba
cooked in every imagin-
able style, as well as
other local catch.

Bolonia

Chiringuito Los Troncos
Playa de Bolonia
Tel: 956-688 603
L & D daily. €
Informal wood-beamed
cabin, serving light tasty
tapas and fish, espe-
cially grilled sardines, in
a relaxed beachfront
garden.

Cádiz

**Casa Paco (El Rincon
del Jamon)**
Plaza San Augustin, 5
Tel: 956-250 183
L & D daily. €
This is a good-value,
neighbourhood tapas
bar serving hearty
portions of tasty home-
cooked food.
A cosy, friendly
atmosphere prevails
and lots of laughter
oozes out into the
secluded side street
where there are a few
tables for outside dining.

El Balandro
Alameda de Apodaca, 22
Tel: 956-220 992
L & D daily. €–€€
www.restaurantebalandro.com
Understated but smart,
this is a formal restaurant
with a long bar and win-
dows overlooking the bay.
The menu is wide ranging
with superb *jamón ibérico*
and an extensive wine
and sherry list.

La Catedral
Plaza de la Catedral, 9
Tel: 956-252 184
L & D daily. €–€€
www.miraalsur.com/lacatedral
With its forest of para-
sols on the cathedral
square, this restaurant
ought to feel touristy,
but doesn't. Floodlit at
night, its setting is
romantic and the menu
features quality sea-
sonal produce including
excellent fresh fish from
the Bay of Cádiz.

La Commercial
Jose del Toro, 8
Tel: 956-211 914
L & D daily. €€
This contemporary,
intimate restaurant has
been stylishly designed
and attracts an up-
market clientele. Its
menu features well-
presented modern
Andalusian cuisine.

La Marea
Paseo Maritimo, 1
Playa Victoria
Tel: 956-280 347
L & D. €
An informal, welcoming
chiringuito set on

wooden decking in the
middle of Playa Victoria.
Quite good food and
drinks are served until
late into the night by
friendly staff.

Conil de la Frontera

**Restaurante Francisco
la Fontanilla**
Playa de la Fontanilla
Tel: 956-440 802
L & D daily. €–€€
Located right on the
sand, with an authentic
maritime feel and decor,
this is a traditional,
popular spot that serves
superb sea bream.

*El Puerto de Santa
Maria*

Casa Flores
Ribera del Río, 9
Tel: 956-543 512
L & D daily. €€
Casa Flores is a small,
classy restaurant with a
far-reaching reputation
for superb shellfish and
salt-baked fish from the
bay. Dishes are prepared
with careful attention to
detail and served in
rather formal, private
surroundings.

Romerijo
Ribera del Marisco
Tel: 956-541 254
L & D daily €
A lively informal eatery
for seafood on the river-
front, Romerijo is very
popular with locals. Good
value fresh-catch,
steamed or fried and
priced by the
kilogramme.

Jerez de la Frontera

La Carbona
Calle San Francisco de
Paula, 2
Tel: 956-347 475
L & D daily. €€
Very spacious, sociable
dining room under the
cavernous vaulted ceil-
ings and arches of a con-
verted sherry bodega.
Specials include sword-
fish or Sanlucar prawns
a la plancha, cooked on
the grill in an open
kitchen.

Bar Juanito
Calle Pescadería Vieja, 8–10
Tel: 956-334 838
L & D daily. €
Thriving local tapas bar
in Jerez old town. Tables
fill a canopied alley that
resonates with the ani-
mated conversation of
families and friends. A
long list of *raciones*
includes vermicelli with
prawns, artichokes and
excellent manchego.

El Laga Tio Parilla
Plaza Becerra, 5
Tel. 956-338 334
L & D daily. €
On the edge of the
Romany gypsy quarter,
authentic good value
tapas and sherry in a
buzzing atmosphere with
twice-nightly flamenco
performances.

Bar Las Bridas
Paseo de la Rosaleda, 4
Tel: 956-304 5 66
L & D daily. €€
A choice of menu or
tapas offering superb
fish and shellfish and a

very warm welcome.
Specialities include
squid and hake.

Los Caños de Meca

El Caña
Avenida Trafalgar
Tel: 956-437 034
L & D daily. €
An informal bar restaurant with limited opening times but a perfect spot to watch the sunset, from a decked terrace perched above the cliffs.

Sanlucar de Barameda

Casa Balbino
Plaza del Cabildo, 11
Tel: 956-360 513
L & D daily. €
At the heart of old Sanlucar, this is a renowned and popular bar /restaurant. Locals and visitors sit on barrels and at tables in the square to feast on an extensive choice of seafood, including lobster.

Casa Bigote
Bajo de Guia
Tel: 956-362 696
L & D daily. €€
One of the famed seafood establishments in Bajo de Guia, with a choice of tapas and more substantial fare. Specialities include fresh sea bream or prawns. The paella is particularly good.

Casa Juan
Bajo de Guia
Tel: 956-362 6 95
L & D daily. €€
Another mouth-watering choice on Bajo de Guia

where the house special is *arroz con langostinos* (rice with prawns), though the monkfish is better. A broad dining terrace has views across the river to Doñana.

Vejer

El Jardín del Califa
Plaza de España, 16
Tel: 956-447 730
L & D daily. €€
For a sense of Vejer's Moorish past, Arabic dishes (including cous cous and lamb tagine with almonds and plums) are served in an enclosed and pleasant patio garden with Moroccan decor

Restaurante Trafalgar
Plaza de España, 31
Tel: 956-447 638
L & D €€–€€€
A tidy, bright dining room spreads out smartly around the edge of Plaza España, overlooking the fountain. The excellent menu is varied, with a few vegetarian options and a slight bias towards meat over fish. Specialities include suckling pig.

Zhara de los Atunes

Casa José María
Plaza Marqués de Tamarón, 3
Tel: 956-439 338
L & D daily. €€
An inviting, down-to-earth place with warm traditional décor and service, specialising in fresh seafood, including sea urchin and meats.

Tarifa

La Casa Amarilla
Calle Sancho IV El Bravo
Tel: 956-681 993
L & D daily. €€–€€€
www.lacasaamarilla.net
La Casa Amarilla has a welcoming ambience of low ceilings, wooden tables, warm service and a chattering crowd sitting on barrels at the bar. Well chosen and prepared Andalusian specialities include acorn-fed *jamón* and locally caught tuna.

Misiana
Calle Sancho IV El Bravo,
Tel: 956-627 083
L & D. €–€€
www.misiana.com
Catering to Tarifa's fashionable crowd, this is smart, modern lounge bar at the corner of Misiana hotel, with trendy décor and a cosmopolitan array of tapas and cocktails.

La Sacristia
San Donato, 8
Tel: 956-681 759
L & D. €€–€€€
www.la sacristia.net
An eclectic restaurant designed to make best use of the arches and corners of a brick courtyard at the heart of the hotel. The menu is a contemporary mix of Moroccan and Andalusian

Bamboo Café Lounge
Paseo de la Alameda, 2
Tel: 956-627 304
B, L & D. €
A mellow café with a Moroccan flavour. The place to linger over a late breakfast .

PRICE CATEGORIES

Prices for three-course meal per person with a half-bottle of house wine:
€= under €20
€€ = €20–€40
€€€ = €40–€60

RIGHT: Café Central, a popular café in Tarifa.

EXPLORING THE WHITE TOWNS

Following a route linking a selection of the so-called *pueblos blancos* (white towns) is an excellent way of sampling the western interior of southern Spain. The higher you go, the whiter and prettier they get

Seville

The lowlands of Andalucía are characterised by large white-washed agricultural villages from which landless labourers used to go out to till the big arable farms of the river plains. Though certainly "white", these villages are bleak and functional; not all members of the white town species are charming or pretty. But the higher you climb into the sierras, where the terrain is more rugged, the smaller and more pic-turesque the towns and villages (both are called *pueblos*) become.

In the hills, large monocultures give way to smallholdings, herding and forest crops such as chestnut and cork. Glimpsed from the road or rail-way, whether framed in forest green or tucked under a vertiginous fang of rock, the mountain *pueblos* are dra-matic. They are usually crowned by a crumbling Moorish fortress and an imposing church erected as a victory statement by the Christians following the Reconquest.

The regional tourist authorities have striven to establish the white towns as the great attraction of the Andalusian interior. Some *pueblos* bear the official sign "Ruta de los Pueblos Blancos"; others, often no less attractive, do not. The major promotion concentrates on the prov-ince of Cádiz and the western half of the province of Málaga. As some

50 or 60 *pueblos* are commended in a number of leaflets, a little inside knowledge may help.

Regional differences

Some of the *pueblos* netted in the official trawl belong to the Atlantic coast, running from the Bay of Cádiz to the Straits of Gibraltar. These tend to be very different from those accessed from the Costa del Sol, for here tourism, though not absent, is less direct. There is large-scale migration of labour to Madrid,

Map
on page
118

LEFT: view of Jimena de la Frontera from its castle.
BELOW: Olvera's massive Iglesia de la Encarnacíon.

The whitewashed villages must make the most of abrupt terrain and fend off summer heat. Hollow clay roof tiles channel rainwater and improve ventilation. Interior courtyards provide privacy as well as a welcome refuge from heat, while exterior windows are kept small to keep out the summer glare. Thick walls of stone and mortar provide insulation. The yearly application of lime-wash not only reflects the sun's rays, but also serves as a disinfectant.

Barcelona or the coasts; the remaining townsfolk or villagers pursue a traditional pattern of life and the odd stranger remains a rarity.

That said, great efforts have been made to improve facilities in the villages in recent years, in particular for young people, who are apt to drift away to the cities. You may be surprised to find the occasional nightclub, for example, and also a number of towns with a municipal swimming pool. The mountain roads have also improved considerably.

Tourist infrastructure is still fairly limited in all but the best-known towns and villages, with mainly basic hotels and restaurants. The best way of exploring the *pueblos blancos*, therefore, is to set up base camp in Ronda *(see page 127)*, well placed for the more easterly *pueblos blancos*, Arcos de la Frontera, Olvera or Grazalema, the last also a good base for walkers.

CASARES–GAUCÍN LOOP

Holidaymakers on the Costa del Sol, who want to sample the white towns without travelling too far, can make an easy day excursion to Casares and Gaucín. To reach **Casares ❶**, take the signposted road inland 10 km (6 miles) west of Estepona. The town surges dramatically into view, its white-walled, red-roofed houses rising up the far side of a deep rocky gorge. At the top, in earthy red brick, stand the shell of its ruined church and all that now remains of its Moorish fort.

The town has been discovered, but not spoilt: menus have English translations but the food is still Spanish. On any summer evening the central plaza will echo with that special Spanish roar, created by most of the town's male population talking to each other at the tops of their voices. From Casares's summit there are some splendid views to the peaks of the Sierra Bermeja and, in

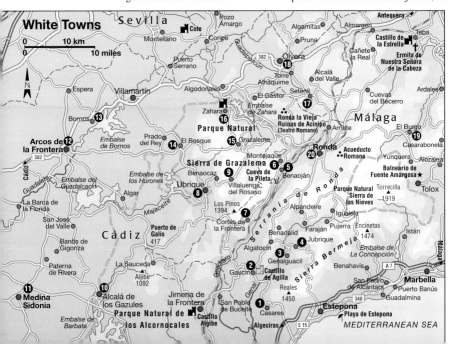

the opposite direction, to the valley of the Río Genal.

Gaucín

Running on a spine between the the Genal and the Río Guadiaro, the Ronda–Algeciras road has a string of white towns. Gaucín, on the main road, with roughly 2,500 inhabitants, is the largest of these; most have a population in the region of 1,000, and some, such as Alpandeire, have shrunk well below this figure.

After the Reconquest of 1492 and their nominal Christianisation, these townspeople all joined the *Morisco* (converted Muslim) rebellion of 1570. Resentment smouldered on for centuries and bred a wary people, whose villages were accessible only by steep mule track.

The construction of well-engineered roads has opened up the towns. Their populations increase markedly in the summer months, when migrant workers return to stay with elderly relatives for the holidays and fairs, and in some cases to rebuild and modernise their family homes.

Gaucín ❷ sits high up, spread across a saddle between rocky peaks. It was discovered by foreign visitors long before Casares, and its Fonda Nacional has been catering for British visitors since the early 19th century, when it was a stop on the road between Gibraltar and Ronda. Today it is only open for meals, but the owner will show you two ancient visitors' books with entries, mainly in English, from the 1870s onwards. Most entries are enthusiastic about the stabling, food, cheap prices and absence of bedbugs, though a few complain about the temper of the innkeeper Don Pedro Reales, who was always quarrelling with his wife.

Gaucín has a well-restored Moorish castle, perched high above the town. From here you can see Gibraltar and the coast on a clear day. It was in this castle that one of the

great heroes of Spanish history, Guzmán the Good *(see page 108)*, sacrificed his son rather than surrender to the Moors.

From Gaucín, continue to **Genalguacil** ❸, off the MA356, in the heart of the Sierra Bermeja. Its name means "Vizier's Garden", and it exhibits a certain hill-station gaiety, exemplified by the fine municipal swimming pool. This local renaissance is essentially Spanish, as there is no special provision for foreign tourists and no hotel. But there is a shady campsite down by the bridge over the Río Genal between Algatocín and Jubrique.

From here the route back to the coast at Estepona is bendy but beautiful, taking in a number of tiny white villages, chief of which is **Jubrique** ❹. The village climbs almost vertically up the side of a gorge, with steps in its main streets.

AROUND RONDA

Ronda *(see page 127)* is another good springboard for exploring the white towns. The Río Guadiaro

Map on page 118

Brightening the whitewash – a pot of geraniums in Jubrique.

BELOW: a backstreet in Casares, one of the more visited of the *pueblos blancos.*

Time passes slowly in the white towns, particularly in the afternoons, when local men like to while away the hours playing cards in the local bars.

BELOW: picture of a pregnant mare in the Cueva de la Pileta near Ronda.

(joined lower down by the Genal) rises above Ronda to debouch in the Mediterranean a little north of the Rock of Gibraltar.

The railway hugs it closely much of the way down; a minor road (MA501) also follows it in a switchback fashion, rising to the white towns of **Benaoján** ❺ and **Montejaque** ❻, renowned for their *embutidos* (tinned pork products) and mountain-cured hams, then plunging down to the station of Jimera de Líbar before rising again to Cortes de la Frontera.

On the way it is well worth stopping to visit the **Cueva de la Pileta** (tours daily 10am–1pm and 4–5pm, 6pm in summer; admission charge), prehistoric caves with spectacular wall-paintings, discovered in 1905 by a local farmer who was looking for guano (bird droppings) to fertilise his fields. If there is no one around, wait at the entrance to the caves and one of the caretakers, the grandson or great-grandson of the farmer, will eventually emerge with the previous group of visitors. Inside are paintings of sheep, cattle,

horses and fish believed to date from around 25,000 BC, as well as impressive stalactites and stalagmites and a subterranean lake.

Cortes de la Frontera ❼ is a pleasant, medium-sized *pueblo* (pop. 5,000) perched on a high shelf above the Guadiaro. It is clad in the trademark whitewash, with the exception of its distinguished stone town hall dating from the mid-18th century. It also has a bullring of masonry and a fine *alameda* or public promenade. Cortes derives its relative wealth from the cork forests which stretch for over 48 km (30 miles) to the west.

From Cortes, the road winds westwards through the forest, emerging into occasional clearings with fairytale cottages (the witches' variety), to the remote crossroads of **Puerto de Galis**.

The most industrial of the sierra towns is **Ubrique** ❽. This is deep in hunting country, as indicated by the great many stag heads and photographs mounted on the walls of the town's bars and restaurants, whose menus are biased towards game. Goats, which are also prolific, are herded for more than their milk, as the town prospers on a centuries-old reputation for leather craft.

A few kilometres east of Ubrique is **Villaluenga del Rosario** ❾, a tiny village carved into the rock that somehow finds space for a bullring. It is a serenely peaceful retreat where elderly locals rest on their sticks in a small, shady square. From here, another 10 km (6 miles) further north is Grazalema, a *pueblo blanco* par excellence and the hub of the Parque Natural Sierra de Grazalema *(see page 122)*.

BETWEEN UBRIQUE AND CÁDIZ

South of Ubrique, a flower-dotted route winds down through the

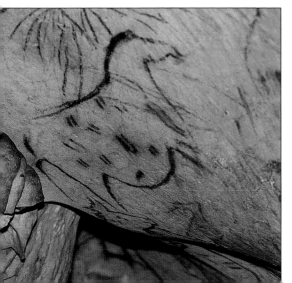

extensive **Parque Natural de Los Alcornocales**, forests of wild olive and cork oak. The source of the cork used to plug sherry bottles, many of the cork oaks are rusty-red from the waist down where their cork has been harvested.

At Puerto de Galis the road splits, offering a choice of routes to the Mediterranean. Secondary roads take in the "de la Frontera" towns of **Jimena** and **Castellar**, each with a crumbling 13th-century Moorish castle. Indeed, place names that include the word Frontera date from the two-and-a-half centuries before 1492, when the area was the frontier between Christian Spain and the surviving Kingdom of Granada.

Alternatively, the scenic A375 continues to another hill town at the geographical heart of Cádiz, Alcalà de los Gazules (*see below*). The undulating arable farms and bull-breeding pastures of the province of Cádiz contain several of the larger *pueblos blancos*. Alcalá de los Gazules, Medina Sidonia and Arcos de la Frontera (all on eminences above the plain) are approved White Towns. All three were strongholds of Moorish tribes until the Reconquest, when they passed into the hands of Spanish nobles who then abandoned them in favour of the larger cities.

Alcalá de los Gazules ⑩, with several wayside restaurants on the Cádiz road, is the most Moorish, its flat-topped houses climbing up to the church and fort. **Medina Sidonia** ⑪, bearing the name of the Spanish Armada's admiral, the Duke of Medina Sidonia, excites some expectations. In fact, a windswept place on top of a conical mound, its monuments are mostly ruinous, but it has a fine main square.

Arcos de la Frontera ⑫, squeezed onto a thin limestone ridge, precariously balanced above a river valley, is the westernmost *pueblos blancos* and one of the most spectacular. Arcos deserves investigation, for though less visited than famous Ronda, it is no less breathtaking, narrowing to medieval lanes so tight that scuffs along sandstone corners testify to the challenge of driving into the

Map on page 118

Many sierra villages have their own municipal pools. It is worth taking your swimming costume with you when touring the area.

LEFT: bull country east of Cádiz.
BELOW: evidence of the cork industry.

El Bosque is renowned for its mountain trout.

centre. A lingering reputation for witchcraft adds to the intrigue of the cobbled labyrinth.

Semana Santa and the Feria de San Miguel (29 September), are celebrated with bull-running, a terrifying thought in Arcos's exceptionally narrow, walled streets.

Easily discovered in the highest, oldest part of town is the **Plaza del Cabildo**. On the lip of the crag's near-vertical precipice, it benefits from far-reaching views across the River Guadalete and beyond. A luxurious parador hotel converted within the Casa del Corregidor, the 11th-century walls of the Castillo de los Duques (privately owned) and a 15th-century Gothic church, **Santa Maria de la Asunción**, flank the square.

Just to the north of Arcos is low-lying **Bornos** ⑬, on the shores of a reservoir squeezed out of the waters of the Guadalete. Above its white-washed walls rise the remnants of the palace-castle of the Riberas and other grand but gutted buildings. From the desiccated lakeside beach, with its makeshift bars, there is a superb view of the Sierra de Grazalema. Its decayed grandeur and raffish character make Bornos a perfect foil for the pristine mountains rising across the tranquil water.

The Parque Natural Sierra de Grazalema

East of Arcos de la Frontera, the A372 tilts up through sunflower fields to **El Bosque** ⑭. This refreshing town, with its tinkling fountains and an old waterwheel, is surrounded by pine trees, sloping down to a clear river abundant with trout a speciality in the local restaurants.

The wooded hills mark the start of the **Parque Natural Sierra de Grazalema** (controlled access). Close to El Bosque's bullring is the park's head office and main information centre (tel: 956-727 029), where maps are available and free hiking permits, obligatory for the three walks in the park – Garganta Verde, Pinsapar and El Torreón *(see page 123)* – can be obtained.

The park's rugged terrain, where an unusual microclimate has preserved some ancient Mediter-

ranean forest and a precious wildlife habitat, extends almost to the border with Málaga province. At its northern and eastern limits it meets Zahara de la Sierra and Grazalema, which have smaller visitor's centres.

A cascade of pretty whitewashed houses snuggled into the lush foothills of the peak of San Cristóbal, **Grazalema ⑮** is a welcoming, ebullient place, and a good base for exploring the area. The town lays claim to the region's highest rainfall, and its wroughtiron balconies and geranium-filled window boxes are often coated with snow in winter.

The town earns its living from ceramics and woollen products, crafted according to long-established traditions, as well as tourism. For outdoor activities around the town, Horizon Aventura (tel: 956-132 363; www. horizonaventura.com) organises hiking, mountain biking, climbing, caving, 4x4 trips, kayaking, paragliding and bungee jumping.

Alternatively, a rewarding drive through the park follows the spectacular CA531 from Grazalema to Zahara. The route passes the starting point for two of the park's walks (permits required), the **Garganta Verde** – a densely vegetated ravine – and the **Pinsapar** – a conservation area devoted to pre-Ice Age, dark green Spanish fir.

Halfway to Zahara the road twists and climbs to 1,357 metres (4,511 ft) at **Puerto de las Palomas**, where birds of prey (Bonnelli's, booted and golden eagles, griffon vultures and buzzards) circle watchfully, high overhead.

The village of **Zahara de la Sierra ⑯** wraps itself like a helter-skelter around an isolated, sheer outcrop, twisting down from the ruined 12th-century castle at its peak. An important Moorish town, it was a significant Christian conquest in 1483, and seems little changed. A cared-for place, where a humble pride can be seen in swept steps and immaculately tended flower beds, unassuming Zahara enjoys majestic views across olive groves and the reservoir at the foot of its hill.

Map on page 118

Grazalema is plastered like a martlet-nest on the rocky hill, and can only be approached by a narrow ledge... The wild women, as they wash their parti-coloured garments in the bubbling stream, eye the traveller as if a perquisite of their worthy mates.

– RICHARD FORD
A Handbook for Travellers in Spain, 1855

BELOW LEFT AND RIGHT: views of Zahara de la Sierra.

Map
on page
118

TIP

Olvera is the starting
point for a 38km
(24-mile) "vía verde",
a hiking and cycling
path following a dis-
used railway track.
The route runs from
Olvera to Puerta
Serrano west of
Algodonales on the
Ronda–Seville road.
Visit www.ffe.es/vias
verdes for more details
or enquire at the
tourist office near the
Iglesia de la
Encarnacíon.

BELOW: the sugar-
cube houses of Olvera.

North of Ronda

One of the most publicised sights in
the region is **Setenil** ⑰, a small
white town set not on a hilltop as is
usually the case but in a ravine of the
Río Guadalporcun, 20 km (12 miles)
north of Ronda. It has two or three
streets of semi-cave houses whose
roofs are formed by overhanging
rock, giving their neat white facades
the appearance of mushroom stems
under a spreading crown. It is worth
stopping for lunch or a drink at one
of its characterful bars.

A few kilometres further north,
passing under the walls of the little
hilltop village of **Torre Alháquime**,
you come to **Olvera** ⑱, a white
town par excellence. With around
12,000 inhabitants it is larger than
its neighbours. Its silhouette is dramatic: a Moorish keep and the
imposing Iglesia de la Encarnacíon
rise above tightly packed houses
sloping down to a clear perimeter,
where the countryside begins.
Famous as the refuge for outlaws in
the 19th century, Olvera today has
a reputation for religiosity. A monument to the Sacred Heart of Jesus

on a natural outcrop of rock dominates the lower town, and pilgrims
have been known to crawl for miles
on their hands and knees, in fulfil-
ment of a vow, to the popular sanctuary of the Virgen de los Remedios.

Olvera's streets are neat and somewhat stern. The handsome facades
make few concessions to the floral
trimmings so ubiquitous in many
pueblos blancos. However, the local
fair, late in August, is one of the most
lavish in the region, lasting for five
nights, until 5am or later, with stalls,
sideshows, bars, song and dance;
during the day there are football
matches, clay-pigeon contests and
two or three novice bullfights held
in a portable ring. Olvera is also the
starting point for one of Andalucía's
most spectacular Vías Verdes *(see
margin tip)*.

The last white town in this section
is **El Burgo** ⑲, out on a limb east of
Ronda, on the road to Málaga via
Coín, and an alternative base to
Ronda for exploring the Parque Natural de la Sierra de las Nieves. It has
two hotels on Calle Mesones *(see
page 237 for details)*.   ❑

RESTAURANTS & BARS

Restaurants

Arcos de la Frontera

El Convento
Calle Marqués de Torresto, 7
Tel: 956-700 721
L & D daily. €€
This upmarket, formal choice set in the patio of a *casa palacio* has a reputation for traditional sierra recipes, biased towards game. The menu features, rabbit, partridge, lamb, venison and *jamón iberico*.

Parador Casa del Corregidor
Plaza del Cabildo
Tel: 956-700 500
L & D daily. €€–€€€
Enjoy spectacular views from this parador's excellent restaurant. There is always a well-priced set menu, but for a splurge opt for the *menú gastronómico* offering 10 different regional specialities.

Benaoján

Molino del Santo
Boulevardia Estación de Benaoján
Tel: 952-167 151
L& D daily. Closed mid-Nov–mid-Feb. €€ –€€€
Hotel-restaurant with beautiful terrace overlooking a stream. The menu includes Andalusian and international options, using organic ingredients.

El Bosque

Las Truchas
Avenida de la Diputación s/n
Tel: 956-716 061. €€
Long-established hotel-restaurant just outside El Bosque. The excellent restaurant has local specialities, including trout for which the town is known.

El Burgo

Posada del Canonigo
Calle Mesones, 24
Tel: 952-160 185
L & D daily. €
Rustic hotel-restaurant serving well-prepared Andalusian fare.

Gaucin

Hotel Restaurante La Fructuosa
Calle Convento 67
Tel: 952-151 072
May–Oct Wed–Sat, D only. €€
www.lafructuosa.es
Well-prepared local and Moroccan cuisine in delightful hotel restaurant.

Grazalema

Restaurante Mirador de Grazalema
Avenida Juan de la Rosa, s/n
Tel: 956-132 319
L & D. €€–€€€
Floor-to-ceiling windows offer panoramic views over the sierra from this spacious restaurant. Specials include beef, Serrano ham and trout.

Mesón El Simancon
Plaza Asomadero
Tel: 956-132 421
L & D. €–€€
www.elsimancon.com
A packed, tiny dining room that feels like a cosy hunter's lodge with hams hanging from the ceilings and stuffed stag heads on the walls. Game is the house speciality, especially venison.

Bar Zulema
Calle Agua
Tel: 956 132 402
L & D daily. €
A bustling haunt where locals gather inside to prop up the bar and watch sport on TV, while the good range of tapas attracts a hungry crowd to outdoor tables on the traffic-free Calle Agua.

Jimena de la Frontera

Mesón Campoy
Mesila de los Angeles, 36
Tel: 956-641 060
L & D. Closed Wed. €–€€
Local and international dishes, plus good pizzas.

Zahara de la Sierra

Mesón Los Estribos
Calle Fuerte, 3
Tel: 956-123 145
L & D. €
A tiny, very friendly family-run restaurant near the castle, overlooking the reservoir.

PRICE CATEGORIES

Prices for three-course meal per person with a half-bottle of house wine:
€= under €20
€€ = €20–€40
€€€ = €40–€60

RIGHT: propping up a bar in Zahara de la Sierra.

RONDA

Nothing can detract from Ronda's incomparable setting, perched above the El Tajo gorge. It also has fine Mudéjar and Renaissance architecture, one of the finest bullrings in Spain, and Moorish and Roman remains

Seville
Ronda

Dramatically spanning the El Tajo gorge, **Ronda** ⑳, along with the cave-riddled surrounding region, has a long and fascinating history. Prehistoric relics such as the wall-paintings of the nearby Cueva de la Pileta *(see page 120)* are evidence of human settlement from as early as 25000 BC. Ancient Iberians also populated the area, but it was the Romans who established the first significant settlement here.

The site's impressive geography made the place a natural fortress. After the Muslim invasion of 711 Ronda became one of the Moors' most important towns, known as Madinat Runda, and examples of Moorish architecture can still be seen in the old town.

Early in the 11th century, the Berber Abu Mur displaced the caliphal government, making Ronda an independent *taifa*. Later, after Christian forces had retaken Seville in 1248, the the town was at the forefront of tensions between Christian Seville and Muslim Granada. But Muslim rule lasted until 1485 when, as one of the last strongholds of the Kingdom of Granada, it was conquered by the Christians after a seven-day siege. It was soon given a city council with the same rights as Seville.

By the 18th century the old Arab town, La Ciudad, was becoming too small for the growing population, and so, in 1793 the Puente Nuevo (New Bridge), now the symbol of the city, was built over the Tajo, connecting La Ciudad with a new quarter known as El Mercadillo. The city prospered, and in 1784 Ronda's neoclassical-style Plaza de Toros was also built.

Not long after this, however, the town was practically destroyed by Napoleon's forces during the Wars of Independence.

Maps:
City 128
Area 118

LEFT: the El Tajo Gorge.
BELOW: Ronda's Plaza del Toros.

Finery and frills at Ronda's feria, *held in September and a highlight in southern Spain's festival diary.*

Famous visitors

Ronda was one of the first small Spanish cities (it has around 35,000 inhabitants today) to earn a place on the tourist map. It was mentioned by early geographers and travellers, from Strabo and Pliny the elder to Ibn Batuta, the 14th-century Arab geographer and explorer, but received its most enthusiastic write-up in Richard Ford's *A Handbook for Travellers in Spain* (1855): "There is but one Ronda in the world, and this Tajo, cleft as it were by the scimitar of Roldan, forms when the cascade is full… its heart and soul. The scene, its noise and movement, baffle pen and pencil, and, like Wilson at the Falls of Terni, we can only exclaim, 'Well done, rock and water, by Heavens!'"

Ford wrote this lyrical description in the heyday of the Romantic movement, when Andalucía drew Scottish artists David Wilkie and David Roberts, Frenchman Théophile Gautier, the great lithographer Gustave Doré, and many others.

In 1906 the Hotel Reina Victoria on the edge of the El Tajo was completed, and it quickly became popular as a retreat for the officers of the Gibraltar garrison. In 1913 the poet Rainer Maria Rilke stayed here for several weeks and wrote *The Spanish Trilogy*, including his eulogistic lines on observing a shepherd tending his flock on the hillside: "Even today a god might secretly enter that form and not be diminished."

Later came swashbuckling Ernest Hemingway and Orson Welles to fraternise with the leading matador Antonio Ordóñez, and the painter David Bomberg.

Approaches to the city

With such a legacy of international interest, Ronda has a lot to live up to and probably raises too many expectations in first-time visitors. The inevitable has happened: urban

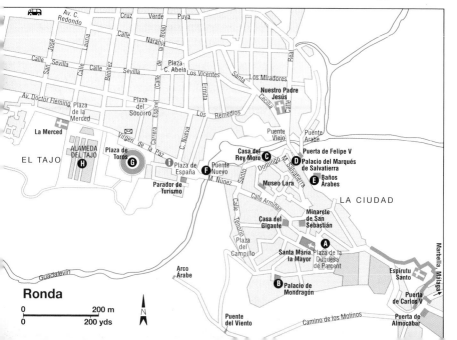

Ronda

0 _____ 200 m
0 _____ 200 yds

N

sprawl, an industrial estate and bleak municipal housing have encroached upon the town.

It is therefore wise to approach Ronda with circumspection. The best routes into town, yielding the best views of the old city, are from Algeciras and San Pedro de Alcántara. If you enter from Seville or from Granada, take the ring-road around the town, as if aiming for San Pedro, and then double back into Ronda on the unblemished flank, leading into La Ciudad, the old city.

La Ciudad

The road enters La Ciudad via the **Barrio de San Francisco**, which is like a small mountain *pueblo* picked up and deposited under the city walls. There is a lively market here every Sunday and an important animal fair early in October. The most striking building, reached through the 13th-century horseshoe arch of the **Puerta de Almocabar**, is the fortress-like church of **Espíritu Santo**, the first to be built after the recapture of Ronda from the Moors in 1485.

The first vehicle-accessible turning on the left as you ascend leads into the **Plaza de la Duquesa de Parcent Ⓐ**, a pretty square with cypresses, medlars and oleanders inside low box hedges. Flanking the plaza are an early 18th-century barracks, now the town hall; a 19th-century boys' school on the site of the Moorish fortress (left ruinous after the Peninsular War); the convents of the Poor Clares and of the Little Sisters of the Cross; the Iglesia Santa María la Mayor; and the law courts.

The 13th-century **Iglesia Santa María la Mayor** (10am–6pm, until 8pm in summer; admission charge) is built on the site of Ronda's main mosque. Consecrated after the Reconquest, it was later considered too small and was replaced by this church, begun in the Gothic style in the late 15th century and completed in the 18th century. Evidence of the original mosque can be found in the mihrab (niche indicating the direction of Mecca), visible in the entrance, and the minaret, which is now the bell-tower. Facing the square is an arcade with a gallery, where priests and notables would watch bullfights before the permanent bullring was built.

As you leave the church look out for the quirky **Museo del Bandolero** (Bandit Museum, Calle Armiñàn, 65; daily 10.30am–6.30 pm, until 8.30pm in summer; admission charge; www.museobandolero.com), dedicated to the region's reputation for banditry in the 19th century.

On the same street, the **Museo Lara** (Calle Armiñàn, 29; daily; admission charge) has an interesting selection of clocks, weapons, scientific paraphernalia and archaeological finds, as well as a collection of popular art.

Not far from here, on the Plaza Mondragón, is the **Palacio de Mondragón Ⓑ** (Mon–Fri 10am–7pm,

Icon of the Virgin inside the Iglesia Santa María la Mayor, Ronda.

BELOW: courtyard of the Palacio de Mondragón, now the Municipal Museum.

Map on page 128

Sculptural detail on the main facade of the Palacio del Marqués de Salvatierra, built in the 18th century for the Marqués de Moctezuma.

Sat–Sun 10am–3pm; admission charge), a grand townhouse of Moorish origins (1314) with a Renaissance stone facade, cobbled porch with mounting block, front patio dating from around 1570 and Mudéjar-style rear patio. Formerly the home of kings and governors, as well as Alistair Boyd (Lord Kilmarnock), author of several books on Spain, including *The Road from Ronda*, it is now the city museum, concentrating mainly on archaeological finds in the region.

There are relatively few remaining examples of domestic building dating from the Muslim era, but the nearby **Casa del Gigante** (not open to the public) has a patio with 14th-century arabesque stucco work.

An alley leads from the Plaza de Mondragón into the **Plaza del Campillo** (open on one side to the mountains). Halfway down a steep slope are the remnants of an outer wall and gateway, through which winds a track down to the market gardens and abandoned watermills in the valley.

From the Plaza del Campillo,

Calle Tenorio leads back to the main road bisecting the old city. The steep **Cuesta de Santo Domingo** leads down past the **Casa del Marqués de Santa Pola** (with basements preserving some traces of Moorish wall-painting) to the so-called **Casa del Rey Moro** ● in Calle Santo Domingo. This is an 18th-century pastiche with hanging gardens (designed by the French landscape gardener Jean-Claude Forestier in 1912) through which the **Mina de Ronda**, a long staircase cut inside the rock, descends to the river bed, emerging through a keyhole arch (the gardens and Mina de Ronda can be visited; admission charge).

The so-called Water Mine is the one feature that is thought to date from the Moorish era. During times of siege, it was manned by a chain of Christian captives, who passed up pitchers of water to supply the citadel, "whose fierce king" – according to a romantic travel book of 1923 – "drank only from the skulls of enemies; cutting off their heads and making them into goblets inlaid with splendid jewels".

Another of Ronda's fine buildings is the 18th-century **Palacio del Marqués de Salvatierra** ● (provided the family isn't in residence, guided tours of the palace are conducted on the hour from 11am–2pm and 4–7pm; admission charge). Its interesting facade, showing Spanish colonial influences, reflects the fact that it was built for the Marqués de Moctezuma, the Governor of South America. The fine wrought ironwork is a speciality of Ronda; you will see other examples in *rejas* (window grilles) and on balconies throughout the town.

Below the palace, Calle Marqués de Salvatierra leads down to the **Puerta de Felipe V**, a mini triumphal arch built in 1742 and commemorating Spain's first Bourbon monarch. Down the slope, the

Puente Viejo (Old Bridge) crosses the gorge, offering an impressive upward view of the Tajo.

To the right is the so-called **Puente Árabe** and, a short walk away, the **Baños Árabes** ❸ (Arab Baths; Mon–Fri 10am–7pm, Sat–Sun 10am–3pm; admission charge), dating from around 1300. Sited at the confluence of two rivers near the city gates, the baths were used by travellers entering the city. As is common in Muslim societies today, they were built next to a mosque, spiritual and bodily purification being interdependent. The baths have been fully restored and comprise a reception area, cold room, warm room and, closest to the wood-fired oven, a hot room. From this point, a rough pebbled track leads up under the Salvatierra palace to the third of the medieval city gates.

The Puente Nuevo

The **Puente Nuevo** ❺ (New Bridge) crosses the gorge at its deepest and narrowest point and is a uniquely assertive feat of engineering, more like a solid causeway with apertures than an aerial span over the abyss. The Puente Nuevo was constructed entirely of stone between 1751 and 1793. Once it was open, tightly corseted Ronda spilled out onto the tableland known as the Mercadillo, until then used mainly for markets and fairs.

Many have fallen to their death from the bridge. Indeed, its architect José Martín de Aldehuela plunged to his death while inspecting the structure shortly before its completion. Much later, in the 20th century, the bridge gained notoriety in Ernest Hemingway's *For Whom the Bell Tolls,* which describes local fascists being thrown to their deaths from the bridge by the Republican forces during the Spanish Civil War.

Few can resist the opportunity to peer over the railings at the waters of the Guadalevín river flowing 98 metres (321 ft) below. A small prison *(carcel)* used to exist in the middle of the bridge.

Plaza de Toros

The **Plaza de Toros** ❼ (daily Nov–Feb 10am–6pm, Mar–mid-Apr

Map on page 128

BELOW: Ronda is famous for bullfighting and has one of Spain's oldest bullrings.

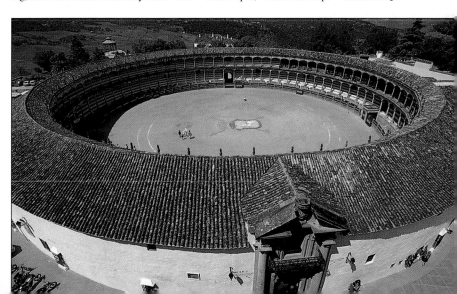

A meeting of like minds – Orson Welles pictured with Antonio Ordóñez (1932–98), one of Ronda's greatest ever bullfighters. Ernest Hemingway, another great fan of Ordóñez, based his collection of short stories The Dangerous Summer *on Ordóñez's rivalry with fellow bullfighter Luis Miguel Dominguín.*

BELOW: view from the Alameda del Tajo.

10am–7pm, mid-Apr–Oct 10am–8pm; admission charge; audioguide available: www.rmcr.org) is not the oldest bullring in Spain, as is often claimed, but it is far and away the largest and most elegant of the early plazas. It was inaugurated in 1785, though had been in use before that. Indeed, a corrida held the previous year resulted in a partial collapse of the arena killing 10 spectators. Besides being of architectural beauty, the ring is considerably different from more modern plazas in its technical layout. With a diameter of 66 metres (72 yards), it is one of the widest rings in the world.

Ronda has produced many notable figures in the bullfighting world. Pedro Romero, of the influential Romero dynasty, laid down the modern rules of bullfighting in the 18th century, starting the tradition on foot, equipped with a sword and *muleta* (small cloth). Born in Ronda in 1754, Pedro Romero is credited with having killed over 5,600 bulls in his career without ever suffering a major injury. From a family noted for its longevity – his father lived to 102 – Pedro Romero killed his last bull in the Madrid bullring at the incredible age of 79.

The other great Ronda-born dynasty is the Ordóñez family, which has produced several generations of prominent matadors over more than a century.

The bullring's **Museum** is of real interest, detailing the origins and evolution of bullfighting, including Ronda's role in these, with documents, deeds, historic posters, costumes, memorabilia, paintings, etc.

In September, on the Saturday of the *feria*, the bullring stages a *corrida goyesca*, introduced by the Ordóñez family in 1954 to mark the 200th anniversary of Pedro Romero's birth. The torreadors, and many members of the audience, dress in the costumes of the period, as shown in Goya's series of etchings, *The Tauromachia*, which are on display in the bullring's museum.

Paseo places

A little higher up than the Plaza de Toros on the same side of the street is the **Alameda del Tajo ❶**, a shady public promenade dating from 1806, which ends in a balustrade on the brink of a sheer drop. "The view from this eminence over the depths below, and the mountain panorama," wrote Richard Ford, in his *Handbook for Travellers*, "is one of the finest in the world." Few will accuse him of hyperbole.

It is not necessary to go beyond the Alameda (or the neighbouring church of La Merced, which once housed the arm of Santa Teresa of Ávila) other than to reach the **Hotel Reina Victoria** on the highest point of the new town. With the coming of newer, more luxurious hotels including the parador on the edge of the gorge, this once-famous establishment has lost some of its Edwardian atmosphere. However,

Map on page 128

it is worth paying it a visit to see the room in which Rainer Maria Rilke stayed, which has a few mementoes, and to enjoy a drink on the terrace at sunset.

Despite its claim to an aristocratic and warlike past, and its delight in legends of brigands and smugglers, Ronda has for long been a lively commercial centre for almost 30 smaller towns and villages. This is borne out in the **Calle de la Bola**, a traffic-free shopping street running from the bullring due east for more than a kilometre. Ronda's answer to Las Ramblas of Barcelona or Calle Sierpes in Seville, it is packed both before lunch and for the evening *paseo*.

Around Ronda

Ronda is a stop on one of the great train journeys of southern Spain, the Algeciras–Bobadilla route, which meanders through the valley of the Río Guadiaro via the white towns of Gaucín and Jimena de la Frontera.

The town is also a good base for excursions by car. Just a few kilometres west of town are the remains – theatre, forum and public baths – of

the 1st-century BC Roman town of **Acinipo** (Tues–Sun 10am–5pm; free admission) at Ronda La Vieja.

Further afield, southeast of Ronda, the **Parque Natural Sierra de las Nieves** stretches almost to Marbella. It is famous for a rare species of prehistoric fir, the *pinsapo*, which grows only above 1,000 metres (3,200 ft), and also for the *Capra pyrenaica* or ibex; some pairs of golden eagles also survive. Access by jeep trail via the towns of **El Burgo** *(see page 124*, **Yunquera** or **Tolox** *(see pages 154–155)* is relatively unrestricted.

West of Ronda, the **Parque Natural Sierra de Grazalema** *(see page 122)* covers an area of almost 50,000 hectares (120,000 acres), including 13 villages, mainly in the province of Cádiz. The flora and fauna on this side are more varied, but access is strictly controlled, and some of the routes in the *pinsapares* (which also exist here) are closed during the summer months as a precaution against forest fires. The main park office is in the small town of El Bosque *(see page 122)*. ❑

Welcome to the Parque Natural Sierra de las Nieves, whose wildlife includes the ibex.

RESTAURANTS & BARS

Albacara
Calle Tenorio
Tel: 952-161 184
L &D. €€€
www.hotelmontelirio.com
Comfortable, traditionally styled restaurant in a hotel occupying a historic house. Good-quality regional and international dishes.

Casa Santa Pola
Santo Domingo, 3
Tel: 952 879 208. €€€
Housed in a pretty mansion built over a 9th-century mosque next to the

Puente Nuevo. Creative interpretations of Andalusian cuisine.

Don Miguel
Villanueva, 4
Tel: 952-878 377
L & D daily. Closed mid–late Jan. €€–€€€
Spectacular setting at the edge of the Ronda gorge, with a pleasant terrace for al fresco dining. Spanish and international food.

El Amócabar
Plaza Ruedo Alameda 2
Tel: 952-875 977

L & D daily. €€
Great local cooking in unpretentious restaurant popular among locals.

Jerez
Paseo Blas Infante, 2
Tel: 952-872 098
L & D daily. €€–€€€
Directly across from the Plaza de Toros. Eat in the tasteful dining room or out on the covered terrace. Regional cuisine.

Pedro Romero
Calle Virgen de la Paz, 18
Tel: 952-871 110
L & D daily. €€€
Touristy, but serving good Andalusian fare. It is across from the Ronda

bullring, and many bullfighters have eaten here. The *Rabo de Toro* (oxtail stew) is superb.

Tragabuches
Calle José Aparicio, 1
Tel: 952-190 291.
L & D. Closed Mon and Sun evenings. €€€–€€€€
Stylish, modern restaurant serving innovative Andalusian dishes. Considered one of the best restaurants in Spain.

● ● ● ● ● ● ● ● ● ● ● ●
Price includes dinner and a glass of wine, excluding tip.
€€€€ €40 and up,
€€€ under €40,
€€ under €30, € under €20.

THE COSTA DEL SOL

The Costa del Sol's resorts offer something for every taste. They range from glamorous Marbella to brash Torremolinos, and from family-focused Fuengirola to exclusive Puerto Banús

I t is impossible to write about the Costa del Sol without some degree of regret about what a lovely coast it must have been with its small sandy bays and fishing villages, connected to each other by no more than dirt roads, backed from end to end by a dramatic line of sierras. But that is just a distant memory now, and the only way you will see that scene is on grainy black-and-white photographs sometimes on display in hotels and bars. These days large built-up resorts lie almost end to end from Sotogrande to Nerja. So many golf courses are found here that it has been dubbed the "*Costa del Golf*".

But if the Costa is scenically and ecologically a disaster, it can still be fun. The climate is good year-round, the sea is warm and the sandy beaches are still there, immaculately maintained by the local authorities. The array of attractions appeals to visitors of all ages, tastes and backgrounds.

Málaga

Málaga ❶ is the largest city, capital and gateway of the Costa del Sol. Although historic and with some interesting attractions, for many years it was largely overlooked by visitors who, for the most part, just passed through the airport on the

way to the resorts. In recent years all that has changed, and Málaga has become a city destination in its own right, especially since the opening of the long-planned Picasso Museum. The city has been given a thorough make-over. Attractive new hotels have been built in the centre and along the beach, and Calle Marqués de Larios – the main shopping street, west of the Cathedral – is now a pleasant pedestrian zone. New motorways along the coast allow through-traffic to pass around the

Maps:
Area 136
City 138

LEFT: the popular resort of Nerja, east of Málaga.
BELOW: Málaga, the gateway to the Costa del Sol, is worth exploring in its own right.

Costa del Sol, Antequera and La Axarquía

MEDITERRANEAN SEA

city rather than clogging the centre, and ambitious plans are in place to run some streets underground, allowing more areas of the old city to become pedestrianised.

For a long time the city had no decent beach, but a massive programme involving the import of millions of tonnes of sand and the removal of unsightly shacks has vastly improved both Málaga's beaches, which lie east of the city centre, and others along the coast.

Málaga's history

Originally Phoenician, Málaga sided briefly with Carthage before becoming a Roman *municipium* (a town governed by its own laws). In 711 it fell to the Moors, and was the port of the Kingdom of Granada until 1487, when it was taken by the Christians after a four-month siege followed by brutal burnings.

On several occasions the city has been a place of revolt. It was on Málaga's San Andrés beach that the rebel General Torrijos and his 52 companions were shot in 1831. In revolt against the repressive government of Fernando VII, this young Spanish general landed on today's Costa del Sol, encouraged by an invented story that the Málaga garrison would join him. Instead it surrounded and captured him.

In 1931, and again at the start of the Civil War five years later, left-wing citizens burned Málaga's churches and convents. The city held out against General Franco's Nationalists until 1937; when it finally fell, its refugees were bombed and shelled as they escaped up the coast road towards Almería.

Main sights

Málaga's most prominent landmark is the **Catedral Ⓐ** (Mon–Sat 10am–6.45; admission charge; Sun for Mass). Built in fits and starts between 1528 and 1782, it is still unfinished, as one of its twin towers is missing – the other rises an impressive 100 metres (330 ft) above street level. From that, it gets its nickname, *"La Manquita"*, the One-Armed Lady. The highlight of the interior is the choir, completed in 1662 by the great Granada sculptor Pedro de Mena.

On the square in front of the Cathedral's western facade is the **Palacio Episcopal**, now a venue for temporary art exhibitions.

Picasso Museum

A short walk from the Cathedral, on Calle San Augustín, is the magnificent Buenavista Palace, built between 1516 and 1542 by Diego de Cazalla and housing the **Museo Picasso Ⓑ** (Tue–Thur and Sun 10am–8pm, Fri–Sat 10am–9pm; admission charge; www.museopicassomalaga.org), dedicated to Málaga's most famous son. Comprising 155 paintings, drawings, sculptures, ceramics and prints, spanning Picasso's entire career, the bulk of the collection was donated by Cristina and Bernard Ruiz-Picasso, Picasso's daughter-in-law and grand-

Map on page 138

Picasso sculpture in the Casa Natal, the former home of Picasso on Plaza Merced, a short distance from the Museo Picasso.

BELOW: wedding party outside Málaga's Cathedral.

The leafy courtyard of Málaga's Museo de Artes Populares.

son. They range from works such as a portrait of his younger sister Lola, painted when he was just 15, to familiar Cubist works from 1910 onwards.

The family home on nearby Plaza de la Merced, where Picasso spent the first 10 years of his life, has been restored, and functions as the **Casa Natal** (Mon–Sat 10am–2pm and 5–8pm; Sun 10am–2pm; admission charge; www.fundacionpicasso.es), primarily a study centre and reference library, but with a collection of family photographs, sketches and pots.

The fortifications

Málaga's historical sights are mainly evident on the high ground at its eastern end , dominated by the **Alcazaba** ● (Tues– Sun 9.30am– 8pm; admission charge), and the Castillo de Gibralfaro above it. The route up to the Alcazaba passes through a maze of pretty gardens to the **Arco del Cristo** (Gateway of Christ) – where the Catholic Monarchs celebrated

Mass following their conquest of the fortress in 1487 – and then to an old palace housing an archaeological museum. At the foot of the route is the **Teatro Romano** (Roman Theatre; Tues–Sat 10am– 2.30pm and 5–8pm, Sun 10am– 2.30pm).

Connecting the Alcazaba with the **Castillo de Gibralfaro** ● (daily 9am–7.45pm; admission charge) formidable double walls with square turrets ascend the hill. Named from the Arabic Jebel al Faro (Lighthouse Hill), this immense structure was founded by Abd-al-Rahman I in the 8th century and enlarged in the 14th century. A rocky path climbs beside the wall to a height of 130 metres (425ft), though you can also drive up here from behind the hill. A *mirador* offers superb views over the harbour and down on to the Plaza de Toros *(see page 139)*, but for a beer (or more) with your view stop off at the luxurious Parador de Málaga Gibralfaro.

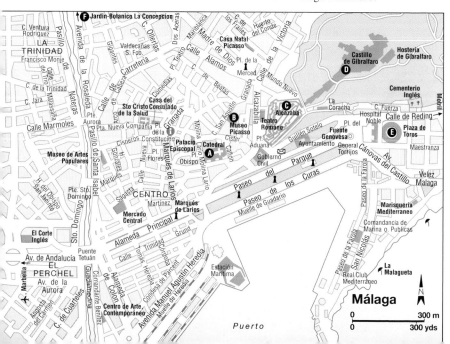

Other sights

The city centre offers a few more sights. Just below the Castillo the **Plaza de Toros** ❸ (Bullring) has a small museum (Mon–Fri 10am–1pm and 5–8pm; admission charge), although it is not as good as those in Ronda, Córdoba or Seville. Between the bullring and the seafront the area known as **La Malagueta** has good restaurants and bars. The local speciality if *fritura malgueña*, mixed fried seafood.

Also on this side of town, off the Avenida de Príes, is the **Cementerio Inglés** (English Cemetery). Founded in 1830, it was Spain's first Protestant cemetery, and Captain Robert Boyd, the Englishman who financed Torrijos's revolt and died with him, was one of the first to be buried here. Before then, Málaga's Protestants were buried on the beach below the high-water mark, where the sea washed their bones out of the sand.

On the other side of the city centre near the dry river bed of the Guadamedina, which divides the city, are two very different museums. Occupying a 17th-century palace at Pasillo de Santa Isabel, 10, the **Museo de Artes Populares** (Museum of Popular Arts; Mon–Fri 10am–1.30pm and 4–7pm, Sat 10am–1.30pm; admission charge) is packed with oddities relating to traditional life in the area. Closer to the port, in Málaga's old wholesale market on Calle Alemania, is the **Centro de Arte Contemporáneo** (Tues–Sun 10am–8pm; free admission; www.cacmalaga.org). It has works by leading national and international artists, including Roy Lichtenstein.

On the northern outskirts of Málaga (off the Antequera road 4 km/2½ miles from town), the **Jardín Botánico La Concepción** ❻ is a pleasant place in which to while away a few hours. A tropical garden with lakes and waterfalls, it was created in the mid-19th century by a local aristocratic family (Tues–Sun 10am–dusk; 90-minute guided tours; admission charge).

WEST OF MÁLAGA

From the start, **Torremolinos** ❷ epitomised the best and the worst of

Maps:
Area 136
City 138

TIP

Just west of Torremolinos, the fishing quarter of La Carihuela retains a certain Spanish feel, and is famous for its excellent seafood restaurants.

BELOW:
Calle San Miguel, the main shopping street in Torremolinos.

The Good-Time Costa

The year 1932 is regarded as a turning point in the making of the Costa del Sol. Legend has it a certain Carlota Alessandri bought a piece of barren hillside at Montemar, west of Torremolinos. Asked what she intended to plant there, she replied haughtily: "Plant? I shall plant tourists!"

After World War II, the Marquis of Najera, a Spanish nobleman, took up residence in Torremolinos. In his wake came well-to-do Spanish families, and European diplomats and colonial officials unwilling to adjust to a retirement devoid of constant sunshine. In the 1960s Torremolinos became a magnet for bohemians, including Hemingway and the American novelist James Michener, who based his book *The Drifters* on characters plucked from the Costa del Sol's lotus-eaters.

While Torremolinos throbbed with life on the fringe, further down the coast the Spanish nobleman Ricardo Soriano, the Marquis of Ivanrey, was inviting his wealthy friends to the village of Marbella. The Marquis's nephew, Prince Alfonso von Hohenlohe of Liechtenstein, was so impressed that he bought a decaying farmhouse on the outskirts of the fishing village for £2,000

(US$3,000), turned it into a hotel and named it the Marbella Club. Visitors included King Leopold of the Belgians, the Duke and Duchess of Windsor, Gina Lollobrigida, Sophia Loren and Frank Sinatra.

Inevitably, the rest of the world refused to be left out of the fun, and so between Torremolinos and Marbella a string of bucket-and-spade resorts sprang up. Increasing numbers of these holidaymakers decided that the Costa del Sol was to be their playground too, with many staying on to set up bars and restaurants.

More money flooded in during the 1970s, when the 1973 oil crisis and Middle East turmoil persuaded many rich Arabs to seek safer havens for their riches. The late King Fahd himself (then Prince), together with 60 relatives and minions, set up one of his many homes in a multi-million-dollar palace complete with mosque and heliport.

More recent celebrities on the Costa have included local boy Antonio Banderas and his wife, US actress Melanie Griffith, who own a house in Los Monteros just outside Marbella; Bruce Willis, who has a home in Estepona, and Julio Iglesias, who has a house near Coín. Jennifer López attracts plenty of attention during her frequent visits to Marbella, and Prince Andrew, a keen golfer, frequents Sotogrande's Valderrama course.

There has also been a dark side to the money-fuelled hedonism. If it was Arab and British money that cemented the Costa del Sol as an international investment centre, it was the Costa del Sol's proximity to the cannabis plantations in Morocco's Rif Mountains just across the Straits of Gibraltar, and the absence of an extradition treaty between Spain and Britain, that helped the coast gain the dubious title of the Costa del Crime. The fortunes generated by drug trafficking have seen the growth of a sophisticated extension of the European underworld. A booming local economy and the ease with which a foreign face goes undetected aid the crooks, while the hostility of nearby Gibraltar to the local Spanish authorities proves a stumbling block to solving many crimes and gathering evidence. ❑

LEFT: Antonio Banderas and friends.

mass tourism on the Costa, and it is no different today. The town is busy and cosmopolitan (though in no sense sophisticated) and not particularly attractive, apart from the surviving kernel of the old town. That said, the 8 km (5 miles) of fine beaches, even if somewhat overcrowded, are a great attraction.

From its main drag, the pedestrianised **Calle Miguel**, a series of steps winds down to the attractive **Paseo Marítimo**, where just to the west the rocky promontory of the **Castillo de Santa Clara** divides the Bajondillo and Carihuela parts of town. La Carihuela, to the west around the headland, used to be a small fishing village, and even today fishermen in their brightly coloured, flat-bottomed boats catch the sardines that you see skewered and grilled at the many beachside *chiringuitos* lining the promenade.

The seafront continues west to **Benalmádena Costa ❸**, one of several gleaming-white marina villages. At first glance it seems like an extension of Torremolinos, but although it has its fair share of bars and restaurants it is nowhere near as brash. Three Moorish watchtowers and the neo-Moorish Castillo El Bil-Bil, built in the 1930s, are focal points along the beach, and the large Torrequebrada complex houses one of the Costa del Sol's biggest casinos. Its other half, **Benalmádena Pueblo**, located inland high above the sea, is much more unspoilt, and home to a surprisingly good museum of Pre-Columbian American art (Mon–Fri; closed 2–4pm and Sat–Sun; admission charge).

Rather more typical attractions of the Torremolinos/Benalmádena area include Benalmádena's **Selwo Marina** (www. selwomarina.com), which has a dolphinarium, a "penguinarium on ice", and offers the opportunity to swim with sealions, and **Teleférico Benalmádena** (late

Mar–Oct; www.teleferico.com), operating spectacular cable-car rides over the area, as well as falconry displays and horse-riding displays. In a similar vein are **Tivoli World** (www. tivolicostadelsol.com), the largest amusement park on the coast, with more than 40 rides; **Sea Life** (www. sealife.es), containing Europe's largest shark collection at Puerto Marina, and **Crocodile Park** (www. crocodile-park.com), with hands-on displays in Torremolinos.

Fuengirola

A few kilometres further west along the coast, although the gap gets smaller every year as the towns expand, is **Fuengirola ❹**, which has been extremely popular with the British – as the numerous bars offering full English breakfasts, fish and chips, pints of beer and giant TVs screening British premier-league football matches testify. The best of the hotels are found on the very long **Paseo Marítimo** that stretches all the way down to Sohail Castle on the hill above the Río Fuengirola. With views up and down the coast,

Map on page 136

For a simple but delicious lunch on the beach, buy some grilled sardines from one of the many chiringuitos.

BELOW: Fuengirola's magnificent but busy beach.

Fuengirola's Tuesday market in the Fairgrounds (eastern side of town) is one of the best of many markets on the Costa del Sol. The town also holds a market at the marina on Sunday.

BELOW: fun for everyone, but especially the young, at Parque Acuático, Mijas.

the castle was originally built in 956, some 250 years after the Moorish conquest of Spain, by Abd-al-Rahman III, the best-known of the Umayyad caliphs. Fuengirola grew up under its protection.

Even after the Christian conquest of Granada it survived for a few years, and was not finally captured and levelled until 1497. The present castle was built in 1730 to hamper trade with Gibraltar, which the British had occupied in 1704. Eighty years later, in 1810, it was connected with one of the more shameful (from a British point of view) episodes of the Peninsular War. A British expedition of 800 men under General Blayney landed here and advanced on Mijas, but found the country too difficult and retreated to the castle. Here Blayney disposed his troops "with the utmost contempt of military rules" and as a result was forced to surrender to 150 Polish troops who were fighting for the French.

The area around the castle is being smartened up. The best hotel in town, the Beatriz Palace & Spa, has recently opened west of the castle on the one quiet piece of beach left in Fuengirola.

Mijas

The mountain village of **Mijas ❺**, 8 km (5 miles) above Fuengirola, markets itself as a typical *pueblo,* but actually has more in common with the coast than with inland Spain. Its shops sell sheepskin jackets, local pottery and the usual souvenirs; you can take a *burro* taxi (donkey taxi) or visit a "miniature" museum to see the reputed 2,000 most curious (and tiny) things in the world. Mijas also has Spain's only square *plaza de toros,* though for the most part the bullfights held here are for the consumption of foreign visitors and not comparable to what you would see in Málaga or other more serious plazas.

Despite all this, the village does have some appeal. The air is fresher up here, and there are fine views down to the coast. With its clean white houses and green shutters, this village is a good example of the Spanish genius for giving even tourist traps a certain enchantment.

Of the attractions in this area, the **Parque Acuático Mijas** (www.aquamijas.com), next to the the busy A7 road on the outskirts of Fuengirola, has a full array of water amusements, and the **Hipódromo** racetrack, which also doubles as an arena for the El Cartujano Andaluz horse show (www.elcartujano.com).

Marbella

The next resort of any size is **Marbella ❻**, long associated with wealthy celebrities and aristocrats. This is reflected in the plethora of 5-star hotels on the beach front, including the Marbella Club *(see page 240)*, established by Prince Alfonso von Hohenlohe in 1953 and the acorn from which Marbella's exclusive reputation grew. The town's main thoroughfare, Avenida Ramon y Cajal, is usually jammed with traffic, but just north of its centre an old town survives. At its heart is the lovely **Plaza de los Naranjos**, planted with orange trees and overlooked by the 16th-century Casa del Corregidor, one of the town's few old buildings and home to the tourist office. On a hot summer night this plaza, set from side to side with dining tables, becomes one vast open-air restaurant, and can delight even hardened Costa-watchers.

Although Marbella has its own marina, few visitors will be able to resist a visit to **Puerto Banús ❼** just west of town (the best way of getting there is on the little ferry that travels between the marinas), where the jetties are fringed with palm trees, and the neo-Andalusian-style architecture – mock minarets and Moorish arches – is pristine white. The main attraction is the many large yachts – a misnomer if ever there was one – and the opportunities for celebrity-spotting. For those who can afford them, there are numerous good fish restaurants and pricey boutiques around the marina.

Unlike the resorts further east, this part of the Costa del Sol is both cosmopolitan and sophisticated. Wherever you go you will see designer boutiques, international banks, huge estate agents, luxury-car dealers and gourmet restaurants.

Map on page 136

Marbella, Queen of the Costa del Sol.

BELOW: Puerto Banús, the Costa's most exclusive marina.

The hinterland

There are numerous little villages in the hills behind Marbella, some of which were once genuine mountain *pueblos*, but almost all of them have been gentrified, and many are inundated by British retirees. **Benahavís**, about 10 km (6 miles) inland from Marbella, past the exclusive Atalya Golf Club, is a good example of this – more than half of its population is foreign, and it is self-consciously pristine and quaint.

For a more Spanish experience, consider a half-day drive into the Sierra Bermeja, stopping for lunch in the Refugio de Juanar, 19 km (12 miles) from Marbella. Take the C337 off the coastal N340, twisting into the hills through fir and eucalyptus trees, with views of the coast to the rear. After 12 km (7 miles), past the village of **Ojén**, a signposted side road on the left leads to the Refugio de Juanar, a parador until the Spanish government sold it to the workers for the symbolic sum of one peseta.

A pleasantly simple place, decorated with hunting trophies, the hotel is where General de Gaulle chose to finish his memoirs. It has a good restaurant (barbecues on the terrace on summer weekends), and lunch here can be followed by a 2.5-km (1½-mile) stroll to the *mirador* overlooking the sierra and the coast, or a more strenuous hike through the forest following signposted trails to Ojén or **Istán**.

West of Marbella

It was to **San Pedro de Alcántara**  that the early British and American expatriates escaped when Marbella expanded out of recognition. A few kilometres west of Puerta Banús, the original village stands more than a kilometre from the sea, and thus retains a degree of Spanish character. North of here the bendy but beautiful 376 heads north to Ronda.

Estepona ❾, the most westerly of the Costa's swollen fishing villages (25 km/15½ miles from Marbella), now a largish town, has avoided too many high-rises, and retains an old quarter of narrow streets and bars, while its long

Willy the Whale sets the tone for family-oriented Estepona.

BELOW: Estepona's promenade.

esplanade has a certain elegance. It also has some historical interest. Phoenician, then Roman – the remains of Salduba aqueduct are near by – it was fortified by the Moors and then the Christians when they retook the town in 1456. It also has one of the little round watchtowers built when Barbary pirates plagued the coast in the 16th century.

The area around Estepona is developing fast. A number of resort-style hotels with spas have sprung up, and there are numerous attractions for children. The biggest of these is nearby **Selwo Aventura** (www. selwo.es), a safari park offering close-up views of some 2,000 mammals from every continent, including elephants, giraffes, rhinos and tigers. Tours can be made on foot or in four-wheel drive trucks. Added attractions include the largest walk-through aviary in Europe, with over 1,000 birds, camel rides, overhead walkways, plus activities such as archery.

Fore a more Spanish experience, Estepona is a good springboard for exploring the white towns of Cac-eres and Gaucín, which can be visited on an easy day circuit *(see page 118)*.

The least changed section of the Costa del Sol lies closest to Gibraltar in the province of Cádiz, where the main highway runs a few kilometres inland. Here, belatedly, the Spanish authorities are trying to prevent building on the very edge of the waves. Where the road returns to the coast, near the mouth of the Río Guadiaro, you'll find the plush marina-resort of **Puerto Sotogrande**, along with the exclusive Valdemarra golf course. In the early evening the marina bars offer lovely views of the sun setting over Gibraltar. From here it is an easy run of some 50 km (30 miles) back to Marbella.

EAST OF MÁLAGA

This section of the Costa del Sol is quite different from its western counterpart. In general, the mountains recede further from the sea – at least until Nerja – and the resorts here are neither as large and crowded as Torremolinos and Fuen-

Map on page 136

The must-have accessory is a yacht.

BELOW: sand, sea and a perfect climate in Estepona.

Tiled fountain in the grounds of the parador at Nerja, built in the late 1920s at the request of Alfonso XII. The parador is situated on a cliff above the beach, which is accessed by lift.

BELOW: Nerja's Balcony of Europe.

girola nor as sophisticated as Marbella and Puerto Banús. Though not undeveloped, the east is much quieter. A new motorway runs far inland, taking much of the traffic away from what was formerly a slow and overcrowded coastal road.

From Málaga city centre the road initially passes some good city beaches, each offering a large choice of *chiringuito* restaurants, and after an ugly cement works **Rincón de la Victoria** comes into sight with tall blocks of flats lining an otherwise attractive shallow bay.

Inland diversion

At **Torre de Benagalbón**, just past Rincón, a road heads inland, climbing past the emerald-green fairways of yet another golf course to the tiny villages of Benaque and Macharaviaya. They first appear far below the road, tentacles of white houses set against the grey peaks of the Sierra de Tejeda. Immediately below, on the valley sides, are their vineyards.

Macharaviaya ⑩ is the smaller and more charming of the two, with cobbled streets and a huge dilapi-

dated church, hinting at the village's former importance. In fact, in the 18th century Macharaviaya had a monopoly on the manufacture of playing cards. Its factory even supplied the Americas. In the church's crypt are memorials to the industry's founders, the Gálvez family, powerful Spanish colonialists who extended Spanish influence up the west coast of America as far as San Francisco Bay. Alas for Macharaviaya, the Gálvez family eventually petered out, its monopoly lapsed and the factory closed.

Benaque ⑪, slightly larger, is at the end of a road to nowhere, the village that time forgot and a world away from the Costa del Sol. It is the kind of place where you might still see the local housewives outside its one grocery shop, haggling over the price of trousers with a pedlar who has brought them on a bicycle. The only industry here is sieving and packing raisins.

Back on the coast

After Torre de Benagalbón, the small community of **Benajarafe** sits

across from the long, open (and often deserted) **Playa de Chilches**. Just past there is the medium-sized resort of **Torre del Mar**, which has an attractive marina. After that, sporadic development interrupts the coastal plain and its fields of sugar cane, as do pockets of plastic agriculture *(see page 216)* encroaching from the provinces of Granada and Almería.

Coves and caves at Nerja

The main resort on the eastern side of the coast, **Nerja** ⑫, 52 km (32 miles) east of Málaga, has seen spectacular growth in recent years. It has not all been well controlled, but it remains an attractive town, backed by the Sierra de Tejeda and with a series of pretty, sandy coves near by.

Follow signs to the so-called Balcón de Europa (the Balcony of Europe), a marble-paved projection above a headland, set with palms and decorated with a couple of cannons recovered from the sea. Alfonso XII gave it this name in 1885, and indeed there is nothing ahead but the Mediterranean, with Africa somewhere beyond the horizon. The king was here to commiserate with the townfolk in the wake of a devastating earthquake.

Tucked below the balcony to the east is a small sandy cove with fishing boats and a popular *chiringuito* called "Papagaya", while, beyond, the coast curves away in a big crescent of cliffs backed by mountains.

Maro, 3 km (2 miles) round this curving bay, has its own balcony, a palm walk above surrounding market gardens, with fine views east. Unmissable from the coast road is the **Puente del Águila**, a four-tiered aqueduct built in the 19th century to transport water from a local spring to the San Joaquín sugar factory.

Turn away from the coast for Nerja's other attraction. Here, in 1959, five young boys went on a bat-hunting expedition, felt warm air coming from a crack in the rocks and stumbled upon the **Cuevas de Nerja** (Nerja Caves; July–Aug 10am–2pm and 4–8pm; Sep–June 10am–2pm and 4–6.30pm; admission charge). Every day, busloads of foreign visitors pour into Nerja to see these astonishing underground caverns, one of which has been fitted out as an auditorium. The chambers are all well lit with paved walks; soft music echoes among the stalactites.

The caves are a staggering sight, if only for their immense size. They were inhabited 20,000 years ago, and a skeleton – of a woman who apparently died of a mastoid infection – is displayed in a glass case.

Beyond Maro, the Sierra de Tejeda drops sharply down to the sea, and the Costa del Sol gives way to the Costa Tropical of Granada province *(see page 198)*. Here, steep, stony hillsides protect small rocky coves, and if you manage to climb down you can still bathe alone, quite possibly beside a farmer's avocado plantation. ❑

Map on page 136

The Cuevas de Nerja first opened to the public in June 1960, when a French ballet company presented Swan Lake *there.*

BELOW: the 19th-century aqueduct at Maro.

RESTAURANTS & BARS

Best Areas

The resorts of the Costa del Sol are packed with restaurants of every type and in every price bracket, from the exclusive gastronomic temples of Marbella and Puerto Banús to inexpensive *chiringuitos* on the beach. Málaga is a great source of good and reasonably priced restaurants, as well as characterful bars.

PRICE CATEGORIES

Prices for three-course meal per person with a half-bottle of house wine:
€= under €20
€€ = €20–€40
€€€ = €40–€60
€€€€= more than €60

Benahavis

Taberna del Alabardero Resort Hotel
Cerro de Artola, s/n
Ctra San Pedro to Ronda, km 167. Tel: 952-812 794
L & D daily. €€€
Located just east of the San Petro to Ronda road, this beautifully designed complex, set in lush gardens, serves international and Spanish cuisine using local produce.Try the tester menu.

Benalmádena

Casa Fidel
Maestro Ayala, 1
Benalmádena Pueblo
Tel: 952-449 165
L & D. Closed Wed D, Tues. €€
A favourite among Costa del Sol diners, in the picturesque old village of Benalmádena. Fish available, but lamb is the speciality.

El Balcón
Santo Domingo, 7
Tel: 952-568 273
L only Mon–Sat. €€€
This restaurant is run by Málaga's official hotel school and the food is innovative and tasty.

La Rada
Avenida España, s/n
Tel: 952-791 036
L & D. Closed Wed. €€€
This large bar and restaurant at the eastern end of Estepona serves really fresh fish in an informal atmosphere.

Ventorillo de la Perra
Avenida de la Constitución, s/n, Arroyo de la Miel
Tel: 952-441 966
L & D. Closed Mon. €€€
A pleasant old roadside inn on the road between Torremolinos and Arroyo de la Miel, serving local and international dishes.

Estepona

Alcaría de Ramos
Urb. El Paraíso
Tel: 952-886 178. €€€
Owner José Ramos is a winner of Spain's national gastronomy prize. Classical Spanish dishes, beautifully presented, in a lovely setting.

Fuengirola

El Bote
Paseo Marítimo, s/n
Torreblanca del Sol
Tel: 952-660 296
L & D. Closed Tues. €€
Spacious and popular, serving fresh fish dishes, right next to the beach at the eastern end of Fuengirola's seafront promenade.

La Langosta
Francisco Cano, 1
Los Boliches
Tel: 952-475 049
D only. Closed Sun. €€
This small restaurant has been a popular venue since it opened in the 1960s. It was the first place on the south coast to serve lobster, which is still the house speciality.

Patrick Bausier
Rotonda de la Luna, 1
Tel: 952-585 120
L & D daily. €€€
The owner of this classic French restaurant was a student of Paul Bocuse, the *grand-père* of nouvelle cuisine. But don't worry, you won't go hungry.

Málaga

Antigua Casa de Guardia
Alameda Principal, 18
Tel: 952- 214 680
L & D. €€
A Málaga institution since 1840. There are no tables or chairs, but a long wooden bar upon which the tab is chalked up. Huge old barrels hold a selection of Málaga wines.

LEFT: pavement dining at Santiago in Marbella.

Astorga

Gerona, 11
Tel: 952-346 832
L & D. Closed Sun. €€€
The food here, both fish and meat, has earned this lively, friendly restaurant the reputation of being one of the city's best, and reservations are essential.

Café de Paris

Calle Velez Málaga, 8
Tel: 952-225 043
L & D. Closed Sun. €€€
www.rcafedeparis.com
On a back street near the lighthouse, this sophisticated restaurant serves imaginative dishes. The *menu degustación* is a good way to sample the house specialities. Reservations essential.

El Chinitas

Moreno Monroy, 4
Tel: 952-210 972
L & D daily. €€€
Traditional-style Andalusian restaurant with attached tapas bar, just off the Pasaje de Chinitas in the old part of city.

Escuela de Hostelería

Finca La Consula, s/n
Churriana
Tel: 952-622 562
L only. Closed Sat and Sun
€€€
Málaga's official hotel and catering school, 8 km (5 miles) west of the city, serves some of the best food on the coast in a magnificent setting. Reservations essential.

Pitta Bar

Echegaray, 8
Tel: 952-608 675
L & D. Closed Sun.
No cards. €
Located between the cathedral and the Picasso Museum. The food is tasty Middle Eastern.

Marbella

Altamirano

Plaza Altamirano, 3
Tel: 952-824 932
L & D. Closed Mon. No cards. €
In the old town, this is a very popular, modest establishment serving excellent seafood at good prices.

Aquavit

Plaza del Puerto
Puerto Bánus
Tel: 952-819 127.
L & D. €€
Funky restaurant serving Fusion dishes and 45 different vodkas.

El Portalón

N340 km 178
Tel: 952-861 075
L & D. Closed Sun. €€€
Across the street from the Marbella Club, this restaurant combines the atmosphere and flavours of Castile.

La Chêne Liège

La Mairena, s/n, Elviria
Tel: 952-852 061
D only, closed Tues. €€€€
A 10-minute drive into the hills east of Marbella is rewarded with splendid views and some of the best French cuisine you'll find anywhere.

La Hacienda

Urb. Las Chapas, s/n
Tel: 952-831 267
L & D. Closed Mon, Tues and mid-Nov—mid-Dec. €€€€
Set in a villa in the hills east of Marbella, this restaurant was among the first top-class international dining spots on the Costa del Sol. The French-Belgian cuisine has adapted local recipes. Reservations recommended.

La Meridiana

Camino de la Cruz, s/n,
(near mosque)
Tel: 952-776 190
L daily, D in winter only.
Closed Jan. €€€€
This elegant dining spot is a favourite among the resort's famous guests. Reservations essential.

La Pesquera

Plaza de la Victoria, s/n.
Tel: 952-765 170
L & D. €€
Open all day, this informal bar and restaurant in the old town serves seafood and grilled meats. There are several other branches at locations in and around Marbella.

Santiago

Paseo Marítimo, 5
Tel: 952-770 078
L & D. Closed Nov. €€€
Famous for its superfresh seafood, this long-established restaurant has an adjoining Castilian-style tapas bar.

Mijas

El Mirlo Blanco

Plaza de la Constitución, 13
Tel: 952-485 700
L & D. €€€
Overlooking a square in the old part of Mijas, a long-established restaurant serving Spanish and Basque specialities.

Venta El Higuerón

Málaga—Fuengirola motorway exit 217
Tel: 952-119 163
L & D. €€€
A roadside inn has stood here since 1840. It offers a range of Spanish dishes, including some Asturian specialities.

Nerja

Casa Luque

Plaza Cavana, 2
Tel: 952-521 004
L & D. Closed Mon. €€€
Authentic Spanish food in an old Andalusian house, near the Balcón de Europa. Pleasant patio for al fresco dining.

Pepe Rico

Almirante Ferrandiz, 28
Tel: 952-520 247
L & D, D only summer.
Closed Jan—Feb. €€€
In the centre of Nerja, in an old Spanish house with cool patio. International cuisine with a Scandinavian touch.

Torremolinos

El Roqueo

Carmen, 35, La Carihuela
Tel: 952-384 946
L & D. Closed Tues and Nov.
€€€
In Torremolinos's fishing quarter, La Carihuela, every other house is a seafood restaurant, and they're all good. This one, facing out onto the seafront promenade, is among the best known.

Frutos

Ctra de Cádiz km 228 (next to Los Alamos petrol station)
Tel: 952-381 450
L & D. Closed Sun. €€€
Midway between Torremolinos and the airport, a spacious restaurant known for its hearty helpings of traditional Spanish fare.

ANTEQUERA AND LA AXARQUIA

The highlights of the uplands behind Málaga and its coast include one of Andalucía's most venerable towns, ancient dolmens, and hills dotted with perched villages redolent of Spain's Muslim past

Behind the hedonistic, high-rise resorts of the Costa del Sol, the province of Málaga quickly reverts to a procession of deeply rural mountain chains, with only the occasional north–south river valley facilitating communications. The peaks are at their highest and bleakest around Ronda (*see pages 127–133*), west of which the landscape becomes tamer. While for the most part the scenery is unexceptional, there are areas of beauty to discover, most notably the belt of hills that makes up the Axarquia. To the north the uplands give way to plains which are surveyed by the venerable town of Antequera.

Ancient Antequera

Towns don't come much more ancient than **Antequera ⓭**, which stands at a strategic crossroads between the cardinal points of Córdoba, Málaga, Seville and Granada. It was old before the Romans arrived, and although the title they gave it, *Antikaria*, rings suggestively of antiquity, it was simply the name of a pre-existing Iberian settlement.

Modern Antequera is the service and shopping hub of the northern part of Málaga province. Suburban sprawl quickly yields to a centre of narrow streets leading to an immaculately preserved core of historic buildings. Rising out of the mass of white houses are many belfries: Antequera claims to have more churches in proportion to its population than anywhere else in Spain.

The natural place to begin sightseeing is the **Plaza San Sebastián**, on which stands a 16th-century church of the same name with a baroque-Mudéjar tower and a Renaissance facade, an example of the town's architectural richness. Behind the tourist office, a straight street, **Calle Zapateros**, leads uphill away

Map on page 136

LEFT: Garganta del Chorro near Alora.
BELOW: view over Antequera.

Antequera's elegant Plaza San Sebastián is a good place to begin a tour of the town.

BELOW: Dolmen de Menga, the oldest of Antequera's dolmens.

from the noise and traffic, around a dog-leg to the monumental gateway of the **Arco de los Gigantes** (Giants' Arch), dedicated in 1585 to Felipe II. Through the arch you step into the **Plaza Santa María**, overlooked by the Renaissance church of **Real Colegiata de Santa María la Mayor**. One side of the square looks over the Roman ruins of the **Termas Romanas** (Roman Baths), and access to the Muslim fortress of the **Alcazaba** is also off the square. At the top of the Alcazaba, standing proud above the city, is the keep to which a belfry was added in the 16th century.

On the way downhill from this complex of monuments is the **Museo Municipal** (closed Mon and Tues, Sat and Sun pm, admission charge), housed in the Baroque **Palacio de Nájera**. Although it has eight galleries of art and ecclesiastical silverware, most visitors are drawn to the archaeology section and to one piece in particular, the **Efebo de Antequera**. This 1½-metre (5 ft) high bronze figure of a youth has been described as the most beau-

tiful Roman find in Spain, even without the glass eyes that once filled its hollow sockets. It was cast in the 1st century AD and probably served as a lamp or candle holder.

Antequera's dolmens

In Antequera's suburbs, on the way out towards Granada, are three massive prehistoric dolmens. Two of these, the **Dolmen de Menga** and the **Dolmen de Viera**, stand together in a park created around them (closed Mon and Sun pm). Menga is the oldest, dating from 2500 BC, and also the most impressive: an assembly of 31 stones, the largest weighing 180 tonnes. Its construction testifies to an advanced Copper Age civilisation capable of mobilising, coordinating and feeding a sizeable labour force working to a shared purpose.

The third dolmen, **Romeral** (closed Mon and Sun pm), stands alone in a surprisingly peaceful location behind a small industrial estate. Dating from around 1800 BC, It is the most recent, but it is also the most interesting as it demonstrates use of architectural concepts. A long tunnel

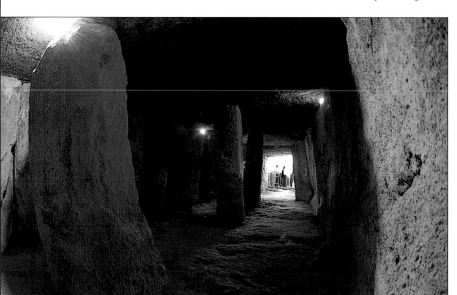

of finely laid stones, roofed by great slabs, leads into a perfectly round, domed chamber at the heart of the dolmen, 5 metres (17 ft) in diameter and almost 4 metres (13 ft) high, created by concentric courses of stones.

Hikes and flamingos

In the hills behind Antequera is one of Andalucía's foremost beauty spots, **El Torcal** , reached by the c3310 towards Villanueva de la Concepción, which passes above the town, giving views of the rooftops, church towers and Alcazaba rising out of them. Over the other side of the pass of La Boca del Asno ("The Ass's Mouth"), there is a turning to El Torcal at the top of the sierra. The visitors' centre (open daily) and car park is at the base. From here there is an easy walk to a viewpoint or two marked hiking routes *(see below)* through the distinctive rock formations. The towering limestone outcrops eroded by wind and rain into abstract sculptures not unlike piles of sandwiches have fanciful names such as El Cara Perro, El Sombrero, El Tornillo, La Tortuga.

Don't set off too late in the day, as it is easy to get disorientated in the labyrinth of rocks, depressions, corridors, crevices, cliffs and ledges.

There is another distinctive rock east out of Antequera, towards Granada, the **Peña de los Enamorados** ("Lovers' Leap"), named after the legend of a Christian boy and Muslim girl who, forbidden to marry, threw themselves off the top. Beyond the rock is **Archidona** , a sloping white town above olive groves, with medieval walls and an octagonal main square.

The plains north of Antequera don't look very promising, but they hide one place of interest, the salty lagoon outside the town of **Fuente de Piedra** . This is the largest natural lake in Andalucía and it is famous for its colony of flamingos,

although you will be lucky to see any without high-powered binoculars as the lake expands and shrinks with the weather and can be distant from the road around it. There is a visitors' centre with a lookout point on a rise 1 km (½ mile) from the town (closed Mon).

Mountains of Málaga

There are two routes between Málaga city and Antequera. The obvious and quickest is the motorway down the Guadalmedina valley, skirting the side of the **Montes de Málaga** . Although declared a *parque natural*, the landscape here is largely man-made, as these hills were planted with pine forests to prevent flooding in Málaga city. There are views of the coast and city from various points along the C345 road, which also takes you past the visitors' centre at Lagar de Torrijos.

From Roman times until the 1870s, these hills were important for their vineyards. Málaga's strong, sweet wine made from moscatel and Pedro Ximénez grape varieties was known all over Europe. Then disaster

Map on page 136

TIP

El Torcal offers two marked walking routes: the *ruta verde* (green route, 1.5km/1 mile), a fairly gentle 45-minute walk, or the longer and more demanding *ruta amarilla* (yellow route, 3km/2 miles) which takes about two hours.

BELOW: climbing the distinctive limestone outcrops of El Torcal.

A backstreet in the old spa town of Carratraca.

struck. In just a few years the vines here, as in much of the rest of Europe, were destroyed by the phylloxera bug; but while other areas were replanted with resistant stock, Málaga's vineyards never fully recovered, perhaps because the taste for sweet wines was already diminishing. Wine is still made in Málaga, both in the Montes de Málaga and the Axarquia, but in much smaller quantities.

Lakes and waterfalls

The alternative route to the coast is by way of the Guadalhorce valley and **Alora** ⑱, a sloping white town of narrow streets beneath a restored castle with a church beside it. Just up the valley from here is what should be Andalucía's principal beauty spot, the **Desfiladero de los Gaitanes** or **Garganta del Chorro** ⑲, a tall, thin gorge of rock barely wide enough for the river Guadalhorce to slip through.

In 1921 King Alfonso XIII came to open a dam built at the head of the gorge holding back the three uninspiring reservoirs upstream which comprise "Málaga's Lake District". To impress him, a catwalk of concrete and iron, the **Caminito del Rey**, was built on the rock face along the gorge with a bridge spanning the chasm. This marvel of engineering, however, was allowed to fall into disrepair over the years and is now closed – which doesn't stop the tourist authorities boasting about it. Almost as impressive is the railway line from Málaga that crosses a girder bridge and plunges into a tunnel beside the Caminito del Rey. Access to this spot of natural and man-made beauty is restricted for safety reasons, but the gorge, railway, remains of the walkway and a tall sliver of waterfall can be viewed from Bar Restaurant El Pilar across the river.

Heading towards Ardales from the gorge, the road passes through a nature reserve of large smooth rocks in scattered pine woods. A signposted turning off this road leads to the abandoned village of **Bobastro**, where a Mozarabic community – Christians living under Muslim rule – cut a church out of the rock. The forms of its horseshoe arches can still be seen.

Spa towns

South and west from the Guadalhorce valley there is little of interest along the meandering B roads except scattered towns trying to revive their fortunes. On a hillside near Ardales is **Carratraca** ⑳, a small spa town on a steep hillside which today gives no hint of the success of its sulphur springs in the 19th century, when it attracted the celebrities of the time, including Byron, Dumas and Empress Eugénie of France, and incorporated three casinos. The once grand neoclassical-style baths are now dated, and the emphasis is on the serious treatment of angina, asthma and other respiratory diseases.

There is another reincarnated 19th-century hydro at **Tolox** ㉑, a

Map on page 136

long drive to the west, on the edge of the wild, underpopulated karst mountains of the eastern Sierra de Ronda. It goes by the uninspiring name of the Balneario de Fuente Amargosa ("Bitter Fountain"). Again, facilities are dated, but the waters are beneficial in the treatment of respiratory diseases and kidney stones. Past visitors have included various famous bullfighters and Primo de Rivera.

Coín ㉒, on the back road between Málaga and Marbella, can at least claim more recent success and glamour. It made a name for itself as the location for *Eldorado*, a British TV soap opera about expats living lives of idleness and intrigue in the sunshine. The serial was prematurely pulled from the schedules in 1993 after little more than a year on air, its relative lack of popularity blamed on its capacity to arouse envy rather than empathy among its viewers.

LA AXARQUIA

If you want pretty countryside within reach of the coast, save your time for the Axarquia, the district extending back from the coast between Rincón de la Victoria and Nerja *(see page 147)* as far as the peaks of the Sierra de Almijara. The roads into and around the Axarquia are, in the main, narrow, winding, steep and sometimes badly surfaced, but the scenery is worth the discomfort.

The district's official capital is **Vélez-Málaga**, an industrial town not worth the trouble of exploring, although it does have two churches converted from mosques and the remains of a castle if you can find your way up to it. Better, though, to stay on the road up the valley which avoids the town centre. Soon after you leave the outskirts of Vélez-Málaga you will see the tantalisingly sited **Comares ㉓**, which balances on the top of a rocky mountain peak. A steep winding road takes you up to it from the valley floor, green with citrus and tropical-fruit trees, through slopes dotted with olive trees. There are few points of interest in the town except a badly eroded stack of stone (all that is left of the castle) which stands outside the cemetery. The charm of a visit is

View from the castle of Vélez-Málaga, the capital of the Axarquia.

BELOW: Tolox.

Map
on page
136

TIP

Interesting guided walking tours of Frigiliana have been devised by expat David Riordan, who lives in the town. The tours are a fascinating lesson in noticing the clues that uncover the history, culture and traditions not just of Frigiliana but of other such villages and towns. Contact Frigiliana Tours, tel: 952-534 240.

BELOW:
impeccable Frigiliana.

mostly in the panoramic views, but the town has genuine atmosphere and a "Muslim Route" of blue-and-white ceramic footprints inlaid in the streets and alleyways leads you on a pleasant walk around the town.

Colourful Cómpeta

For the most picturesque part of the Axarquia head west from Vélez-Málaga towards the de facto capital of the region, **Cómpeta** ㉔. The patchwork of fertile hills around it is surprisingly populous, with modern villas and old *cortijos* all the way up the slopes to the summits. The terraced hillsides are planted with a great variety of crops, including oranges, subtropical fruit trees, olive trees, almonds and small vineyards. A typical feature of the older farmhouses is a *pasero*, an inclined rectangular enclosure for drying grapes into raisins.

When, after all the curves, you finally reach Cómpeta it can come as a surprise, not only for its size but for the composition of its population – this is a popular area for foreign house-buyers, and the main square is dominated by estate agents. Aside from that, Cómpeta is an attractive place, a dense labyrinth of streets and steps and houses built on various levels, picturesque and tastefully colourful in almost every corner. It may pull in the tourists and the foreign home-buyers, but Cómpeta remains a wine town (making sweet Málaga wine) and its main fiesta, on 15 August, is the Night of Wine, dedicated to wine-pressing.

Mosques and minarets

Of the several designated tourist routes around the Axarquia, the most worthwhile is the Ruta del Mudéjar, linking villages that still bear distinct traces of their Muslim past. The nearest of them to Cómpeta is **Archez**, where the church tower is a perfect 15th-century brick minaret. Outside the village (take the top road) is a delightful surprise from modernity, an extraordinary fantasy residence made up of three hobbit-like igloos with psychedelic decoration set in a stepped vineyard garden. Built by four artists working to the principles of Gaudí and Hundertwasser, it is private property but can be admired over the wall.

Salares, tucked into a valley at one remove from the rest of the Axarquia, is arguably the most unspoilt village in these hills. Its church tower is a 13th-century minaret. At the bottom of the village an Arab bridge crosses a verdant little valley planted with orange trees. A 5-km (3-mile) walk (allow up to three hours) departs from the far end of the bridge from the village.

There is still the prettiest and best-preserved and presented of all the towns, **Frigiliana** ㉕, to go. Being near the coast, particularly the popular resort of Nerja *(see page 147)*, it receives lots of visitors but avoids being spoilt. Despite new buildings going up, the town centre retains a perfect cluster of stepped streets. ❑

RESTAURANTS & BARS

Restaurants

Alfarnate

Venta de Alfarnate
Ctra Málaga–Granada km 513
Tel: 952-759 388
L & D daily. €
Claims to be the oldest *venta* (roadside inn) in Andalucía, dating from 1691. The house speciality is *huevos a lo bestia*: fried eggs with pork, chorizo and morcilla.

Antequera

Caserio de San Benito
Ctra Málaga–Córdoba, km 108
Tel: 952-034 000.
L. Closed Mon, and Tues–Thur Sep–June. €€
Restaurant in a traditional country house. Specialises in grilled meats, lamb chops, rice with rabbit and Antequera's thick chilled tomato soup, *porra*. Good wine list.

El Angelote
Plaza Coso Viejo, s/n
Tel: 952-703 465
L & D. Closed Mon. €
This popular, lively restaurant in the heart of town, near the museum, serves traditional Andalusian dishes.

Los Dolmenes
Cruz El Romeral
Tel: 952-845 956
L & D daily. €
An inexpensive place to try Antequera's cuisine after visiting the dolmens

(it is off the roundabout near Romeral). Follow a first course of *porra* with the *plato de los montes* – chorizo, pork, fried eggs, chips and fried peppers.

Comares

Molino de los Abuelos
Calle Plaza s/n.
Tel: 952-220 404
L & D daily. €
A delightful cafeteria, restaurant and hotel in a restored old building in which some of the original features have been preserved. On the main square of town.

Cómpeta

El Pilón
Calle Laberinto, Cómpeta
Tel: 952-553 512
L & D daily. €
English-run restaurant with a terrace looking over the rooftops of the town to the hills beyond. The filling *menú del día* is well cooked and excellent value. The dishes have a local emphasis and include rabbit and lamb, but there is enough choice to please a vegetarian. Baguette sandwiches also available for a lighter lunch.

La Posada Mesón Mudéjar
Calle Álamo, 6, Archez
Tel: 952-553 106. €€
"Authentic grandmother's recipes" are

the backbone of the menu here, which focuses on lamb (cooked with honey or in creamy sauce) and fish such as "Mudéjar-style" hake and salmon. Alternatively, there are scrambled eggs flavoured with locally gathered herbs. The delicious home-made desserts vary according to season. Also a hotel with five rooms.

El Chorro (Alora)

El Pilar
Ctra El Chorro-Parque Natural Ardales
No phone. L & D daily. €
As its car park is the only place to get a decent view of the Garganta del Chorro, it's convenient to call in here for a snack or meal of home cooking.

Frigiliana

The Garden Restaurant
Calle Real, 12
Tel: 952-533 185
L & D daily. €
English-run restaurant on two terraces serving barbecued meat and fish.

Teba

Molino de las Pilas
Ctra Vieja de Ronda, km 2
Tel: 952-748 622
L & D daily. €
A restored farmhouse-cum-olive-oil mill near Teba, west of Antequera. Local menu. Also a hotel.

PRICE CATEGORIES

Prices for three-course meal per person with a half-bottle of house wine:
€= under €20
€€ = €20–€40

RIGHT: El Angelote in Antequera.

CÓRDOBA

Capital of al-Andalus in the 10th century, Córdoba is a labyrinth of winding alleyways and Moorish patios. Its supreme monument is La Mezquita, its fabulous Mosque

The furthest north of Andalucía's great Moorish cities and not easily accessible on a day trip from the Costa del Sol, **Córdoba ❶** receives significantly fewer visitors than Granada and Seville. Partly for that reason, but also due to its particular charm – the gracious old town spreads around its extraordinary Mosque on a bend in the River Guadalquivir – it is often the city that people who do take the trouble to visit end up liking best.

It is possible to visit Córdoba for the day from Seville (a 30-minute journey on the Seville–Madrid AVE train) but it is well worth staying a night or two *(see page 244)* and perhaps also taking in Medina Azahara *(see page 167)*.

The city's history

Córdoba is one of the oldest cities in Spain. In 206 BC it was invaded by the Romans, who later made it the capital of the Roman province of Further Spain. In 572, after nearly eight centuries of Roman rule, the Visigoths took control of the city.

In 711 it fell to the Moors, and In 756 Abd-al-Rahman I, Amir of the Umayyad dynasty, established it as an independent emirate ruling most of the Iberian Peninsula.

Abd-al-Rahman III raised the city to the status of Caliphate in 929 and ushered in a golden age. Considered to be one of the cultural capitals of the world, second in wealth and culture only to Constantinople, the city was a respected centre of science and art. It had the first street lighting in Europe and a library containing over 400,000 volumes. Estimates of the population at that time range from 500,000 to one million.

This prosperity came to an abrupt end with the rebellion of Muhammad II al-Mahdi in 1009, a development that led to the disintegration of the

Maps:
City 162
Area 169

LEFT: view of the old town of Córdoba from the Puente Romano.
BELOW: festive mood in the Judería.

Caliphate and triggered a long decline in the city's fortunes.

By the time Córdoba was reconquered in 1236 by Fernando III, the city was in ruins. During the ensuing years it was repopulated by people from northern Spain. In 1382 Alfonso XI ordered the construction of the Alcázar, which became the residence of Queen Isabel towards the end of the 15th century.

Monument to the Moors

Córdoba's most important monument, the **Mosque** , La Mezquita (Mon–Sat 10am–7pm, Sun 9am–10.45am and 2–7pm; admission charge), is the third-largest mosque in the world and the oldest building in day-to-day use in the Western world. Its dominant feature is the bell-tower, which has its origins in the 10th-century minaret.

Construction of the Mosque over the site of a Visigothic cathedral began in 786 at the order of Abd-al-Rahman I. The initial design was for an open courtyard *(sahn)* for ablutions, now known as the Patio de los Naranjos (orange trees), and a covered area that could accommodate as many as 10,000 worshippers. Three expansions later – by Abd-al-Rahman II in 833, under al-Hakam II in 926, and finally by al-Mansur, who was chief minister of Hisham II, in 978 – it was completed.

The architectural style evolved with each addition, reaching the greatest splendour and technical mastery in what came to be known as the caliphal style of architecture during the Caliphate of al-Hakam. Features to note are great skylighted domes for extra interior light, and an ingenious engineering system comprising clustered pillars bearing intersecting lobed arches to support the domes.

After Fernando III reconquered Córdoba in 1236, small Christian chapels were added in 1258 and

Carlos V initiated the construction of the Christian cathedral inside the Mosque. Later, however, he appeared to regret the decision, saying, "Had I known what this was, you would not have done it, for what you are building here can be found anywhere; but what you have destroyed exists nowhere."

BELOW: the distinctive red-and-white pillars and arches of La Mezquita.

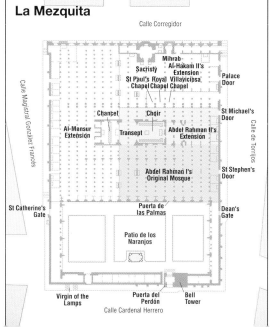

La Mezquita

Calle Corregidor

Mihrab
Sacristy — Al-Hakam II's Extension
St Paul's Royal Villaviciosa — Palace Door
Chapel Chapel Chapel

Chancel — Choir — St Michael's Door

Al-Mansur Extension — Transept — Abdel Rahman II's Extension

Calle Magistral González Francés

Calle de Torrijos

Abdel Rahman I's Original Mosque — St Stephen's Door

St Catherine's Gate — Puerta de las Palmas — Dean's Gate

Patio de los Naranjos

Virgin of the Lamps — Puerta del Perdón — Bell Tower

Calle Cardenal Herrero

1260. Nearly three centuries later, in 1523, during the reign of Carlos V, the Christian cathedral was built in the centre of the Mosque. Whether inadvertent or not, the incongruous mix of architecture and culture combines to produce a place of utter fascination. Inside are hundreds of columns – 856 to be exact – most supporting double-horse-shoe arches. The different-coloured columns, fashioned from various types of stone, present a constantly mesmerising interplay of architecture and light.

Touring the Mosque

Walking through the original Mosque of Abd-al-Rahman I, you reach the Mosque's first extension, added by Abd-al-Rahman II in 833 (a slight ramp in the floor is evidence of the extension). To the left is the rear of the cathedral's *coro* (choir). Further on is the vaulted ceiling of an aborted church, planned in the 15th century. To the left you will see the domed Capilla de Villaviciosa, where the old Mosque's mihrab (indicating the direction of Mecca) would have been. Through a cutaway you can see the Capilla Real next door, redecorated in the 14th century in Mudéjar stucco. This was the mosque's *maqsura* (royal enclosure).

Continuing straight ahead, you enter al-Hakam's extension. He extended the southern wall to the river and built an opulent new mihrab (seen through the railings), decorated with dazzling mosaics and a stunning star-ribbed dome that was subsequently copied throughout Spain. The bejewelled side rooms formed Hakam's *maqsura*.

The third extension of the Mezquita by al-Mansur is functional rather than aesthetically pleasing. It widened the prayer hall and courtyard to accommodate Córdoba's growing population.

Construction of the cathedral within the Mosque required the removal of 60 of the original columns and some of the most beautiful stucco work. The contrast in styles is a jolt to the senses. In the cathedral, human images – taboo in Islamic art and architecture – abound in paint, stone and wood, particularly in the massive paintings of Christ and the saints.

The cathedral is of Gothic design with later additions in plateresque and baroque styles. Especially noteworthy are the mahogany choir stalls, carved by the Andalusian sculptor Pedro Duque Cornejo and depicting the lives of Jesus and the Virgin Mary in life-like detail. The magnificent golden altarpiece contains 36 tableaux of the *Life of Christ*.

The **Cathedral Museum** (Tesoro Catedralicio) contains religious art from the 15th to 20th centuries. Among its treasures is a stunning monstrance weighing over 164 kg (440 lbs) and fashioned from solid silver by the renowned goldsmith Enrique Arfe. It was used for the first time during the Corpus Christi celebrations of 1519.

Maps on pages 160, 162

TIP

For a postcard-perfect view of La Mezquita's tower, framed by whitewashed houses decked with pots of geraniums, visit the Calleja de las Flores (northeast of the Mosque), the vainest, most photographed street in Córdoba.

BELOW: the dome above the Mosque's *mihrab*.

Statue of the Archangel Raphael on the Puente Romano.

The town

Across from the Mosque (on Calle Torrijos), in a 16th-century former chapel is the **Palacio de Congresos**, a convention hall housing the regional tourism office and a lovely courtyard café, the ideal place for a cool drink or beer. From here it is a few steps to the river, crossed by the **Puente Romano ⑬** (Roman Bridge), a good place to come at sunset for views over the old town. On the bridge is one of many images of Córdoba's patron saint, the Archangel Raphael, candles burning at his feet. In the river bottom, overgrown with rushes where ducks paddle, are the remains of three Arabic watermills, the **Molinos Arabes**.

On the far side of the bridge is the **Torre de la Calahorra ⑭** (May–Sept 10am–2pm and 4.30–8.30pm, Oct–Apr 10am–6pm; admission charge), a 14th-century watchtower which houses a museum depicting the glories of al-Andalus with wax fig-

ures and a 50-minute diorama, with audioguides in several languages.

Back on the north bank of the river, a few blocks downriver from the Mosque is the **Alcázar de los Reyes Cristianos ⑮** (Tues–Sun am; closed 2–4.30pm and Mon; admission charge), a palace built by Alfonso XI in the 14th century, over the site of previous Visigoth and Moorish fortresses. For many years it was the home of the Catholic Monarchs, who received Columbus and planned the reconquest of Granada here. Following the fall of Granada in 1492, the palace was used by the Court of Inquisition, and then functioned as a civil jail and military prison.

Inside, the highlight of the palace is the **Hall of the Mosaics**, featuring Roman mosaics and a Roman stone sarcophagus dating from the 2nd or 3rd century AD. Outside, you will note that four towers guard the walls, and the tops of those that are

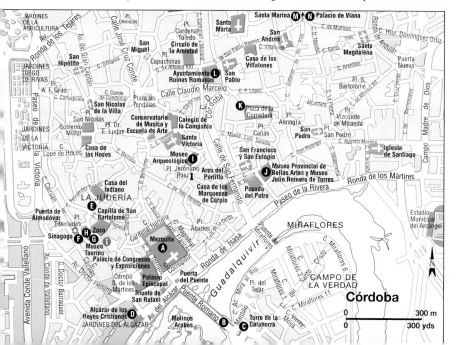

open to visitors provide an excellent platform from which to take photographs of La Mezquita. The extensive gardens are a peaceful place, the design of which includes a series of rectangular ponds similar to, but not as stunning as, those at the Generalife in Granada.

Pretty patios

Monumental Córdoba is golden, but its *barrios* or neighbourhoods are usually pristine white, kept limewashed by house-proud owners. The city's old quarter, a compact warren of whitewashed houses, winding alleys and flower-filled patios, spreads out around the Mosque.It is best visited on foot, as many of the streets are hardly more than narrow alleyways. The houses generally present a blank facade to the street, broken only by an entryway closed by a *cancela*, wrought-iron gate. Through this gate is glimpsed a patio, shaded by a palm, furnished with ferns, perfumed with jasmine, air-conditioned by a bubbling fountain.

Whether the intimate heart of private homes or elegant courtyards of great buildings, the patio was developed as a survival technique – a cool oasis in the long hot summers. Calle Albucasis and Calle Manríquez (close to the northwest corner of the Mosque) are two streets with especially beautiful patios. Córdoba celebrates its courtyards during the first half of May, when many private patios are opened to the public.

The Judería

The area northwest of the Mosque is Córdoba's medieval Jewish quarter, **La Judería ⓔ**, entered through the **Puerta de Almodóvar**, one of the city's ancient gates.

If Córdoba is known for the splendour of its 10th-century achievements in art, architecture and science, a part of its glory is attributed to the Sephardim community, the Spanish Jews who settled here during the time of the Roman emperors, when they were allowed the same rights as other inhabitants of Baetica, Roman Spain.

Under the Visigoths Jews were persecuted so severely that they welcomed the Muslim invaders. In exchange, they enjoyed long periods of peaceful coexistence, and a flowering of Sephardim culture during which many achieved rare heights in diplomacy, medicine, commerce and crafts.

Sepharad simply means Spain in Hebrew. More than 500 years after King Fernando and Queen Isabel expelled the Jews from Spain in 1492, some Jews of Spanish descent still speak an archaic Spanish dialect. Were Columbus to come back to life today, he would find it easier to converse with the Sephardic Jews in, say, Istanbul than with modern *Madrileños*.

Córdoba's **Sinagoga ⓕ** (Tues–Sat 10am–2pm, Sun 10am–1.30pm; free admission) is one of only three medieval synagogues remaining in

Detail on a Roman sarcophagus in the Alcázar de los Reyes Cristianos.

BELOW: strolling across the Puente Romano from the Torre de la Calahorra.

Statue of the great Jewish philosopher Maimonides in the Plaza Tiberiades in the Judería.

BELOW: a statue of Seneca the Younger, who was born in Córdoba, near the Puerta de Almodovar in the old city walls.
RIGHT: the Judería, the former Jewish quarter.

Spain, where once there were hundreds (the other two are in Toledo). Córdoba itself had 26 synagogues between the 10th and 15th centuries. This survivor, built in 1315, is entered through a patio off the narrow Calle Judíos. Segments of Hebraic inscriptions and family history remain on the walls. The upper gallery, where women were seated, and the niche where the Torah was kept are still intact.

Many Córdoban Sephardim achieved high status, either at the Muslim court or within the Jewish community. One was Maimonides, one of the greatest philosophers of Jewish history. A rabbi and Talmudic scholar with an Aristotelian bent, Maimonides was born in Córdoba in 1135. By this time, fanatic Berber sects, the Almohads, had changed the political landscape, initiating a period of unrest and repression. To escape the repression, Maimonides's family fled to Morocco, and he eventually settled in Egypt. But Córdoba still claims him as a native son.

Near the Synagogue, in the **Plaza Tiberiades**, under the bower of an enormous jasmine vine, is a statue of Maimonides, dedicated in 1965. He presides over the tiny square with kindly dignity, his slipper rubbed shiny by thousands of passers-by, possibly hoping some of his great wisdom might rub off on them.

Bullfighting memorabilia

In the plaza named after Maimonides is a different sort of monument. Opening off a beautiful patio, in the house said to have belonged to Maimonides's family is the municipal **Museo Taurino** Ⓖ (Bullfighting Museum; currently closed for restoration, but check to see if it has reopened). This is one of the most comprehensive of its genre in Spain, and the normal quota of bulls' heads is complemented by some splendid suits of light *(trajes de luces)*, posters *(carteles)*, a large library, and permanent exhibitions dedicated to the local *toreros* Lagartijo, Machaquito, Guerrita and Manolete. The last, who dominated Spanish bullfighting in the 1940s, was eventually

killed by a bull in the Plaza de Toros of Linares on 28 August, 1947.

Craft quarter

Behind the museum, again on Calle Judíos, is the **Zoco** , a cluster of craft workshops around a central courtyard. Here artisans work in both traditional and modern styles, in silver filigree (for which Córdoba has long been famous), leather, wood and ceramics. Near by, in a 16th-century house on Calle Tomás Conde, No 3, the street leading into Plaza Maimonides, **Artesanía Andaluza** features an excellent selection of Córdoban crafts, particularly ceramics. One of the exhibition rooms off the central patio has an ancient well.

East of the Mosque

The area of the old town northeast of the mosque is also full of attractive little streets and plazas. Take Calle Encarnación and then Calle Horno del Cristo to reach Plaza de Jerónimo Páez, where the **Museo Arqueológico** ❶ (Archaeological Museum; Tues 3–8pm, Wed–Sat 9am–8pm, Sun 9am–3pm; admission charge for non-EU visitors), housed in a fine Renaissance palace (currently being extended with a modern wing), has good displays of artefacts from the Bronze Age through Roman and Moorish times. Of particular interest are the finds from Medina Azahara *(see page 167)*, the 10th-century palace of Abd-al-Rahman III.

The other highlight of the old town east of the Mosque is the **Plaza del Potro** (an easy walk from the mosque along the interesting Luis de Cerda and Lucano streets), which is mentioned in Cervantes's *Don Quixote*. It is named after a small statue of a colt on the 16th-century fountain in the centre of the square. The 13th-century inn on one side of the plaza, where Cervantes

once stayed, houses a municipal arts-and-crafts centre and a branch of the tourist office. Modern paintings hang where horses and mules were stabled.

On the other side of the square is the 15th-century Hospital de la Caridad (Charity Hospital), home to two small but noteworthy, museums. The **Museo Provincial de Bellas Artes** ❶ (Fine Arts Museum; Tues 2.30–8.30pm, Wed–Sat 9am–8.30pm, Sun 9am–2.30pm; admission charge for non-EU visitors) is entered through a courtyard, elegantly tiled on one side.

The collection, largely based on works of art from disentailed monasteries and convents, is wide-ranging: a haunting head of Christ, dating from 1389; several paintings by the local master of baroque, Antonio del Castillo Saavedra (1616–68); Pedro Duque Cornejo's clay sketches for his carving of the Ascension in Córdoba Cathedral; works by the Seville artist Juan de Valdés; a wonderful painting by Joaquín Sorolla of a woman with downcast eyes and a red hat, and a

Map on page 162

Córdoba's craft tradition lives on in the Judería.

BELOW: patio in the Palacio de Viana.

Classic portrait of an Andalusian beauty by Julio Romero de Torres in Córdoba's museum of the artist's work.

whole section devoted to Córdoban sculptor Mateo Inurria, including a life-size sculpture of the Roman philosopher Seneca the Younger, another native Córdoban, looking wise and wizened.

In addition, just across a delightful patio enhanced by a fountain and busts, is the ever-popular **Julio Romero de Torres Museum** (Tues pm–Sun am; closed Tues am, Sun pm and Mon; admission charge), devoted to the works of a well-known local painter who specialised in mildly erotic portraits of sultry Andalusian women. The museum contains over 50 works donated by the artist's family.

Plaza de la Corredera

A little to the north of here is the **Plaza de la Corredera** , from this direction accessed through the main entrance in the south façade (its other entrances and exits are known as the High and Low arches). This impressive plaza is rectangular in shape and consists of a lower colonnaded level and three upper floors, embellished with galleries and balconies supported by semi-circular arches. Built by the Magistrate Corregidor Ronquillo Briceno in the late 17th century, the building is Castilian in style and the only one of its kind in Andalucía. It has been used for bullfights and public executions.

In 1896 the central area was converted into a covered market – the roof was removed during the 1950s. These days it hosts a general market on Monday to Saturday, a flea market (*rastro*) on Sunday morning, and shoppers can treasure-hunt in any number of second-hand shops under the arcades.

A few blocks up from this plaza, on Calle Capitulares, is a curious architectural landmark, Córdoba's **Ayuntamiento** (Town Hall), built in the late 1980s in a modern style, but incorporating the ruins of a Roman amphitheatre in its foundations. Beside it rise the columns of a Roman temple.

Just across from the Town Hall is the church of **San Pablo**, a Romanesque building fronted with spiral columns.

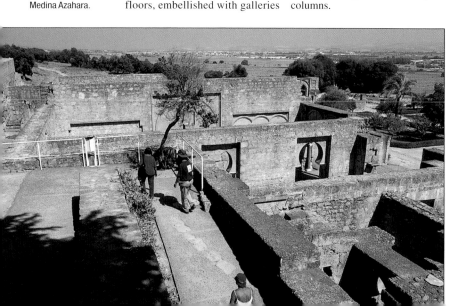

Bulls and convents

Continuing north along Alfaros brings you to **La Marina**, another interesting neighbourhood, named for the beautiful Gothic church of **Santa Marina** . This is the *barrio* of bullfighters, hence the extravagant homage to Manolete in front of the church. Around the corner from here, in the **Convent of Santa Isabel**, the Clarisa nuns keep up an old Andalusian tradition of making almond-based biscuits to sell to the public.

Near Santa Marina (along Calle Morales) is the **Palacio de Viana** ⓝ (summer 9am–2pm; winter 10am–1pm and 4–6pm; Sun 10am–2pm, closed Wed and the first two weeks of June), a 15th-century palace which belonged to the Marquis of Viana. Finding it difficult to maintain such a large establishment, the family advertised the palace for sale in a French newspaper. It was acquired in 1980 by a local savings and loan bank, the Caja Provincial de Ahorros de Córdoba, and converted into a museum. A year later it was declared a historic and artistic monument of national character. Its most unusual feature is the incorporation of 13 entirely different patios. On entering the first patio, note that the corner column has been deliberately omitted to facilitate the entrance of horse-drawn carriages. The 38 rooms and galleries inside the house are crammed with antique furniture, tapestries, porcelain, etc, and include an extensive library.

In the hills

No visit to Córdoba is complete without a visit to **Medina Azahara** ❷ (May–mid-Sept Tues–Sat 10am–8.30pm, until 6.30pm rest of the year, Sun 10am–2pm all year; admission charge for non-EU visitors), the city-palace of Abd-al-Rahman III, in the foothills of the Sierra Morena, just 8 km (5 miles) west of Córdoba. If you do not have your own transport, note that special buses for Medina Azahara leave from Avenida Alcázar in Córdoba at 11am–Tues–Fri, 10am and 11am Sat, Sun and holidays.

The palace, reputedly built in honour of Abd-al-Rahman III's favourite concubine, the Syrian-born

Maps:
City 162
Area 169

Córdoba has a lively custom of the tapeo, *stopping at one or several* tabernas, *neighbourhood bars. Good* tabernas *in the old quarter are Guzmán and Taberna Sociedad de Plateros, Both in the Judería.*

BELOW:
the Upper Basilica at Medina Azahara.

Al-Zahra, the Flower, was famous for its size and splendour. Its construction was said to have involved 10,000–12,000 workmen, and materials were brought from Constantinople as well as North Africa.

Life inside the palace was full of pomp and ceremony and was luxurious in the extreme, as witnessed by the mystic Ibn-al-Arabi. To impress an embassy of Christians from the north of Spain, the Caliph "had mats unrolled for a distance of 5 km (3 miles) from the gates of Córdoba to the entrance of the palace, and a double rank of soldiers stationed along the route, their naked swords meeting at the tips like the rafters of a roof."

Inside the palace, "the Caliph had the ground covered with brocades. At regular intervals he placed dignitaries whom they took for kings, for they were seated on splendid chairs and arrayed in brocades and silk. Each time the ambassadors saw one of these dignitaries they prostrated themselves before him, imagining him to be the Caliph, whereupon they were told, 'Raise your heads! This is

but a slave of his slaves!' At last they entered a courtyard strewn with sand. At the centre was the Caliph. His clothes were coarse and short: what he was wearing was not worth four dirhams. He was seated on the ground, his head bent; in front of him was a Koran, a sword and fire. 'Behold the ruler,' the ambassadors were told."

Despite its grandeur, the palace had a short life. After the breakup of the Caliphate of Córdoba early in the 11th century, it was utilised by various factions, then sacked. Many of the materials were used on constructions in Seville and other places and, over the next 900 years, it was allowed to fall into disrepair.

It was not until 1910 that the arduous work of excavation began. This work continues today, though the expanding suburbs of Córdoba are encroaching on parts of the site not yet excavated, causing considerable controversy.

The Sierra Morena

Continuing west, the Córdoba to Seville river road (C431) passes

BELOW: the rush hour in Priego de Córdoba.

through a rich agricultural region of fruit and citrus orchards, wheat, sugar beets and cotton. After the autumn cotton harvest, fluffs of cotton border the road like snowdrifts.

At **Almodóvar del Río**, on a hill dominating the river valley, is a picture-book castle, built by the Moors and later embellished. Halfway between Córdoba and Seville, on the Guadalquivir river, is **Palma del Río ❸**, famed for its citrus groves and as the birthplace of the popular bullfighter, El Cordobés. The 15th-century **Convent of San Francisco** in Palma was a springboard for missionaries bound for the New World, such as Fray Junipero Serra, who established California's missions. The monastery has been converted into a small hotel and restaurant where, in season, the menu features venison and boar taken in the nearby **Sierra Morena**.

This mountainous region, happy hunting ground of the aristocracy, has become very popular for its *monterias*, formalised hunts, where on a single day up to a hundred deer are shot.

Wine and oil

South of the capital (main road to Málaga, N331) is Córdoba's wine region, centred on the towns of **Montilla ❹** and **Moriles**, where wine has been made since the 8th century BC. Comparisons with sherry are inevitable, for Montilla wines are produced by the *solera* system of blending in the same way as the more widely marketed Jerez wines. These days, a light, young white wine, rather similar to the Vinho Verde from northern Portugal, is being produced around here.

The oldest winery is **Bodegas Alvear** in Montilla (tours weekdays at 10am, noon and 4pm). Other wineries are open by appointment only. The region celebrates its wine festival in the last week of August.

Map below

The long-standing feud between Julius Caesar and Pompey came to its bitter end when Caesar annihilated the forces of Pompey's sons, Gnaeus and Sextus, at Munda, now Montilla, on 17 March 45 BC.

BELOW: the grape harvest, Montilla.

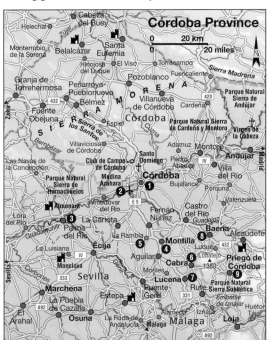

Córdoba Province

0   20 km
0   20 miles

Map on page 169

Other towns in the region worth a visit are **La Rambla ❺**, with more than 50 ceramic workshops; **Cabra ❻**, with the 13th-century sanctuary of the Virgin of the Sierra; and **Lucena ❼**, which was a totally Jewish town in the caliphal epoch, specialising in trade and crafts. Lucena is still a centre for copper, brass and bronze workshops. Outside the town are many furniture factories where newlyweds from all over Andalucía come to furnish their homes at factory prices.

Adjoining the vineyards is Córdoba's olive-oil region, centred on **Baena ❽** (off the main road to Granada), dominated by its Moorish fortress and surrounded by olive-covered hills, hence the presence of the interesting **Museo del Olivar y el Aceite** (Olive-Grove and Olive Oil Museum; Tues–Sat 11am–2pm and 6–8pm; admission charge).

Beyond Baena the terrain becomes more craggy, with villages such as **Luque**, built against a grey rock, and **Zuheros**, with its Moorish castle, two museums, and maze of narrow streets. High above the village is the interesting prehistoric **Los Murcielagos Cave** (limited opening hours; tel: 957-694 545; Mon–Fri 10am–2.30pm and 5–7pm).

Priego de Córdoba

The jewel of the province is the town of **Priego de Córdoba ❾** situated on a bluff above the Río Salado, a saltwater river. Known as the capital of 18th-century Andalusian baroque architecture, Priego has several beautiful churches in this style, notably **La Asunción**, with a white-and-gold dome in the Sagrario chapel, and **La Aurora**. The **Fuente del Rey** is a monumental baroque fountain with 139 spouts. Locals say that when the water level is high enough to cover the private parts of Neptune's statue, there will be sufficient water for the crops.

During the 18th century, Priego's thriving silk industry brought prosperity to the town. The fine buildings, including a number of noble mansions with handsome wrought-iron balconies and window grilles, date from that time. The old quarter of town, where passageways are no more than an arm's breadth, dates from Moorish times. Here, neighbours keep up the curious custom of carrying an image of a favourite saint, complete with tiny altar in a carry-case, from house to house. A complex schedule allows each family to keep it for one day.

South from Priego, almost to the Málaga and Granada borders, is Córdoba's lake region, stretching from **Iznájar** and all along the tributaries of the Río Genil. Here, numerous species of wildlife are sheltered, including some that are threatened with extinction. Among the rarer examples is one of Europe's last colonies of white-headed ducks. ❑

BELOW: belfry of the church of San Pedro in Priego de Córdoba.

RESTAURANTS & BARS

Restaurants

Almudaina
Jardines de los Santos
Martires, 1
Tel: 957-474 342
L & D. Closed Sun L (all
year), Sun D (mid-Jun–Aug).
€€€
Installed in a 15th-
century house near the
Alcázar gardens, serving
local recipes based on
fresh produce. Seven
dining areas, around a
central courtyard, deco-
rated with antiques.

Bar Santos
Magistral Gonzales
Francís, 3
(no phone). B, L & D. €
Just across from La
Mezquita, this is a small
and typical Spanish bar –
don't expect seats –
serving authentic tapas.
A pleasant change from
the more touristy places
hereabouts.

Bodegas Campos
Los Lineros, 32
Tel: 957-497 643. L & D.
Closed Sun. €€€
Colourful restaurant in a
former wine cellar near
the Julio Romero de
Torres museum, serving
variations on classical
Córdoba cuisine.

Casa Pepe de la Judería
Calle Romero, 1
Tel: 957-200 744
L & D. €€€
At the entrance to the
Judería, a typical Andalu-
sian townhouse, deco-

rated with bullfighting
themes and paintings,
with an interior courtyard.

Círculo Taurino
Calle Manuel María de
Arjona, 1. Tel: 957-481 862.
L & D. Closed Sun. €€€
Bullfighting is the theme
at this restaurant. *Rabo
de toro* (braised bull's
tail) stars on the menu
along with other Andalu-
sian classics.

El Caballo Rojo
Cardenal Herrero, 28
Tel: 957-475 375
L & D daily. €€€
Long-established restau-
rant near the Mosque.
The menu includes Moor-
ish dishes based on
medieval recipes.
Reservations essential.

El Churrasco
Romero, 16
Tel: 957-290 819
L & D daily. Closed Aug. €€
The name suggests
grilled meats, but there
is much more besides. A
good place to try
salmorejo, a thick Cór-
doban version of gaz-
pacho. Best to reserve.

Posada de Vallina
Corregidor Luis de la Cerda,
83. Tel: 957-498 750
L & D daily. €€
Innovative dishes such
as *berenjenas al ver-
mouth y arroz griego*
(eggplant with vermouth
and Greek rice). The
building, facing the
Mezquita, has original
Roman columns.

La Albacería
Corregidor Luís de la
Carda, 73
Tel: 957-487 050
B, L & D. $
Close to the tourist
office west of La
Mezquita. Good tapas,
tasty ice creams and
desserts.

Los Marqueses
Tomás Conde, 8
Tel: 957-202 094
L & D. Closed Mon.
€€–€€€
A charming restaurant in
a 17th-century palace in
the Judería. Mediter-
ranean cuisine. Good-
value lunch Mon–Sat.

Palma del Río
Hospedería San Francisco
Avenida Pío XII, 35
Tel: 957-710 183
L & D daily. €€€

Restaurant in the hotel
of the same name, in a
restored 17th-century
monastery. Basque and
Andalusian cuisine.

Montilla

Las Camachas
Ctra Córdoba–Málaga km 48
Tel: 957-650 004
L & D daily. €€
A rambling old roadside
restaurant where the
landed gentry of the wine
district dine out. Hearty,
good food, and Montilla
wines on sale.

PRICE CATEGORIES

Prices for three-course
meal per person with a
half-bottle of house wine:
€= under €20
€€ = €20–€40
€€€ = €40–€60

RIGHT: quintessentially Córdoban.

JAÉN AND ITS PROVINCE

Mountain nature reserves and towns filled with
Renaissance architecture and gourmet olive oil in
abundance are the main attractions of a province
more often driven through than explored

Amassive, undulating sea of 60
million olive trees, Jaén province is often thought of as a
place to hurry through rather than
somewhere worth stopping to
explore. Named *Giyen* ("caravan
route") by the Arabs who conquered
it in 712, throughout history it has
been trudged across by armies,
saints and traders on their way
between central Spain and the great
cities of Andalucía.

If any of these travellers of old
did halt here, it was to fight a battle.
In 208 BC the Romans defeated the
Carthaginians at the battle of Baec-
ula, a key step in the Romanisation
of Spain. At Navas de Tolosa, in
1212, a coalition of Christian monarchs from northern Spain scored
their first decisive victory in their
reconquest of the Peninsula against
the Muslim "occupiers". For a long
time in the late Middle Ages, Jaén
was the contested frontier between
the Moorish Kingdom of Granada
and the Christian Kingdom of
Castile, leaving it with a legacy of
more castles per square kilometre
than any other region of Europe.

Jaén became a war zone agin in
the 19th century when, at the battle
of Bailén on 19 July 1808, a Spanish
victory against French forces meant
that the tide began to turn against
Napoleon in the Peninsular War.

All armies gone, Jaén remains a
region of transit with different kinds
of trade caravans – trains and lorries
– rolling across its plains and hills.
But Jaén is worth devoting time to.
There is more here than transport
corridors and interminable lines of
smoky green-grey olive trees
marching over the hills in defiance
of the contours, and the locals well
know it. "*A quien Dios quiso bien,
casa le dio en Jaén*", they say:
"Whomever God wished well, He
gave a house in Jaén." If nothing

Map
on page
174

LEFT:
Jaén's massive
Cathedral, viewed from
the Castillo Santa
Catalina.
BELOW:
La Iruela, in the
Parque Natural
Sierra de Cazorla.

else – and there is much else – the province has all those castles to admire, but it also has Spain's largest nature reserve and two exquisite Renaissance towns which are by far the best places to begin a visit.

Beautiful Baeza

Column detail on the Isabelline Palacio de Jabalquinto in Baeza.

The astounding richness of both Baeza and Úbeda gives the lie to books that suggest that there is little of architectural interest in Andalucía outside the great Moorish cities. Their splendid honey-coloured palaces, churches and civic buildings, dating largely from the wealthy 15th to 17th centuries, have a cherished rather than lived-in air, as if history had left them frozen in their glory days.

Despite their similarities, each is different from the other. **Baeza ❶** – the sight of which at dusk prompted the poet Federico García Lorca to remark: "*Borrachera espléndida de romanticismo!*" ("What a glut of romanticism!") – is the smaller of the two. Its historic centre is so compact that you could walk around it in half an hour, although it deserves a far more leisurely visit.

The natural starting point for a stroll is the little square off the bottom of the large and unharmonious Plaza de la Constitución, the **Plaza del Pópulo**, also called the Plaza de los Leones after the lion fountain in the middle of the square, built using stone from the ruined Roman town of Cástulo. At the head of this square is the **Casa del Pópulo**, containing the tourist information office and beside it two monumental gateways, the **Puerta de Jaén** and the **Arco de Villalar**.

The other handsome Renaissance building on the square, the **Antigua Carnicería**, was built as Baeza's slaughterhouse or butcher's shop.❸

If you head uphill from here and bear left you will soon reach the **Cathedral** (Oct–Mar 10.30am–1pm

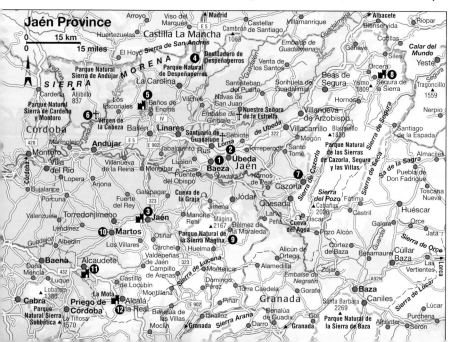

Jaén Province

and 4–6pm, Apr–Sept 10.30am–1pm and 5–7pm; free admission), remodelled in the 16th century but including some of its earlier Gothic elements. Its main door looks down onto a quiet cobbled square surrounding a quaint triumphal arch of a fountain, the **Fuente de Santa María**. The former Seminario de San Felipe Neri opposite the Cathedral (on the lower side of the square) is adorned with the fading red calligraphic *vitores* dating from between 1668 and 1720: graffiti by former students of the school in praise of someone or something of their fancy.

Downhill to the right of the seminary is Baeza's finest building, the **Palacio de Jabalquinto** (patio only: Thur–Sat 10am–2pm and 4–6pm; free admission), which has a decorative Isabelline facade framed by two pillars and topped by a gallery of arches. At the bottom of the slope you emerge on the Paseo de la Constitución. Across this and one street back is the **Ayuntamiento** (Town Hall), once used as an old prison which has ornate window surrounds on its upper floor.

Elegant Úbeda

A stone's throw from Baeza, on an adjacent hill, is **Úbeda ❷**, where a group of monumental palaces and churches forms the core of a modern town. The ensemble is largely the work of the architect Andrés de Vandelvira under the patronage of two noblemen, Francisco de los Cobos and his nephew Juan Vázquez de Molina, both powerful and ambitious secretaries to the emperor of Spain.

With one exception, all the buildings worth seeing are contained within the area circumscribed by the old city walls, of which only fragments remain. The centrepiece of this network of small streets of museum-like calm is the **Plaza de Vázquez de Molino**, an open-plan public space planted with clipped hedges and ornamental trees. At one end of it stands the domed chapel of **El Salvador**, commissioned by Francisco de los Cobos as a family pantheon with an extravagant interior. The north side of the square is formed by two other imposing buildings, the former Dean of

Church and fountain on the Plaza de Vázquez de Molino, Úbeda.

LEFT: cathedral wedding in Baeza.
BELOW: Baeza's Plaza del Pópulo.

Oil Wealth

The Romans planted olive trees across what are now Jaén, Córdoba and Seville above the Río Guadalquivir. After milling, the oil was transported downriver to the sea, to be shipped to Rome. Later, the Moors extended the cultivation of the olive across much of the Peninsula. They called it *az-zait*, "juice of the olive". From this derives the Spanish *aceite*, the generic word for oil. The tree in Spanish is *olivo*, from the Latin, but the fruit, *aceituna*, is from the Arabic.

These days, when harvesting the olives a vibrating machine is used to shake the trees, and plastic crates rather than baskets are used to collect the fallen olives; a tractor rather than a mule hauls the olives to the mill; and great stainless-steel vats have replaced the clay amphorae of yore. At the mill, the olives are thoroughly washed, then crushed to release the oil. The oil is extracted by purely mechanical means and, unlike other vegetable oils, can be consumed without further refining and purification.

Modern methods have brought a dramatic improvement in the finished product. The old-fashioned *almazaras* may have pre-sented a romantic image, with their mule-driven stone presses, but the process was slow, the olives often bruised and rotted in the sun while awaiting their turn, and the oil was more often than not rancid and highly acidic. Today's continuous presses and temperature controls ensure a much higher and consistent quality.

The oil is filtered into a series of settling tanks. The oil rises to the top and is drawn off, while the sediment and water content settle to the bottom. The resulting product is pure virgin olive oil, first pressing.

The quality of that oil depends on several factors, such as variety of olive, soil and climate, but, most importantly, how the olives were picked, transported, stored and milled. The best oil, labelled "extra virgin" or "fine virgin", comes from olives which are picked ripe and milled immediately. Its colour can vary from pale gold to amber to greenish-yellow, depending on the type of olive. It is usually completely clear after filtration. New oil has a slight bitterness, appreciated by many people, which disappears with a few months' maturation. Two, even three pressings can be made from the same olive pulp.

The product is used extensively in Andalucía. In a typical village home the housewife serves the midday meal. The fish, croquettes, pork and potatoes are all fried in olive oil. The salad is dressed with olive oil. For breakfast, toasted slabs of bread are lavishly drizzled with olive oil.

Everything from glowing complexions (before commercial moisturisers, Spanish women used olive oil and water whipped together) to strong hearts and good digestion have been attributed to olive oil. To encourage production of the highest-quality oil, a control board authorises a few select *denominación de origen* labels, or "guarantee of origin", for virgin oils.

There are 20 such DOEs, 10 of them in Andalucía: the sierras of Magina, Segura and Cazorla in Jaen, the Sierra de Cádiz, Priego de Córdoba, Baena (also in Córdoba), Poniente de Granada, Montes de Granada, Antequera (Málaga) and Estepa in Seville province. ❑

LEFT: Jaén province is carpeted with olive trees.

Málaga's residence, converted into a parador (*see page 246*), which has a delightful patio and the **Palacio de las Cadenas**, by Vandelvira, now the Town Hall. On the other side of the square are the **Antiguo Pósito** (the Old Granary) and, set back a little, **Santa María de los Reales Alcázares**. This last is the third largest church in the province after the cathedrals of Jaén and Baeza, and is essentially 13th-century incorporating part of an old mosque and fortress and with a conspicuous Renaissance facade.

Wander away from the square, and in two directions you quickly pass through the city walls and are faced with an endless vista of olive trees. In the other two directions, north and west, there are other buildings to discover, notably the **Palacio Vela de los Cobos** (behind the Town Hall), which has a gallery of arches along its top floor ending with a white marble column in one corner, and the **Casa de las Torres**, an early 16th-century mansion with a Plateresque facade framed by two towers.

If you crave relief from the smugness of the Renaissance, you will find it in the **Iglesia de San Pablo**, a church built in the 13th century. Its main, southern door is late Gothic and its west door Romanesque.

In the square outside the church is a monument to one Renaissance man who was anything but worldly, vain and materialistic. The poet, mystic and Carmelite monk John de Yepes, better known as St John of the Cross (San Juan de la Cruz in Spanish), died in obscurity in Úbeda in 1591 after a life of physical and mental suffering, having been imprisoned in Toledo and on two occasions saved from death by starvation only "by divine intervention". He left a lasting legacy to Spanish literature, however – and one of its best titles – in his *Dark Night of the Soul*.

A step or two up the street from the church and square, tucked away down an alleyway, is the delightful **Casa Mudéjar**, a 14th-century building of humble elegance with a porch of horseshoe arches, a pretty patio and carved capitals and door-

Map on page 174

Lion outside the Palacio de las Cadenas.

BELOW: the Palacio de las Cadenas, Úbeda's Renaissance Town Hall.

Sunflowers, an alternative source of oil to the ubiquitous olive.

ways. It functions as Úbeda's **Museo Arqueológico** (Archaeological Museum; Tues 9am–3pm, Wed–Sat 9am–8pm, Sun 9am–3pm; free admission).

The one building of renown which stands outside the line of the old city walls is the **Hospital de Santiago**, next to the bullring. It is considered to be the masterpiece of the mature Vandelvira for its facade, patio and, above all, arcaded staircase.

Up on a hilltop not far from Úbeda is a town which gets fewer visitors than it deserves. **Sabiote** has Arab ramparts and a Moorish castle treated to a Renaissance facelift by Vandelvira. Several of the town's noble mansions have carved portals and coats of arms.

Provincial centre

After such concentrated architectural beauty, the city of **Jaén ❸**, perched halfway up a hillside with its back to the sierras, can come as an anticlimax, especially as it is often clogged by traffic. All the monuments are in the old part of the city, at the top, and if you arrive by

car it's best to park downhill and brace yourself for the hike up steep streets towards the **Cathedral** (Mon–Sat 8.30am–1pm and 4–7pm or 5–8pm in summer, Sun 9am–1pm and 5–7pm; free admission), a Renaissance work of the 16th and 17th centuries. In the Capilla Mayor is a singular relic, one of three cloths in Christendom claimed to be indelibly stamped with the face of Jesus Christ after being used by Veronica to wipe the sweat from his face as he went towards his crucifixion.

From one corner of the Cathedral, Calle Maestra Martínez de Molina leads past the tourist information office and around the contours into the prettiest corner of the city, San Juan. On the discreet square of Plaza Santa Luisa de Marillac is the **Palacio de Villardompardo** (Tues–Fri 9am–8pm, Sat–Sun 9.30am–2.30pm; admission charge for non-EU nationals), a 16th-century mansion built by Fernando de Torres y Portugal, Count of Vilardompardo and Viceroy of Peru, now a cultural centre and folk museum of more depth, literally, than at first meets the

eye. It lies on top of a complete suite of Arab baths (**Baños Arabes**), the largest and arguably best-restored example in Spain, their chambers divided by horseshoe arches and lit by star-shaped skylights. The baths were built in the 11th century, but after the Christian reconquest of the city turned into a tannery.

The city has other fine buildings to see, but if time is short you may just want to look into the **Museo Provincial** (Tues 3–8pm, Wed–Sat 9am–8pm, Sun 9am–3pm; admission charge for non-EU nationals) to see one of the best collections of Iberian sculptures (5th century BC) in Spain, and then drive up the hillside beyond the busy streets above the Cathedral to the **Castillo de Santa Catalina**, a crumbling Arab castle which offers spectacular views. In the 1960s it was extended by building a "castle-style" parador (*see page 246*) next to it.

Into the hills

Having seen what the towns have to offer, it is time to head for the mountains. Jaén has a greater extension of protected wildlife areas than any other province in Spain, including four designated *parques naturales*. Two of these protect chunks of the large, empty Sierra Morena to the north. The most accessible of them is the gorge-pass of the **Desfiladero de Despeñaperros ❹**, which funnels the motorway and mainline railway between Madrid and the plains of La Mancha and the cities of Andalucía. The last town on the motorway before the frontier with Castilla-La Mancha is **La Carolina**, a "new town" laid out by order of Carlos III in 1767 as a lead-mining community, and populated with immigrants from Central Europe. Much more ancient is the enormous 10th-century castle overlooking the plains from **Baños de la Encina ❺**, as if waiting for one last army to come and lay siege to it.

The other *parque natural* in Jaén's stretch of the Sierra Morena is to the north of the Iberio-Roman town of Andújar and encompasses within its borders one of Andalucía's most popular shrines. It takes a 33-km (20-mile) drive from the main road along winding roads to get to the **Santuario**

Map on page 174

View from the mirador at the Castillo de Santa Catalina, Jaén.

LEFT: visiting the Castillo de Santa Catalina. **BELOW:** Jaén's immense Cathedral.

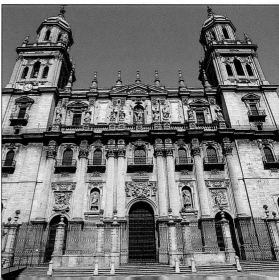

Welcome to the Parque Natural de las Sierras de Cazorla, Segura y las Villas, best accessed from the town of Cazorla.

de la Virgen de la Cabeza ❻. Every April half a million pilgrims make the trip on foot, horseback or by car to pay homage to the diminutive statue of the Virgin contained therein. Outside the church stands an elegy to the idealism and futile sacrifice of war: a simple stone tablet which tells how Capitán Cortés, leading 250 rebel troops and a handful of local villagers, defended the sanctuary against eight months of Republican onslaught during the first year of the Civil War.

Spain's largest reserve

There are even more appealing mountains in the east. The forested limestone ridges and deep, steep valleys of the **Parque Natural de las Sierras de Cazorla, Segura y las Villas** comprise Spain's largest nature-and-game reserve and take up almost one-fifth of the province of Jaén. Aside from its importance in terms of wildlife preservation – it has a rich population of eagles and vultures amongst other birds, and its endemic species of plant include a singular carnivorous

species – the reserve has symbolic significance, as it is here that Andalucía's principal river, the Guadalquivir, rises. To begin with, this modest stream is forced north by the mountains into the reservoir of Embalse del Tranco, but as soon as it finds a way through the Sierra de Cazorla it sets off westwards, along the base of the Sierra Morena, picking up speed as it passes through Córdoba and Seville, finally emptying into the Atlantic. Another important river, the Segura, also rises within the reserve, but flows the other way, to the Mediterranean.

The nature reserve has a visitors' centre, but it is a long way inside the park's boundaries. The best point of access is **Cazorla** ❼, which clings to a steep slope under a rocky ridge and looks out onto an endless view of olive trees. It centres on the Plaza de la Corredera, with its fine town hall, but another good square is the Plaza de Santa María, which has lively terrace cafés in summer.

The road into the reserve from Cazorla passes under the Templar castle of **La Iruela** *(see picture on*

page 173) before leading over the Puerto de las Palomas pass to bring you winding down to a crossroads, the Empalme del Valle. The only thing to do here is turn up the valley northeast, unless you want to visit the parador (*see page 246*)– a modern luxury hotel in a stunning setting – or go in search of the source of the Guadalquivir (a round trip of almost 40 km/25 miles from the crossroads).

The valley road takes you to the Torre del Vinagre visitors' centre, which has displays on the sierras' geography and wildlife, as well as an adjacent botanic garden. A hunting museum is a reminder of the days when wildlife was to be hunted rather than given protection: General Franco bagged a record-breaking deer in Cazorla in 1959.

After the visitors' centre, the road continues north and runs beside the reservoir. From here a scenic route follows the gorge of the Guadalquivir towards Iznatoraf, but if you have the time it is worth continuing to the end of the lake into a more open, much less wooded land-scape. This is surveyed by **Segura de la Sierra ❽**, an important town under Muslim rule, from which times it retains a castle with impressive views. In the 16th century, as Spain's empire was expanding, Segura made a fortune by cutting down the trees around it and shipping the timber down the Guadalquivir to build ships. Today, the town lives from its olive oil, for which it enjoys a *denominación de origen*. This is also a popular area for hang-gliding: there is a "free flight resort" near Segura on the top of Mt El Yelmo (1,809 metres/6,000 ft).

Faces in the floor

The remaining *parque natural* covers a compact massif reaching to 2,165 metres (7,103ft) between Jaén city and Cazorla, the **Sierra Mágina**, where olive trees cover the lower slopes and then give way to scrub vegetation and crags. The prettiest parts are to the north and the south: the area around Albánchez de Mágina and Torres is worth driving through, and there are good views from the Huelma to Cambil road.

Segura de la Sierra was the birthplace of Jorge Manrique, a 15th-century courtier and poet.

BELOW: Cazorla.

Map on page **174**

TIP

For more information about Spain's *vías verdes*, long-distance cycling and hiking tracks along disused railway tracks, see *Cycling*, page 227.

BELOW: high views in Jaén's castle country.

The name Mágina is thought to mean "magic" or "mysterious", and it is fitting that it should be the location for one of the best-known paranormal enigmas of Spain. On the eastern slopes of the sierra is **Bélmez de la Moraleda** , an undistinguished little town which would receive no visitors at all were it not for a phenomenon which has been occurring since 1971. Since then a multitude of ghostly, monochrome faces have been appearing in the concrete floor of a house supposedly to the bafflement of scientists – although it only seems to be paranormal enthusiasts who care either way.

You can see this for yourself by following the signs to the "Casa de las Caras" (or the "Nueva Casa de las Caras" – because another house has been experiencing similar receptivity in a concrete floor). Both houses are advertised as being open weekends only, but if you visit on a whim at other times you may be lucky and find someone who will let you see the faces in return for a tip.

Three castles

The southeast corner of Jaén province is agricultural, but three olive-processing towns built around castles are worth a visit. The first two form part of a 55-km (33-mile long) cycle way (also used by hikers), the Vía Verde del Aceite ("The Olive Oil Green Way") from Jaén city along a disused railway line which passes through two illuminated tunnels. **Martos** ❿ is considered the epicentre of world olive- oil production although it is not a *denominación de origen* – such distinction is reserved for the better oils produced on the sierras to the east.

Alcaudete ⓫, a dusty town above a sea of olive trees, has a castle built by the Knights of Calatrava in the 13th and 14th centuries. At **Alcalá la Real** ⓬, meanwhile, in the far south, the abbey church of Santa María la Mayor was built on the site of the former mosque in the Moorish fortress of La Mota after the Renconquest, and its presence there creates a strangely postmodern effect. ❑

RESTAURANTS & BARS

Restaurants

Alcalá la Real

El Rey de Copas
Crta de Frailes s/n
Ribera Alta
Tel: 953-593 305
L & D. €
A small restaurant of growing reputation, although so far ignored by food writers because of its location in a village 10km (6 miles) from a small town. Creative cuisine combining choice fowl, and some seafood, with imaginatively-transformed vegetables.

Jaén city

Casa Vicente
Francisco Martín Mora, 1
Tel: 953-232 222
L & D. Closed Sun D. €€
Popular family restaurant near the Cathedral, serving traditional Jaén dishes and game in season. There is also a good *mesón* (tavern) serving tapas.

Horno de Salvador
Road to the castle
Tel: 953-230 528
L & D. €€
One of Jaén's best restaurants. If you are not sure what to order, ask for the sampler menu, the *menú de degustación*: not cheap but at least it keeps the final bill under control. Closed Sun night, Mon and July.

La Caseria de Piedra
Carretera de Los Villares
km. 7, Jabalcuz
Tel: 953-315 136
L & D. €
A stone hotel surrounded by woods southwest of Jaén. Dishes such as rabbit with garlic are accompanied by regional wines..

Parador de Santa Catalina
Tel: 953-230 000
L & D daily. €€€
www.parador.es
The spectacularly located parador, 4 km (2½ miles) west of Jaén, has an excellent, baronial-looking restaurant. Worth coming for the views alone.

Taberna La Manchego
Calle Bernardo López, 12
Tel: 953-232 192
L & D daily. €
Authentic bar and restaurant, serving good tapas and daily specials.

Andújar

Don Pedro
Gabriel Zamora, 5
Tel: 953-501 274
L & D. €€
Regional dishes at good prices. Pleasant outdoor dining in the summer.

Baeza

Juanito
Paseo Arca del Agua, s/n
Tel: 953-740 040
L & D. Closed Sun, Mon D.
€€€
Spacious and friendly,

one of the best-known restaurants in Andalucía has based its reputation on its owner's missionary zeal in recovering traditional recipes.

Restaurant Vandelvira
Calle de San Francisco, 14
Tel: 953-748 172
L & D. Closed Mon and Sun D. €€
Attractive restaurant set in the Convento de San Francisco. Good meat, game and local specialities.

Cazorla

Cueva de Juan Pedro
Calle de la Hoz 2
Tel: 953-721 225
L & D. No cards. €
Literally a hole in the wall, this tiny, informal cave-restaurant specialises in grilled meat.

Úbeda

Mesón Navarro
Plaza del Ayuntamiento, 2
Tel: 953-790 638
L & D. €
Centrally located in the historic area of town, serving a good value *menú del día*. If you happen to overshoot lunchtime many items on the menu – including meats, salads and starters, seafood and fish – are available as tapas and *raciones* at the bar.

PRICE CATEGORIES

Prices for three-course meal per person with a half-bottle of house wine:
€= under €20
€€ = €20–€40
€€€ = €40–€60

RIGHT: the Parador de Santa Catalina

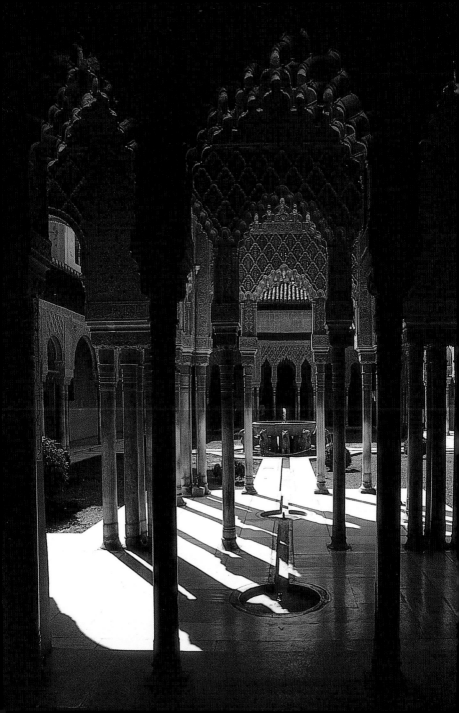

GRANADA

The last city to fall to the Reconquest, Granada epitomises the refined culture of Moorish Spain. Its exquisite Alhambra is the most impressive medieval Moorish palace in the world

L egend has it that, when the Moors were finally ousted from the Kingdom of Granada in 1492, their defeated king, Boabdil, could not contain his tears as he looked back at the magnificent city his ancestors had forged over nearly seven centuries and which he had been obliged to surrender . The site of this legendary moment of sadness is a pass in the hills 13 km (8 miles) south of Granada. It is called El Suspiro del Moro, the Moor's Sigh.

These days the view from this spot is less impressive, as the foreground is dominated by the sprawl of Granada's modern suburbs, which seem determined to fill the fertile farming plain (the *vega*), with housing estates and shopping centres. To get a truer appreciation of the old city of **Granada ❶** it is better to begin with a view from a vantage point closer in.

The **Mirador de San Cristóbal ❹**, on the road which winds up and out of Granada in the direction of Murcia (No. 7 bus from the city centre), provides the best view of all, and is an excellent starting point for the newcomer to Granada. Across the valley of the Darro river, the Moorish fortress-palace of the Alhambra seems to grow out of the burnt sienna rock and the dark-green vegetation, asymmetrically in

harmony with the natural landscape. Behind it are the snowcapped peaks of the Sierra Nevada, at one's feet the old quarter of the Albaicín.

Maps:
City 186
Area 197

Hub of the old city

When Granada became an independent Moorish kingdom at the beginning of the 11th century, the royal court was in the **Albaicín ❸**, and not transferred to the Alhambra opposite until 250 years later. Today, with its network of steep erratic streets, steps and alleyways,

LEFT: the Alhambra's Patio de los Leones.
BELOW:
view of Granada's Cathedral from the Albaicín.

The 11th-century baths on the Carrera del Darro are worth visiting. For a luxurious modern version of a traditional Arab hammam, *visit Aljibe Banos Arabes, San Miguel Alta, 41, tel: 958-52 2 867, www.aljibes sanmiguel.es*

it is still easy to imagine what the Albaicín must have been like when it was the hub of Moorish Granada with its 30 mosques, its potters and weavers, and its women fetching water from the *aljibes* (public water tanks), still used as recently as the 1960s. Today, the Albaicín is a desirable place to live and an atmospheric place in which to stroll, even if it keeps most of its secrets behind the tall walls of its typical house-patio complexes, known as *carmenes*.

The best place to begin a walking tour of the Albaicín is along the **Carrera del Darro**, the little river valley separating the Albaicín and Alhambra hills, which starts just north of Plaza Nueva. Several old properties along this route have been converted into interesting hotels. At No. 31) are the 11th-century Arab baths, **El Bañuelo ●** (Tues–Sat 10am–2pm; free admission). Entered through a leafy patio, the baths are perfectly restored with sunlight play-

ing through the stars and octagons pierced through the roof. A little further along is the **Museo Arqueológico** (Tues–Sat 9am–8.30pm, Sun 9am–2.30pm; admission charge for non-EU nationals), with finds from prehistoric times to the Islamic era.

Turn left at any point along here to zigzag up through the Albaicín, where the smells of jasmine, of damp, of heat or of cooking take over from car fumes, where the sound of burbling water is common, and where mules are occasionally still used to carry bricks and bags of cement. Little trace of Islamic architecture remains, as churches and convents – several enclosed orders still function here – rapidly supplanted the mosques after the reconquest of Granada. One survivor is the **Palacio de Dar al-Horra** (Queen's House), on the other side of the Albaicín, built for King Boabdil's mother in the mid-15th

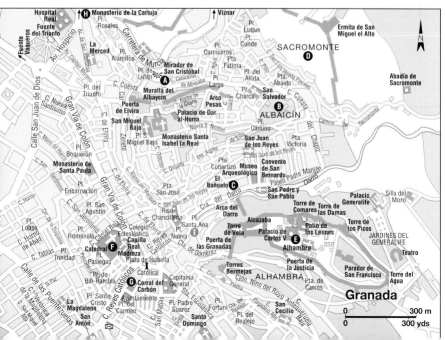

century. It is behind the convent of **Santa Isabel la Real**, also a former Moorish palace.

The Holy Hill

Up the hill north of the Albaicín is **Sacromonte ⓓ**, literally, the "Holy Hill". This was once a well-known cave quarter inhabited by a strong gypsy community ,but these days only a handful of caves still offer *zambras,* gypsy fiestas of flamenco music and dance. Past the caves is the **Abadía de Sacromonte** (Tues–Sun 11am– 3pm and 4–6pm; admission charge), a late 15th-century abbey founded on the site where the remains of four Christian martyrs were discovered, including the patron saint of Granada, San Cecilio. It has five fascinating subterranean chapels.

The Alhambra

Everything else in Granada, however, is merely a foretaste for the one building everyone comes to the city to see, the **Alhambra ⓔ** *(see box on page 189 for opening hours and ticket information)*. No other monument in Spain has exerted such fascination over travellers and historians over the centuries, or inspired so many poets, composers, painters and writers.

That the palace-fortress, its gardens and the summer residence, the Generalife, can still be termed "the best-preserved medieval Arab palace in the world" is nothing short of a miracle given the Alhambra's history after the defeat of Boabdil. An earthquake in 1522 and an explosion in 1590 caused significant damage. During the Peninsular War, Napoleonic troops used the Alhambra as a garrison and destroyed part of its ramparts. Further destruction was undertaken in 1626 by Carlos I (known as Emperor Charles V outside Spain), who decided to build a palace in the confines of the Alhambra in a style of jarring incongruity. Then, 50 years later, the palace's mosque was knocked down to make way for the Church of Santa María.

It was largely thanks to the "discovery" of the Alhambra by 19th-century writers and artists that the monument was at last recognised as unique. Mérimée, Chateaubriand,

Typical window in the Albaicín, the higgledy-piggledy hub of Moorish Granada on the hill opposite the Alhambra. In the 14th century the population of the Albaicín was 400,000, twice that of today.

Maps: on page 186

BELOW: the Alhambra, seen from the Albaicín.

Gustave Doré and Victor Hugo were all profoundly influenced by their stay in Granada, while Washington Irving *(see page 193)*, Théophile Gautier and Richard Ford enjoyed the extraordinary privilege of lodging within the Alhambra itself, in the quarters where Carlos I spent his honeymoon.

In 1870 the Alhambra was declared a national monument and restoration began, although the first efforts were geared more to creating the ideal image of a fairy-tale castle as envisioned by the romantics of the day than a faithful recreation of the building. It wasn't until the 1920s that a measure of historical rigour was applied to the restoration, a painstaking process that continues to this day, carried out by a permanent staff of architects and craftsmen.

Form and function

The Alhambra is made up of three principal parts: the Royal Palace, the Alcazaba or fortress, and the Medina, where up to 2,000 members of the royal household lived but which today is mainly given over to gardens. Further up the slope stands a fourth part of the complex, the summer palace of the rulers of Granada, the Generalife.

The Alhambra largely dates from the 14th century, but it is better thought of as an accumulation of buildings over time. When in 1238 Muhammad Ben Nasr founded the Nasrid dynasty that was to rule Granada until 1492, he held court in a castle where today's Alcazaba stands. It wasn't until his descendant Yusuf I became king 100 years later that building on the new palace began. The reign of this Nasrid king, and that of his son Muhammad V, which together lasted from 1333 to 1391, saw the construction of all the most important elements of the royal palace as we know them today.

The core of the Alhambra is the

The German historiographer Hieronymus Münzer, who visited the Alhambra in 1494, only two years after it had been captured by the Christians, wrote: "There is nothing like it in Europe: it is so magnificent, so majestic, so exquisitely fashioned that, looking at it, one cannot be sure that one is not in paradise."

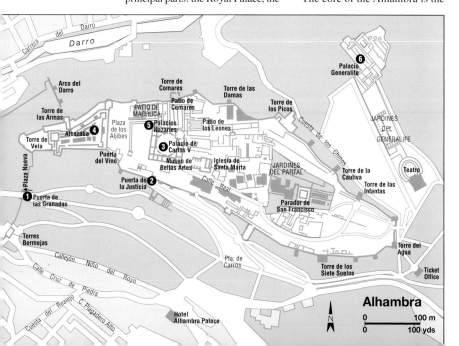

Alhambra

0   100 m
0   100 yds

Royal Palace (the Casa Real or Palacios Nazaries), a fantasy of delicate arches, intricate carving and trickling fountains. Unlike the self-confident grandeur of the Mosque in Córdoba, or the restrained elegance of the Almohads' Giralda in Seville, the Alhambra has an almost ephemeral quality, and, indeed, the carved patterns and inscriptions on plaster which are the most striking decorative feature were regarded as no more permanent than today's wallpaper; successive rulers would remove the work of their predecessors and have it replaced with inscriptions more to their liking.

Built with clay bricks, mortar and wood, the whole palace is the architectural expression of a civilisation in its twilight years, when the once formidable military might of Muslim Spain had been replaced by the intense, if relatively brief, cultural flowering of Nasrid Granada.

The intrigues that unfolded in the rooms of the Royal Palace, pitting the sultan Mulay Hassan and his favourite concubine, the Christian-born Zoraya, against his wife Aixa and their luckless son Boabdil, would spark a civil war and precipitate Granada's eventual downfall.

Map on page 188

Approaching on foot

If your legs and lungs are up to it, it is well worth starting out from the **Plaza Nueva**, at the foot of the Alhambra hill in central Granada, and walking up the shaded Cuesta de Gómerez and through the **Puerta de las Granadas ❶** (Gate of the Pomegranates), built on Carlos I's orders in 1536. It is decorated with three pomegranates, symbol of the city (the Spanish word for pomegranate is *granada*, although the city's name has a different origin; it comes from the name given to the city by its sizeable Jewish population during Visigoth days, Garnatha).

As you approach the Alhambra, on the left-hand side you'll see the impressive **Puerta de la Justicia ❷** (Gate of Justice or Bib Xaria), one of the main entrances to the palace, on which are engraved the Islamic symbols of a hand and a key. As every tour guide will tell you, the Moorish leg-

The word granada *means pomegranate and the fruit is a recurring motif in the stonework of the Alhambra, in particular on the Puerta de las Granadas.*

BELOW LEFT: the Puerta del Vino.

Opening Times, Tickets and Transport

The Alhambra is open daily year-round (Nov–Feb 8.30am–6pm, Mar–Oct 8.30am–8pm). Although tickets can be bought on the day at the ticket office (next to the car park), which opens from 8am until one hour before the Alhambra closes, they sell out quickly, as numbers are restricted. It is advisable, therefore – and essential at peak times – to purchase tickets in advance. They are available by phone (tel: 902-224 460), over the counter at any branch of the BBVA bank in Spain, or via the website www.alhambratickets.com. One person can buy a maximum of five tickets. Leave plenty of time to pick up pre-booked tickets, as the queue for these can also be long.

Only 300 visitors are admitted to the Nasrid Palaces every 30 minutes; your ticket will show the time slot in which you may enter (once inside, you can stay as long as you like). If you buy a ticket on the day during a busy period you may have to wait several hours for this, but you can visit other parts of the complex in the meantime.

Parking, though plentiful, is quite expensive. If you don't want to walk up to the site (a bit of a hike on a hot day), take the special minibus service that runs from Plaza Nueva every 15 minutes.

The name Alhambra comes from the Arabic ga'lat al-Hamra, the Red Castle. According to the Moorish historian Ibn al-Khatib, it was called this because construction continued far into the night, to the light of torches, and the palace had a red glow when viewed from a distance.

BELOW: view from the Torre de Vela.

end insisted that Christian visitors would never enter this gate until the hand reached down to grasp the key.

Visitors arriving by coach or car follow a ring road, which avoids the city centre. They join pedestrians in the queue outside the ticket office, at the bottom of the car park.

The Palacio de Carlos V

Once inside the complex, you can stroll along the garden pathway, through the former medina, the surrounding town, following the signs to "Palacios Nazaries", until you reach the imposing **Palacio de Carlos V 3**. Although glaringly out of place among the Nasrid architecture, this is one of the most outstanding examples of Renaissance architecture in Spain, with its unique circle-within-a-square layout.

Off the central courtyard is the **Museo de la Alhambra** (Tues–Sat 9am–2.30pm; free admission), which has well-arranged exhibits of Spanish Islamic art. Upstairs is Granada's **Museo de Bellas Artes** (Museum of Fine Art), Tues–Sat 9am–2.30pm; admission charge).

The Alcazaba

Leaving the palace, you reach the **Plaza de los Aljibes**. This square commands the first of many magnificent views over the Albaicín and Sacromonte. If you have half an hour to spare before your allotted time in the Royal Palace, this is the best time to tour the **Alcazaba 4** (if you visit later, its stark military aspect will come as an anticlimax after the splendour of the Nasrid Palaces). The massive fortress juts out like the prow of a ship on the Alhambra hill.

Make your way across the **Plaza de Armas** (which has a small snack bar selling beers, sandwiches and soft drinks), where you can view the foundations of the soldiers' domestic quarters, and climb up to the **Torre de Vela**. Isabel had a bell installed in this tower after the fall of Granada to symbolise the Christian triumph (bells are banned under Islam).

One last stop before the Nasrid palaces is the illuminating **Sala de Presentación**, in a Moorish *aljibe* (water cistern) under the Palace of Carlos, an introduction to the Alham-

bra covering both its history and the techniques and materials used in its construction.

The Nasrid Palaces

The **Royal Palace ❺** (Palacios Nazaries), the highlight of the visit, comprises three distinct parts, leading from the most public areas to the most private quarters, ending up with a visit to the baths or *hammam*. Inside the entrance to the palace is the *mexuar*, where citizens of Granada were received and justice was meted out; from here, you enter the *serail*, where official, diplomatic life took place; and finally, the *harem*, the monarch's private quarters.

The *mexuar* is the least well preserved part of the palace, having been converted into a chapel shortly after the expulsion of the Moorish court and also damaged by the 1590 explosion. At the end of the main room is an oratory with a glimpse of the intricate geometrical motifs so prolific elsewhere.

From here a small courtyard (Patio del Mexuar) leads to the **Cuarto Dorado** (Golden Room),

where the sultan's visitors were received. The entrance to the *serail*, through the left-hand door at the end of the patio, follows a zigzag route, thus protecting its access. Within this part of the palace diplomatic life was intense, especially in the latter half of the 14th century when the power of the Moors in Spain was draining away. Central to this part of the Alhambra is the **Patio de Comares** (also called Patio de los Arrayanes/Courtyard of the Myrtles), which, with the reflection of the buildings in the water of the pool, is an outstanding example of the symmetry of Islamic art. Critics refer to this as "the Parthenon of Arab art in Spain".

At one end of this patio is the **Torre de Comares**, in the ground floor of which is the majestic **Salón de Embajadores** (Ambassadors' Hall), perhaps the room which leaves the most lasting impression on visitors. The domed ceiling, representing the firmament, is inlaid with cedar and reaches a height of over 15 metres (50 ft). The sultan used to sit with his back to the light,

Map on page 188

The Mores believe Granada Ly's Directly under Paradise And that they differ both no more Than th'upper Roomes do from the Floure.
– PHILIP THICKNESSE, *A Year's Journey through France and Spain*, 1789

LEFT: the Plaza de los Aljibes.
BELOW: view over the Torre de las Armas from the Torre de Vela.

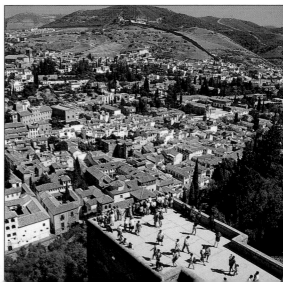

One of the 12 lions comprising the central fountain of the Patio de los Leones.

BELOW: detail in the Sala de los Abencerrajes.
RIGHT: Sala de las Dos Hermanas.

facing entering visitors, thus keeping an advantage over them.

From the Patio de Comares you pass into the *harem*, accessed from the **Patio de los Leones** (Patio of the Lions). The domestic quarters of the sultan, his wives and the sultan's mother (a key figure in Moorish court life) lead off this central courtyard – the **Sala de los Reyes** (Hall of the Kings); the **Sala de los Abencerrajes** (Hall of the Abencerrajes) and the **Sala de las Dos Hermanas** (Hall of the Two Sisters).

Amid the overwhelming richness of the *harem* as a whole, several architectural and decorative features are distinctive. First there is the anti-earthquake device, a lead plate inserted at the top of the 124 white-marble pillars. Next, the 12 lions themselves, surrounding the central fountain: according to one theory, the lions represent the Twelve Tribes of Israel, and the two marked with an equilateral triangle on the forehead symbolise the Chosen Tribes.

The paintings on leather in the Sala de los Reyes, where human figures appear, were probably done by

Castilian artists who sought refuge in Granada from the reign of terror of Pedro the Cruel. Look for the traces of "blood" in the fountain in the Sala de los Abencerrajes, "proof" of the veracity of the legend which tells of how 36 members of the Abencerraje family (Boabdil's family's rival clan) were beheaded one by one as they entered – a sultan's revenge for his mistress's infidelity.

Exit the patio via the Sala de las Dos Hermanas, with its cupola said to be decorated with more than 5,000 cavities, to reach the **Baño de Comares** (Royal Baths), titled chambers with star-spangled domed roofs. From here you can wander down to the area where the 19th-century American author Washington Irving lived in "delicious thraldom" while writing his bestseller *Tales of the Alhambra (see box opposite)*.

The Generalife

The itinerary continues through an open garden area, flanked by the **Palacio del Partal** (the oldest part of the complex) and unrestored parts of the exterior walls, as you head for

the Nasrids' summer palace, the **Generalife** ❻, whose gardens are perhaps the most magnificent in Spain. The sound of running water is particularly soothing for anyone who has had enough of heat and monuments, although it is questionable whether the Italianate layout of the present gardens owes anything to the Moors, who were more interested in roses, aromatic herbs and fruit and vegetables than in trimmed cypress hedges.

The gardens and adjoining palace are all that remain of what was once a much larger estate. The likeliest explanation for the name Generalife is that it derives from the Arabic *Gennet al-Arif* ("architect's garden"). The River Darro was diverted 18 km (11 miles) to feed this oasis of fountains and waterfalls. Only a part of the old summer palace remains, including the **Patio de la Acequia**, with its long and narrow central pond flanked by water spouts, and the **Patio de los Cipreses** (Courtyard of the Cypresses). Despite the name, there is only one cypress tree here now, the dead trunk of a venerable tree that

was supposedly witness to the illicit encounters between Zoraya, the sultan's concubine, and her Abencerraje lover, a liaison that led to the massacre of the Abencerraje family in the Sala de los Abencerrajes *(see opposite page)*. Ascending from here is the **Escalera de Agua**, a stairway whose banisters hold channels of rushing water.

Alhambra hotels

Before descending to the city, there are two hotels on the Alhambra hill worth visiting for different reasons. Nudging up to the Alhambra itself is the 15th-century **Monasterio de San Francisco**, now one of the most desirable hotels in the state-run parador chain. A room here needs to be booked in advance and does not come cheap *(see page 247)*, but you can always stroll in to the public areas and enjoy a drink or lunch on the terrace, which has views of the Generalife in the distance.

The **Hotel Alhambra Palace**, meanwhile, is a kitsch imitation of its namesake, and was built in 1910

Map on page 188

Detail on a fountain in the Generalife.

LEFT:
the Patio de la Acequia in the Generalife.

Alhambra Tales

Washington Irving, more than anyone else, helped put Granada on the map, with his *Tales of the Alhambra*, written following a visit in 1829 when the American author was travelling through Spain as a diplomat. Although the monument had been maintained by the Spanish rulers following the Reconquest, the Bourbon dynasty that acceded to the Spanish throne in the early 18th century was less attached to it, and it fell into disrepair.

By the time Irving arrived and set up headquarters in the Alhambra, the palace had become home to a colourful bunch of squatters. Ironically, it is thanks to the fact it was inhabited that the monument survived, even if it was the worse for wear, rather than being dismantled and carted away piecemeal for building materials.

Irving's fanciful tales of lovesick princesses and hidden Moorish treasure captivated the imagination of bourgeois society when the book was first published in 1832, and the many visitors who followed in the author's wake to see for themselves this magical place soon made the authorities aware that it was a major attraction that needed to be preserved.

*Isabel La Católica
receives Columbus
on the Plaza de
Isabel La Católica.*

when Granada was enjoying an economic boom thanks to its sugar industry. It has a hanging terrace with a superb view over part of the city and beyond to the *vega*, which in 1829 the American writer Washington Irving described as "a blooming wilderness of grove and garden and teeming orchard", but is now disappearing under housing estates.

The city centre

Most of Granada's other sights lie in the narrow streets of the city centre and the best way to visit them is on foot. Rising out of the hubbub is the **Cathedral** Ⓕ (Mon–Sat 10.45am–1.30pm and 4–8pm; Sun 4–7pm; admission charge), built on the site of the main mosque of Granada and considered one of the most important examples of Renaissance architecture in Spain. The warm, honey-coloured exterior, however, contrasts with the austere interior. Next to the Cathedral, accessed from Calle Officios, which runs alongside the east side of the Cathedral, is the much more appealing **Capilla Real** (Royal Chapel; open daily; closed

1–4pm; admission charge), the mausoleum of the so-called "Catholic Monarchs", Fernando and Isabel. The black-lead coffins of this famously pious and pro-active double act are on public display in the crypt, along with those of their luckless daughter, remembered by history as Juana the Mad, and her philandering husband, Felipe the Fair. Above the family vault, the chapel has superb iron grillework and a lavish baroque altarpiece. The sacristy, on the way out, houses an exquisite collection of primitive Flemish paintings.

Across the street from the chapel is the **Madraza** (currently being restored), the Arab university founded in the 14th century by Yusuf I, of which only the oratory remains from the original building (across the patio on the left); its intricate Arabic decoration was covered over for centuries, only to be rediscovered under a layer of plaster in 1893.

Next to the Madraza, pass through the Alcaicería, a warren of souvenir shops designed to resemble an Arab

souk, to reach central Granada's main traffic artery, the Calle de los Reyes de Católicos, which intersects with the Gran Vía del Colón at Plaza de Isabel La Católica, dominated by a statue of Queen Isabel receiving Columbus.

Across Reyes Católicos is the attractive **Corral del Carbón ❼**, built as an inn in the 14th century but later used as a theatre and coal depot (hence the *carbón* part of its name), and now housing, among other premises, a branch of the tourist office.

One of the best squares for cafés is the lively **Plaza de Bib-Rambla**, immediately south of the Cathedral. It is a popular place to come in the early evening for a beer or aperitif before going shopping. The adjacent streets are a rich source of restaurants, though most don't open until 9pm or later.

Outside the city centre

Two attractions outside the historic centre are worth visiting. If you have a special interest in baroque art and architecture it is worth seeking out the **Monasterio de la Cartuja ❽** (Apr–Oct 10am–1pm and 4– 8pm, Sun 10am–noon and 4–8pm; Nov–Mar 10am–1.30pm and 3– 6.30pm; admission charge), north of the centre (bus No. 8). Its richly ornamented church is an outstanding example of Churrigueresque, a Spanish extrapolation of baroque.

Offering a very different experience, and a particularly enjoyable one for children, is the **Parque de las Ciencias** (Tues–Sat 10am–7pm, Sun 10am–3pm; admission charge; www.parqueciencias.com) in the Avenida del Mediterráneo, southwest of the centre (take bus Nos. 4, 5, 10 or 11). It offers plenty of hands-on exhibits, a planetarium, a butterfly house, an observation tower, temporary exhibitions, etc.

Around Granada

Granada's most famous son is the poet and playwright Federico García Lorca, who was shot dead by Franco's Nationalists at Viznar, north of the city, on 19 August 1936, during the first weeks of the Spanish Civil War. He was born in

Maps:
City 186
Area 197

Poet and playwright Federico García Lorca, born near Granada in 1899.

LEFT: entrance to Calle Officios, alongside the Cathedral.
BELOW: topping a turret on Granada's Cathedral.

Fuentevaqueros **❷**, 16 km (10 miles) northwest of Granada, where the house where he was born has become a museum, the **Museo Casa-Nata**l (closed Mon).

Further in the same direction, amid olive-dotted hills, is the attractive white town of **Montefrio ❸**, built on a steep hillside around a rock. Its main church is the highly unusual **Iglesia de la Encarnación**, neoclassical in its simplicity, perfectly round and capped by a broad dome. But more intriguing is the 16th-century Gothic **Iglesia de la Villa**, which now serves as **El Centinela** (Tues–Sat am only), a museum dedicated to the border conflicts between Muslim and Christian Spain during the Middle Ages.

East of Granada

East of Granada, the motorway towards Almería and Murcia leaves the *vega* behind to cross the wooded Sierra de Huétor. Over the other side of the Puerto de la Mora pass (1,390 metres/4,560 ft) it drops down into an ancient lake bed in the middle of which sits **Guadix ❹**.

Although this city has a monumental centre radiating from the cathedral beneath the restored 11th-century fortress of the alcazaba, what visitors come here to see is the southern suburb, the **Barriada de las Cuevas**, a cluster of bluntly pointed mud hills pockmarked by hundreds of inhabited caves in various states of conservation and restoration, ranging from hovels to luxury homes.

Around 3,000 people out of a population of just over 20,000 live underground, almost all of them by choice rather than out of necessity (as was historically the case). Caves maintain their temperature at around 18°C (64°F) year-round because of the insulating properties of the clay into which they are dug. They are therefore said to be comfortably cool in summer and correspondingly warm in winter. The only drawback is the lack of natural light. Several caves around Guadix have been turned into cave hotels *(see page 249).* There are caves in almost all the villages around Guadix, notably **Purullena**,

Outside Montefrio, at Peña de los Gitanos (off the road towards Illora), there is a large group of Megalithic dolmens standing on private land but open to visitors who telephone in advance (tel: 628-305 337).

BELOW: Granada's Parque de las Ciencias.

1 -CATEDRAL
2 -SAN CRISTOBAL
3 -SAN MIGUEL BAJO
4 -ALBAYCIN
5 -SAN NICOLAS
6 -EL SALVADOR
7 -CERRO DEL ACEITUNO
8 -SAN MIGUEL ALTO
9 -SACROMONTE
10 -TORRE DE LA VELA
11 -ALHAMBRA
12 -CARMEN DE RODRIGUEZ ACOSTA
13 -STA. Mª DE LA ALHAMBRA
14 -HOTEL ALHAMBRA PALACE
15 -SILLA DEL MORO
16 -AUDITORIO MANUEL DE FALLA
17 -CARMEN DE LOS MARTIRES
18 -LLANO DE LA PEROIZ

which is also well known for its ceramics industry.

In Guadix, the natural centre of the cave quarter is the bright white church of the **Iglesia de las Cuevas** on **Plaza del Padre Poveda**, which has a cave chapel on the far side of the nave. Opposite the church is a municipal cave museum which illustrates life in a cave a century or so ago. The scrape marks of the adzes used to dig it can be seen in the ceiling, proving that it hasn't been restored using modern materials as many other caves have.

For an overview of Guadix, you need to make for the balcony at the quarter's highest point, behind the Colegio Padre Poveda. It takes some finding, but the walk there offers a chance to see a variety of cave houses close up. The view is surreal: half-houses stuck haphazardly to banks of clay which sprout white chimneys seemingly at random.

On the outskirts of Guadix, the motorway from Granada forks sending a southern branch heading into Almería past the Renaissance fortress of **La Calahorra** ❺ (Wed only) and, just over the provincial border, **Fiñana** ❻, which has a 12th-to 13th-century Almohad mosque thinly disguised as a chapel – if it is closed you can see all there is to see by peering through a small glass window in the door.

The northern branch of the motorway makes for Murcia, but an inconspicuous turn-off from it leads towards **Gorafe** and the lip of a canyon where 180 prehistoric dolmens have become the pretext to create the **Parque Megalítico del Mediterráneo** ❼. Most of the dolmens are in a poor state of conservation but there are good explanatory signboards.

Snowy mountains

North–south communications in the province of Granada are restricted

Pots for sale in Purullena, known for its caves and ceramics industry.

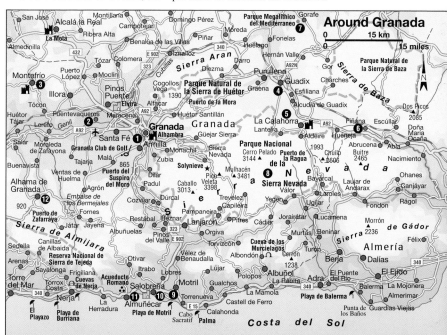

by the **Sierra Nevada** , the second-highest mountain range in Europe after the Alps. Its peaks are the highest in the Iberian Peninsula: Mulhacén 3,481 metres (11,421 ft) and La Veleta 3,398 metres (11,149 ft). National park status protects the rare vegetation of the mountains: the highest zones are frosty desert where only lichens grow, but lower down the tundra is inhabited by indigenous plant species of wolfsbane, violet, camomile, narcissus, thistle and saxifrage.

Synonymous with the mountain range is the southernmost ski resort in Europe, and also one of the continent's highest, with pistes descending from up to 3,300 metres (10,827 ft). Only 32 km (20 miles) southeast of Granada, it has reliable snow cover from December until April, and sometimes as late as May. Being largely above the tree line, it is not scenically spectacular, and its two stations – **Pradollano** at 2,100 metres (6,890 ft) and **Borreguiles** at 2,645 metres (8,677 ft) – aren't likely to win any beauty contests. But it makes up for that with the

brilliant sunshine of its southern European climate and the proximity of Granada and the coast.

It's not too difficult to go even higher. An unsurfaced road – claimed to be the highest road in Europe – crosses the range from the ski resort to Capileira in the Alpujarras (*see page 208*), but it can only be used by authorised vehicles. The national park, however, offers a minibus shuttle from its **Hoya de la Mora** visitors' centre (tel: 630-959 739) above the Pradollano ski station, almost to within reach of the summit of La Veleta. The ascent takes about three hours, and you can either return with the bus or walk down.

The Costa Tropical

From the heights of the Sierra Nevada, skiers and walkers look down upon Granada's Mediterranean coast, a world away from the rest of the province. This short, indented strip of shore is now officially called the "Costa Tropical" because of its abundant subtropical orchards growing bananas, mangoes, avocados and other fruit. As a succession of mountainous headlands, Granada's coast has so far avoided becoming an extension of the Costa del Sol. The joining up of the coastal motorway between Almería and Málaga, however, threatens to deliver mass international tourism here too.

The main town of the Costa Tropical is the port of **Motril** , but it has little to lure tourists except a museum explaining the once-important sugar industry. Europe's last sugar refinery is still going at neighbouring **Salobreña** , the most attractive town on this strip of coast, where the bright white houses of the old town pile around a tall rock that culminates in a well-kept Moorish castle. Beside the sugar canes on the

BELOW: on the slopes of the Sierra Nevada.

coastal plain below the town is a small, family-oriented resort.

Almuñécar , next along the coast, is an ancient town which has surrendered itself to tourism – its Velilla beach is a prime example of insensitive, short-term planning, but it does have historic monuments to show off. Chief of these is the ruined castle on a low hill overlooking the Parque del Majuelo, where there are the remains of a Roman fish-salting factory which once exported its products across the empire. Roman Almueñécar (Sexi) was fed by a 7-km (4½ mile) long series of aqueducts: with the aid of directions from the tourist office, the line of these can be followed up the lush valley towards Jete.

A few more curves around the coast road bring you to the small resort of **La Herradura**, which has an attractive beach between two headlands, Cerro Gordo and the Punta de la Mona. Beneath the latter is a beautiful cove beside the pleasure boat harbour of Marina del Este. La Herradura is a well-known scuba diving centre; there are plans to create an underwater park offshore, with prefabricated wrecks and ruins to dive over.

Into hot water

Granada province has one more town worth seeing, although being lost in the middle of unpopulated farmland en route to Vélez-Málaga from the coast, it demands a special effort to reach. **Alhama de Granada**  nudges up to the edge of an attractive gorge (overlooked by a balcony behind the Iglesia del Carmen), but its attraction lies in the spa hotel down a mini-gorge of its own below the town. The waiting room for guest-patients using the baths, and the source of the thermal waters, is a 12th-century Moorish chamber built of horseshoe arches.

The complex can only be visited during the afternoon (daily 2–4pm). If you need somewhere to pass the time while waiting for it to open, you can join the bathers in the river outside the hotel, where a series of improvised pools is fed by a steady stream of surplus thermal water.   ❏

Map on page 197

The coast below Granada is known as the Costa Tropical, where the growing of avocados, bananas guavas, papayas and custard apples has largely replaced the traditional sugar cane.

BELOW: Salobreña.

RESTAURANTS & BARS

Restaurants

Granada city

Granada has a good range of restaurants and bars. The area around the Cathedral is best for traditional meat and fish menus, especially around Plaza Bib-Rambla and streets off Reyes Católicos. The Albaicín is known for its *carmen* restaurants (old houses with pretty terraces often overlooking the Alhambra), though it also has a growing number of funky Moroccan bars with rugs, cushions, candles, mint tea and more, especially along Calle Calderería Nueva, leading up into the Albaicín from Calle de Elvira. One of many good things about Granada is that, as in Almería, bars still serve free tapas with drinks.

Chikito
Plaza del Campillo, 9
Tel: 958-223 364
L & D. €€€–€€€€
This long-established restaurant (the poet Lorca was a regular) is one of the best restaurants in the region. Chef Antonio Torres serves consistently good regional dishes such as *rabo de toro* (braised ox tail) and *bacalao* (baked cod) along with more innovative fare. It's best to reserve, especially on weekends.

Cunini
Calle Pescadería, 14
Tel: 958-250 777
L & D. Closed Mon. €€€

This friendly restaurant close to the Cathedral is the best place for fresh seafood in Granada. Tent-like terrace for outdoor dining in summer.

La Mimbre
Avenida del Generalife, s/n
Tel: 958-222 276
L only. Closed Sat. €€
This is a small restaurant in an unbeatable location at the very foot of the Alhambra walls, with outdoor dining on shaded terrace in summer. Traditional Granada dishes.

Parador San Francisco
Alhambra
Tel: 958 221 440
www.parador.es
If you are spending the day at the Alhambra this is an excellent place to come for a leisurely lunch (or dinner if you are here in the evening). The shady terrace at the rear has lovely views over the Generalife, and there is a good-value set-price lunch.

Méson El Trillo
Callejon de Aljibe de Trillo, 3
Tel: 958-225 182
L & D. Closed Tues. €€€
Delightful and very well respected *carmen* restaurant in the Albaicín. Superb Spanish cuisine with strong Basque influences. Combine a morning visit to the Albaicín with the good-value set lunch.

Rabo de Nube
Paseo de Los Tristes
Tel: 958-220 421
No cards. L & D. €
Lovely location on this scenic and quiet stretch alongside the Río Darro, the river valley between the Alhambra and Albaicín hills. There are tasty *bocadillos* (sandwiches) and pasta dishes.

Rincón de Lorca
Calle Tablas, 4
Tel: 958-253 211
L &D daily. €€
Located in the Hotel Reina Cristina, this is one of Granada's most reliable restaurants, serving regional dishes prepared with a modern touch. Less staid than the restaurant, the friendly hotel bar, alongside the hotel, is also good for *raciones* and daily specials.

Ruta del Veleta
Ctra Sierra Nevada km 5
Tel: 958-486 134
L & D. Closed Sun evening.
€€€
On the old road to Sierra Nevada, 5 km (3 miles) from the city, this spacious restaurant has served good food for decades. Also has an outdoor terrace. Classic Spanish food. Best to reserve.

Sevilla
Calle Oficios, 12
Tel: 958-221 223
L & D. Closed Sun evening.
€€

This Granada classic situated alongside the Cathedral, opened in 1930 and remains a good place to sample traditional dishes such as *Jamon con Habas* (cured ham with broad beans) or *Tortilla Sacromonte*.

Terraza las Tomasas
Carril de San Agustín 4
Tel: 958-224 108
L only Mon–Tues, L & D Wed–Sat. Closed Sun. €€€
Delightful Albaicín *carmen* where the regional cuisine is almost as good as the superb view over the Alhambra.

Vía Colón
Gran Vía de Colón 13
Tel: 958-220752. L & D. €
A cafeteria-restaurant next to Cathedral with a contrived interior of sculpted plaster and white columns. A good place to come for breakfast or a light, informal meal.

Almuñecar

Bodega Francisco
Calle Real, 14
Tel: 958 630 168
L & D .€
Atmospheric and popular bar serving tasty tapas.

El Chambao de Joaquin
Tel: 958-640 044. L daily. €
A hut at the end of La Herradura beach which looks from a distance like a hovel but is cunningly sophisticated inside and very popular

with foreigners. The menu concentrates on paella, fish and seafood. It is worth coming for the giant paella prepared on Saturday and Sunday lunchtimes.

Jacqui-Cotobro
Edificio Río Playa, s/n
Playa de Cotobro
Tel: 958-631 802
L & D. €€
L & D. Closed Mon.
The simple dining room with bare brick walls gives little indication that this beachside restaurant is famous all over Spain for its Belgian-French cuisine. The best plan is to order the *menú degustación*, including a wide choice of three different courses, plus dessert. Reservations are recommended.

La Galeria
Paseo Puerta del Mar, 3
Tel: 958 634 118
L & D. €€
Innovative international cuisine prepared by a Belgian chef. There is a good-value lunch menu.

Guadix

Comercio
Mira de Amezcua 3
Tel: 958-660 500
L & D. €
Restaurant and 20-room hotel in the city centre of town. Home-cooked dishes such as lamb with honey.

Riofrio

Meson Riofrio
Plaza San Isidro
Tel: 958 321 361
L & D. €
Having always been a popular beauty spot and place for weekend family outings to the river, Riofrio now also serves as a service area for the A92 (Granada–Málaga/ Seville) motorway. There is also a fish farm here, and trout features prominently on the menu. Riofrio is 4km (2.5 miles) from Loja in the direction of Archidona.

Salobreña

El Peñón
Playa del Peñón
Tel: 958-610 538
L & D. €€
There is no missing this restaurant which occupies one side of the distinctive rock which divides Salobreña's two beaches.

The best part of it is the shaded terrace overhanging the sea where you can relax over your fish or seafood – and often be entertained by local boys diving from the rocks.

Pesetas
Calle Bóveda 13
Tel: 958-610 182
L & D. €
As well as good food (mainly fish), this restaurant next to the Iglesia del Rosario at the top of Salobreña's old town offers an incomparable view from its rooftop terrace.

PRICE CATEGORIES

Prices for three-course meal per person with a half-bottle of house wine:
€= under €20
€€ = €20–€40
€€€ = €40–€60
€€€€= over €60

THEY CAME, THEY SAW, THEY PLANTED

From intimate patios to the magnificent gardens of the Alhambra, Andalucía is a magnet for gardeners from all over the world

Fertile soil and abundant sunshine make Andalucía a gardener's paradise, and the region is home to some outstanding gardens, including Seville's María Luisa Park and the gardens of the Generalife in the Alhambra. For the Muslims, gardens were intimate places appealing to all the senses. Aromatic plants such as mint and basil were key elements, along with the soothing sound of running water. Moorish homes were arranged around interior courtyards that provided a scented refuge from the heat.

After the Moors departed, the reigning style was the Italian garden of the Renaissance, designed to impress with symmetrical layout, manicured aspect, statues and fountains. The Generalife gardens we see now owe more to this style than to the Moorish.

Colourful imports

Each subsequent wave of settlers brought with them their preferred plants. The Phoenicians, Greeks and Romans introduced olive trees, date palms and vines. The Muslims brought orange trees and a great many herbs and flowers native to Asia. Explorations of new continents added to this botanical wealth. Geraniums came from southern Africa, mimosas from Australia, wisteria from Asia and bougainvillea from South America.

ABOVE: though designed several centuries later, the El Partal gardens in the Alhambra successfully unite some of the oldest sections of the Nasrid Palace.

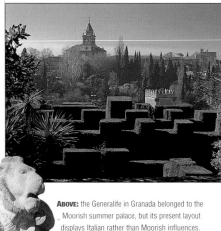

ABOVE: the Generalife in Granada belonged to the Moorish summer palace, but its present layout displays Italian rather than Moorish influences.

LEFT: a statue in the Jardín de los Leones in Seville's María Luisa Park. Lions are a recurring motif in Andalucía, whether in the mysterious Patio of the Lions in the Alhambra or the conquering lion of Castile, which crops up everywhere.

BELOW: a tiled fountain in María Luisa Park's Plaza de América, Seville. Donated to the city by Duchess Marie Louise of Orléans in 1893, the park contains many delightful features.

BELOW: geraniums are often considered the quintessential Andalusian pot plant, brightening many a white wall. Yet, like so many of Andalucía's plants, they originated from elsewhere, in this case South Africa.

THE WONDER OF WATER

Using their considerable engineering skills, the Romans were the first to harness Andalucía's water resources. Their canals and aqueducts turned the region into the breadbasket of the empire, and they built baths over several natural springs. But it was the Muslims who, adapting and improving on the Roman irrigation system, regarded water as an aesthetic element as well. Fountains, pools and elaborate channels, such as the "water stairway" in the Generalife gardens of the Alhambra, cooled the air and filled it with soothing sound. Water had a symbolic significance for the Muslims. Gardens were divided into four sections separated by channels of water representing the four Rivers of Life.

Taking a leaf out of the Moors' gardening book, Christian landscapers also used water for dramatic effect, especially with exquisite fountains, such as in the Palacio de Viana in Córdoba, a sumptuous 15th-century palace noted for its gardens incorporating 13 different patios.

BELOW: mirador in La Concepción botanical gardens in Málaga. Look-out points are popular features in parks, gardens and nature reserves.

THE ALPUJARRAS

Over the Sierra Nevada from Granada are the deep, leafy valleys of the Alpujarras, one of Spain's most charming corners. The countryside between its bright, white villages makes for excellent walking

Once a poor, remote and self-contained world of its own, the gigantic mountainsides and plunging valleys of **Las Alpujarras** first became known to the world in the 1950s because of a book written by Gerald Brenan, an English intellectual, who had taken refuge there from civilisation 30 years before. In recent decades his example has been followed by innumerable other migrants from northern Europe with a variety of similar motives – urban escapees, downsizers, alternative lifestyle-seekers, artists, neo-pastoralists, nature-lovers – and the Alpujarras fame has been given a fillip by another book by a refugee Englishman, called Chris Stewart, whose best-selling *Driving over Lemons* is an autobiographical account of his life as sometime smallholder and sheep-shearer in the area.

Many of the native inhabitants, meanwhile, have been migrating the other way, towards the comforts of the city. Despite improvements in communications between the Alpujarras with the outside world, young men and women are not anxious to take on subsistence hill farming in the mould of previous generations.

Memories of the Moors

It's easy to get the impression the newcomers are gatecrashing a way of life that has been going on for ever, but population-replacement is nothing new in the Alpujarras, and tradition is not as deep-rooted as it first might seem. When the Kingdom of Granada fell to Christian forces in 1492, its Muslim inhabitants were driven into the Alpujarras with the promise that they would be able to carry on their lives here as before. After a brief period of toleration, however, they were forced to choose between baptism or exile. Most chose the former, becoming

Map on page 206

LEFT: typical restaurant terrace in Pampaneira. **BELOW:** crossing a gorge near Trevélez.

Characteristic chimneys in the village of Pampaneira.

Moriscos, nominal Christian, who discreetly maintained their Muslim traditions. But when a series of decrees sought to ban their traditional costume, their use of Arabic and even their bathing ritual, the *Moriscos* of the Alpujarras revolted. The rebellion was bloodily crushed, the Moriscos driven into exile and the Alpujarras resettled with yet another wave of immigrants, this time from northwest Spain – indeed, several of the villages of the Alpujarras have Galician names.

Despite this historic handover of religion and culture, the Alpujarras retain a strong air of Arab influence, and it is this which makes them so attractive. Although many hill terraces have fallen into disrepair and become overgrown, they are still fed by the same ingenious system of irrigation channels appearing out of nowhere and slipping silently out of sight among the chestnut trees as they distribute the meltwaters of the Sierra Nevada according to a strict rationale. The occasional mulberry tree is a reminder of the *Moriscos'* once-important silk industry – the mulberry leaves being the food plant of the silkworm.

Village architecture

Above all, the lingering influence of the departed Muslims is evident in the architecture of the villages, which has its closest echo in the Atlas Mountains of Morocco. The houses are built onto each, as if at random – "a confused agglomeration of boxes, one box rising above another, and so on to the top", as Gerald Brenan saw them.

This creates higgledy-piggledy street patterns of shaded, narrow lanes and alleys widening and constricting again for no apparent reason, and often stepped or ribbed to prevent pedestrians and pack-mules slipping on a frosty day. Smaller villages will have only one road in and out; in other directions they peter out into intriguing-looking paths which wander past disused threshing floors.

Traditionally, the houses of the Alpujarras were built using the materials available close to home, and those that have not been mod-

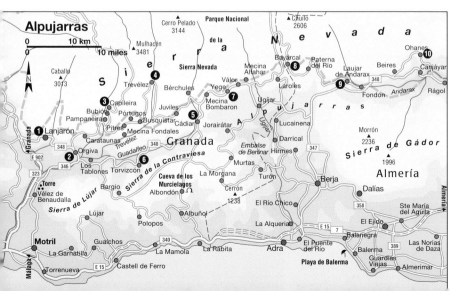

ernised with brick, aluminium and double-glazed windows still blend harmoniously into the landscape. Older houses usually consist of two storeys: the upper one for human habitation, the ground floor for livestock and farming equipment. The flat roof, supported by chestnut beams and spread with *launa,* an impermeable gravel of decomposed slate, served as a place for hanging out the washing, the line being attached to the tall, white chimney.

A circuit of the Alpujarras

A circuit of the Alpujarras looks fairly short on the map, but the roads are steep and winding, so progress is slow. You will need a full day to tour the area, and at least one overnight stay if you want to enjoy some walking *(see below).*

The point of access coming from Granada is the spa of **Lanjarón ❶**, which has turned its spring water into one Spain's most popular bottled brands. It is also a serious health spa with extensive facilities. Its one monument – the ruins of a Moorish castle on a rock adrift

from the rest of Lanjarón – can be seen from the ring-road around the bottom of town.

From here, the road descends into **Orgiva ❷**, the main shopping and service town of the western Alpujarras, and again there is no intrinsic charm making it worth a stop. Best to turn left at the crossroads before you enter the town, and take the main road through the Alpujarras towards Trevélez and Pitres.

From this point the road climbs inexorably, passing by two typical Alpujarran villages, Carataunas and Soportújar. Beyond them you reach a pass from which a narrow road takes off to the left. It may be the last thing you expect to find, but 7 km (4½ miles) along this side road and up a dirt track is a Buddhist meditation and retreat centre, **O Sel Ling**, which is open to visitors for three hours (3–6pm) every afternoon. In 1986, the fifth son of two of the pioneers of O Sel Ling made international headlines when he was declared to be the new embodiment of the late Lama Yeshe – one of very few Westerners to be acknowledged

Map on page 206

Wine for sale in Lanjarón. The fruity red wine of the area is drunk young and unbottled.

LEFT:
hilly but heavenly, the Alpujarras is a great area for walking.

Walking Country

To really experience the Alpujarras fully you need to stop the car and take to the footpaths and mule tracks – usually centuries old and sometimes stone-paved – that wind around the terraces, connecting the villages and hamlets. Such paths are not always signposted or clearly marked on maps, but at least there is usually abundant shade and water available en route while you sit down and think which way to go. Spring and early summer are exceptionally pretty times for being outdoors here because of the abundant wild flowers.

If you want to be safe and do some serious walking there are two long-distance paths through the Alpujarras – the GR7 (or E4, the so-called "Mediterranean Arc" running from Greece to Tarifa) crosses the southern flank of the Sierra Nevada in seven daily stages, and the GR142 will take you around the whole area in 13 days. The GR140 crosses the Almerian Alpujarras. Despite the gradients, the Alpujarras are good cycling country too.

Even if you don't want to walk too far, you can find much of interest in and around the villages.

by Tibetan Buddhism to be a re-incarnated spiritual master.

Poqueira and Trevélez

Continuing on from here, the main road suddenly rounds a corner and enters the deep ravine of the **Barranco de Poqueira**, the most scenic and most visited part of the Alpujarras. It contains three villages spaced out on the south-facing hillside. The first (the lowest of the three) is **Pampaneira**, at the entrance to which a sign welcomes you with an invitation to stop and live here. Assuming you don't do that, you can enjoy a view of the flat, gravel-spread roofs and hobbitish chimneys as you pass above the village.

As the road climbs out of the valley, there is a detour to the left leading to the two higher villages of **Bubión** and **Capileira** , the latter perhaps the best-kept and most typical of all those in the Alpujarras. Although the road continues past Capileira and over the top of the Sierra Nevada, descending past the ski resort on the other side *(see page 198)*, it is closed to traffic. You can,

Pony-trekking is another exhilarating way of exploring the Alpujarras. Look out for signs in the main villages, such as this one in Bubión, or enquire at any of the tourist offices.

BELOW: Bubión.

however, take a minibus from the **Sierra Nevada National Park** visitors' centre above Capileira to the higher slopes.

The main road through the Alpujarras continues beyond the Bubión and Capileira turn-off and across the Barranco de la Sangre (the "Valley of Blood"), named after a battle that was fought here during the *Morisco* rebellion.

Down the slope are two pretty villages to explore, **Mecina Fondales** and **Ferreirola**. The road passes through the towns of **Pitres**, **Pórtugos** (just after which there is a spring flowing with rusty-coloured, iron-rich water) and **Busquistar**, before swinging into a large, almost uninhabited valley at the head of which, on the lower slopes of Mt Mulhacén, stands **Trevélez** . The highest village in Spain, sited at 1,476 m (4,843 ft), it puts its altitude to good use for the dry-curing of hams known throughout Andalucía. But don't expect to see any pigs here. The pork shoulders are imported from elsewhere to hang in the curing cellars at the bottom of the village, where they acquire their distinctive flavour and the privilege of being called Jamón de Trevélez. Although the lower part of this village seems like one big tourist shop, the two upper parts *(barrios)* are attractive.

Sierra de la Contraviesa

Shortly after Trevélez, the road passes above what looks like another typical Alpujarran village but is actually a hotel modelled to look like one, complete with a dummy church tower. Round the next corner and the best scenery, the prettiest villages and most of the tourists have been left behind. You can make a round trip back to Orgiva by turning right after Juviles and Bérchules and heading downhill to the undistinguished **Cádiar ⑤**, on the valley floor. From here, take the road towards the coast and turn off onto the minor road that follows the ridge of the Sierra de la Contraviesa through high-altitude vineyards before descending to the small town of **Torvizcón ⑥**, where fruity red wines (known as "Costa"

wine) are made to be drunk unbottled, still young. Along the valley from here is Orgiva.

Yegen

If, on the other hand, you are determined to travel through the Alpujarras all the way to Almería – or if you have an interest in literary connections – keep to the high road after Bérchules. Most of the villages in the eastern Alpujarras have lost their charm to the cult of indiscriminate home improvement using modern materials. One such village, however, stands out from the rest because of its reputation – although it would be easy to drive through it without realising that it is known to Hispanophiles everywhere.

It was to **Yegen ⑦** that the young Gerald Brenan made his way, along with his considerable book collection, to get some reading done after two years' active service on the Western Front during World War I. Disappointingly, Brenan's adopted village has all but forgotten him. Few of the locals will tell you with any confidence where he lived, even

Map on page 206

You can order serrano ham in any bar in Granada (or elsewhere in Spain), but somehow it tastes better in Trevélez.

BELOW: the main square, Trevélez.

Colourful cotton rugs are some of the rustic crafts on sale in the Alpujarras. Others include leatherwork and ceramics.

though the house is not at all tricky to find. Privately owned and not open to visitors, it is just below the square in which stands a reproduction of the Alhambra's Patio de los Leones. A plaque on the wall recalls the man who put this otherwise nondescript town on the international map.

Brenan's account of the periods he spent in Yegen between 1920 and 1934, *South from Granada*, became a classic travel book. While in Yegen he was visited by some of his literary friends from Britain, including Virginia Woolf and Lytton Strachey, who found that too much olive oil caused him indigestion and muleback riding exacerbated his piles.

During his time in Yegen, Brenan fathered an illegitimate child by a village girl, but rather than settle down with her, he married an American poetess. After periods back in Britain, he eventually settled permanently in southern Spain, and died near Málaga.

Moriscos and Moors

After Yegen, the road climbs through the last settlements of Granada

province, including **Válor**. This was the birthplace of Don Fernando de Córdoba y Válor, a nobleman descended from the caliphs of Córdoba. On 24 December 1568 he reclaimed his ancestral Muslim religion under the name of Ibn Umayya (or Aben Humeya), and was crowned "King of Córdoba and Granada" by his fellow *Moriscos*, who were by now in open revolt against the repression ordered by Felipe II in Madrid. Less than a year later, in October 1569, Ibn Umayya was assassinated, almost certainly by his own followers but the revolt went on without him for almost two more years.

By coincidence rather than because of all this, in mid-September Válor celebrates the most well-known of the Alpujarras' many festivals of Moros y Cristianos (Moors and Christians) – ritualised mock battles and negotiations in which the Muslims at first gain the upper hand but are finally "persuaded" to convert to Christianity. Although it nominally celebrates the Christians' final ascendancy in Spain's wars of religion, like similar fiestas else-

Map on page 206

where, it is really no more than an excuse for the populace to dress up and have fun.

Beyond **Laroles**, which has a fine 16th-century domed bell-tower, is the provincial border between Granada and Almería. **Bayarcal** ❽ is the first village on the other side. It stands above a rocky valley and below the Puerto de la Ragua, a pass across the Sierra Nevada and a popular spot for cross-country skiing.

The Almerian Alpujarras

From here the road drops down into the tamer, drier landscapes of the Almerian Alpujarras to enter the sprawling **Laujar de Andarax** ❾, which was the last toehold in Spain of Boabdil "the Unlucky", ex-ruler of Muslim Granada before he was forced into permanent exile in Africa. Although the modern town is something of a mess, serving as a destination for school trips and excursions by city-dwellers, it does have a handsome Mudéjar church in the centre, and a town hall built of three levels of brick arches standing on the main square.

Beyond Laujar is a succession of low-altitude Alpujarran towns of which **Fondón**, the first, is the most interesting. Here the *Morisco* rebellion was ostensibly brought to an end in 1570 by a peace supposedly signed between Don Juan de Austria, half-brother and emissary of Felipe II, and Ibn Umayya's successor, his cousin Abén Aboo. The latter, however, went on fighting, moving from cave to cave until he was assassinated in March 1571. The Moriscos were finally expelled from Spain in 1609.

Already, there are signs of the arid landscapes so characteristic of Almería, even if they are spruced up here and there by the occasional vineyard or citrus orchard. The remaining towns and villages are of only passing interest, but one of them is worth making a detour to see. Halfway up a great mountain slope, and on the road to nowhere, is **Ohanes** ❿, known for its sweet table grapes, its small centre a pleasant complex of narrow streets and whitewashed houses – in all, a suitable souvenir of the best of the Alpujarras. ❏

RESTAURANTS & BARS

Restaurants

Capileira

Casa Ibero
Parra, 1
Tel: 958-763 256
L & D. Closed Sun evening and Mon. No cards. €
No-frills establishment offering innovative Moroccan-inspired dishes at low prices.

Fondón

Camping Puente Colgante
Camino Benecid, s/n
Tel: 950-514 291. L & D. €
Restaurant attached to the campsite below the town, next to the river. Tasty *menu del día*.

Mecina Fondales

L'Atelier
Calle Alberca, 21
Tel: 958-857 501. L & D. €
A cosy vegetarian/vegan restaurant and guest-house in a converted village house. The owner chef, Jean-Claude Juston, ran successful restaurants in London

before moving to the Alpujarras, where he also runs cookery courses.

Pitres

Balcón de Pitres
Tel: 958-766 111. L & D. €
Part of a campsite and cabin complex with panoramic views. The restaurant stands beside a curvy swimming pool, which is open to the public.

Puerto de la Ragua

Posada de los Arrieros
Tel:950-524 001. L & D. €€
A restaurant and 12-room hotel on the way up

to the Puerto de la Ragua from Bayarcal, and on the GR7 long-distance footpath. Typical Alpujarreno food served.

Trevélez

Mesón La Fragua
Barrio Medio
Tel: 958-858 573. L & D. €
Fine views from the upstairs dining room.

• • • • • • • • • • • • •
Price includes dinner and a glass of wine, excluding tip.
€€€€ €40 and up, €€€ under €40, €€ under €30, € under €20.

ALMERÍA AND ITS PROVINCE

Spain's sun-rich southeastern province is a region of
stark desert landscapes concealing some
surprising beauty spots and providing some
unconventional science lessons

lmería is Mediterranean Spain
in the raw; a land governed by
the sun, and home of Europe's
only desert. The attractions here
may not at first be obvious, but they
are surprisingly numerous, however
often you have to endure drab, dusty
kilometres through what the British
travel writer Rose Macaulay called
the "burnt, cactus-sharp, breathless
sprawl of hills" between them.

Such a tough terrain takes a little
more effort to explore than the other
provinces of Andalucía, and the joy
of touring here lies not in long
scenic drives – although there are
some stretches of untamed, lonely
grandeur to enjoy – but in stumbling
upon unexpected oases of interest.
The best of these are an education in
the enjoyable sense of the word, and
a tour around Almería could almost
be seen as a do-it-yourself geogra-
phy-and-science field trip.

Fall and rise

Of all the provinces of Spain,
Almería has arguably had the most
historical ups and downs. In the
Copper Age it had the most ad-
vanced civilisation in western
Europe, but its next period of glory
wasn't until after the arrival of the
Muslims in Spain, when the Caliph
of al-Andalus founded the port of
Almería as one of his principal life-

lines with the east to trade on equal
terms with the famous Alexandria.
Even when the Caliphate disintegrated, Almería kept its head held up
as one of the *taifas*, or splinter kingdoms, into which Spain was divided.

But the Christian Reconquest of
Spain at the end of the 15th century
heralded a change in the times. The
new rulers turned their gaze west-
ward to the riches available across
the Atlantic, leaving Almería, still
looking unfashionably east, to lan-
guish as a redundant limb of the

Map
on page
214

LEFT: lighthouse in the
Parque Nacional de
Cabo de Gata.
BELOW: the Alcazaba,
Almería.

Road to somewhere. These days booming Almería is well connected with the rest of Andalucía.

empire. The province fell into obscurity and rural poverty – despite a brief recovery in the 19th century based on mining and the export of grapes – so much so that even the proudest inhabitants would reluctantly admit that there was some truth in its cruel nickname, "*el culo de España*": "the backside of Spain". The Civil War and post-war periods further exacerbated the decline, and countless migrants departed from Almería in search of work in northern Spain or abroad.

But then, in the 1970s, two economic miracles took hold, and in starkly contrasting ways Almería began to turn its biggest resource, sun power, into gold. While poor migrants were heading one way out of hardship, tourists started to head the other way for pleasure, and parts of Almería's coast began to develop as an overspill of the Costa del Sol.

More significantly, Almería's warm winter temperatures were

found to be ideal for a peculiar system of agriculture which could meet the needs of growing consumerism in northern Europe (*see page 216*).

It was largely this agricultural revolution which turned Almería's fortunes around: in a decade or so, the province went from being the poorest in Andalucía to being one of the richest in Spain. But a heavy price was paid, and is still being paid, in the spoiling of the landscape – although to anyone who remembers the times when there was no work, or whose parents or grandparents were forced to emigrate, this is not an important consideration.

Shrink-wrapped shoreline

Production figures suggest that the greenhouse boom has passed its peak and ceded to North Africa, where labour is cheaper than in Europe. But there are few signs of this in the so-called "Costa del Plástico", more properly called the

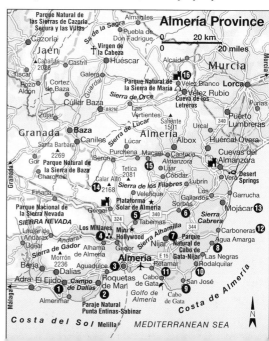

Campo de Dalias, which bulges out into the sea from the foothills of the Sierra de Gádor. When Gerald Brenan first passed by here in the 1920s, he complained of "a delta of stone and rubble… it might have been the wilderness of Sinai", without a single house or tree. On his return in the 1950s, he found that underground springs had been tapped to irrigate fields of corn and fruit orchards.

It is hard to believe that this intensively farmed, semi-industrialised strip of coastal plain was ever considered infertile. Presiding over its economic empire is **El Ejido ❶**, a town that mushroomed overnight from being unmarked on most maps to having the second-largest urban population in the province – and a bank for every 1,500 inhabitants.

On the coast, meanwhile, there is just space between the greenhouses for two high-rise resorts, **Aguadulce** and **Roquetas del Mar ❷**, and the smaller **Almerimar**, where you can take a break from the beach and learn about the methods of modern greenhouse farming from one of its leading exponents – Clisol (tel: 620-843

385). The only relief from hot holidaymakers and hothouses is provided by the **Paraje Natural Punta Entinas-Sabinar**, a wetland protected from development on behalf of its birdlife.

The port and its protector

The city of **Almería ❸**, over a small range of hills to the east, comes almost as a relief after the shrink-wrapped plains. It has grown since Brenan came upon it as "a bucket of whitewash thrown down at the foot of a bare, greyish mountain", although its growth is still hemmed in by the steepness of the bone-dry slopes behind it. If it gets little rain, it gets lots of sunshine, claiming to have more hours (3,217 on average) than any city in Europe.

Even if both its location and flavour make it a resolutely Mediterranean city, it hardly seems aware of its own shoreline, preferring to let the commercial and passenger port block the best sea views. Indeed, the city's most conspicuous monument is a piece of intrusive quayside equipment, the **Cable Inglés,** a rail-

Map on page 214

TIP

For more information on the wildlife of the Cabo de Gata, *see page 56.*

BELOW: Almería is an upbeat city with a thriving port.

Plastic Agriculture

Until a few decades ago, the pattern of Andalucía's agriculture was dictated solely by tradition. Farmers grew the crops which their forebears had always grown, largely for their own or local consumption, using centuries-old methods.

Then, in the late 20th century, came improved communications with the rest of Spain and Europe, and the prospect of profits from the consumer economy. Now supermarket buyers in distant countries indirectly decide what is grown in large parts of Andalucía.

Nowhere is the trend more obvious than in Almería, which has led the way in a new style of get-rich-quick farming since the 1970s. Back then, the idea seemed nothing short of revolutionary to farmers used to a subsistence living. If winter temperatures could be kept above a particular, critical level, it was proposed, then delicate summer fruit and vegetable plants could be forced to crop in December and January to feed the whims of northern European shoppers.

Whole swathes of the province consequently disappeared under plastic greenhouses whose purpose was to coddle the tomato or melon plants, giving them those few vital extra degrees of warmth above the outside temperature without the need for artificial heating. Not only was it apparent that Almería could beat the seasons: land cultivated under plastic proved to be five times at least productive than the same land left exposed to the weather.

The result of the greenhouse miracle was spectacular. What was once Andalucía's poorest province became its wealthiest. The unofficial capital of the industry, El Ejido, rose from obscurity to a financial services centre almost overnight. Fortunes were made not only by enterprising smallholders and venture capitalists but also by a vast ancillary industry that was needed to supply polyethylene sheeting, pipes, wires, fertilisers – and cars and other luxury goods for the nouveaux riches to spend their money on.

Some of the greenhouses are run as hi-tech concerns with plants grown hydroponically and farmers dressed in white coats watching computer screens rather than the weather. Others are more conventional, low-key market gardens, providing employment for a family of four or five people who work hard from autumn to spring and rest during the summer, when midday temperatures under plastic would cause a human to faint.

But while money was being made, the landscape was being smothered. It is estimated that around 3 per cent of the surface of Almería is now farmed in this way. Across the whole of southern Spain, plastic covers land equivalent to an area the size of Ibiza.

Critics of the "plastic farming" complain of the lack of planning, the strain on the watertable and the excessive use of chemicals – pests and diseases, too, flourish in frost-free winter gardens – and the pollution that their disposal causes. But as Spanish agriculture elsewhere has slipped into crisis, most people in Almería believe the gains far outweigh the costs. However, there are signs that the boom may be ending, as southern Spain now has competition from the countries of North Africa, which are almost as close to the markets of northern Europe but have a fraction of the labour costs. ❑

LEFT: plastic dominates parts of the coastal plain.

way pier which was formerly used for loading ore onto ships but now stands preserved as a dark, dense, satanic hulk.

Looming proudly over the port and the huddle of flat-roofed houses which form the old part of town is the great fortress of the **Alcazaba** (Tue–Sun; admission charge), built by Abd-al-Rahman III, first Caliph of al-Andalus, to protect the walled trading settlement that stretched from the castle walls to the sea. It's a short, easy climb from the old town to the gateway of the fortress, and once inside you continue climbing through three enclosures, the first being a garden, the last a Christian castle planted as an indestructible victory pennant on the highest point of the Muslim city.

As you ascend, there are views over the city, port and coast. From the second enclosure you can look down on the **Centro Rescate de la Fauna Sahariana** (Centre for the Rescue of Saharan Fauna; visit by permit only; am only), a research station whose purpose is to nurture breeding stocks of the endangered gazelles of the western Sahara.

Almería's Cathedral

Back down below in the city centre, which gradually smartens towards the broad, shady 19th-century **Paseo de Almería**, there are few monuments worth the trouble of seeking out. The Plaza Vieja or Plaza de la Constitución is a pleasant assembly of buildings, however, and the 16th-century **Cathedral** (closed Sat pm and Sun; admission charge) is unavoidable because of its bulk – it was built with defence in mind against attacks by pirates and rebel Muslims. Its bulky golden exterior largely belies the graceful vaulting and superb wood carving of the choir inside, although on one outside wall is a delightful reminder of Almería's interest in all things solar: the Sol de Portocarrero, a carved personified sun named after the 16th-century bishop who commissioned it. In the side chapels you will find paintings by Ribera, Murillo and Alonso Cano.

At night the city centre comes alive; as bars and cafés take over the narrow streets and alleys in the triangle roughly marked by the Puerta

Map on page 214

A characteristic Madonna wreathed in clouds and cherubs by Murillo in Almería's Cathedral.

BELOW:
Almería's Cathedral.

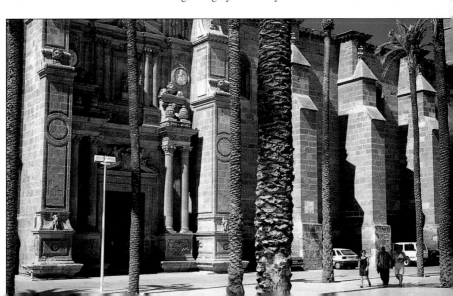

de Purchena, the Cathedral and the top end of Plaza Marqués Heredia. Almería has a famous tradition of tapas; as in Granada, one comes included in the price of each glass of beer or wine.

From copper to celluloid

Until the building of the Alcazaba, the omphalos of Almería was a short way inland, in the corridor between the Sierra de Gádor and the Sierra Alhamilla. The walled Copper Age settlement **Los Millares ④** (closed Mon and Tues), between a gulley and the Río Andarax, near Santa Fe de Mondújar, could be said to be one of the prehistoric cradles of Europe, as it was occupied from around 2700 to 1800 BC by the first community in the western Mediterranean to work metals. Of particular archaeological importance is the necropolis, with a hundred collective tombs of which one has been restored.

The road beyond Los Millares, following the Río Andarax, leads into the fertile valleys of the Alpujarras (*see page 205–211*). Going in the opposite direction, around the

back of the Sierra Alhamilla, you enter the desert of Tabernas. With so much of Almería being parched and uncultivated it is often hard to tell where the desert technically begins and ends (there are no sand dunes to spell it out), but the bald hills, badlands and dry ravines were close enough to the archetypal deserts of North America to draw the Italian film-maker Sergio Leone here to shoot his "spaghetti westerns".

Tabernas ⑤ probably never had much glamour as the low-budget Hollywood it likes to pretend it used to be, but three of the former western sets have been saved for posterity and are commercially run as tourist attractions in continuance of the western theme. The most developed of them is **Mini Hollywood** (daily, admission charge), the former fake frontier town of El Fraile, to which a zoo and swimming pool have been attached.

On the other side of Tabernas is something not of past but present and future importance. The **Plataforma Solar de Almería** (visits by appointment Wed and Thur am, tel: 950-387 900) is a long-running research project into the use of solar power as a source of unlimited energy. The first banks of reflectors concentrating the sun's rays onto a receiving dish at the top of a white tower were set up in the 1970s in response to the first oil crisis, but only recently has the technology become sufficiently effective to lead to Europe's first viable solar power station.

Karst landscape

The desert scenery continues to the coast, but halfway there it is punctuated by a beauty spot sunk out of sight amid the threadbare hills. This is an area called the **Yesos de Sorbas**, an instance of karst scenery formed not by chalk, as is more common, but by gypsum. There is a visitors' centre to explain the features of gypsum

TIP

Almería is famed for its generous – and free – tapas, which are served with every glass of wine or beer you take in a bar, the portions becoming more generous and scrumptious the more you drink.

BELOW: Café La Rambla, Almería, a typical café-bar.

karst at **Sorbas** ❻, a town built above a gorge-cum-river meander. To see the karst landscapes you can either start a 38-km (24-mile) hike from the visitors' centre or take the winding minor road to the hamlet of **Los Molinos del Río Aguas**, park there and walk up and down the valley of the Río Aguas ("Waters River") – ask for a map at the Sorbas centre. Los Molinos is also home to Sunseed, a charity run by volunteers pioneering low-cost technologies for poor communities living in semi-arid environments in developing countries.

Caves are typical of karst scenery, and the **Cuevas de Sorbas** have been opened for visitors (on the hour every hour, but by prior reservation only; tel: 950-364 704; loose clothing and appropriate shoes essential) who are willing to forgo concrete paths and electric lighting in favour of cave helmets and miners' lamps.

Desert cape

On the east coast of Almería, the desert meets the sea in the bewitching landscapes of the **Parque Natural Cabo de Gata-Nijar**. The town of **Nijar** ❼ is something of an incongruous ally in this nature reserve. It stands inland, above the motorway to Murcia, overlooking a valley of plastic greenhouses, and is only worth visiting for its craft shops and working potteries.

More because of its topography than conscientious planning restrictions, the coast from Agua Amarga to the cape (*cabo*) has not been spoilt by tourism. **Agua Amarga** ❽ is a small, pleasant resort with a sandy beach squeezed between two headlands and streets that peter out into dirt tracks on the settlement's edges. **San José** ❾, to the south, is larger and more developed, but still in proportion to its surroundings. Between these two the coast is only sporadically accessible by surface road and there are empty beaches if you are prepared to walk to them. Halfway along this stretch of coast is **Rodalquilar** ❿ and its eerily disused gold mines, which had been worked to the point of unprofitability by the end of the 1960s.

The Cabo de Gata proper, one of the Iberian Peninsula's few volcanic

Map on page 214

Nijar is known for its working potteries and attendant ceramics shops.

BELOW: the Wild West at Mini Hollywood.

Ancient Caves

Twenty thousand years ago, human beings dipped their fingers in ochre and traced the outlines of fish and deer on cave walls in southern Spain. Today, evidence of these early cave-dwellers is still coming to light. Indeed, archaeologists have a difficult time keeping up with the past. Almost daily, a plough or a bulldozer uncovers traces of early human endeavour.

Finds that reach the hands of the archaeologists throw essential light on prehistoric man. One discovery occurred in the cave of the Boquete de Zafarraya, on the border of Málaga and Granada provinces, where investigators' torches revealed the large bones and lower jawbone of a Neanderthal man, possibly dating back 85,000 years. Other traces of Neanderthal occupation have turned up in caves at Piñar (Granada), Vera (Almería) and on the Rock of Gibraltar.

There are abundant indications that, as the last Ice Age receded (around 40,000 years ago), Cro-Magnon man took up residence in Andalusian caves. Regarded as our direct ancestor, he was an artist, used tools and was skilled in hunting. Arrow and spear heads and other evidence of his presence

have been found in the Almerian caves of Zájara at Vera, and Ambrosio at Vélez Blanco.

Evidence of religious rites is common. Near Vélez Blanco in Almería province, the Cueva de los Letreros shelters prehistoric inscriptions that include the Indalo, depicting a man holding an arc over his head. This symbol was long believed to ward off the "evil eye" and it has been chosen by Almería's artists to represent the province.

One significant discovery occurred on 12 January 1959, when five boys playing on a hillside near the hamlet of Maro, in Málaga province, came across an immense grotto, now known as the Cuevas de Nerja (see page 147). Investigators found evidence that it was inhabited at least 15,000 years ago, and that it had also been used as a burial chamber. Remains of shellfish and the bones of goats and rabbits have been found, as well as wall paintings depicting deer, horses and fishes. Drawings representing a female deity and red-painted pebbles indicated that religious rites had taken place.

Another fascinating cave to visit is La Pileta (see page 120) near Ronda, where limestone galleries scoured out millennia ago by an underground river provided shelter for man as long ago as the Upper Palaeolithic period, when he daubed the image of a stag's head on a wall. La Pileta was discovered in 1905 when José Bullón Lobato, whose family still owns the cave, was searching for guano (bird droppings) to fertilise his land. Seeing a large hole, he let himself down 30 metres (100 ft) by rope into a chamber. Penetrating further, he noted human remains and wall-paintings. Later exploration turned up human skeletons, silex (fused quartz), bones, stone tools and ceramics from the Neolithic period.

Some caves had been known about for centuries, but for one reason or another were not fully explored. This was the case with the Aracena cave in Huelva province, which was flooded until the early 20th century. When the water was pumped out, dazzling stalactites and stalagmites formations were revealved, now known as the Gruta de las Maravillas (the Grotto of the Marvels). ❏

LEFT: there are extensive cave systems in southern Spain, thanks to its karst and limestone.

landscapes, is best approached from San José. You can drive down a dirt track to two beautiful un-built-up beaches – **Playa de los Genoveses** and **Playa de Monsul**, setting for a scene in *Indiana Jones and the Last Crusade* – but thereafter you can only follow the track by foot as it continues around the cliffs to the cape.

To get to the cape by car, you have to approach it from the Almería side by way of the village of **San Miguel de Cabo de Gata ⑪**, beyond which a long flat road follows the beach and passes salt pans visited by flamingos before climbing steeply up to the lighthouse to meet the end of the track from San José.

Cartoon capers

Going the other way from Agua Amarga it is a different story. After climbing over the headland encouragingly named Punta de los Muertos ("Dead Men's Point") you plunge into a strip of modern mass tourism beginning with **Carboneras ⑫**, named after the old charcoal-burning industry which thrived here until all the available trees had been cut

down. This curious town combines a magnificent broad sandy beaches with a cement works, desalination plant and power station whose chimney spoils the view for miles around.

A belt of steep hills to the north of Carboneras has so far inhibited the apartment blocks, hotels, shops and restaurants from becoming a continuous sprawl down the coast of Almería, but they resume once you descend to the coast south of Mojácar. The village of **Mojácar ⑬**, itself, however, is geographically and metaphorically raised above the excesses of the coast, a cluster of white cubic buildings amongst which you can never be sure where tradition ends and make-believe begins. According to a local rumour, which some old-timers treat as fact, Mojácar was the real birthplace of Walt Disney (under the name of José Guirao), not Chicago as reference books state; despite investigations, no link has ever been proved.

Marble mountains

Of the several mountain ranges that stride west to east across Almería, the

The more remote beaches on the Cabo de Gata do not have facilities such as sunbeds and parasols. As the beaches are exposed, you are advised to bring your own.

BELOW: San José.

Map on page 214

Vera, north of Mojácar, has Spain's first official nudist hotel, the Vera Playa Club. It operates a strict non-dress code: nudism is obligatory around the pool during the day, but prohibited in the evening and in the restaurant.

BELOW: off the east coast of Almería.

highest and most impressive is the Sierra de los Filabres, which for 60 km (37 miles) reduces the choice of north–south route to two roads. One of these crosses the chain from Tabernas to Macael, over a 1,247-metre (4,091-ft) pass, and serves a group of villages including the bellicose Líjar, which waged its own non-violent hundred years war with France.

The other route, between Gérgal and Serón, goes even higher (1,970 metres/6,464 ft) and leads almost past the door of the Hispano-German observatory at **Calar Alto** ⑭ (2,168 metres/6,937 ft; visits on Wed by prior arrangement, tel: 950-632 500). Both these roads lead down into the Almanzora valley, where everything seems to be coated in marble dust. Spain's marble industry has its headquarters at **Macael** ⑮, which supplied the stone for the Alhambra and the Mosque at Córdoba.

Los Vélez

In the far north of the province, across yet another mountain range, the Sierra de las Estancias, and the Murcia–Granada motorway, is the district of Los Vélez, dominated by a double act of towns, Vélez Blanco and Vélez Rubio. The epithets "White" and "Blond" are thought to have been bestowed on them by the Muslims, who were referring to the colours of the local earth. By far the more interesting is **Vélez Blanco** ⑯, which has an improbably tall 16th-century Renaissance castle, still handsome even if it has been reduced to a shell by the removal of its magnificent patio to the Metropolitan Museum in New York.

Near the town is the Cueva de los Letreros, which is more than just another rock shelter decorated by prehistoric artists. Here was found the drawing which has become the symbol of Almería, a stick figure of an ancestral god holding aloft a rainbow. He was christened the Indalo after St Indaletius, an apocryphal preacher supposedly dispatched by the Apostles to evangelise Almería in the 1st century AD, and is to be seen everywhere in the province, on banks, street signs and trucks, a sign of local pride and bringer of good luck. ❑

RESTAURANTS & BARS

Restaurants

Almería City

Amarga Sound Café
Plaza Marqués Heredia 7
(no phone)
B, L & D. €
The best place for breakfast in the city. At other times of day tapas are available. Sit inside or outside on the square.

Bellavista
Urb Bellavista, Llanos del Alquian
Tel: 950-297 156
L & D, closed Sun evening and Mon. €€
Almería's best restaurant is in drab surroundings 7km (4½ miles) from the city centre (take the motorway towards the airport and turn off at the Viator exit). The menu, strong on fish and seafood, changes daily.

Club de Mar
Muelle de las Almadrabillas, s/n
Tel: 950-235 048
L & D. €€€
Within Almería's yacht club and near the beach, this classic restaurant has built a solid reputation on its fresh seafood.

La Gruta
Ctra N340 km 436
Tel: 950-239 335
D only. Closed Sun and Nov. €€
Unusual setting, inside a cave overlooking the sea between Almería and Aguadulce. Grilled meat is the speciality.

Veracruz
Jaun 10
Tel: 950-251 220
L & D. €€
Near the beach in Almería, specialising in seafood.

Almerimar

Club Naútico
Puerto Deportivo, Dársena 1
Tel: 950-497 162
L & D. €€
There are great views of the marina through the windows of this yacht club restaurant. Rice and fish dominate the menu, and vegetables are from the restaurant's own greenhouses.

Garrucha

El Almejero
Explanada del Puerto, s/n.
Tel: 950-460 405
L & D. Closed Mon and Nov. €€
Dine on fresh fish and prawns on the terrace overlooking the fishing port where the catch is unloaded.

Huercal-Overa

Ballabona
Autovía del Mediterráneo
(N340/E15) km 543
Tel 950-134 902. €
Not many motorway service areas are recommendable, but this one is worth pulling in for. In the cool, spacious dining room a very reasonably priced menú del día is served including good fish. Also a hotel.

Instinción

La Kabila
C/ Ejido s/n. L & D.
Tel: 950-601 802
This unusual place mixes Alpujarran with Middle Eastern influences (there is an Arabic tea shop). It is also a hotel with 11 simple but welcoming rooms.

Lucainena de las Torres

Venta El Museo
Plaza Maestro Paco
Tel: 950-36 42 00. L & D. €
A pair of restaurants in the Sierra de Alhamilla, between Sorbas and Nijar. The main restaurant serves rustic dishes, such as meaty stews; the other is for gourmet cuisine. They share a well-stocked cellar. The Venta is also a hotel.

Mojácar

Casa Juana
Calle Enmedio, 27
Tel: 950-478 009
L & D. Closed Wed & Jan. €€€
In a renovated village house in the centre of Mojácar, this cosy and stylish restaurant serves Spanish dishes with a French touch.

El Palacio
Plaza del Cano, 3
Tel: 950-472 846
L & D. Closed Wed and winter. €€
Imaginative local and international dishes, in a Mojácar house.

Roquetas de Mar

Albaida
Avenida de las Gaviotas, 94
Tel: 950-333 821
L & D. Closed Wed, Jan. €€
Excellent fresh seafood.

San José

La Chumbera
Paraje Los Ventorrillos
950 168 321. €€€
Agua Amarga's best restaurant serving a creative variation of Andaluz cuisine. Reservation essential.

Mesón El Tempranillo
Puerto Deportivo 6-7
Tel: 950 380 206. Closed Nov. €
Restaurant in San José's marina specialising in fresh fish, seafood and rice dishes but also offers pork and lamb.

Vera

Terraza Carmona
Manuel Giménez 1
Tel: 950-390 760
L & D. Closed Mon and mid-Jan. €€
This long-established restaurant offers a good combination of local dishes (mainly fish) as well as international fare in a bustling atmosphere.

PRICE CATEGORIES

Prices for three-course meal per person with a half-bottle of house wine:
€= under €20
€€ = €20–€40
€€€ = €40–€60
€€€€= over €60

TRANSPORT

GETTING THERE AND GETTING AROUND

GETTING THERE

By Air

Southern Spain has frequent air links with the rest of Europe and North Africa and is within 2½ hours' flying time of London. Most transatlantic flights operate via Madrid.

Málaga and Seville airports have daily scheduled connections with international destinations. **Iberia** (www.iberia.com; UK tel: 0845 6012854) and **British Airways** (www.britishairways.com; UK tel: 0870 8509850), often operating with its franchise partner GB Airways, offer the most comprehensive service. British Airways also flies to Jerez de la Frontera.

In addition, several **budget airlines** operate flights to Southern Spain. **easyJet** (www.easyjet.com; UK tel: 0871 759 0100) flies to Málaga from London Stansted. **Monarch** (www.flymonarch.com; UK tel: 0870 0405040) flies to Almería from Birmingham and Manchester, Granada from London Gatwick, and Málaga from several UK airports. **Ryan Air** (www.ryanair.com; UK tel: 0871 246 0000) flies to Seville from London Stansted and Liverpool, Jerez from London Stansted, Almería from London Stansted, and

Granada from London Stansted and Liverpool. Large numbers of visitors also arrive by charter flights.

Gibraltar, serviced by GB Airways (www.gbairways.com; UK tel: 0870 850 9850), is another good point of entry, especially for the Cádiz area.

On arrival

Airport porters have set charges, often displayed, for handling baggage. Trolleys are available in bigger airports. For transport from the airport see *Airport Transfer* under Getting Around.

By Sea

Other than cruise liners, the only sea passages between the UK and Spain are from Portsmouth to Bilbao and Plymouth to Santander, both in northern Spain. These services are operated by **Brittany Ferries** (www.brittanyferries.com; UK tel: 08705 360 360).

Trasmediterranea vessels, carrying passengers and vehicles, ply the routes between Almería, Málaga, Algeciras and Cádiz, and ports on the African coast and on the Canary Islands (www.trasmediterranea.es).

There are frequent services across the Straits of Gibraltar, both by ferries and hydrofoils, from Algeciras to the Spanish

enclave of Ceuta and/or Tangier in Morocco (a popular day-trip). A small number of hydrofoils also operate from Tarifa (just west of Algeciras), but only for EU passport-holders.

By Rail

Rail travel to Spain from other European countries can be organised through **Rail Europe** (www.raileurope.com; UK tel: 08705 186 186), which offers a variety of saver passes for different periods of travel, as well as for senior citizens and under-25s.

AVE and Talgo

Rail services in Spain are operated by RENFE). It operates a range of different trains, the fastest of which is **AVE**. This high-speed rail service links Seville to Madrid in 2½ hours (some trains also stop in Córdoba). An AVE link to Málaga is due to open in 2007, which will reduce the Madrid–Málaga run to 2 hours 15 minutes (2½ hours on stopping trains).

The special AVE track is also used on other services, such as the Madrid–Málaga **Talgo**, which is also fast and very comfortable. AVE and Talgo services are best booked in advance.

Timetables and reservations are available through the RENFE website (www.renfe.es/ingles).

ABOVE: the open road, Almería. The road network in southern Spain has improved dramatically in recent years.

By Road

Road access to Andalucía has improved dramatically in recent years, as part of a massive expansion of the motorway system throughout Spain. It is now possible to drive on four-lane highways virtually all the way from the French border at La Junquera to Seville. For advice on driving in Andalucía see *Getting Around*.

An alternative for those travelling from Britain is the **ferry service** from Portsmouth or Plymouth to Bilbao or Santander on the northern Spanish coast, then south via Madrid *(see By Rail opposite)*. Four-lane *autovías* link Granada, Córdoba, Málaga, Seville, Cádiz and Huelva. The *Autovía de Andalucía*, from Madrid to Córdoba and Seville, has slashed driving times, and the age-old bottleneck created by the Despeñaperros Pass, which cuts through the Sierra Morena, has been removed.

Entry from Portugal's southern coast – served by Faro airport – is quickest via the bridge across the Guadíana river at Ayamonte.

Driving requirements

When driving your own vehicle in Spain you must have third-party insurance (arrange European cover before leaving home), a valid EU or international driving licence with photocard, and the vehicle log book/registration document. It is also sensible to get European breakdown cover, and you must carry a fluorescent warning triangle to set up on the road in case of accident or breakdown. Lead-free fuel is widely available. For speed limits, information on fines and seat belt requirements, see *Getting Around*.

When planning your trip, avoid peak holiday times. Easter and the first weekend of August (when many North African migrant workers travel home for their annual holidays) are particularly busy.

By bus

Eurolines (UK tel: 08705 808 080; www.eurolines.co.uk) operates a comfortable **bus service** from the UK to Andalucía's main cities (Málaga, Seville, Granada, Algeciras and Córdoba), with journey times of around 30 hours plus depending on changes. There are daily services to the region from Barcelona and Madrid.

GETTING AROUND

Airport Transfer

IIf you decide to take a bus into town from any of these airports, you will need to have small change, as drivers will not be able to give change from notes.
Almería
Bus No 20 (€0.80) leaves for the city centre from outside the arrivals terminal every 30 minutes from 7am–10.30pm, less frequently at weekends. A taxi from the airport costs around €12.
Granada
Granada's airport is 16 km (10 miles) from the centre. There is a limited bus service from around 8am–6pm. Taxis cost about €20 (more to hotels within the grounds of the Alhambra).
Jerez
The airport is 10 km (6 miles) from the centre. There is no public transport into town. A taxi costs around €11.
Málaga
The airport is 10 km (6 miles) from the city centre. Bus No 19 (€1) leaves from the city bus stop outside the arrivals hall every half

hour from 7am–11pm. Alternatively, the train station is a five-minute walk from the terminal: trains run every 30 minutes from 7am–11.45pm to Málaga to the east and Fuengirola to the west (stops include Torremolinos and Arroyo de la Miel). Tickets to either destination cost about €1.35. A taxi from the airport to Málaga costs around €12.

Seville

The airport is 8km (5 miles) from the centre, but heavy traffic can mean the journey takes about half an hour. A bus from the Amarillos Tour company (€2.30) – look for the "Aeropuerto de Sevilla" sign – leaves from outside the arrivals terminal to the city centre every half hour from 6.45am– 3.15pm and 4.45pm–11.15pm and hourly at weekends. A taxi from the airport to the centre costs around €20.

Public Transport

Inter-city buses

Regular bus services run between Andalucía's cities and towns. This is a cheap and generally comfortable way to travel (buses on longer journeys show films and have a toilet) and can be preferable to the train on some routes.

For example, the journey between Seville and Granada (or Córdoba and Granada) is quicker and less expensive by bus than by train, as the latter involves an inconvenient and time-consuming change. Tourist offices can provide bus and train timetables for comparison on key routes.

Bus stations and buying tickets

You can buy bus tickets immediately prior to travel, but arrive early for popular routes (such as Seville–Granada) or better still book the day before.

Bus stations usually have an information booth where staff will direct you to the bus company serving your route. In most cases this will be **Alsina Graells**: (www.alsinagraells.es, tel: Almería: 950 238 197, Córdoba: 957 278 100, Granada: 958 185 480, Seville: 954 418 811), the main company serving the inter-city routes in Southern Spain.

When taking a taxi to the bus station ask for the *Estación de Autobuses*. Note that Seville has two stations, Plaza de Armas (serving Huelva and Madrid) and El Prado de San Sebastián (near the Parque de María Luisa), serving Granada, Córdoba, Málaga and further east.

City buses

Buses can be a good and inexpensive way of getting around the main cities. Diagrammatic plans of the various routes are posted at bus stops, making it easy to find your way around. Passengers pay on the bus (small change necessary).

In **Granada**, the Alhambra and Albaicín are served by special minibuses (prices are on a par with the normal bus service).You can pick up both services, which are frequent, from the Plaza Nueva, at the foot of the Alhambra Hill.

Open-top tourist buses

Seville and Granada both have open-top hop-on, hop-off buses linking the main tourist sites. These offer a commentary on the sights you pass and can be a good way of seeing them if time is short.

Trains

As a rule, buses tend to be a better bet than trains when it comes to getting around Andalucía. The journey between Seville and Granada, for instance, often involves an inconvenient change at Bobadilla. That said, the AVE is convenient (though relatively expensive) for travelling between Seville and Córdoba: it takes just 30 minutes.

Seat reservations are advisable on the high-speed AVE and the Talgo, where seats are allocated on purchase. It is also best to reserve seats if you are travelling at peak periods (Christmas, Easter, July–August, and at long weekends). You can book online on the RENFE website: www.renfe.es/ingles.

Children under 12 years of age travel at reduced cost.

The Al-Andalus Express

A train ride in the grand style of the Orient Express is offered by the Al-Andalus (not to be confused with the regional Andalucía Express service). Operating April–October, this deluxe train visits

BELOW: in Granada minibuses run from the Plaza Nueva to the Alhambra.

DISTANCES

Almeria to:
Córdoba 332 km (206 miles)
Granada 166 km (103 miles)
Seville 422 km (262 miles)
Malaga: 219 km (136 miles)
Málaga to:
Cordoba 187 km (116 miles)
Granada 129 km (80 miles)
Seville 219 km (136 miles)
Seville to:
Córdoba 166 km (103 miles)
Granada 256 km (159 miles)

Seville, Córdoba, Granada, Ronda and Jerez. Information from Iberrail, tel: 915-715815/915-716 692, www.alandalus expreso.com.

Taxis

Taxis are readily available in major centres and fares are officially controlled; in urban areas fares are by meter, outside towns fixed rates apply.

Car Hire

To rent a car you will need to be over 25 and possess a valid EU (with photo; not the UK's old green paper version) or international driving licence. US and Canadian licences are also usually accepted. Scores of car hire companies offer their services. International chains such as **Avis**, **Europcar** and **Hertz** have airport offices, and offer collect and deliver service. Smaller local companies can be cheaper and will arrange to meet you on arrival if you book beforehand.
Avis (www.avis.com)
● Almería: tel: 950-298 221.
● Granada: tel: 958-446 455.
● Jerez de la Frontera, Cádiz: tel: 956-150 005.
● Málaga: tel: 952-048 483.
● Seville: tel: 954-449 121.

Europcar (www.europcar.es)
● Almería: tel: 950-292 934.
● Granada: tel: 958-245 275.
● Jerez de la Frontera: tel: 956-150 098.
● Málaga: tel: 952-048 518.
● Seville: tel: 954-254 298.

Hertz (www.hertz.com)
● Almería: tel: 950-292 500.
● Córdoba (railway station): tel: 957-402 061.
● Granada: tel: 958-242 577.
● Jerez de la Frontera: tel: 956-150 038.
● Málaga: tel: 952-233 086.
● Seville: tel: 954-449 125.

Advice for drivers

Driving in Spain is on the right, but actually often in the centre of the road. The best advice is: be prepared to take evasive action at all times in the face of local devil-may-care attitudes. Traffic from the right has priority except on roundabouts or unless otherwise signalled.

The **speed limit** in built-up areas is 50 kph (30 mph), on open roads 90 kph (55 mph) or 100 kph (62 mph), and 120 kph (75 mph) on motorways.

Civil Guard motorcycle patrols, out in force on holiday weekends, brook no nonsense and can administer heavy, **on-the-spot fines** for driving offences (they will issue a receipt; keep this and present a copy to your car hire company). Radar traps are common. Secondary roads have been improved and can be much more pleasant to use than main highways, which are often clogged with heavy transport.

Seat belts are obligatory in the front and back seats of vehicles. Children under the age of 12 must not travel in the front seat.

Motorways

Southern Spain's motorways (autopista) have been extended and improved in recent years. The following stretches of motorways have tolls (peaje): the AP4 (formerly A4) Seville–Cádiz; the AP4 Seville–Jerez; the A7 Málaga–Estepona. Tolls can be paid in cash or using a major credit card. It can be worth paying the extra to travel on a toll road, as they tend to be considerably quieter than other routes.

ABOVE: a great way to travel.

Motorcycles

Mopeds can be hired in main centres. They are ideal for short excursions, but make sure you are fully covered by insurance. Helmets are compulsory.

Cycling

Cycling is an idyllic way to enjoy the beauty of Andalucía's scenery, though intense heat makes it hard going in summer. The region has several *vías verdes*, cycling and hiking routes running along disused railway lines: there is one from the white town of Olvera to Puerta Serrano west of Algodonales; the Via Verde del Aceite, a 55-km (33-mile) cycle ride southwest from Jaén city; and three *vías verdes* in Huelva (a 49km/30-mile route from Ayamonte to Gibraleón; a 36-km/22-mile route between San Juan del Puerto and Velverde del Camino; and a 17km/10½-mile route between Puerto de la Laja and Mina La Isabel). For more information visit www.ffe.es/viasverdes.

Bikes can be taken on most regional trains providing they are not in the way of other passengers.

ACCOMMODATION

SOME THINGS TO CONSIDER BEFORE YOU BOOK THE ROOM

Choosing a Hotel

Spain may no longer be the bargain it once was, but accommodation still offers good value. Hotels are officially rated from one to five stars. Five-star establishments are in the luxury category with all the comforts one would expect in a first-class hotel. Bear in mind that the rating has more to do with the amenities offered than the quality of the service.

The ratings do not take into account charm or friendly atmosphere. Small, **family-run** places in the lower categories can be more comfortable than large soulless establishments with gilded fittings and marble halls. Some amenities offered by large hotels may be a positive disadvantage – do you want a *discoteca* under your window or a rooftop nightclub above your bed? Hotel prices are posted at the reception desk and behind your room door. IVA (value added tax) is added on top. There is a maximum and minimum price, but often the maximum rate is applied year round. Hotels in Seville are more expensive than the equivalent elsewhere in Andalucía, and a hefty premium is charged during Holy Week and the April Fair. There is no obligation to take breakfast or other meals, except at boarding

houses. In any case, breakfast in smaller hotels often consists of little more than coffee, bread and jam, and better value can be obtained in the nearest bar.

If the **blue plaque** at an establishment's door carries the sign "**Hs**", this signifies that it is a *hostal*. These also have star ratings but offer fewer facilities and are worth seeking out if you are on a tight budget. "**HR**" and "**HsR**" signify *hotel residencia* and *hostal residencia*, meaning there is no restaurant or meal service.

At the bottom of the market are the *pensión* (boarding house), the *fonda* (inn) and *the casa de huéspedes* (guesthouse). These are small and spartan, but usually clean. They may not run to carpets and the beds may sag, but most are perfectly adequate considering the low price.

Paradors are state-run hotels. Sometimes the service can be a little glum, but they are often located in unrivalled positions, sometimes in modern buildings but often in old castles, palaces and convents.

Motels are not common in Spain, but you will find some on main highways. Thousands of apartments have been built in tourist areas and if you are planning to stay more than a few days it is worth renting one. In

summer they are usually fully booked, but off-season it should be possible to negotiate a reasonable price.

Hotel vouchers, in books of five or 10, can be exchanged for accommodation at participating hotels of three–five stars. The system offers a considerable saving on normal rates. Schemes on offer include: Bancotel, Ibercheque, Hotel Color, Talonario 10, all of which are available at travel agents. El Corte Inglés have their Bono Hotel, available from their in-house travel agency.

The Red Andaluza de Alojamientos Rurales (RAAR) publishes a catalogue in several languages listing members' accommodation available in rural areas and has a reservation service, tel: 902-442 233, fax 950-271 678, www.raar.es.

Prices: In a pensión, expect to pay about €28 for a double room. In one- and two-star *hostals*, prices range from €35–50. Hotel prices run roughly from €40 for a one-star establishment to €125 or €150 for a four-star. A double in a five-star hotel is usually in the €150–250 bracket. Paradors usually charge €100–150 for a double. **Note on addresses: s/n in an address signifies *sin número* (no number); ctra means *carretera* (highway). Hotel names are in bold print.**

ACCOMMODATION LISTINGS

SEVILLE CITY AND PROVINCE

ACCOMMODATION

Alfonso XIII
San Fernando, 2
Tel: 954-917 000
Fax: 954-216 033 €€€€
www.westin.com/hotelalfonso
Old-style elegance in
this all-time classic
hotel of Seville, built in
Neo-Mudéjar style in the
1920s and centring
upon a splendid patio.
Great location too,
within walking distance
of the main sights and
the Parque de Maria
Luísa. Notable Spanish
and Japanese restau-
rants, plus outdoor
pool. Sometimes has
special offers out of
season.
**Apartmentos-Suites
Santa Cruz**
Plaza de los Venerables
Barrio de Santa Cruz
Fax: 954-563 806 €€€
www.barriosantacruz.com/
apartments

A group of traditional-
style buildings that have
been combined to form
an interesting selection
of apartments, each
one well decorated and
retaining their charac-
ter. In the heart of the
Barrio de Santa Cruz.
Bécquer
Reyes Católicos, 4
Tel: 954-228 900
Fax: 954-214 400 €€€€
www.hotelbecquer.com
This long-established
four-star hotel has an
excellent location a
short walk from the
river, around the corner
from the Plaza de
Toros, and a five-
minute walk from the
Cathedral. It has a
charming style, with
spacious rooms, a nice
restaurant, spa and,
importantly, its own
private parking.

Casa Imperial
Calle Imperial, 29
Tel: 954-500 300
Fax: 954-500 330 €€€€
www.casaimperial.com
Hotel set in a restored
16th-century palace just
behind the Casa de
Pilatos, with four patios
and a restaurant. There
are 24 suites, each dec-
orated elegantly and
differently, with enor-
mous bathrooms.
Casa Numero 7
Calle Virgenes, 7
Tel: 954-221 581
Fax: 954 214 527 €€€€
www.casanumero7.com
Situated near the
Jardines Murillo on the
edge of the Barrio de
Santa Cruz, this is an
attractive small hotel in
an old mansion
arranged around a tiny
inner courtyard. Individ-
ually decorated rooms.

Casa Romana
Trajano, 15
Tel: 954-915 170
Fax: 954-373 191 €€€
www.hotelcasaroma.com
Found in a quieter, yet
rather Bohemian area
of Seville this boutique-
style hotel is about a
20-minute walk from
the Cathedral, via the
pedestrianised Sierpes
shopping street. A tra-
ditional building has
been enhanced with
complementing furni-
ture and high-tech
facilities. The service
includes national and
international newspa-
pers, a Jacuzzi on the
terrace and parking
facilities. 26 rooms.
Doña María
Don Remondo, 19
Tel: 952-224 990
Fax: 954-219 546 €€€€
Well situated close to
the cathedral, with
rooms of varying size,
some with antiques.
Also has a roof-top
swimming-pool.

BELOW: the impressive central patio of the Alfonso XIII Hotel, Seville.

PRICE CATEGORIES

Price categories are for
a double room without
breakfast:
€ = under €50
€€ = €50–90
€€€ = €90–150
€€€€ = more than €150

Hostal Londres
San Pedro Mártir, 1
Tel: 954-212 896
Fax: 954-503 830 €
Old-fashioned hotel with
plain yet comfortable
rooms, some with bal-
conies. Well-positioned
near shops and historic
centre.

Hostería del Laurel
Plaza de los Venerables, 5
Tel: 954-220 295
Fax: 954-210 450 €€€
www.hosteriadellaurel.com
In one of the best loca-
tions in the Barrio de
Santa Cruz, this small
hotel and restaurant is
very popular with foreign
visitors. The rooms are
small but comfortable.

Hotel Patio de la Cartuja
Calle Lumbreras, 8
Tel: 954-900 200
Fax: 954-902 056 €€
www.patiosdesevilla.com
This hotel is housed in
a restored "Corral de
Vecinos" (a home
shared by several fami-
lies). The rooms are
modern if simply deco-
rated, and some have
kitchenettes. Well
located next to the
Alameda de Hércules,
Seville's booming
nightlife area.

Inglaterra
Plaza Nueva, 7
Tel: 954-224 970
Fax: 954-561 336 €€€€
www.hotelinglaterra.es
Comfortable and
friendly hotel that has
been recently refur-
bished. Overlooks the
very central Plaza
Nueva, complete with
Irish bar.

La Casa del Maestro
Almudena, 5
Tel: 954-500 007 €€€
www.lacasadelmaestro.com
The maestro in question
is Manuel Serrapi
Sánchez, one of

Seville's most
acclaimed guitarists,
who was born nearby in
1904 and later made
this his home. It is off
the main tourist beat but
very close to the Casa
de Pilatos and a com-
fortable walk from the
Barrio Santa Cruz. The
décor blends elegantly
with the surroundings,
and the terrace is a
peaceful haven in the
midst of this city.

Las Casas de la Judería
Callejón de Dos Hermanas, s/n
Tel: 954-415 150
Fax: 954-422 170 €€€€
Three old palaces in the
Santa Cruz quarter
were restored and con-
verted into this delight-
ful boutique hotel
comprising 95 rooms
(including some suites)
arranged around inner
courtyards and with
Moorish-inspired décor.

Las Casas de los Mercaderes
Calle Alvarez Quintero, 9–13
Tel: 954-225 858
Fax: 954-229 884 €€€
Centred on an 18th-
century patio, this
friendly, well-run and
centrally located hotel
is one of the best in its
category.

Las Casas del Rey de Baeza
Plaza Cristo de la Redención, 2
Tel: 954-561 496
Fax: 954-561 441 €€€
Tucked away on a small
square close to the
lovely Casa de Pilatos,
this hotel comprises 44
rooms in a sympatheti-
cally renovated town
house that was owned
by a duke until very
recently. Facilities
include a roof-top pool,
free use of bicycles and
even private parking – a
real luxury in central
Seville.

Los Seises
Calle Segovias, 6
Tel: 954-229 495
Fax: 954-224 334 €€€€
www.hotellosseises.com
A unique location in part
of the 16th-century
Bishop's Palace, beauti-
fully restored and strik-
ingly decorated to blend
old elements with mod-
ern design. Rooftop pool
with view of the Giralda.

Macarena
Calle San Juan de Ribera, 2
Tel: 954-375 700
Fax: 954-381 803 €€
www.solmelia.com
An elegant, old-style
exterior conceals a
large, modern, comfort-
able hotel across the
street from the
Macarena basilica. With
331 rooms, it's a
favourite with business
guests, but quite a
stretch from the main
tourist sights.

Maestranza
Gamazo, 12
Tel: 954-561 070
Fax: 954-214 404 €€
www.hotelmaestranza.es.
From the outside, and
inside, this hotel is
thoroughly *Sevilliano* in
its style and ambience
and situated just a
hundred metres or so
from the Cathedral. All
the rooms – in a variety
of sizes – have mod-
ern facilities and the
hotel has plenty of old-
fashioned charm.

Novotel Sevilla Marques del Nervion
Avenida Eduardo Dato, 71
Tel: 954-558 200
Fax: 954-534 233
www.accorhotels.com
This modern hotel is
just a few minutes from
the railway station and
directly outside the
Sevilla football club stadium. Also has private
parking.

Petit Palace Marqués Santa Ana
Jimios, 9–11
Tel: 954-221 812
Fax: 954-228 993 €€€€
www.hthoteles.com
This hotel chain spe-
cialises in renovating
historical properties
whilst retaining their
ambience, but adding
all kinds of high-tech
facilities, and this
hotel, which opened in
2005, is a perfect
example. It occupies a
19th-century building
in a quiet side street
close to the Cathedral
and, very importantly,
has its own parking.
Doubles and family
rooms. Another hotel in
the same chain, **Petit
Palace Santa Cruz** (*see
same website*), on
Calle Muñoz y Pavón,
close to the Cathedral,
is due to open in 2006.

Puerta de Triana
Calle Reyes Católicos, 5
Tel: 954-215 404
Fax: 954-215 401 €€
www.hotelpuertadetriana.com
Conveniently located,
near the river and the
main shopping area, but
also within easy walking
distance of the Cathe-
dral. Friendly efficient
and good value, with
attractive reception
area. Rooms are small
but adequate. A simple
breakfast is included.

San Gil
Calle Parras, 28
Tel: 954-906 811
Fax: 954-906 939 €€€
www.fp-hoteles.com
This hotel around the
corner from the
Macarena basilica, on
the northern edge of
the old town, offers spa-
cious lodging in rooms
with modern furniture
and decor, centred on a
more traditional patio

with Seville *azulejo* tiles. There is also a small swimming pool on the roof.

Simon
Calle García de Vinuesa, 19
Tel: 954-226 660
Fax: 954-562 241 €€
www.hotelsimon.com
Located in the centre of the city, not far from the Cathedral, offering pleasant but no-frill lodgings in an 18th-century house around an Andalusian patio.

Apartamentos-Suites Santa Cruz
Plaza de los Venerables, Barrio de Santa Cruz
Fax: 954-563 806 €€
www.barriosantacruz.com/apartments
Found in the heart of the pretty Barrio de Santa Cruz, this is a group of traditional style buildings offering an interesting selection of 17 varying sized apartments, each beautifully decorated in an individual manner.

Zaida
Calle San Roque, 26
Tel: 954-211 138
Fax: 954-213 612 €€
www.andalunet.com/zaida
This intimate budget hotel is located in a delightful, restored 18th-century townhouse with an attractive Mudéjar-style courtyard and halls graced with Moorish arches.

Alcalá de Guadaira

Oromana
Avenida de Portugal, s/n
Tel: 955-686 400 €€
www.hoteloromana.com
Andalusian country manor set among pines, 15 km (9 miles) east of Seville, just off the A-92 motorway.

Carmona

Alcázar de la Reina
Plaza de Lasso, 2
Tel: 954-196 200
Fax: 954-140 113 €€€
www.alcazar-reina.es
Stylish hotel comprising around 69 spacious rooms (some suites available) on the edge of Carmona's old quarter. It combines tasteful, classic architecture with modern comfort.

Casa de Carmona
Plaza de Lasso, s/n
Tel: 954-143 300
Fax: 954-190 189 €€€€
www.casadecarmona.com
Dating from the 16th century, this building was in ruins until a caring and very effective renovation in the early 1990s made it into one of the best hotels of its kind in Spain. The rooms and public areas are filled with antiques, paintings and books and the ambiance is one of old-world elegance combined with modern comforts. The Loggia and small pool area is a peaceful, cool, haven.

El Triguera
5 km (3 miles) west of Carmona
Tel/fax: 955-953 626 €€
Delightful country farmhouse set in the middle of a bull-breeding ranch. It offers seven double rooms and two singles, all furnished in traditional style. Facilities include a pool surrounded by orange trees. Meals are available on request.

Parador Alcázar del Rey Don Pedro
Alcázar, s/n
Tel: 954-141 010
Fax: 954-141 712 €€€
www.parador.es

A Mudéjar-style building on a hill overlooking the town, with spacious rooms and a great view overlooking the surrounding countryside.

Castilleja de la Cuesta

Hacienda San Ignacio
Real 194,
Tel: 954-160 430
Fax: 954-161 137 €€€
www.haciendasanignacio.com
Installed in a rambling 17th-century Andalusian manor at the edge of this town, just east of Seville, off the motorway to Huelva, .

Cazalla de la Sierra

La Cartuja de Cazalla
Ctra Cazalla–Constantina km 55
Tel: 954-884 516
Fax: 954-884 515 €€
www.cartujadecazalla.com
This small hotel, a few kilometres from the village, stands within an old Carthusian monastery which was abandoned in the 19th century and is now in the process of being restored.

Las Navezuelas
Ctra SE196, km 43
Tel: 954-884 764 €€
Country hotel in a restored 16th-century olive mill surrounded by a large farm estate, with a cosy, friendly, and informal atmosphere.

Posada del Moro
Paseo del Moro, s/n
Tel: 954-884 858 €€
www.laposadadelmoro.com
In a modern section of the village, gleaming white 15-room hotel and a restaurant serving local specialities.

Gerena

Cortijo El Esparragal
Ctra de Mérida, km 21
Tel: 955-782 702
Fax: 955-882 783 €€€
www.elesparragal.com
This is one of a number of working ranches just north of Seville which have been converted to welcome paying guests. Owned by a Marquis, it stands on a 3,000-hectare (7,500-acre) estate.

Los Jinetes

Hacienda de Los Jinetes
Ctra local SE-110
Tel: 651-813 336 €€€
Found down a track, just to the west of the very small town of Los Jinetes – between Seville and Carmona – the building dates from the 16th century and was once a Crown holding. The spacious rooms combine antiques and modern facilities, including large beds and walk-in showers.

Sanlúcar La Mayor

Hacienda Benazuza
Virgen de las Nieves, s/n
Tel: 955-703 344
Fax: 955-703 410 €€€€
Built on the site of an old farmhouse, a sumptuous Moorish fantasy palace, 20 km (12 miles) from Seville.

PRICE CATEGORIES

Price categories are for a double room without breakfast:
€ = under €50
€€ = €50–90
€€€ = €90–150
€€€€ = more than €150

HUELVA CITY AND PROVINCE

Huelva city

Tartessos
Avenida Martín Alonso Pinzón, 13
Tel: 959-282 711
Fax: 959-250 617 €€
There is not a lot of choice in Huelva itself, but if you need to stay here this is a modern medium-sized hotel with a corner location in a quiet area of Huelva city. Restaurant and bar.

Almonaster la Real

Hotel Casa Garcia
Avenida San Martin, 2
Tel: 959-14 31 09 €
www.hotelcasagarcia.com
There are 22 individually decorated rooms, some with balcony, at this charming yet inexpensive small hotel in a converted house at the entrance to the village. Has a good restaurant plus a bar that is open all day.

Aracena

Finca Valbono
Ctra de Carboneras, km 1
Tel: 959-127 711
Fax: 959-127 679 €€
An attractively converted Andalusian farmhouse tucked into quiet woodland just outside Aracena. It offers a warm and rustic welcome and charming rooms in either the main house (containing six rooms) or bungalows in the grounds.

Los Castanos
Avenida de Huelva, 5
Tel: 959-12 63 00 €
This very central option is a converted town mansion, with 33 simple but decent rooms.

Sierra de Aracena
Gran Vía, 21
Tel: 959-126 175 €€
A family-run hotel in the centre of the town, with a neo-Mudéjar façade and 42 simply furnished but comfortable rooms.

Ayamonte and environs

Confortel Islantilla
Ctra La Antilla–Isla Cristina, km 3, Isla Cristina
Tel: 959-486 017
Fax: 959-486 070 €€€€
www.confortelhoteles.com
Alarge, modern and comfortable beachfront hotel belonging to a small chain of Spanish hotels. Situated next to a wide sandy beach, and near a golf course.

Cortijo Los Millares
Ctra Almonte–Villanueva de los Castillos, km 22, Sanlúcar del Guadiana
Tel: 959-485 411
Fax: 959-485 410 €€
www.losmillares.com
A stylish country hotel with 25 spacious rooms forming part of a large hunting and sheep-raising estate located 40 km (25 miles) north of Ayamonte. A great escape, with log fires in winter, hearty breakfasts and lovely gardens.

Parador Costa de la Luz
El Castillito, s/n
Tel: 959-320 700
Fax: 959-364 462 €€€
www.parador.es
Modern parador in a superb situation on a hill overlooking the village of Ayamonte, the Guadiana river, with Portugal on the opposite shore.

Riu Canela
Paseo de los Gavilanes, s/n, Playa Isla Canela
Tel: 959-477 124
Fax: 959-477 170 €€€€
This is a large, modern hotel, near the beach and surrounded by pleasant gardens. Closed Nov–Mar.

Doñana and environs

Cortijo Los Mimbrales
Ctra del Rocío-Matalascanas A483
Tel: 959-442 237
Fax: 959-442 443 €€
www.cortijomimbrales.com
Situated between El Rocio and Matalascanas, right on the edge of the National Park, this country mansion is set in 1,000 hectares (2,470 acres) of grounds with a traditional Arabic pool. Rooms are individually decorated, with traditional furnishings and tiled floors. There are 24 doubles, plus villas and suites.

BELOW: the Roman bridge at Niebla in the province of Huelva.

Tierra Mar

Matalascañas Parc,
120 Sector M
Tel: 959-440 300
Fax: 959-440 720 €€€
www.atlanticclub-hoteles.com
Matalascañas, a vastly
overbuilt beach resort,
has little to recommend
it except that it is next
to Doñana. This beach-
side hotel is a good
base for exploring the
national park. All ameni-
ties and about 500
metres from the golf
course.

Toruño

Plaza Aecbuchal, 32
Tel: 959-442 323
Fax: 959-442 338 €€
A small hotel in the
hamlet of El Rocío, this
is a favourite with visiting bird watchers, not
least because some
rooms have views over
the Doñana marshes.

El Rocío

Hotel Toruno

Plaza Acebuchal, 32
Tel: 959-44 23 23
€ (except during Romería
when rates are much higher)
A stand-alone bal-
conied mansion near
the church and wet-
lands. Of the 30 good
rooms, one-third over-
look the lake and there
is a roof deck equipped
with telescopes for
birdwatching.

Isla Cristina

El Paraiso Playa

Avenida de la Playa
Tel: 959-33 02 35 €–€€
www.hotelparaisoplaya.com
A friendly converted
house, set back from
the beach (2 minute
walk) amid eucalyptus
trees. Rooms are light
and airy and there is a
small outdoor pool.

Isla Cristina Palace Hotel

Avenida Parque, 148
Tel: 959-34 44 99 €–€€
www.islacristinapalace.com
A modern 5-star, 5-
storey hotel set around
a large pool and shel-
tered by thick umbrella
pines from both the
road and the beach (to
which there is direct
private access). There
are elevated sea views
from many rooms.
Facilities include
sports centre and spa.

Sol y Mar

Avenida de la Playa
Tel: 959-33 20 50 €
One of few places that
are right on the beach
promenade. All rooms
face straight out to sea
but are fairly basic, as
are facilities and
meals.

Mazagon

Parador Mazagon

Ctra Huelva–Matalascanas
Tel: 959-53 63 00 €€
In a cliff-top setting
amid forest, a low-rise
building that has been
tastefully designed in
keeping with its peace-
ful surroundings. 60
rooms are large with
wooden verandahs and
most have ocean
views. There is a pool
in landscaped gardens
and private access
down steep steps to a
stunning stretch of
beach.

Palos de la Frontera and environs

Hostería de la Rábida

La Rábida, s/n
Tel: 959-350 035 €
Five-room hostelry, sim-
ple but comfortable,
next door to the 15th-

ABOVE: breakfast at the Parador San Cristobal.

century Monastery of
La Rábida.

La Pinta

Rábida, 75, Palos de la Frontera
Tel: 959-350 511
Fax: 959-530 164 €
Unpretentious, friendly
30-room hotel situated
in the centre of the
town of Palos. The
restaurant serves
some interesting
dishes.

Parador Cristobal Colón

Ctra Huelva–Matalascanas,
km 24, Mazagón
Tel: 959-536 300
Fax: 959-536 228 €€€
www.parador.es
A modern parador in a
tranquil, pine-shaded
spot overlooking a
sandy beach, with
rooms opening onto a
garden.

Punta Umbria

Barcelo Punta Umbria

Avenida del Oceano
Tel: 959-49 54 00 €–€€
www.barcelo.com
A huge modern com-
plex that compensates
for its size by copying

traditional Andalusian
features. Five-star facilities include very spa-
cious rooms, two pools
and a spa. There is pri-
vate access through
pine-clad dunes to a
lovely beach.

Sierra de Aracena

Hotel Galaroza Sierra

Ctra Sevilla–Lisboa
Tel: 959-12 23 37/12 32 15
www.hotelgalaroza.com
A very presentable,
peaceful hillside hide-
away, occupying three
sides around a wide
terrace with lovely
sierra views. Rooms
are subtly decorated.
There is a small pool
and good restaurant
overlooking Galaroza
village and church.

PRICE CATEGORIES

Price categories are for
a double room without
breakfast:
€ = under €50
€€ = €50–90
€€€ = €90–150
€€€€ = more than €150

JEREZ, CÁDIZ AND THE COSTA DE LA LUZ

Cádiz City

Atlántico
Avenida Duque de Nájera, 9
Tel: 956-226 905
Fax: 956-214 582 €€€
www.parador.es
This parador occupies a modern but stylish building in Cádiz's old town.

Hospederia Las Cortes de Cádiz
Calle San Francisco, 9
Tel: 956-22 0 489/211 048
Fax: 956-21 26 68 €€
www.hotellascortes.com
Mid-19th-century house in the heart of old Cádiz. 36 pretty bedrooms are set around a bright atrium, each with period furnishings and individually named, rather than numbered, in celebration of the 1812 liberal parliament. Also a roof terrace with city views.

Hotel Playa Victoria
Glorieta Ingeniero La Cierva, 4
Tel: 956-20 5 1 00
Fax: 956-263 3 00 €€€
www.palafoxhoteles.com
Well-designed, modern hotel on Cadiz's southern Playa Victoria, with direct access to the beach. More than half of the 188 spacious rooms have balconies with Atlantic views. The hotel has a swimming pool, terrace bar and secure parking.

Algeciras

Reina Cristina
Paseo de la Conferencia, s/n
Tel: 956-602 622
Fax: 956-603 323 €€€
Surrounded by luxuriant gardens, this stately 1900s hotel is a classic, its ambience recalling days gone by.

Conil de la Frontera

Hotel Almadraba Conil
Calle Senoras Curas, 4
Tel: 956-456 037
Fax: 956-44 45 19 €€
www.hotelalmadrabaconil.com
A delightful, light and airy 18th-century Andalusian house, in the centre of Conil, faithfully restored with beamed ceilings, ceramic tiled floors, whitewashed arched columns and a sunny, plant-filled patio. The 17 rooms are cosy, clean and quiet. A terrace has lovely views across the village rooftops to the sea.

Conil Park Hotel
Playa de La Fontanilla
Tel: 956-043 000
Fax: 956-04 30 43 €€€
www.conilparkhotel.com
With a stunning clifftop location above quiet Playa Fontanilla, this tasteful, modern hotel, just five minutes' walk from Conil, has been designed in keeping with the traditional village architecture. Panoramic sea views are enjoyed from the pool, gardens and most of the 180 rooms. In addition there are also bungalows to accommodate families of 4–6.

El Palmar Zahora

Sajorami Beach
Playa de Zahora
Tel: 956-437 424
Fax: 956-437 072 €€–€€€
www.sajoramibeach.com
Occupying an exclusive spot on its own secluded bay to the

north of Cape Trafalgar, this rustic collection of bungalows, houses and rooms made from natural materials (wood, stone and thatch) have an alternative, laid-back feel and are clustered around an ocean-front seafood restaurant with high, wide, sunset viewing windows.

El Puerto de Santa María

Casa No 6
Calle San Bartolome, 14
Tel: 956-877 084
€€–€€€
www.casano6.com
A tranquil haven, only two streets from the bustling restaurant district in the heart of El Puerto, this 19th-century house, centred on a sunny open courtyard, has been lovingly renovated to offer spacious, rooms with original wooden doors and high, beamed ceilings. The owners (one of whom is English) are friendly and helpful.

Los Cantaros
Calle Curva, 6
Tel: 956-540 240
Fax: 956-541 121 €€€
www.hotelloscanteros.com
Friendly, comfortable and reasonably priced modern hotel, conveniently located one block from the town's famous "seafood promenade".

Monasterio de San Miguel
Larga, 27
Tel: 956-540 440
Fax: 956-542 604 €€€€
Tasteful and comfortable, installed in a former 18th-century

monastery which still retains the original cloisters, chapel and enclosed garden.

Jerez de la Frontera

NH Avenida Jerez
Avenida Alvaro Domecq, 10
Tel: 956-347 411
Fax: 956-337 296 €€
www.nh-hotels.com
A typical member of the popular chain, this is comfortable and functional modern hotel, and with an excellent location in an exclusive area of town.

Hotel Bellas Artes
Plaza del Arroyo, 45
Tel: 956-34 84 30
Fax: 956-16 96 33 €€–€€€
Romantic, beautifully restored casa palacio, centrally located with views from a roof terrace to the cathedral opposite. 19 individual, enchantingly decorated rooms with period colours and exposed stone (some with curtained roll top baths), centred on a cool, peaceful atrium. Service is warm and welcoming.

Los Jandalos
Calle Nuno de Canas, 1
Tel: 956-327 2 30
Fax: 956-326 030 €€€
www.jandalos.com
Smart, comfortable hotel, with a "Manhattan" touch to the décor.

Newly converted from a historic mansion on the site of the Williams & Humbert winery, with a spa in the former bodega. 59 rooms include duplex rooms and suites. Well located for the Royal Equestrian School and city centre.

Hotel Torres
Arcos, 29
Tel: 956-323 400
Fax: 956-321 816 €
www.hoteltorres.com
Centrally located, this is probably the best budget-option in a city that is generally short on such accommodation.

Jerez
Avenida Alvaro Domecq, 35
Tel: 956-300 600
Fax: 956-005 001 €€€
www.jerezhotel.com
In the leafy, residential part of town, this is a popular and comfortable hotel. Attractive pool and tennis courts.

Montecastillo
Ctra de Arcos, km 9
Tel: 956-151 200
Fax: 956-151 209 €€€€
www.montecastillo.com
A few kilometres outside Jerez, near the motor-racing track, a sprawling and luxurious neo-Moorish palace adjoining a golf course designed by Jack Nicklaus.

Villa Jerez
Avenida de la Cruz Roja, 7
Tel: 956-153 100 €€€€
www.villajerez.com
A sister hotel to Montecastillo, this is a romantic luxury hotel situated in lovely gardens in the heart of town. There are 18 plushly furnished rooms, plus a pool, gym and beauty salon.. Some special offers occasionally available, so it is worth checking the website.

ABOVE: playing on the Playa de Santa Maria, Cádiz.

Los Caños de Meca

Hostal Mar de Frente
Avenida Trafalgar, 3
Tel: 956-437 025
Fax: 956-437 2 91 €€
Perched on a cliff, with private access to one of the most picturesque coves in Cádiz, this unassuming hotel offers views towards Cape Trafalgar. Although new, the building has a traditional layout, overlooking an attractive floodlit fountain courtyard. There are 15 cheerful rooms, including two superior attic rooms with terraces.

Hotel La Brena
Avenida Trafalgar, 4
Tel: 956-43 73 68
Fax: 627-42 43 43 €€–€€€
www.hotelbrena.com
Welcoming small hotel and restaurant with 7 spacious, attractive rooms, each individually decorated and very comfortably furnished. The two attic rooms are vast, with lovely sea views. There is a private garden and, useful in this one street village, a car park.

San Roque

Casa Señorial La Solana
N340, km 116, Torreguadiaro
Tel: 956-780 236 €€
An atmosphere of faded elegance pervades this 18-room country hostelry, set in a tastefully restored 18th-century mansion surrounded by a large garden.

Suites Hotel
San Roque Club, N340, km 126
Tel: 956-613 030
Fax: 956-613 013 €€€€
www.sanroqueclub.com
This former mansion of the Domecq sherry dynasty has been tastefully converted to a luxurious hotel, offering superb facilities and extensive grounds, incorporating two championship golf courses, Other sports facilities include a horse-riding centre.

Sanlúcar de Barrameda

Los Helechos
Plaza de la Madre de Dios, 9
Tel: 956-367 655
Fax: 956-369 650 €€
www.loshelechos.com
Friendly atmosphere in a classic Andalusian setting, around a central courtyard with colourful potted plants. In the centre of town.

Posada de Palacio
Caballeros, 11
Tel: 956-364 840 €€
www.posadadepalacio.com
Welcoming ambience in an 18th-century aristocratic town house, with rooms arranged around a central patio. There is also a roof-top terrace. Closed January–February.

TRANSPORT

ACCOMMODATION

ACTIVITIES

A – Z

LANGUAGE

Tartaneros

Tartaneros, 8
Tel: 956-362 044
Fax: 956-360 045 €€€
At the top end of Sanlú-
car's main boulevard,
the Calzasa del Ejercito,
this hotel is installed in a
neo-classical house, dec-
orated with antiques.

Tarifa and environs

Dos Mares

Ctra Cádiz–Málaga, km 80,
Tel: 956-684 035
Fax: 956-681 078 €€€
This is a cheerful, mod-
ern hotel right on the
windsurfing beach of
Los Lances.

Hurricane Hotel

Ctra Cádiz-Málaga, km 77
Tel: 956-684 919
Fax: 956-684 329 €€€
www.hotelhurricane.com
Situated next to the

windswept beach west of
town, this low-lying hotel
is popular with the wind-
surfing set and horse-
trekkers (there are
stables on the
premises). It has a laid-
back ambience, a pool
and good restaurant.

Posada La Sacristia

San Donato, 8
Tel: 956-68 17 59
Fax: 956-68 51 82 €€€
www.lasacristia.net
This boutique hotel has
been converted from a
17th-century corner
house, in the heart of
the old town, and is
listed among 100 "Hip
Hotels of the World".
Each of the 7 double
rooms is uniquely fur-
nished, with iron beds,
crisp white linen, floaty
curtains, jasmine
scented shower rooms
and exotic touches.

There is also a high
quality Moroccan
inspired bar/restaurant.

Vejer de la Frontera

Casa Cinco

Calle Sancho IV El Bravo, 5
Tel: 956-455 029
Fax: 956-451 125 €€€
www.hotelcasacinco.com
The names of the four
individually decorated
guest rooms – See,
Hear, Touch, Aroma –
give some idea of
the approach at this stylish and comfortable
guest house lovingly run
by two ex-Londoners. The
breakfast changes daily.

Convento de San Francisco

La Plazuela, s/n, Vejer de la
Frontera
Tel: 956-451 001,
Fax: 956-451 004 €€

www.tugasa.com
Basic but comfortable
lodgings comprising 25
rooms in a restored
17th-century convent in
the hilltop village of
Vejer, overlooking the
coast. Meals are served
in the former refectory.

Hotel La Casa del Califa

Plaza de Espana, 16
Tel: 956-447 7 30
Fax: 956-451 625 €€–€€€
www.casadelcalifa.com
True to the Islamic her-
itage of Vejer, this
atmospheric hotel in
the centre is a maze of
stone passageways
leading to 18 rooms,
individually designed
with Moroccan furnish-
ings and two suites
with panoramic views.
There are terraces and
a flower-filled patio
restaurant serving Ara-
bian dishes.

THE WHITE TOWNS

Arcos de la Frontera

Cortijo Fain

Ctra de Algar, km 3
Tel: 956-231 396 €€
cortijofain.en.eresmas.com
Three kilometres (2
miles) from the village
of Arcos, in a rambling
17th-century country
manor in the middle of
an olive grove.

El Convento

Calle Maldonado, 2
Tel: 956-702 333
Fax: 956-704 128 €€
Tiny 11-room hotel
occupying part of a for-
mer convent. It's right
around the corner from
the Arcos's parador,
and some rooms enjoy
the same views, at half
the price.

Cortijo Mesa de la Plata

Arcos–El Bosque road, km 4.5
Tel: 956-704 774 €€
www.cortijomesade-
laplata.com
Delightful semi self-
catering option (the lit-
tle bungalows have a
small kitchen area) on a
rustic but modern cor-
tijo. Bar, restaurant and
swimming pool.

Hacienda El Santiscal

Avenida El Santiscal, 129
Tel: 956-708 313
Fax: 956-708 268 €€€
www.santiscal.com
Rustic hotel in a 15th-
century country manor
with a central courtyard,
next to the Arcos reser-
voir. A good base for
horse-riding, which is
popular in the area.

Los Olivos

Paseo Boliches, 30
Tel: 956-700 811
Fax: 956-702 018 €€
This is a pleasant and
comfortable small hotel
in an old Andalusian
town house in the lower
part of the village, with
rooms arranged around
a central courtyard.
Good value.

Parador de Arcos de la Frontera

Plaza del Cabildo, s/n,
Tel: 956-700 500
Fax: 956-701 116 €€€
www.parador.es
The splendid views
from this hotel, which
is perched on a cliff at
the very top of the vil-
lage, are worth a visit
in their own right. The
rooms are very large

and furnished in typical
parador style. Try and
get one of the rooms
that look over the cliff.

Benaoján

El Molino del Santo

Barriada Estación, s/n
Tel: 952-167 151
Fax: 952-167 327 €€€
www.molinodelsanto.com
English-run, 14-room
country inn next to a
stream in the moun-
tains near Ronda, not

far from the Cueva de la Pileta and the Grazalema nature park. Restaurant serves good food.

El Bosque

Hotel Las Truchas
Avda de la Diputacion
Tel: 956-71 6 061
www.tugasa.com
This traditional but stylish hotel, with high wooden ceilings is right opposite El Bosque's bullring and frequented by visiting matadors. Many of the comfortable bedrooms have balconies and there is a wide terrace overlooking the countryside. The restaurant is well known in the area; the special is fresh trout from the nearby Majaceite river. Also has a swimming pool.

Grazalema and environs

Casa de las Piedras
Calle Las Piedras, 32, Grazalema
Tel/fax: 956-132 014 €
www.casadelaspiedras.net
Friendly establishment in the heart of the village of Grazalema, with some rooms in a converted old village house, while others are more like apartments with self-contained kitchens.

Cortijo Huerta Dorotea
Ctra Villamartín-Ubrique, km 12, Prado del Rey
Tel: 956-724 291
Fax: 956-724 289 €€
www.huertadorotea.com
Accommodation is split between 8 rooms in a traditional Andalusian farmhouse, and in Finnish log-cabins (originally imported for

Seville's Expo 92), each with two bedrooms. There is also a horse-riding centre.

Peñon Grande
Plaza Pequena, 7
Tel: 956-132 434
Fax: 956-132 435 €€
Modern hotel, tastefully designed. Rooms have attractive views of the main plaza.

Puerta de la Villa
Plaza Pequea, 8
Tel: 956-132 3 76
Fax: 956-132 087 €€€
www.grazalemahotel.com
A very comfortable refurbished mansion in Grazalema's town centre with 28 good sized, tastefully furnished bedrooms. The small outdoor pool is set right up to the cliff edge, with uninhibited views from the water across the national park. The hotel also has a gym, sauna, Jacuzzi and good restaurant with an innovative local menu.

Villa Turística de Grazalema
Calle El Olivar, s/n, Grazalema
Tel: 956-132 136
Fax: 956-132 213 €€
www.tugasa.com
Part of the Andalusian "Villa Turística" network, with self-catering units (perfect for small groups), in addition to a small hotel.

Jimena de la Frontera and environs

Casa Convento La Almoraima
Finca La Almoraima, s/n, Castellar de la Frontera
Tel: 956-693 002
Fax: 956-693 214 €€€
www.la-almoraima.com
Set in the middle of a huge hunting estate

cloaked in cork oaks, a 17th-century convent restored as a 17-room country hotel offering tranquil, though basic, lodgings.

Castillo de Castellar
Calle Rosario, 3, Castellar de la Frontera
Tel: 956-236 620
Fax: 956-236 624 €€
www.tugasa.com
Dramatically located within the semi-abandoned, walled village of old Castellar, with accommodation in 11 restored village houses with one or two bedrooms.

Hostal El Anón
Calle Consuelo, 34, Jimena de la Frontera
Tel: 956-640 113
Fax: 956-641 110 €€
Delightfully haphazard in its distribution, the result of joining several village houses, this is a long-time favourite rural inn, a good base for excursions into the spectacular surrounding countryside.

Ubrique

Hotel Sierra de Ubrique
Ctra Ubrique-Cortes
Tel: 956-466 8 05
Fax: 956-466 806 €€
www.hotelsierradeubrique.com
This is a new hotel on the outskirts of Ubrique with views across the rolling Sierra from each of the 27 bedrooms. Rooms are comfortable and simply decorated with fittings made from deer antlers – a theme throughout the hotel and a reminder that this is hunting country. The restaurant menu also reflects this with game much in evidence.

Villaluenga del Rosario

Hotel La Posada
Calle Torre, 1
Tel: 956-12 6 119
Fax: 956-463 534
www.tugasa.com
A cosy, hideaway seamlessly integrated into this peaceful village, La Posadal has been renovated within the original walls of the 19th-century town prison. There are seven very quaint rooms with shuttered windows and exposed stone walls. The restaurant, Los Llanos, specialises in local dishes, including cured goat's cheese and *jamón Serrano*.

Zahara de la Sierra

Hotel Arco de la Villa
Paseo Nazari
Tel: 956-123 230
Fax: 956-123 244 €€
www.tugasa.com
This modern hotel has a dramatic cliff-top location, tucked into the mountainside between the rocks just beneath Zahara's spectacular ruined castle. The 17 rooms are comfortable and well equipped with magnificent views of the reservoir and surrounding sierra country. Good food is served in the restaurant.

PRICE CATEGORIES

Price categories are for a double room without breakfast:
€ = under €50
€€ = €50–90
€€€ = €90–150
€€€€ = more than €150

RONDA

Bodega El Juncal
Ctra Ronda–El Burgo, km 1
Tel: 952-161 170
Fax: 952-161 160 €€€€
www.eljuncal.com
On the outskirts of town this beautiful small hotel – just 9 rooms and suites, all beautifully furnished and with a minimalist ambience – is surrounded by landscaped gardens. Relax either in the pool, the Jacuzzi or sauna room, or in loungers on the pool-side terrace. The restaurant specialises in modern Spanish cuisine and fine wines, supplemented by the hotel's homecultivated red wines.

La Fuente de la Higuera
Partido de los Frontones
Tel: 952-114 355
Fax: 952-114 356 €€€€
www.hotelafuente.com
Set on a hill just north of Ronda, this is a rural olive oil mill that has been transformed into a boutique-style hotel in which post-modern decor has been integrated with traditional Spanish architecture. The nine suites each have their own style, original paintings and furniture, open fireplaces, luxury bathrooms and either a private garden or terrace. The restaurant offers tempting and creative Mediterranean cuisine.

Enfente Arte
Calle Real, 40
Tel: 952 879 088
Fax: 952 877 217
www.enfrentearte.com
Laid-back hotel in an old house with deep colours on the walls, subtropical plants everywhere and eclectic furnishings. Its facilities include a roof-top pool, terraces with views, a library and a pool room. All drinks (wine, beer, juice) are included, as is the excellent buffet breakfast.

Parador de Ronda
Plaza de España, s/n
Tel: 952-877 500
Fax: 952-878 188 €€€
www.parador.es
Ronda's parador is justly famous for being spectacularly perched on the edge of the El Tajo gorge, and many of the rooms benefit from the fabulous views this affords. The restored facade of an old building conceals an attractive modern interior. There is a good pool and an excellent restaurant. The only downside is that you must book well in advance.

Polo
Calle Mariano Souvirón, 8
Tel: 952-872 447
Fax: 952-872 449 €€
www.hotelpolo.net
Comfortable, friendly and reasonably priced, and in the centre of the town.

Reina Victoria
Jerez, 25
Tel: 952-871 240
Fax: 952-871 075 €€€
This grand old hotel

built in 1906 is still going strong, and the views over the cliff are still wonderful. Its guest book is full of famous names of the past. Also has a pool.

San Gabriel
Calle José Holgado, 18
Tel: 952-190 392
Fax: 952-190 117 €€
www.hotelsangabriel.com
This 16-room hotel, housed in a restored 18th-century town house in the heart of the old section of Ronda, is comfortable and characterful. It is traditionally furnished, with heavy wooden doors and tiled floors, but with every modern comfort too. It has a pretty patio garden and a good restaurant.

BELOW: the pool of Ronda's Hotel Reina Victoria.

MÁLAGA AND THE COSTA DEL SOL

ABOVE: patio of La Fonda, Benalmádena

Málaga city

Don Curro
Sancha de Lara, 7
Tel: 952-227 200
Fax: 952-215 946 €€€
www.hoteldoncurro.com
A classic Málaga hostelry, with an old-fashioned atmosphere, on a quiet side street off central Málaga's main shopping district.

Hostal Domus
Juan Valera, 20
Tel/fax: 952-297 164 €€
www.hostaldomus.com
This lovely villa, distinguished by its light-blue colour, is an ideal haven just 15 minutes east of the city centre in the pleasant Pedregalejo district. It offers 15 fully-equipped rooms, some of which have disabled access. Facilities include, free Internet access and a solarium. It is close to the best city beaches, too.

Larios
Marqués de Larios, 2
Tel: 952-222 200
Fax: 952-222 407 €€€€

www.hotel-larios.com
This medium sized boutique hotel in a classical-style building on one of Málaga's principal streets is one of the most stylish hotels in Málaga. The rooftop terrace and bar offer good views.

Las Vegas
Paseo de Sancha, 22
Tel: 952-217 712
Fax: 952-224 889 €€
Near the Málaga bullring and next to the city's seafront promenade, with a pool and a large garden.

Málaga Centro
Mármoles, 6
Tel: 952-070 216
Fax: 952-283 360 €€€
www.euro-mar.com
This is one of several good hotels that have recently opened in Málaga. Found just to the west of the city centre, it offers 153 classically decorated and fully-equipped rooms, a pool, cafeteria, car park and the prestigious Guernica restaurant.

Novotel Málaga
Avenida de Velaquez, 126
Tel: 952-248 150
Fax: 952-230 232 €€€
www.accorhotels.com
This very new and modern hotel is between the city centre and the airport, close to the impressive Exhibition Centre and the large hypermarkets. It offers 155 spacious and nicely decorated rooms, all with up-to-date facilities, four with disabled access. It also has an outdoor pool, and private indoor and outdoor parking.

Parador de Turismo Gibralfaro
Monte de Gibralfaro, s/n
Tel: 952-221 902
Fax: 952-221 904 €€€
www.parador.es
This small, luxurious parador is spectacularly situated next to the Castillo de Gibralfaro, the Moorish fortress. Breakfast comes with the best view in town. Reservations are essential.

Benajarafe

Hostal Esperanza
Ctra Málaga–Almería, km 261
Tel/fax: 952-514 388 €€
There are few places to stay on this stretch of the Costa del Sol – just 20 minutes east of Málaga, but this *hostal* opposite unspoiled beaches, is a good option. It offers 35 well-sized and simply furnished rooms, the best of which overlook the swimming pool, away from the road. It also has a good-value restaurant.

Benalmádena

Alay
Puerto Deportivo, s/n
Benalmádena-Costa
Tel: 952-446 000
Fax: 952-446 380 €€€€
This is a large modern hotel situated right next to the lively Benalmádena yacht harbour, one of the nightlife centres of the Costa del Sol.

La Fonda
Calle Santo Domingo, 7
Benalmádena-Pueblo
Tel: 952-568 324.
Fax: 952-568 273. €€€
www.fondahotel.com
Delightful small hotel in the middle of the surprisingly unspoiled village of Benalmádena a few miles inland from the coast. It also offers studios and apartments in nearby buildings.

Estepona

Albero Lodge
Calle Tamesis 15, Finca La Cancelada, N340, km 164
Tel: 952-880 700
Fax: 952-885 238 €€€
www.alberolodge.com

PRICE CATEGORIES

Price categories are for a double room without breakfast:
€ = under €50
€€ = €50–90
€€€ = €90–150
€€€€ = more than €150

TRANSPORT

ACCOMMODATION

ACTIVITIES

A – Z

LANGUAGE

Stylish nine-room hotel in converted villa near the beach, surrounded by gardens with a pool. Rooms are individually and strikingly designed to represent a country or city (from New York to the island of Jerba in Tunisia) and each one has its own patio or terrace. Breakfast is served in the rooms.

Alsatli Spa Hotel
Ctra N-340, km 167
Tel: 952-889 040
Fax: 952-887 060 €€€€
www.alsatlispahotel.com
Situated just south of Puerto Banús, this impressive hotel and spa built right on the beach is the newest resort in this exclusive part of the Costa del Sol. It offers a choice of 234 rooms and 2- and 3-bedroom suites – many of which have views over the Mediterranean and down to Gibraltar. There are six pools including a rooftop one, a beach club and a nearly half-acre large spa.

Atalaya Park
Ctra N340, km 163
Tel: 952-889 000
Fax: 952-889 022 €€€€
www.atalaya-park.es
Not far from the Puerto Banús end of the Estepona municipality, the Atalaya Park is set amidst gardens adjoining a top rate golf course.

El Paraíso
Urbanización El Paraiso
Ctra N340, km 134
Tel: 952-883 000
Fax: 952-882 019 €€€€
www.hotelparaisocostadelsol.com
Modern hotel on a hill to the east of Estepona, next to a golf course and with views over the Straits of Gibraltar.

Hostal Pilar
Plaza las Flores, 22
Tel: 952-800 018 €
Family-run, old-fashioned hotel on an attractive old square in the centre of town.

Kempinski
Playa El Padrón, N340, km 159
Tel: 952-809 500
Fax: 952-809 550 €€€€

www.kempinski-spain.com
Deluxe resort next to the beach a few miles east of the Estepona town centre. Facilities include four swimming pools (one of which is indoor), a fitness centre and beautiful gardens.

Las Dunas
La Boladilla Baja, N340, km 163
Tel: 952-794 345
Fax: 952-794 825 €€€€
www.las-dunas.com
This is a luxurious spa hotel, split into several Andalusian-style buildings next to the beach east of Estepona, with large, sumptuous rooms. A wide range of spa treatments are available.

Fuengirola

Beatriz Palace & Spa
Playa del Ejido
Tel: 952-922 000
Fax: 952-922 005 €€€€
www.beatrizhoteles.com
This rather large and stylish hotel is right on the beach in the most peaceful part of Fuengirola, just past the castle to the south of the town. Its 300 rooms are modern and elegantly furnished and most have Mediterranean views.

El Puerto
Paseo Marítimo Rey España, 32
Tel: 952-470 100
Fax: 952-470 166 €€€
www.hotel-elpuerto.com
This modern, round, high-rise hotel overlooking the fishing port and marina, is the most distinctive building on the busy seafront promenade. The numerous facilities include a spectacular roof-top pool.

Hostal Italia
Calle de la Cruz, 1
Tel: 952-474 193
Fax: 952-461 909 €
Bright and cheerful *hostal* just off the main square. The rooms are small but comfortable with balconies.

Marbella

Coral Beach
N340, km 175
Tel: 952-824 500
Fax: 952-826 257 €€€€
www.hotelcoralbeach.com
This hotel is ringed by palm trees, right on the beach in the heart of Marbella's Golden Mile. It has two restaurants plus a beach club and health centre.

Don Carlos
N340, km 192
Tel: 952-831 140
Fax: 952-833 429 €€€€
www.hoteldoncarlos.com
Rising above the pine woods, near the beach 11 km (7 miles) east of central Marbella, this hotel features a tennis club, a beach club and a lively disco.

El Castillo
Plaza San Bernabé, s/n
Tel: 952-771 739 €
www.hotelelcastillo.com
Well located next to the old town, El Castillo offers basic but characterful and clean rooms for a predominantly young clientele.

El Fuerte
Avenida El Fuerte, s/n
Tel: 952-861 500
Fax: 952-824 411 €€€€
www.fuertehoteles.com
The best option in the centre of Marbella, at the end of the town's seafront promenade, with a tropical garden and rooms with views of the sea. There is a second El Fuerte spa

BELOW: Marbella's sumptuous Puente Romano.

ABOVE: the Marbella Club, established in 1953, remains one of the top places to stay

hotel further along the coast (direction Málaga).

Enriqueta
Calle Los Caballeros, s/n
Tel: 952-827 552 €€
Small, simple hostelry with 17 rooms in a good location not far from the central Plaza de los Naranjos in the old town.

Gran Meliá Don Pepe
José Melia, s/n
Tel: 952-770 300
Fax: 952-779 954 €€€€
www.solmelia.com
This deluxe hotel situated at the western end of the town, and set in magnificent tropical gardens, is widely considered to be one of Marbella's finest.

Lima
Avenida Belón, 2
Tel: 952-770 500
Fax: 952-863 091 €€
www.hotellimamarbella.com
The Lima is conveniently located in central Marbella, one block from the Paseo Marítimo. Comfortable if somewhat old-fashioned, it is a good mid-range choice.

Los Monteros
Ctra N340, km 187
Tel: 952-771 700
Fax: 952-825 846 €€€€
www.monteros.com
Exclusive luxury resort hotel adjoining a golf course near the beach 5 km (3 miles) east of Marbella.

Marbella Club
Ctra N340, km 178
Tel: 952-822 211
Fax: 952-829 884 €€€€
www.marbellaclub.com
This classy 1950s hotel was the birthplace of the Marbella legend. Bungalow-style accommodation set among gardens which spread down to the beach.

Puente Romano
Ctra N340, km 177
Tel: 952-820 900
Fax: 952-775 766 €€€€
www.puenteromano.com
A landmark on the "Golden Mile" west of the town, this is a palatial hotel designed like a Moorish-Andalusian *pueblo*, with gardens and trickling fountains without, and marble galore within.

Rincón Andaluz
N340, km 173
Tel: 952-811 517
Fax: 952-814 180 €€
www.riu.com
This pretty hotel is modelled after an Andalusian *pueblo*, surrounded by luxury villas; near the sea and close to Puerto Banús.

Mijas

Byblos Andaluz
Urb. Mijas-Golf, s/n, Mijas Costa
Tel: 952-473 050
Fax: 952-476 783 €€€€
www.byblos-andaluz.com
This is a truly spectacular hotel and spa set in the middle of a golf course just a few kilometres inland from Fuengirola. It is elegantly designed with large rooms, some of which overlook the two pools and the terrace of the gourmet restaurant.

Hotel Mijas
Urb. Tamisa, s/n
Tel: 952-485 800
Fax: 952-485 825 €€€
www.hotasa.es
Modern, airy hotel with

ample gardens at the entrance to the postcard village of Mijas, offering fine views of the coast.

La Cala Resort
La Cala de Mijas, s/n
Mijas Costa
Tel: 952-669 000
Fax: 952-669 034 €€€
www.lacala.com
There's a relaxed atmosphere at this stylish hotel surrounded by golf courses, with large rooms featuring picture windows overlooking the fairways.

Tamisa Golf
Urbanización Tamisa, 2
Tel: 952-485 800 €€€€
www.hoteltamisagolf.com
This attractive Andalusian-style hotel sits on the edge of the Los Lagos golf course designed by Robert

Trent Jones. It is small and very comfortable, with just 20 spacious rooms and four Junior Suites, all with Internet connections and views over the golf course, as well as a gourmet restaurant and an indoor and outdoor pool.

Nerja

Apartahotel Marinas de Nerja
Ctra N-340, km 289.5
Tel: 952-522 300
Fax: 952-521 153 €€–€€€
www.marinasdenerja.com
One of the many assets of this large complex is its location – just to the west of this busy town and directly on the beach. It has 72 two-bedroom apartments, 107 one-bedroom apartments and 39 studios, all of which are brightly furnished, with large sea-view terraces and a daily cleaning service with towels and bed sheets changed three times weekly. Large pool.

BELOW: a beachfront location in Nerja.

Casa Maro
Carmen 2, Maro
Tel: 952-529 552 €€
www.hotel-casa-maro.com
Cosy small rustic 8-room German-run hostelry on the sea-facing side of the village of Maro, east of Nerja. Its five-table dining room advertises itself as "the smallest gourmet restaurant in the world".

Parador de Nerja
Almuñécar, 8
Tel: 952-520 050
Fax: 952-521 997 €€€
www.parador.es
A modern member of the parador chain, located on a cliff overlooking the beach. Its rooms are arranged around a garden.

Paraíso del Mar
Prolongación del Carabeo, 22
Tel: 952-521 621
Fax: 952-522 309 €€€
E-mail: info@hispanica-colinte.es
Offers a tranquil location on the edge of a cliff, near the parador. Has 12 comfortable rooms, some with breathtaking views.

Ójen

Refugio El Juanar
Sierra Blanca, s/n
Tel: 952-881 000
Fax: 952-881 001 €€€
www.juanar.com
Standing in the middle of a forest in the Sierra just inland from Marbella, this was once part of the parador chain. The 23 pleasant rooms are rustically furnished, with tiled floors and rugs. Some rooms have a fireplace. There is also a good restaurant serving game dishes in season. Pool in summer; log fires in winter. Charles de Gaulle came here to finish his memoirs in 1970.

San Pedro de Alcantara

Taberna del Alabardero Resort Hotel
Cerro de Artola, s/n
Ctra San Pedro to Ronda, km 167
Tel: 952-812 794
Fax: 952-818 630 €€€€
www.alabarderoresort.com
Just east off the San Pedro to Ronda road, a few kilometres inland from the coast, this is as classy as all the other Taberna del Alabardero hotels and restaurants. Surrounded by lush gardens, the rooms are beautifully decorated, spacious and well-equipped with terraces, many overlook its pool and gardens. Gourmet restaurant.

Torremolinos

Amaragua
Los Nidos, 23.
Tel: 952-384 700
Fax: 952-384 945 €€€
www.amaragua.com

Just outside the centre of Torremolinos, this large hotel is dedicated to the sun and the sea. It has 280 rooms, including suites, classically decorated, high-tech facilities, and terraces with views over the large swimming pool and beach. Also has a spa and beauty salon.

Cervantes
Calle Las Mercedes, s/n
Tel: 952-384 033
Fax: 952-384 857 €€€
www.hotelcervantestorremolinos.com
This large, modern hotel is one of the best options for those who want to stay close to the centre of Torremolinos rather than along the coast.

Meliá Costa del Sol
Paseo Marítimo, 11, Playa del Bajondillo
Tel: 952-386 677 €€€
www.meliacostadelsol.solmelia.com
Modern well-run hotel. Every room has a sea-view balcony and the location, right on the beach, is ideal for the town and La Carihuela.

Miami
Calle Aladino, 14
Tel: 952-385 255 €€
www.residencia-miami.com
This small family-run hotel in a traditional Spanish villa next to the Carihuela beach is inexpensive, friendly and informal. Doesn't take credit cards.

Tropicana
Calle Trópico, 6
Tel: 952-386 600
Fax: 952-380 568 €€€
E-mail: hotel-tropicana@spa.es
Good choice right on the beach at the western end of Torremolinos's lively fish restaurant quarter, La Carihuela.

ANTEQUERA AND LA AXARQUIA

Antequera

La Casa de la Fuente
Calle Málaga 18, Villanueva de Algaidas
Tel: 952-745 030 €€
www.lacasadelafuente.com
Luxury bed and breakfast 20 km (12 miles) northeast of Antequera with spacious en suite rooms named after famous painters. Picnics can be provided for lunch. Discounts available for longer stays.

La Posada del Torcal
Ctra La Joya, s/n, Villanueva de la Concepción
Tel: 952-031 177
Fax: 952-031 006 €€€€
www.eltorcal.com/PosadaTorcal
Stylish hilltop hostelry with eight rooms built in the style of a traditional Andalusian farm manor, at the foot of the Torcal nature area.

Parador de Antequera
García del Olmo, s/n, Antequera
Tel: 952-840 261
Fax: 952-841 312 €€
www.parador.es
Airy, spacious modern parador with good views of the sweeping plain of Antequera.

Cómpeta

Balcon de Cómpeta
Calle San Antonio 75
Tel: 952-553 535 €€
www.hotel-competa.com
An Anglo-Spanish-run hotel consisting of 26 rooms and eight independent comfortably furnished bungalows. As well as the main swimming pool there is a children's pool. A baby monitoring service is available.

Frigiliana

Los Caracoles
Ctra Frigiliana-Torrox, km 4.6
Tel: 952-030 609 €€
www.hotelloscaracoles.com
Five igloo-like bungalows, each sleeping 2–4 people, make up this unusual complex near the prettiest village in the Axarquia.

La Posada Morisca
Loma de la Cruz s/n, Ctra Frigiliana-Torrox
Tel: 952-534 151 €€
www.laposadamorisca.com
A comfortable, rustic hotel in which each room has its own terrace and fireplace.

Guadalhorce Valley

Los Limoneros
Apdo de Correos 314
Tel: 952-484072 €€
www.andalucia.com/loslimoneros
Delightful hotel and complementary therapy centre in a restored farmhouse, barn and hayloft in the hills near Alora. Its aim is to create a relaxing informal atmosphere. Swimming pool.

Monda

Castillo de Monda
El Castillo, s/n
Tel: 952-457 142
Fax: 952-457 336 €€€
www.costadelsol.spa.es/hotel/monda
Overlooking the village of Monda midway on the inland road between Marbella and Coin, this 16-room hotel incorporates the ruins of a Moorish fortress. Stylish and comfortable.

Montes de Málaga

Arcadia Artist Retreat
Antigua Venta de Santa María, Almogía
Tel: 952-430 598 €€
www.arcadiaretreat.com
Out-of-the-way guesthouse on a back road between Málaga and Antequera, run by an Italian restaurateur and Slovakian artist. It's meant not only for creative types, as its name suggests, but also for anyone who is in search of peace and inspiration.

Cortijo La Reina
Ctra Málaga Colmenar, km 548.5
Tel: 951-014 000
www.hotelcortijolareina.com
At an altitude of 800 metres (2,600 ft) this country house hotel has views of the surrounding hills and the sea. It stands in its own estate which includes a mature garden. Most rooms have their own fireplaces. Andaluz cuisine is served in the dining room. Also has a pool.

Humaina
Parque Natural Montes de Málaga, Ctra de Colmenar s/n
Tel: 952-641025
www.hotelhumaina.es
A family-run, environment-friendly hotel with a pool, fireplace and well stocked library. Cycling, horse riding and rambling are among the activities available.

Torrox Costa

Hotel Rural Cortijo Amaya
Cortijo Amaya, s/n
Tel/fax: 952-530 245 €€
www.cortijoamaya.com

Located about 1 km (½ mile) from the beach on the hill behind town, and with wide views over the Mediterranean, this small family-run hotel is a real gem. The 14 rooms, including family rooms, are all very comfortably furnished, the public areas and dining room are charming and sports facilities include a tennis court, table tennis, basketball, and an outside swimming pool.

Santa Rosa
Ctra Málaga-Almería
Tel: 952-530 790
Fax: 952-532 527 €€
www.hoteles-santarosa.com
This is a small and comfortable hotel right next to the beach, with its own beach club, where the ambience is formal Spanish. The facilities include a TV lounge, snack bar and garden, and the restaurant's speciality is Axarquian cuisine – especially sardines *al espeto* – freshly caught sardines skewered and charcoal grilled.

PRICE CATEGORIES

Price categories are for a double room without breakfast:
€ = under €50
€€ = €50–90
€€€ = €90–150
€€€€ = more than €150

TRANSPORT
ACCOMMODATION
ACTIVITIES
A – Z
LANGUAGE

CÓRDOBA CITY AND PROVINCE

Córdoba City

Albucasis
Calle Buen Pastor, 11
Tel/fax: 957-478 625 €€
This is a family-run establishment in the heart of the old town offering good value and clean, comfortable lodgings set around a pretty patio.
Al Mihrab
Amistad Córdoba
Plaza de Maimónides, 3
Tel: 957-420 335
Fax: 957-420 365 €€€
www.nh-hoteles.com
If you want to be close to the sights, this is one of the best options in the upper range. Very comfortable if functional rooms in two former mansions looking over the peaceful Plaza Maimónides. Prices very according to demand – good deals are sometimes

available. The rooms overlooking the central patio are preferable to the ones in the annexe. All mod-cons including a Play Station.
Casa de los Azulejos
Fernando Colón, 5
Tel: 957 470 000
Fax: 957 475 496 €€
www.casadelosazulejos.com
This is an absolute delight, an elegant 17th-century house, whose name derives from the wonderful coloured tiles decorating its vaulted ceilings. The style is a mix of Andalusian and Latin American, and the eight pastel-coloured rooms open on to a central patio. In addition there are a very good Fusion Andalusian/Latin American restaurant and a Mexican Cantina. Situated near the Plaza Corredera.

Conquistador
Calle Magistral González Francés, 17
Tel: 957-481 102
Fax: 957-474 677 €€€
www.hotelconquistadorcordoba.com
Córdoba's longest-running hotel at the medium to higher end of the scale, the Conquistador has an unbeatable location, right next to La Mezquita. The rooms are large and comfortable, if rather dated, and some have views of the mosque. Usual amenities, including a coffee shop.
La Hospedería de El Churrasco
Romero, 38
Tel: 957 294 808
Fax: 957 421 661 €€€€
www.elchurrasco.com
With just nine rooms – each individually decorated – this is one of the most stylish hotels in Córdoba. It features an intriguing combination of

the old and the new – fine antiques, plasma TVs and Internet connections, free drinks in the mini-bar and use of the garage and a rooftop terrace/ solarium with great view. It is associated with the restaurant of the same name situated near by.
Lola
Calle Romero, 3
Tel: 957-200 305
Fax: 957-422 063 €€€
www.hotelconencantolola.com
Centrally located hotel with just eight rooms, individually decorated with paintings and bric-a-brac. Some rooms have a terrace with a view of the mosque.

BELOW: one of Córdoba's characteristic patios.

Los Omeyas

Calle Encarnación, 17
Tel: 957-492 267
Fax: 957-491 659 €€
Situated in the Judería, this 27-room hotel, built in traditional style, offers more amenities than you'd expect of an establishment in this price category, including satellite TV.

Maciá Alfaros

Alfaros,18
Tel: 957 491 920
Fax: 957 492 210 €€€
Found in a quieter part of Córdoba, and yet just 15 minutes' walk to the Mezquita, this is a very tasteful hotel with large, modern rooms with a terrace and a balcony overlooking a central patio and swimming pool. Has a good restaurant, too.

Maestre

Romero Barros, 4–6
Tel: 957-472 410
Fax: 957-475 395 €€
www.hotelmaestre.com
This is a good-value hotel situated near the river about half way between La Mezquita and the Plaza del Potro. The rooms overlook an attractive inner courtyard where guests can sit. The management also runs a cheaper *hostal* down the street, as well as a small number of one- or two-bedroom apartments.

Maimonides

Torrijos, 4
Tel: 957-471 500
Fax: 957-483 803 €€€€
www.hotelmaimonides.com
Medium-sized hotel with a pretty Andalusian patio that doubles as a coffee shop. Recently refurbished, it is a comfortable choice, close to the mosque.

Marisa

Cardenal Herrero, 6
Tel: 957-473 142
Fax: 957-474 144 €€
www.hotelmarisacordoba.com
Comfortable and friendly, if a bit old fashioned, this is a good budget option, with a superb position facing the mosque.

Mezquita

Plaza Santa Catalina, 1
Tel: 957-475 585
Fax: 957-476 219 €€
A restored 16th-century home just across from the Mezquita. The ambience is enhanced by sculptures featuring Andalusian themes and antiques. There are 21 rooms: if possible, request one facing the interior patio and, in particular, the one that used to be the old chapel.

Near Córdoba

Al Mihrab

Avenida del Brillante, 5km
Tel: 957- 272 198
Fax: 957-272 198 €€
A friendly neo-Moorish style hotel in the foothills north of central Córdoba, not far from the Parador (see below) and benefiting from the same fantastic views.

Parador de Cordoba

Avenida de la Arruzafa, 33
Tel: 957-275 900
Fax: 957-280 409 €€€
www.parador.es
This is a modern establishment in the parador network that offers fine views and extensive grounds. Situated on a hillside 3 km (2 miles) from the city it is slightly cooler than the city centre, which can be very hot in summer. Usual parador standard of comfort, with spacious rooms, a fine restaurant and a very nice swimming pool.

Cabra

Fuente de las Piedras

Avda. Fuente de las Piedras, s/n
Tel: 957 529 740
Fax: 957 521 407 €€€
Found on the outskirts of Cabra, located on the edge of the Parque Natural Sierra Subbéticas, this is the most modern hotel in the area. The rooms are generously sized, the restaurant is of a high standard and the large pool is set in the midst of nice gardens.

Lucena

Santo Domingo

El Agua, 11
Tel: 957-511 100
Fax: 957-516 295 €€
Opened in 1997, in a former 17th-century convent, 30 rooms arranged around central cloisters.

Montilla

Bellido

Enfermería, 57
Tel: 957-651 915 €
Inexpensive pension in the centre of town, basic but clean and comfortable. The bar dispenses local wine from its own stock of barrels.

Don Gonzalo

Ctra Madrid–Málaga, km 447
Tel: 957-650 658
Fax: 957-650 666 €€
www.hoteldongonzalo.com
Convenient, modern highway hotel on the outskirts of Montilla, in the heart of Córdoba's wine country.

Palma del Río

Hospedería de San Francisco

Avenida Pio XII, 35
Tel: 957-710 183
Fax: 957-710 732 €€
www.casasypalacios.com
This hotel, renowned for its fine food, is in a 15th-century former Franciscan monastery. The attractive rooms look over a lovely patio and gardens.

Priego de Córdoba

Villa Turística de Priego

Aldea de Zagrilla, s/n
Tel: 957-703 503
Fax: 957-703 573 €€
www.villaturisticadepriego.com
This holiday complex of self-catering units, part of the Andalusian "Villas Turísticas" chain, is located in the countryside a few kilometres from the town of Priego.

Zuheros

Zuhayra

Calle Mirador, 10
Tel: 957-694 693
Fax: 957-694 702 €
www.zuheros.com
This is a simple but comfortable hotel, with a good restaurant, situated in the picturesque village of Zuheros at the northern entrance to the Subbética nature park.

JAÉN CITY AND PROVINCE

Jaén city

Parador de Jaén
Castillo de Santa Catalina
Tel: 953-230 000
Fax: 953-230 930 €€€
www.parador.es
This is one of the most impressive paradors in Spain. It is situated on a hill 4 km (2½ miles) west of the city, right next to Jaén's 8th-century Moorish castle and built in a similar style. Offers baronial-style interior, magnificent views of the sierra and the city below, and a great outdoor pool in lovely gardens.

Andujar

Don Pedro
Gabriel Zamora, 5
Tel: 953-501 274
Fax: 953-504 785 €
Modest two-star hotel in the centre of the town, and a good place to sample reasonably priced local specialities.

Baeza

Hospedería Fuentenueva
Paseo Arca del Agua, s/n
Tel: 953-743 100
Fax: 953-743 200 €€
A friendly and tastefully decorated small hotel installed in what used to be a women's prison.
Palacete Santa Ana
Santa Ana Vieja
Tel: 953-741 657 €€
www.palacetesantana.com
A 16th-century building with relaxing, elegant rooms and pretty patios. Within easy walking distance of the centre of town.

Cazorla and environs

Nueva Guadalquivir
Calle Nueva 6
Tel: 953-720 268 €
Excellent value *hostal* located just off the main square with pine and floral décor and satellite TV.

BELOW: the comfortable Palacio de la Rambla, Úbeda.

Parador de Cazorla
Sierra de Cazorla, s/n
Tel: 953-727 075
Fax: 953-727 077 €€€
www.parador.es
Dramatically situated in the heart of the sierra, this modern parador is an excellent base from which to explore the wilderness of Cazorla park. Usual parador facilities, plus a pool and wonderful views.
Sierra de Cazorla
Ctra Sierra de Cazorla, km 2, La Iruela
Tel: 953-720 015
Fax: 953-720 017 €€
www.hotelsierradecazorla.com
A functional but comfortable small hotel situated just outside the village of La Iruela, at the main entrance to the Cazorla park.
Villa Turística de Cazorla
Ladera de San Isicio, s/n
Tel: 953-710 100
Fax: 953-710 152 €€€
www.villacazorla.com
Accommodation in comfortable semi-detached units, some equipped with a kitchenette, on a hillside facing the village of Cazorla.

Úbeda

La Paz
Andalucía, 1
Tel: 953-752 140
Fax: 953-750 848 €€
www.hotel-lapaz.com
In the newer part of Ubeda but within walking distance of the monumental area of town, this is a simple but comfortable budget option, with plenty of facilities, including satellite TV, internet facilities and a cafeteria.

María de Molina
Plaza del Ayuntamiento, s/n
Tel: 953-795 356
Fax: 953-793 694 €€
www.hotel-maria-de-molina.com
Well situated in the heart of the Renaissance centre, hotel María de Molina has 20 tasteful rooms surrounding a central patio. Its restaurant is considered one of the best places in town to experience the regional cuisine of Jaén.
Palacio de la Rambla
Plaza del Marqués, 1
Tel: 953-750 196
Fax: 953-750 267 €€€
www.palaciodelarambla.com
This 16th-century palace continues to be the part-time residence of the Marquesa de la Rambla, but eight rooms – large and furnished with antiques, surrounding an ivy-covered central patio – have been opened to paying guests.
Parador de Úbeda
Plaza Vázquez Molina, 1
Tel: 953-750 345
Fax: 953-751 259 €€€
www.parador.es
One of the oldest hotels in the parador chain, installed in a characterful 16th-century palace in the centre of Úbeda's old Renaissance quarter. Large and comfortable rooms, an attractive patio and all mod cons.

GRANADA CITY AND ENVIRONS

ABOVE: the terrace of the Parador de Granada.

Granada City

Alhambra Palace
Peña Partida, 2
Tel: 958-221 468
Fax: 958-226 404 €€€€
www.h-alhambrapalace.es
At the foot of the Alhambra walls, an ochre-coloured neo-Moorish fantasy with good views over the city. The hotel bar and terrace is a popular meeting place.
Los Alixares
Avenida Los Alixares del Generalife, s/n
Tel: 958-225 575
Fax: 958-224 102 €€
This large, efficiently run four-star hotel with pool is well located near the Alhambra.
América
Real de la Alhambra, 53
Tel: 958-227 471
Fax: 958-227 470 €€€
www.hotelamericagranada.com
This small and intimate family-run hotel has an enviable location within Alhambra grounds. Book well in advance.

Casa Morisca
Cuesta de la Victoria, 9
Tel: 958-221 100
Fax: 958-215 796 €€€
www.hotelcasamorisca.com
Located in the Albaicín, this is a tastefully converted 15th-century house with Moorish-inspired décor, a central courtyard and Alhambra views.
El Ladrón d'Agua
Carrera del Darro, 13
Tel: 958 215 040
Fax: 958 224 345 €€€
www.ladrondeagua.com
Occupying a 16th-century mansion on the picturesque Carrera del Darro, running between the Alhambra and Albaicín hills, this is one of the best new hotels in Granada. A wealth of period details were uncovered during restoration of the building and these blend beautifully with the clean, modern decor. The eight rooms have views of the Alhambra.

Juan Miguel
Acera del Darro, 24
Tel: 958-521 111
Fax: 958-258 916 €€€
www.hoteljuanmiguel.com
Reasonably priced, comfortable option in the busy central district of Granada.
Palacio de Santa Inés
Cuesta de Santa Inés, 9
Tel: 958-222 362
Fax: 958-222 465 €€€
www.palaciosantaines.com
Good location at the foot of the the Albaicín, in a converted 16th-century palace around a traditional Andalusian courtyard. Rooms are individually furnished and some have balconies.
Parador de Granada
Real de la Alhambra, s/n
Tel: 958-221 440
Fax: 958-222 264 €€€€
www.parador.es
Reservations are essential to get into some of the most sought-after rooms in the parador network, in a converted 15th-century Francisco monastery beautifully situated within the Alhambra gardens themselves.
Reina Cristina
Calle Tablas, 4
Tel: 958-253 211
Fax: 958-255 728 €€
www.hotelreinacristina.com
A friendly, comfortable, family-run establishment in an old Granada mansion, nicely placed midway between the cathedral and the Plaza Bib Rambla. Spacious rooms and a good restaurant. Federico García Lorca spent his final days here, before his arrest and subsequent murder by Nationalists.
Triunfo
Plaza Triunfo, 19
Tel: 958-207 444
Fax: 958-279 017 €€€
Situated off the main thoroughfare of Granada, the Gran Vía de Colón, this small and comfortable hotel is convenient for shopping and for visiting the sights in the centre of the city.

PRICE CATEGORIES

Price categories are for a double room without breakfast:
€ = under €50
€€ = €50–90
€€€ = €90–150
€€€€ = more than €150

ABOVE: a good choice in Guadix.

Zaguán del Darro
Carrera del Darro, 23
Tel: 958 215 730
Fax: 958 215 731 €€€
www.hotelzaguan.com
Several historic properties on this picturesque lane at the foot of the Albaicín have been converted into boutique hotels. This delightful three-star hotel has quarry tiled floors, a central courtyard, individually furnished rooms and a cosy bar-cum-coffee shop.

Near Granada

La Almunia del Valle
Camino de la Umbría s/n
Monachil
Tel: 958-308 010 €€€
www.laalmuniadelvalle.com.
An 11-room hotel in a peaceful setting 8 km (5 miles) southeast of the city. Facilities include a bar, restaurant and swimming pool. Home-made olive oil served with meals.

Almuñecar and environs

Almuñecar Playa
Paseo San Cristobal
Tel: 958-639 450 €€
www.playasenator.com
This is a large chain hotel on the beach of Almuñecar with enclosed swimming pool and leafy atrium. Buffet restaurant.

Palacete de Cazulas
Otivar
Tel: 958-644 036 €€€
www.cazulas.com
Bed and breakfast (from September to April only) in a magnificent mansion 20 km (12 miles) inland from Almuñecar.

Tropical
Av Europa, s/n
Tel: 958-633 458
Fax: 958633 458 €€
This is a comfortable, family-run pension with 11 rooms in the centre of town.

Guadix

Comercio
Calle Mira de Amezcua, 3
Tel: 958-660 500
Fax: 958-665 072 €€
www.hotelcomercio.com
his family-run hotel was built in 1905 and it retains a certain period charm in spite of a complete renovation. Aside from comfortable lodgings in 24 rooms, the common areas feature art exhibitions and live music concerts, and the restaurant serves the best food in town.

Cuevas Pedro Antonio de Alarcón
Barriada San Torcuato, s/n
Tel: 958-664 986
Fax: 958-661 721 €€
www.cuevaspedroantonio.com
The rooms of this unusual hotel are caves carved out of the soft rock, emulating the typical troglodyte dwellings of the area.

Loja

La Bobadilla
Ctra Loja–Seville, s/n
Tel: 958-321 861
Fax: 958-321 810 €€€€
www.la-bobadilla.com
This is a super-deluxe hotel resort, built in a superb country palace standing in its own estate in the heart of the countryside. It has a top-quality restaurant, champagne for breakfast, and prices to match.

Motril

La Casa de los Bates
Ctra N340 (Motril–Salobreña), km 329.6
Tel: 958-349 495 €€€
www.casadelosbates.com
A 19th-century country mansion on a hill overlooking the town of Motril and the coast. Breakfast includes exotic fruit juices from the orchards of the Costa Tropical. The grounds include a "romantic" and a botanic garden.

Salobreña

Avenida
Avenida del Mediterraneo 35.
Tel: 958-611 544 €€
www.hotelavenidatropical.com
The best hotel in Salobreña town, on the road to the beach – which is within walking distance.

Hotel Salobreña
Ctra N340 Málaga–Almería, km 323
Tel: 958-610 261 €€
www.hotelsalobrena.com
Situated on a clifftop between Salobreña and Almuñecar. Most room have balconies, but the "club" rooms are more spacious and with spectacular sea views. Facilities include a swimming pool, floodlit tennis court, and a complementary bus service into Salobreña.

Sierra Nevada

Ziryab
Plaza Andalucía, s&n.
Tel: 958-480 512
Fax: 958-481 415 €€€
www.hotelziryab.com
A modern hotel in Granada's ski resort, conveniently close to the ski lifts and reasonably priced.

THE ALPUJARRAS

Berchules

Los Berchules
Tel: 958-852 530 €€
www.hotelberchules.com
Small, family-run hotel at the entrance to the village which aims, it says, to provide comfort rather than luxury. It is a good base for walkers, with a garden and swimming pool for summer; log fires during the winter, plus table games and a small library for the evenings. Special dietary needs can be catered for.

Bubión

Las Terrazas de la Alpujarra
Plaza del Sol, 7, Bubión
Tel: 958-763 034 €
www.terrazasalpujarra.com
Simple but tasteful, and excellent value for money, a favourite with trekkers and bikers as a base to explore the Alpujarras.

Villa Turística de Bubión
Barrio Alto
Tel: 958-763 909 €€
www.villabubion.com
A complex of 43 self-contained cottages, each with fireplace and either a terrace or a garden. There's also a restaurant if you don't feel like cooking.

Busquistar

Alcazaba de Busquistar
Ctra Orgiva-Laujar, km 37, Busquístar
Tel: 958-858 687 €€
A peaceful hotel complex outside Trevelez

built in the style of an Alpujarran village (even sprouting an imitation church tower). Most rooms have a wood-stove or fireplace. There is both an indoor and outdoor, saltwater swimming pool.

Cadiar

Alquería de Morayma
Ctra Cádiar–Torvizon, s/n
Tel: 958-343 221 €€
www.alqueriamorayma.com
Rooms are in a group of five small houses with adjoining shrine and farmhouse which evoke Moorish Andalusian atmosphere in a pristine rural setting. You can play chess on the terrace or swim in the outdoor pool. Has won the Junta de Andalucía's first prize for innovation in rural tourism.

Ferreirola

Sierra y Mar
Tel: 958-766 171 €–€€
www.sierraymar.com
Bed-and-breakfast in a small house at the top of a village away from the main road but on the GR142 long-distance path through the Alpujarras. Rooms are rustic but comfortably furnished, and most have their own terrace. The owners can advise on visits and walks in the area.

Laujar de Andarax
Villa Turistica de Laujar
Cortijo de la villa
Tel: 950-513 027 €€
www.servimar.net/infLaujar.htm
A mini-village of 31 self-contained Alpujar-

ran-style houses or "villas". They range from studios to two luxury suites with private pools. There is also a communal pool and a restaurant.

Mairena

Las Chimeneas
Calle Amargura 6
Tel: 958-760 352 €€
www.alpujarra-tours.com
Beautiful house that has been sensitively restored in a small village near the Granada/Almería border. It is owned by two walking tour leaders, aware of the needs and interests of walkers. Large bedrooms, each with en suite facilities and a private balcony or terrace. There are also three self-catering studios with fireplaces and stunning views.

Mecina Fondales

Mecina Fondales
La Fuente s/n
Tel: 958-766 254 €€
www.hoteldemecina.com.es
Small hotel of 21 rooms (some family rooms available) in a village off the main road through the Alpujarras. Has a restaurant and bar. This is a good area for walking.

Orgiva

Taray
Ctra Tablate–Albuñol, km 18, Orgiva
Tel: 958-784 525
Fax: 958-784 531 €€
Friendly, bright hotel located on its own farm

just outside the village of Orgiva. Decor is cheerful, and the restaurant serves good food based on home-grown ingredients.

Trevelez

La Fragua
San Antonio 4, Trevelez
Tel: 958-858 626
Fax: 958-858 614 €
Comfortable *hostal* at the top of Spain's highest village. Some rooms have balconies and good views. A popular stop for pony-trekking groups.

Yegen

El Rincón de Yegen
Camino de Gerald Brenan
Tel: 958-851 270 €
www.aldearural.com/rinconyegen
Offers simple but comfortable rural accommodation. As well as rooms there is a selection of self-catering cottages. Restaurant, bar and swimming pool. Facilities for the disabled.

PRICE CATEGORIES

Price categories are for a double room without breakfast:
€ = under €50
€€ = €50–90
€€€ = €90–150
€€€€ = more than €150

ACCOMMODATION

ACTIVITIES

A – Z

LANGUAGE

ALMERÍA CITY AND ITS PROVINCE

Almería City

Gran Hotel Almería
Avenida Reina Regente, 8
Tel: 950-238 011
Fax: 950-270 691 **€€€**
www.granhotelalmeria.com
This is Almería's best
hotel, with far-reaching
views over the harbour
and the bay.

La Perla
Plaza del Carmen, 7
950-238 877 **€**
Recently refurbished
and within walking dis-
tance of the Alcazaba.
Modestly priced.

AM Torreluz IV
Plaza Flores, 5
Tel/fax: 950-234 999 **€€**
www.amtorreluz.com
This is a middle-range
hotel that belongs to a
small chain. Its location
on the Plaza Flores is
convenient, the rooms
are clean and modern,
and the price reason-
able. It shares a swim-
ming pool with its sister
hotel AM Congress.

Agua Amarga

Mikasa
Ctra Carboneras, s/n, Agua
Amarga
Tel: 950-138 073
Fax: 950-513 554 **€€€**
www.hotelmikasa.com
More like a private home
than a hotel, in a mod-
ern building, with 20 art-
fully decorated rooms.
Convenient for the
beaches of the Cabo de
Gata nature park.

El Tio Kiko
Calle Embarque s/n
Tel: 950-138 080 **€€€**
www.eltiokiko.com
Small hotel of 27 room
with sea views, swim-
ming pool, jacuzzi and
sauna. Buffet breakfast
offering a wide choice.

Alhama de Almería

San Nicolás
Calle Baños, s/n
Tel: 950-641 361
Fax: 950-641 281 **€€**

This is an old-
fashioned spa hotel
next to hot springs in
the foothills of the
Sierra de Gadór.

Almerimar

Melia Almerimar
Urb. Almerimar, s/n, El Ejido
Tel: 950-497 007
Fax: 950-497 146 **€€€**
www.solmelia.com
This is a large, modern
hotel with all amenities,
including a swimming
pool, and conveniently
situated for the nearby
golf course.

Garrucha

Tikar
Ctra Garrucha–Vera s/n
Tel: 950-617131 **€€**
www.hoteltikar.com
This is a small resort
hotel of just six individually styled suites not
far from the beach.
Facilities include a roof-
top solarium and a pool
in the garden. It aso a
good restaurant.

Los Vélez

Velad al Abyadh
Calle Balsa Parra, 28,
Vélez Blanco
Tel: 950-415 109 **€€**
www.hotelvelad.com
Town hotel incorporat-
ing traditional materi-
als in its construction
including wooden
beams and wrought
iron. No restaurant but
the cafeteria serves
tapas.

Cortijo de la Noria
Ctra Velez Rubio–Puerto
Lumbreras
Tel: 690-346 471/346 463 **€**
www.cordelano.com
Large house 1 km (½
mile) off the A92
motorway in an area of
almonds, olives and
vines, offering bed and

BELOW: Hotel Torreluz in Almería's city centre.

breakfast or two self-contained apartments for short or longer lets.

Mojácar and Environs

El Moresco
Avenida de en camp, s/n, Mojácar
Tel: 950-478 025
Fax: 950-478 262 €€
www.arturogrupocantoblanco.com
In Mojácar itself, rather than on the beach, which is 3 km (2 miles) below the village. Has good views of the surrounding countryside.

El Puntazo
Paseo del Mediterraneo, s/n, Mojácar
Tel: 950-478 285
Fax: 950-478 285 €€
www.hotelelpuntazo.com
This bright, modern hotel is a comfortable and reasonably priced option if you want to be close to the beach.

Finca Listonero
Cortijo Grande, Turre
Tel: 950-479 094 €€
www.fincalistonero.com
Inland from Mojácar, on the edge of the Tabernas desert, this converted Andalusian farmhouse turned seven-room hotel offers gourmet food and tasteful decor.

Mamabels
Calle Embajadores, 5, Mojácar
Tel: 950-472 448 €€
www.mamabels.com
Situated down a flight of steps in Mojácar, this hotel teeters on the very edge of the village. Arty and reasonably priced nine-room pension, with good views of the coast.

Parador de Mojácar
Paseo del Mediterráneo, Mojácar Playa
Tel: 950-478 250
Fax: 950-478 183 €€€

www.parador.es
A splendid beachside location is the main attraction of this modern parador.

Rodalquilar

Paraje de los Albacetes
Tel: 902-995 978 €€
www.hotelrodalquilar.com
Stylish but reasonably priced hotel on a quiet strip of coast, painted in earth colours to blend into the Cabo de Gata Park in which it stands. The rooms are decorated with their own individually-commissioned ceramic murals and other works of art.

Roquetas del Mar

Playacapricho
Urb. Playa Serena, s/n
Tel: 950-333 100
Fax: 950-333 806 €€€€
www.hotelesplaya.com
Modern 330-room resort hotel next to the beach. The first impression is of the enormous glassed-in area containing the lobby, tropical garden and indoor pool. There is also a large outdoor pool.

Playasol
Urb. Playa Serena, s/n
Tel: 950-333 802 €€€
One of the first hotels to open in the burgeoning holiday resort of Playa Serena, near Roquetas de Mar. Next to the beach, and with a spectacular pool.

San José

Cortijo el Sotillo
Ctra San José
Tel: 950-611 100 €€€
www.cortijoelsotillo.com
A hotel built around an old farmhouse in the

country outside San José. Part of the Relais du Silence network and thus promising relaxation and peace.

La Posada del Paco
Correo s/n
Tel: 950-380 414 €€
www.posadadepaco.com
Small hotel with just 20 rooms on the main street of the resort, five minutes from the beach. Modern minimalist decoration.

Sierra de Alhamilla

Balneario de Sierra Alhamilla
Pechina, s/n
Tel: 950-317 413
Fax: 950-160 257 €€
A pleasant small hotel near Pechina, 10 km (6 miles) north of Almería city, built over old Moorish baths, next to a thermal spring.

Sierra de las Filabres

Las Menas de Serón
Ctra A339 Serón–Gergal, km 16
Tel: 950-526 100 €
www.lasmenasdeseron.com
In the middle of the Sierra de las Filabres and as about as far from civilisation as you can get – wonderful if you are looking for silence and walks in the hills.

Las Almendras
Bda. Los Herreras s/n, Lubrín
Tel: 950-528 587 €€
www.lasalmendras.com
Relaxing farmhouse that has been restored using traditional materials, with a threshing floor and old wine press. Four en suite rooms. Through the orchard there is a pool fed with spring water.

Tabernas

Hospederia del Desierto
Ctra N340, km 478
Tel: 950-369 304 €€
www.hospederiadeldesierto.com
Small ochre-coloured hotel in the desert with sauna gym pool and a good restaurant.

Vera

Terraza Carmona
Manuel Jimenez, 1
Tel: 950-390 760
Fax: 950-391 314 €€
www.terrazacarmona.com
Comfortable family-run hotel on the edge of town. The downstairs restaurant is one of the best in Almería.

Vera Playa Club
Ctra Garrucha–Villaricos, km 1
Tel: 950-467 475
Fax: 950-467 476 €€
www.playasenator.com
This is the only nudist hotel in Spain, next to the beach, with a family atmosphere. Clothing is allowed in the restaurant and reception area only.

Sorbas

Urra
Tel: 950-364 532 €€
www.urra-enterprises.com
Eco-friendly field centre near the karst scenery of Sorbas with a choice of guesthouse (three nights minimum stay), self-catering house and camping facilities.

PRICE CATEGORIES
Price categories are for a double room without breakfast:
€ = under €50
€€ = €50–90
€€€ = €90–150
€€€€ = more than €150

TRANSPORT
ACCOMMODATION
ACTIVITIES
A – Z
LANGUAGE

CAMPSITES

Although there are some campsites in wilderness areas, camping in Spain is seen as a cheaper alternative to hotels, not as a way of getting back to nature. Camping outside official sites is not generally allowed, and authorities are especially vigilant in keeping campers off the sides of main roads and off the beaches. Independent campers can try to obtain permission to camp on private property, such as a farm, from the owner.

Official campsites are rated, according to their facilities, as luxury, first, second, or third class. Some have supermarkets and restaurants attached. An **Area de Acampada** indicates something that approximates camping out in the wild. **Campings** (campsites)

in the main tourist areas tend to be too crowded for comfort in July and August.

A full list of campsites is published in the camping guide, *Guía Oficial de Campings*, published by Turespaña (Secretaria General de Turismo), available in bookshops. Not all sites are open all the year, so it is advisable to phone beforehand.

Below is a selection of camp sites, chosen because of their exceptional locations, close to the sea or in or near nature reserves.

Almería

Las Menas
Ctra Seróm–Gergal, km 10, Serón
Tel: 950-526 011
In an abandoned mining town surrounded by pines in the Sierra de Filabres.
Los Escullos-San José
San José, s/n
Tel: 950-389 811
Near the beach, in the

Cabo de Gata nature park. Scuba diving centre. Open all year.
Tau
San José, s/n
Tel: 950-380 166
Tents are pitched in a eucalyptus wood in the Cabo de Gata nature park, a short walk from the sea.

Cádiz

Caños de Meca
Barbate, s/n
Tel: 956-437 120
Near Cape Trafalgar on the Atlantic coast, 600 metres/yds from one of the best beaches in Andalucía.
La Torrecilla
El Bosque, s/n
Tel: 956-716 095
Set in the Sierra de Grazalema nature park.
Los Alcornocales
Jimena de la Frontera, s/n
Tel: 956-640 060
Located near the Los Alcornocales nature park. Open all year.
Los Linares
Parque Natural Sierra de Grazalema, s/n, Benamahoma

Tel: 956-716 275
In the Grazalema nature park. Open all year.
Tavizna
Ctra C-3331, km 49, Puente de Tavizna, Ubrique
Tel: 956-463 011
On the banks of a river near Ubrique in the Grazalema nature park.

Córdoba

Cortijo Las Palomas
Ctra Carcabuey–Zagrilla, km 5
Tel: 957-720 002
This site is situated next to a natural spring in the Sierra Subbética nature park south of Córdoba.
Cortijo Los Villares
Ctra Carcabuey–Rute, s/n, Priego de Córdoba
Tel: 957-704 054
In the Sierra Subbética nature park. Open year round.
El Brillante
Avenida del Brillante, 50
Tel: 957-403 836
At just 1.25 km (¾ mile) north of the Plaza de Colón, this is the closest campsite to the centre of Córdoba.

BELOW: camping in designated campsites is one of the best ways of experiencing Andalucía's natural parks.

Granada

Orgiva
Valle del Guadalfeo, s/n, Orgiva
Tel: 958-784 307
Close to a river, and near the Poqueira valley in the Alpujarras.

Reina Isabel
Ctra Granada–La Zubia, km 4
Tel: 958-590 041
5 km (3 miles) south of the centre, this is a large site with good facilities. Open all year.

Trevelez
Haza de Cuna, s/n, Trevelez
Tel: 958-858 735
Spain's highest campsite, at an altitude of 1,560 metres (5,200 ft).

Huelva

Aracena Sierra
Marimateo, s/n, Aracena
Tel: 959-501 005
In the Sierra de Aracena nature park. Open all year.

El Madroñal
Fuenteheridos, s/n
Tel: 959-501 201
In a chestnut wood in the Sierra de Aracena nature park. Open all year round.

Las Cabañas de Cumbres
Cumbres Mayores, s/n
Tel: 958-710 372
In the Sierra de Aracena nature park. Open all year round.

Jáen

Chopera de Coto Rios
Santiago Pontones, s/n, Coto-Ríos
Tel: 953-721 905
In the middle of the Cazorla nature park.

Fuente de la Pascuala
Ctra del Tranco, km 23, Coto-Ríos
Tel: 953-721 228

In the Cazorla nature park. Open all year.

San Isicio
Camino San Isicio, s/n, Cazorla
Tel: 953-721 280
Two km (1 mile) from Cazorla village.

Málaga

Parque Ardales
Embalse Conde de Guadalhorce, s/n, Ardales
Tel: 952-112 401
In the lake area, north of Málaga.

Pinsapo Azul
Parque Sierra de las Nieves, s/n, La Yunquera
Tel: 952-482 754
In the Sierra de las Nieves park, off the old road from Málaga to Ronda.

Presa La Viñuela
Ctra A-356, km 2, La Viñuela
Tel: 952-030 127
Next to reservoir in the Axarquía region.

Seville

Reserva Verde del Huéznar
Ctra Cazalla–San Nicolás, s/n, Cazalla de la Sierra
Located in the Sierra Norte nature park.

YOUTH HOSTELS

If you are intending to stay in Youth Hostels in Southern Spain it is inadvisable to turn up on spec as some are not open year-round and others may be closed for renovations. For information on facilities and prices, or to make a reservation, contact Inturjoven
Calle Miño, 24
Seville,
Tel: 902-510 000
www. inturjoven.com.

ABOVE: camping is not allowed on the beaches.

Almería

Almería
Isla de Fuerteventura, s/n
Tel: 950-269 788
Fax: 950-271 744

Cádiz

Algeciras
Ctra N340, km 96
Tel: 956-679 060

Cádiz
Diego Arias, 1
Tel/fax: 956-221 939

El Bosque
Molino de Enmedio, s/n
Tel: 956-716 212

Jerez
Avenida Carrero Blanco, 30
Tel: 956-143 901

Córdoba

Córdoba
Plaza Juda Levi, s/n
Tel: 957-290 166
Fax: 957-290 500

Granada

Granada
Ramón y Cajal, 2
Tel: 958-272 638

Sierra Nevada
Estación de Pradollano
Tel: 958-480 305

Viznar
Camino Fuente Grande, s/n
Tel: 958-543 307

Huelva

Huelva
Avenida Marchena Colombo, 14, tel: 959-253 793

Mazagón
Cuesta de la Barca, s/n
Tel: 959-536 262

Punta Umbría
Avenida Océano, 13
Tel: 959-311 650

Jaén

Cazorla
Plaza Mauricio Martinez, 6
Tel: 953-720 329

Málaga

Málaga
Plaza Pio XII, s/n
Tel: 952-308 500
Fax: 952-308 504

Marbella
Trapiche, 2
Tel: 952-771 491
Fax: 952-836 227

Seville

Constantina
Cuesta Blanca, s/n
Tel: 955-881 589

Seville
Isaac Perál, 2
Tel: 955-056 500

TRANSPORT
ACCOMMODATION
ACTIVITIES
A – Z
LANGUAGE

ACTIVITIES

THEATRE & MUSIC, NIGHTLIFE, SHOPPING, SPORTS, SPAS & CHILDREN'S ACTIVITIES

THEATRE & MUSIC

Córdoba

Gran Teatro
Gran Capitán 3
Tel: 957-480 237
www.teatrocordoba.com
Regular performances by city orchestra; recitals; theatre; guitar festival in July.

Fuengirola

Salon Varietés Theatre
Calle Emancipación, s/n
Tel: 952-474 542
www.salonvarietestheatre.com
Theatre in English.

Granada

Auditorio Manuel de Falla
Paseo de los Mártires, s/n
Tel: 958-222 188
www.manueldefalla.org
Year-round orchestral recitals and concerts.

Málaga

Teatro Alameda
Calle Córdoba 9
Tel: 952-213 412
Theatre; musical concerts.
Teatro Miguel de Cervantes
Calle Ramos Marín, s/n
Tel: 952-224 109
www.teatrocervantes.com
Theatre; musical concerts.

Seville

Teatro de la Maestranza
Plaza de Colón, s/n
Tel: 954-223 344
www.teatromaestranza.com
Seville opera house. Orchestra recitals.
Teatro Lope de Vega
Avenida María Luisa, s/n
Tel: 954-590 853
Drama; flamenco; concerts.

NIGHTLIFE

Bars

Spaniards like nothing better than to drink and talk until the early hours. All cities have at least one bar area that comes to life in the evening. The *tapeo* is an accepted custom, in which you move between bars, sampling with every drink a different *tapa*, the tasty tidbits that can run from grilled shrimps to *tortilla* (potato omelette).

In all bars and cafés it is cheapest to drink at the counter. If you sit at a table, the price goes up – and up again on a terrace. Bars with live music charge extra. Bars advertising themselves as "pubs" are usually dimly lit and favoured by the young and hip. An "American bar" is one where the staff is female or there are hostesses, i.e. expect to pay over the odds.

Seville

Seville has a lively nightlife. There are numerous *tapas* bars, including **El Rinconcillo**, considered the city's oldest (founded in 1670). The Santa Cruz area *(see below)*, with its maze of streets and countless bars, is a favourite night-time hot spot for the young set, but many have switched to the newer bars along Calle de Betis, the street running parallel to the Guadalquivir river in Triana, and El Torneo across from La Cartuja. There's a good ambience around the Alameda de Hércules square, as well, and in La Macarena district at the northern end of the Old Town.

Plaza de la Alfalfa is another action-packed part of the city when it comes to bars. **Bar Alfalfa** (corner of Calles Candilejo and Alfalfa) is a traditional place with a cosy setting, while nearby **Bar Gran Tino** (Plaza Alfalfa 2) is always buzzing; wash down a wedge of crumbly Manchego cheese with your Rioja.

In pretty Bario Santa Cruz, students and tourists hang out at **Bodega Santa Cruz** (Mateo Gago) with its barrel tables and traditional tapas. Between here and the bullring, **Bodega San**

ABOVE: sample a tapa or two with your *cerveza* or *café*.

locals at lunchtime, **Tomaquet** (Calle Palangreros 10, behind the main post office) is the place to come for tapas. The surrounding pedestrian streets are good for traditional Spanish bars while the **Plaza Bar** (Plaza de la Constitución) with its terrace seating on the central church plaza is the meeting place for locals and visitors alike.

Granada

Granada knows how to fill the evening hours, thanks to its large student population. Students tend to gravitate towards the area around the Plaza del Principe, the maze-like Albaicín district and the Plaza Nueva. In summer, a good place for bars and outdoor action is the poetically misnamed Paseo de los Tristes (Sad People's Promenade), below the Alhambra. A great place to head here is **Casa 1899**, which has a traditional bodega feel and an excellent range of Spanish wines. A short stroll away, **El Rincón de San Pedro** (Carrera del Darro 12) is a bar with a cool contemporary feel. In central Plaza Nueva, **Café Central** (Calle

Jose (Calle Adriano 10) is an example of a place with earthy Med appeal, full of flat-capped locals playing dominoes and drinking *anís*. And don't miss one of the city's most atmospheric and busiest bars – **El Patio San Eloy** (Calle San Eloy 9) with its hams hanging over the bar, *fino* (sherry) served straight from the barrel and brightly tiled steps providing extra seating.

Fuengirola

Home-sick Brits will find plenty of English-run bars in Fuengirola, especially on the seafront. Head for **Babes** bar (Calle de la Cruz), Fish Alley, where you can indulge in homemade faggots and Tetleys on tap. Nearby **Café Miró** (Calle de Moncaya) specialises in cocktails and imported beers and has a large terrace. Rustic, cavernous and popular with

FLAMENCO FAVOURITES

Not all the best performers are earning millions in New York, contrary to what you may have heard. Even so, you will be fortunate to come across a top-quality authentic flamenco performance. Often it is cheapened to make it more palatable for popular taste. The best performances come spontaneously, when a singer is moved by emotion rather than money, and that is unlikely to happen before a crowd of tourists.

Some of the better flamenco clubs offer solid entertainment that fairly closely approximates the genuine article. The best places to see flamenco are Seville and the Santiago district in Jerez. Most venues open at

around 10pm and stay open until the small hours.

A few recommended venues:
El Arenal, Calle Rodo 7, Seville. Tel: 954-216 492.
El Lagá Tio Parrilla, Plaza del Mercado s/n, Jerez de la Frontera, Cádiz. Tel: 956-338 334.
Jardines Neptuno, Calle Arabial, Granada. Tel: 958-522 533.
Mesón La Bulería, Calle Pedro Lopez 3, Córdoba. Tel: 957-483 839.
Peña Antonio Chacón, Calle Salas 2, Jerez de la Frontera, Cádiz. Tel: 956-347 472.
Tablao Cardenal, Calle Torrijos 10, Córdoba. Tel: 957-483 320.
Tablao Los Gallos, Plaza Santa Cruz 11, Seville. Tel: 954-216 981.

The best flamenco is to be seen at the flamenco festivals and contests held between the end of June and the middle of September in small towns and villages – there's one, or more, every Saturday, somewhere in Andalucia. The best known are the *Potaje* in Utrera (Seville) at the end of June, *La Caracolá* in Lebrija (Seville) in mid-July, the festival in Mairena del Alcor (Seville) at the beginning of September, and *Fiesta de la Bulería* held in the Jerez bullring in mid-September.

In true flamenco tradition, these events never start on time and they tend to be long, drawn-out affairs, lasting into the early hours.

ABOVE: plenty of bars offer live music or club nights.

de Elvira) is good for a coffee or drink while nearby **Antigua Bodega Castañeda** (Calle de Elvira) serves local wines and sherry straight from the barrel.

Other nightlife hotspots on the Costa del Sol are the old town and the seafront in Marbella, the seafront in Fuengirola, the marina in Benalmádena, and the legendary town of Torremolinos.

Málaga

Málaga is a great place to *tapear* – cruise the *tapas* bars – and the best ones are right in the centre, including **Rincón de Mata** (Esparteros 8); **Taberna Rincón Chinitas** (Pasaje Chinitas) and **Bar Logueno** (Calle Marin Garcia 9) which has more than 75 tapas on its menu. An easy stroll in the direction of the cathedral, the **Antigua Casa Guardia** (Calle Alameda 18) is the oldest spit-and-sawdust bar in the city, while **Bodegas El Pimpi** (Calle Granada 62) is a moody, atmospheric bar in a former convent (complete with shrine), with a warren of cavernous bars.

Marbella

Marbella's Plaza de los Naranjos is lined with terrace bars. You can economise by heading around the corner to Calle San Lazaro, a narrow pedestrian street that is home to several long-established tapas bars. **El Encuadernador** (Calle San Lázaro 3) is just one of several appealing drinking dens here. Locals also pile into nearby **Quernecia** (Calle Tetuan 9), tucked down a back street. For cocktails, **Sinatra** bar in Puerto Banús is the top start to an evening out, while **Astral** at Playa Levante in the port has a tempting beachside terrace for sipping a sundowner.

Torremolinos/ Benalmádena

Torremolinos has its fair share of British-owned pubs, especially around the pedestrianised Calle San Miguel. Traditional Spanish bars here include **Bar La Bodega** (Calle San Miguel 40) towards the sea and the bodega **Quitapeñas** (Cuesta del Tajo 3), which serves wines from the barrel and some delectable seafood tapas. Due west, in Benalmádena port, there are numerous bars where you can begin your evening with a cocktail or two.

(see Casinos below).

Nightclubs and Discos

Fully fledged nightclubs are few and far between. If you are looking for a Folies Bergères-type extravaganza, the Sala Fortuna at **Casino Torrequebrada** near Málaga is probably the best bet *(see Casinos below).*

Restaurants and cafés often put on live entertainment. "Sexy shows" usually feature strippers. Remember that a "*sala de fiestas*" may not be a genuine nightclub. Many establishments that use this name are in fact brothels, or bars where prostitutes make their contacts.

Fuengirola

There is no shortage of places to spend the wee hours here. **Babilonia** (Calle Capitan) is a disco with live music and go-go dancers. If you don't fancy discos with techno music and teens, check out **Maxy** (Calle España) which offers a good mix of music appealing to a more mature crowd. There are plenty of places on the Paseo, including the **London Pub** (Paseo Marítimo), a casual yet buzzy bar-club with dancing space and good DJ sounds at weekends. For a typical blarney atmosphere, check out the **Irish Times** (26 Calle Condes San Isidro), which attracts a spirited, mainly Spanish crowd for the Guinness on tap and foot-tapping music.

Granada

Granada offers year-round lively nightlife. In the Albaicín, **El Eshavira** (Postigo de la Cuna 2) is a dimly lit, smoky club with live jazz and sultry flamenco. More jazz can be enjoyed at gritty **Enano Rojo** (Calle de Elvira 91), while **Granada 10** (Carcel Baja 10) is an upscale disco housed in a former theatre. One of the largest and longest-running discos in town is **Zoo** (Puerta Real).

Pick up the bi-weekly flyer *Yuzin* which lists concerts and live acts.

FESTIVALS

Diary of Events: The following is a list of some of the more important or interesting festivals and events in the region. As dates vary each year, it is advisable to check with local tourist offices for exact details of each year's event.

Throughout Andalucía

January New Year, greeted at midnight by eating 12 grapes, one for each chime of the clock; *Fiesta de los Reyes (*Three Kings parades), on the eve of the Epiphany (5 January), when men dressed as kings ride around towns, scattering sweets to children; 6 January is a holiday throughout Spain.

February Carnival celebrations in most towns.

March/April *Semana Santa* processions, from Palm Sunday to Easter Sunday.

June *Noche de San Juan*, midsummer bonfires lit on the beaches at midnight (23 June).

July *Virgen del Carmen*, the patroness of fishermen, honoured with seaborne processions in fishing communities along the coast, particularly Estepona (16 July).

November *Día de los Difuntos* (Day of the Dead), Andalusians honour their ancestors (1 November).

December Spaniards celebrate *Nochebuena* (the Good Night), on 24 December, Christmas Eve, with a family meal followed by the *Misa del Gallo* ("Mass of the Cockerel" – Midnight Mass); the *Día de los Inocentes* (Day of the Innocents) on 28 December is the Spanish equivalent of April Fools' Day.

Cádiz

February The city hosts one of Spain's best-known carnivals.

March/April Coinciding with Holy Week, running of bulls in Vejer de la Frontera and Arcos de la Frontera.

May World Motorcycling Championship at Jerez race track.

May Jerez Horse Fair. Display of horses and horsemanship.

August Sanlucar de Barrameda. Horse races along the beach.

August Sotogrande. International Polo Competition, with matches throughout the month.

September/October Jerez. *Fiesta de Otoño* (Autumn Festival), including sherry harvest festival.

Córdoba

May Córdoba. Festival of the Patios, floral competition with private courtyards opened to public (first week of month); Annual Fair (last week of month).

June *Romeria de los Gitanos* (Pilgrimage of the Gypsies) in Cabra.

July International Guitar Festival at the Gran Teatro in Córdoba.

Granada

January *Día de la Toma* (Day of the Conquest) commemorating the city's capture from the Moors (2 January).

May *Día de la Cruz* festival in Granada.

May/June Corpus Christi marks Granada's annual fair.

June/July International Festival of Music and Dance. One of Spain's leading festivals offers a varied programme of music and dance by national and international companies, with concerts in the Auditorio Manuel de Falla and the Palacio Carlos V in the Alhambra, and dance in the Generalife.

August Pilgrimage sets out from village of Trevelez and heads for the peak of La Veleta in the Sierra Nevada (5 August).

November Granada International Jazz Festival (with emphasis on modern jazz).

Huelva

May *Romeria del Rocío*, Spain's biggest pilgrimage, to the shrine of the Virgin in El Rocio (Doñana), finishing the weekend before Pentecost Monday. A million pilgrims travel on horseback and in decorated wagons.

Jaén

February International chess tournament in Linares.

April *Romeria de la Virgen de la Cabeza*, major pilgrimage in Andújar.

Málaga

July International Music and Dance Festival in the Caves of Nerja.

August Málaga fair, the second biggest in Andalucía. The village of Cómpeta celebrates in *Noche del Vino* (Night of Wine), on 15 August.

September Goyesca Fair in Ronda, with carriage displays and bullfight.

October Fuengirola. *Fiesta del Rosario*, the Costa del Sol's biggest annual fair.

December Festival of Verdiales, celebrating mountain music (28 December).

Seville

April Seville. *Feria* (Spring Fair), the biggest Andalusian festival and most magnificent. The city also hosts an antiques fair in April, with exhibitors from all over Spain.

May/June Corpus Christi celebrations in the city, including performance of the medieval dance, *Los Seises*, in the cathedral.

July Italica. International Festival of Theatre and Dance. Contemporary dance and classical ballet performances by prestigious international companies, held in the Roman amphitheatre.

September Biennial Flamenco Festival (2008, 2010 etc). Lasts throughout the month and represents the very best in flamenco dancing.

Málaga

Like most Andalucian cities, Málaga has more people on the streets at midnight than at midday. If you are a jazz fan there are several clubs here with live music, including **Onda Pasadena Jazz** (Calle Goméz Pallete). **Siempre Asi** (Calle Convalecientes 5) is a chock-a-block place playing rumba, flamenco and hip-swinging Latino. There's more space for a boogie at **Liceo** (Calle Beatas 21), a former mansion. East of the centre, beachside **El Baneario** (Torre de San Telmo) has an all-night music and dancing scene during the summer months.

Marbella

The most famous nightclub on the Costa, **Olivia Valere** (Caretera de Istán) charges a hefty entrance fee, but that's what you pay to bop alongside visiting celebs and the local glitterati. A popular haunt for funseekers, **Navy Disco Bar** (2nd Line, Puerto Banús) offers good live music and an energetic DJ. Back in town, the **House of Silk** (Puerto Deportivo) is a laid-back pre-clubbing place attracting a hip, colourful crowd with its potent cocktails and gorgeous sea views. Wednesday is ladies' night at **Brian's Irish Bar** (Plaza de los Olivos), offering a free extra shot in every drink.

Seville

Seville has a good choice of live music venues. In the thick of clubland on Alameda de Hércules, the **Fun Club** at No. 86 plays a range of sounds, from hip-hop to Latino. Nearby **Habanilla Café** is another hip young hangout (Alameda de Hércules 63) with a good atmosphere. On Calle de Betis, **Boss** is a popular nightclub for serious party people, with a mix of music. Jazz fans can check out the weekly sessions at **La Buena Estrella** (Calle Trajano 51) or the **Jazz Corner** (Calle Juan Antonio Cavestany). In summer there are free evening concerts in the Puerta de Triana.

Torremolinos/ Benalmádena

It is no surprise that one of the Costa's best known drag shows is located here. **Bunny's Nightclub and Cabaret** (Edificio Iris, Avenida Gamonal, Benalmádena Costa; tel: 639-002 425) is a rude and naughty drag show that packs the punters in and gets predictably raucous. Reputedly the largest disco in Europe, **Fun Beach** (Avenida Palma de Mallorca 7) has eight vast rooms. Across the way, the **Palladium** (Avenida Palma de Mallorca 36) has foam parties, theme nights and celebrity DJs.

Casinos

Gambling is a national pastime in Spain. People of all ages pour cash into *"tragaperras"*, the slot machines found in many bars. Every week during the season there is the "Quiniela" football pool. Vast sums are gambled on daily lotteries run by the state or ONCE, the organisation for the blind.

Southern Spain's casinos (in Benalmádena-Costa and Marbella on the Costa del Sol, and in Puerto de Santa María, near Cádiz) are elegant night-time venues, offering the full gamut of American and French **roulette**, **black jack** and other traditional casino games. They all have classy restaurants and top-quality nightclubs and discos, and stay open until late.

Formal dress and identification (ID card or passport) are required. **Casino Bahia de Cádiz**, Ctra Madrid–Cádiz km 650, Puerto de Santa María, Cádiz. Tel: 956-871 042. www.casinobahiadecadiz.es **Casino de San Roque**, Ctra N340 km 127, San Roque, Cádiz. Tel: 956-780 100. www.casinosanroque.com **Casino de Torrequebrada**, Ctra de Cádiz km 220, Benalmádena Costa, Málaga. Tel: 952-446 000. www.torrequebrada.com **Casino Nueva Andalucía**, Hotel Andalucía Plaza, Puerto Banús, Málaga. Tel: 952-814 000. www.casinomarbella.com

SHOPPING

Opening Hours

Shops are generally open from 9.30–10am to 1–1.30pm and from 4.30–5pm to 8–8.30pm Monday to Friday, mornings only on Saturday. Larger department stores such as **El Corte Inglés** do not close at midday. El Corte Inglés has become a Spanish institution, offering a vast range of products, as well as export facilities and a service for foreign tourists.

What to Buy

Purchases worth making anywhere in Spain include quality leather goods, Havana and Canary Islands cigars, porcelain statuary, cultured pearls, bargain-priced alcohol, virgin olive oil, saffron and craftware.

Andalucía offers a variety of handmade products, including intricate fans, embroidery, finely tooled leather goods, earthenware pottery, baskets, Seville tiles, silver jewellery and rugs. Some of the finest **guitars** are made in Granada and Seville.

Exports

Visitors resident in non-EU countries, the Canaries, Ceuta or Melilla can claim back 16 percent tax (IVA) on purchases, but each item must have a value of over 90.15 euros. Shops should have the forms to fill in. The tax refund will normally be sent to your home address, except for travellers leaving via Málaga airport, who can claim the refund immediately from the office of the Banco de España in the airport terminal.

Shopping Areas

Almería

The commercial centre is around the Paseo de Almería, Puerta de

Purchena, Obispo Orbera and Calle de las Tiendas.

What to buy: principal buys are **ceramics and pottery** from Albox, Nijar, Sorbas and Vera; **basketwork** from Almería, Alhabia and Nijar; **jarapas** (rugs made with rags and strips of cotton) from Nijar, Huercal Overa and Berja; **bedspreads and blankets** from Albox, Berja and Macaél; **marble** from Macaél.

Cádiz

The main shopping area is in the delightful warren of streets near the cathedral.

What to buy: **sherry** from Jerez and Puerto de Santa María, such as Harveys, Williams and Humbert, Pedro Domecq and Osborne; **fine leather** from Ubrique; **carpets** from Arcos de la Frontera; **capes and ponchos** from Grazalema; **guitars** from Algodonales; **wickerwork** from Jerez; **saddlery** from Olvera.

Córdoba

For general shopping the busiest area is between the streets Gondomar, Tendillas and Ronda de los Tejares. Of the various markets, the most interesting are held on Saturday and Sunday mornings in the **Plaza Corredera**. **Handicrafts** can be bought at the municipal handicrafts market (Zoco Municipal de Artesanía) behind the bullfighting museum.

What to buy: **silver filigree jewellery**; **Montilla wines** (from *bodegas* in Montilla, 46 km/28 miles from Córdoba); **anís liquor** from Rute (Anís Machaquito, Anís de Raza); **ceramics**, including **Lucena pottery** with geometric green and yellow design and **botijos** (two-spouted drinking pitchers) from La Rambla; **leatherwork**; **decorative metal-work** in copper, bronze and brass, from Espejo and Castro del Río).

Granada

The main shopping area is around Recogidas, Acera de Darro, Gran Vía and Reyes Católicos and the maze of surrounding streets.

ABOVE: look out for quality leather.

Granada offers some excellent handicrafts, many incorporating techniques and designs handed down from the Arabs. You will find a large range of handmade articles in the Alcaiceria (old Arab silk market), near the cathedral.

What to buy: **cured mountain hams** from the Alpujarras; **pottery** – most typical is Fajalauza with a distinctive blue and green design, originally from the Albaicín; **leather**, especially embossed leatherwork; **marquetry** chests, chess boards and small tables; metal craftwork; **lanterns** made to traditional Moorish designs; **rugs, cushions** and **bedspreads** from the Alpujarras; handmade guitars – there are several workshops on the Cuesta de Gomerez leading to the Alhambra; **silver filigree jewellery**.

Huelva

What to buy: **cured hams** from Jabugo; **white wine** from the Condado de Huelva; **pottery** from Aracena and Cortejana; **rugs** from Ecinasola; **embroidery** from Aracena, Alosno and Puebla de

It is a statutory requirement for all businesses dealing with the public (hostelries, garages, transport, shops, etc.) to have a complaints book (*libro* or *hoja de recla-maciones*). Any complaint is registered in the book and sent to the local authority. Any receipts should be attached to the claim. You can also take your complaint to the town hall or the Consumer Advice Office (*Oficina de Información al Consumidor*) if one exists.

Guzmán; **handmade leather boots** from Valverde de Camino.

Jaén

What to buy: **glass and ceramics** from Andújar, Bailen and Ubeda; **carpets and wickerwork** from Ubeda, Jaén and Los Villares; **forged ironwork and lanterns** from Ubeda; **guitars** from Marmolejo.

Málaga

The main shopping area in the city is centred around the streets Larios, Nueva, Granada and Caldereria, and also around Armengual de la Mota and Avenida de Andalucía, where there is an El Corte Ingles. On the outskirts of Málaga are several hypermarkets and shopping complexes such as **Larios**, **Los Patios** and **La Rosaleda**.

What to buy: **leather goods** at factory prices; **Málaga wine**; **pottery** and **ceramics** from Málaga, Ronda, Vélez Málaga and Coín; **embossed copper** (Málaga); **castanets** (Alora); **guitars** (Málaga and Ronda); **basketry** (Vélez Málaga, Benamocarra); **rugs** from Mijas (can be made to order).

Markets: The towns along the Costa del Sol offer a wide variety of street markets. Although colourful and entertaining, they are not necessarily the best place to pick up a bargain.

Monday, Marbella; Tuesday,

BULLFIGHTING

Andalucía is the cradle of bullfighting, the controversial struggle between man and beast, and the town of **Ronda** is regarded as the cradle of modern bullfighting. Many of Spain's top matadors and many of the most respected fighting bulls come from the region.

There are occasional charity fights in winter, but the season really gets under way at Easter with the series of *corridas* (bullfights) during the Seville Fair in April. Seville's **Maestranza** bullring (Paseo de Cristóbal Colón 12.

Tel: 954-224 577, www.real maestranza.com) is the most important arena. Daily fights are held during the fairs in other towns throughout the summer.

Six bulls are killed during a *corrida*, which usually starts at 6pm. **Tickets** are expensive, particularly if you want to be in the shade ("Sombra") and near the *barrera*, the ringside. Cheaper tickets are sold for "Sol", the seating on the sunny side of the arena.

In some communities, bull-runs are held in the streets during local festivities.

Fuengirola and Nerja; Wednesday, Estepona, Rincón de la Victoria; Thursday, Torremolinos, San Pedro de Alcántara, Torre del Mar; Friday, Arroyo de la Miel, Benalmádena Pueblo; Saturday, Coín, Mijas-Costa, Nueva Andalucía; Sunday, Estepona port and Málaga (by the football stadium).

Seville

For general shopping, go to the area behind the El Salvador church; for clothes, Sierpes, Campana, O'Donnell and Velázquez; department stores around Plaza del Duque, and O'Donnell and Velázquez streets.

Seville also has a number of street markets selling handicrafts and bric-a-brac. For handicrafts: daily, Mercado del Postigo; Wednesday and Thursday, Rioja and Magdalena; Friday and Saturday, Plaza del Duque. For secondhand goods and antiques: Thursday, Feria; Sunday, Alameda de Hércules and Parque Alcosa. **What to buy**: **Antiques** around the streets Mateos Gago, Placentines and Rodrigo Caro; **ceramics and tiles** from Santa Ana (factory in Triana) and La Cartuja de Sevilla (factory at Ctra de Merida km 529, tel: 954-392 854); **saddlery and leather items**, **boots** and **chaps**; **fashion**,

Seville's own designers Victorio and Lucchino have a showroom at Sierpes 87; **fans and castanets** and **locally made goods**.

SPORTS

Fishing

Offshore fishing

Boats can often be hired at marinas. Some excursions are available, particularly for the popular sport of shark fishing.

Inland fishing

It is possible to catch tench, carp, pike, black bass and trout. Permits can be obtained from branches of the Caja Rural savings bank. Licence legislation varies from province to province, so check details with local tourist offices.

Golf

Southern Spain, particularly the Costa del Sol, is a golfer's paradise, with Europe's biggest concentration of golf courses. Details from the **Andalusian Golf Federation**, Sierra de Grazalema 33, Málaga, tel: 952-225 590. www.golf-andalucia.com

Almería

Cortijo Grande Golf Club, Cortijo Grande s/n, Turre, tel: 950-468 176; www.cortijogrande.net. 18 holes.
Golf Almerimar, Urb. Almerimar s/n, El Ejido, tel: 950-497 454; www.meliagolfalmerimar.solmelia .com. 18 holes.

Golf Playa Serena, Urb. Playa Serena s/n, Roquetas de Mar, tel: 950-333 055; www.golfplaya serena.com. 18 holes.
La Envía, Ctra Parador–Enix km 10, Vicar, tel: 950-559 641; www.laenvia.com. 18 holes.
Marina Golf Mojácar, Avenida del Mar s/n, Mojácar, tel: 950-133 235; www.marinagolf.com. 18 holes.

Cádiz

Alcaidesa Links, Cortijo Las Aguzaderas, Ctra N340 km 125, San Roque, tel: 956-791 040; www.alcaidesa.com. 18 holes.
Almenara, Avenida Los Cortijos s/n, Sotogrande, tel: 956-582 054. 27 holes.
Club de Golf Valderrama, Avenida de los Cortijos s/n, Sotogrande, tel: 956-791 200; www.valder ramma.com. Venue of the 1997 Ryder Cup. 18 holes.
Costa Ballena, Crta Chipiona–El Puerto s/n, Rota, tel: 956-847 070; www.costaballena.com. 18 holes.
Dehesa Montenmedio, Ctra N340 km 42, Vejer de la Frontera, tel: 956-451 216. 18 holes.
El Campano Golf, Ctra Cádiz–Málaga km 14, Chiclana, tel: 956-493 081. 9 holes.
La Cañada, Avenida Profesor Tierno Galván s/n, Guadiaro, tel: 956-794 100; www.lacanadagolf.com. 9 holes.
Montecastillo Golf, Ctra de Arcos s/n, Jerez de la Frontera, tel: 956-151 213; www.monte castillogolf.com. 18 holes.
Novo Sancti Petri Golf, Novo Sancti Petri s/n, Chiclana, tel: 956-494 005; www.golf-novo sancti.es. 18 + 9 holes.
Real Club de Golf Sotogrande, Paseo del Parque s/n, Sotogrande, tel: 956-785 014;

www.golfsotogrande.com.
18 + 9 holes.
San Roque Club, Ctra de Cádiz
km 126, San Roque, tel: 956-
613 030; www.sanroqueclub.com.
18 holes.
Vista Hermosa Golf, Casa
Grande s/n, Urb. Vista Hermosa,
El Puerto de Santa María,
tel: 956-541 968. 9 holes.

Córdoba

Club de Campo Córdoba,
Avenida de Arruzafa s/n,
Córdoba, tel: 957-350 208;
www.golfcordoba.com. 18 holes.
Club de Golf Pozoblanco,
San Gregorio 2, Pozoblanco,
tel: 957-339 171;
www.cordoba-es.com/pozoblanco.
9 holes.

ABOVE: mulling over the day's catch.

Granada

Granada Club de Golf, Avenida
Los Corsarios s/n, Las Gabias,
Granada, tel: 958-584 436;
www.granadaclubdegolf.com.
18 holes.
Los Moriscos, Urb. Playa
Granada s/n, Motril, tel: 958-
825 527. www.moriscosgolf.com
9 holes.

HUNTING

You are legally entitled to
import two hunting guns with
100 cartridges. It is advisable
to contact the **Andalusian
Hunting Federation** (Federación
Andaluza de Caza), Los
Morenos s/n, Archidona, tel:
952-714 871 for details of
licences, restrictions and
seasons, as some species
are protected and others have
a quota ceiling.

For the serious, hunting is
available in controlled areas
and state-run game parks
such as Cazorla in Jaén
where it is possible to hunt
wild goat *(capra hispanica)*,
deer or **wild boar**. Organised
parties, known as *"monterias"*,
take part in shoots in the
Sierra Morena, where deer
and boar abound.

Huelva

Club de Golf Bellavista, Ctra
Huelva–Aljaraque km 6, Huelva,
tel: 959-319 017; www.golfbella
vista.com. 18 holes.
Isla Canela Club de Golf, Paseo de
los Gavilanes s/n, Playa de Isla
Canela, Ayamonte, tel: 959-477
263; www.islacanela.es. 18 holes.
Islantilla Golf Club, Ctra Isla Antilla–
La Antilla s/n, Isla Antilla, tel:
959-486 039; www.islantillagolf
resort.com. 18 + 9 holes.

Málaga

Alhaurín Golf & Country Club, Ctra
Fuengirola–Alhaurín el Grande km
15, Alhaurín el Grande, tel: 952-
595 800; www.alhauringolf.com
18 + 9 holes.
Aloha Golf, Urb. Aloha s/n,
Nueva Andalucía, Marbella,
tel: 952-907 085. www.clubde
golfaloha.com. 18 + 9 holes.
Añoreta Golf, Urb. Añoreta Golf
s/n, Rincón de la Victoria,
tel: 952-404 000. www.anoreta
golf.es. 18 holes.
Atalaya Golf & Country Club,
Ctra de Benahavís km 1,
Estepona, tel: 952-882 812.
www.selected-hotels.com.
18 + 18 holes.
Club Miraflores, Ctra de Cádiz
km 199, Mijas-Costa, tel: 952-
932 876. www.mirafloresgolf.com.
18 holes.

El Coto de la Serena, Ctra de
Cádiz km 63.5, Estepona, tel:
950-333 055. 9 holes.
El Paraíso Golf Club, Ctra de
Cádiz km 167, Estepona, tel:
952-883 835; www.elparaisogolf
club.com. 18 holes.
Golf Club Las Brisas, Calle
Londres 1, Nueva Andalucía,
Marbella, tel: 952-813 021;
www.lasbrisasgolf.com. 18 holes.
Golf Río Real, Urb. Río Real s/n,
Ctra de Cádiz km 185,
Marbella, tel: 952-765 733;
www.rioreal.com. 18 holes.
Guadalhorce Club de Golf, Ctra
de Cártama km 7, Campanillas,
tel: 952-179 378; www.guadal
horce.com. 18 + 9 holes.
Guadalmina Club de Golf, Urb.
Guadalmina Alta s/n, San Pedro
Alcántara, tel: 952-883 455;
www.guadalminagolf.org.
18 + 18 + 9 holes.
La Cala Golf & Country Club,
La Cala de Mijas s/n, Mijas-Costa,
tel: 952-669 033;
www.lacala.com. 18 + 18 holes.
La Dama de Noche, Camino del
Angel s/n, Río Verde, Marbella,
tel: 952-818 150; www.golfdama
denoche.com. Floodlit course, 9
holes.
La Duquesa Golf & Country Club,
Urb. El Hacho s/n, Manilva,
tel: 952-890 725; www.golfla
duquesa.com. 18 holes.

La Quinta Golf & Country Club, Urb. La Quinta s/n, Benahavís, tel: 952-762 390; www.laquinta-golf.com. 18 + 9 holes.

La Siesta Golf, Calle José de Orbaneja s/n, Urb. Sitio de Calahonda, Mijas-Costa, tel: 952-933 362; www.geocities.co/lasiestagolf. 9 holes.

Lauro Golf, Alhaurín de la Torre, km 76, tel: 952-412 767; www.laurogolf.com. 27 holes.

La Zagaleta, Ctra de Ronda km 9, Benahavís, tel: 952-855 453; www.lazagaleta.com. 18 holes.

Los Arqueros Golf, Ctra de Ronda km 166.5, San Pedro Alcántara, tel: 952-784 600. 18 holes.

Los Naranjos Golf Club, Urb. Nueva Andalucía s/n, Marbella, tel: 952-812 428; www.losnaranjos.com. 18 holes.

Marbella Club Golf Resort, Ctra de Cádiz km 188, Marbella, tel: 952-830 500. www.marbellacc.net. 18 holes.

Mijas Golf, Camino Viejo de Coín km 3, Urb. Mijas Golf, Mijas-Costa,

tel: 952-476 843. www.mijas golf.org. 18 + 18 holes.

Montemayor Golf Club, Ctra de Cádiz km 166, Benahavís, tel: 952-937 111. 18 holes.

Santa María Golf & Country Club, Urb. Elviria, Ctra N340 km 192, Marbella, tel: 952-831 036; www.santamariagolfclub.com. 18 holes.

Torrequebrada Golf, Ctra de Cádiz km 220, Benalmádena-Costa, tel: 952-442 742; www.golftorrequebrada.com. 18 holes.

Seville

Club Zaudin, Ctra Bormujos–Mairena km 2, Seville, tel: 954-153 344; www.clubzaudin.com. 18 holes.

Las Minas, Ctra Isla Mayor km 1, Aznalcázar, tel: 955-750 678; www.lasminasgolf.com. 9 holes.

Real Club Pineda, Avenida Jerez, s/n, Seville, tel: 954-611 400. 18 holes.

Real Club de Golf de Sevilla, Ctra Sevilla–Utrera km 3, Seville, tel: 954-124 301; www.sevillagolf.com. 18 holes.

Horse-riding

Riding is available for all levels, from beginners, paying by the hour, to advanced treks through the sierras.

Cádiz

Cortijo Las Piñas, Ctra N340 km 74, Tarifa, tel: 956-685 136; www.cortijolaspinas.com

Dehesa Montenmedio, Ctra N340 km 42, Vejer de la Frontera, tel: 956-451 216.

Dos Mares, Ctra N340 km 79, Tarifa, tel: 956-684 035; www.grupo-mares.com

Hipica Novo Sancti Petri, Urb Novo Sancti Petri, Chiclana, tel: 956 496 352; www.hipica-novo.com

Hurricane Hotel, Ctra N340 km 77, Tarifa, tel: 956-684 919; www.hurricanehotel.com

Rancho Huerta Dorotea, Ctra Villamartín–Ubrique km 12, Prado del Rey, tel: 956-724 291.

Rancho Los Lobos, Estación de Jimena de la Frontera, tel: 956-640 429; www.rancholos lobos.com

San Roque Club Equestrian Centre, Suites Hotel, San Roque s/n, tel: 956-613 030; www.sanroqueclub.com

Córboda

Club Hípico, Ctra Trassierra km 3, Córdoba, tel: 957-271 628.

Granada

Cabalgar-Rutas Alternativas, Bubión, Alpujarras s/n, tel: 958-763 135. One- to 10-day treks in the Alpujarras; www.riding andalucia.com

Dallas Love, Ctra de la Sierra, Bubión, tel: 958-763 038; www.rusticblue.com/horseriding.htm

Málaga

Club Hipico Alhaurín, Ctra Fuengirola–Alhaurin el Grande km 15, Alhaurin el Grande, tel: 952-595 970.

El Ranchito, Ctra N340 km 235, La Colina, Torremolinos, tel: 952-383 063.

Club Hipico Elviria, Urb. El Platero, Elviria, tel: 952 835 272.

Lakeview Equestrian Centre, Urb. Valle del Sol, San Pedro de Alcántara, tel: 952-786 934.

Los Monteros Riding School, behind Los Monteros golf course, Marbella s/n, tel: 952-770 675.

Seville

Centro Ecuestre Epona, Ctra Madrid–Cádiz km 519, Carmona, tel: 954-148 310; www.epona-spain.com

El Vizir, Hacienda El Visir s/n, Espartinas, tel: 955-710 020.

Centro Equestre Epona, Carmona, tel: 608-155 359.

Hípica Puerta Príncipe, Alcalá de Guadaira s/n, tel: 954-860 815.

Cortijo las Navezuelas, Cazalla de la Sierra, Ctra Sevilla SE196 km 42, tel: 954-884 764.

Rancho el Rocío, Puebla del Río s/n, tel: 955-771 212.

BELOW: getting into the swing.

ABOVE: beautiful to watch – or hire one by the day.

Marinas

Almería
Adra Marina,
tel: 950-401 417.
Aguadulce Marina,
tel: 950-343 115.
Almeria, tel: 950-230 317.
Almerimar Marina, El Ejido,
tel: 950-497 350.
Club de Mar, Almería,
tel: 950-230 780.
Garrucha Marina, tel:
950-460 048.
Roquetas de Mar Marina,
tel: 950-320 789.
San José Marina, Níjar,
tel: 950-380 041.

Cádiz
Chipiona Yacht Harbour,
Chipiona, tel: 956-373 844.
Club Náutico, Barbate,
tel: 956-431 907.
Club Náutico Sancti Petri,
Chiclana de la Frontera,
tel: 956-496 169.
Puerto América, Cádiz,
tel: 956-224 220.
Real Club Náutico,
Cádiz, tel: 956-213 262.
Rota Yacht Harbour, tel:
956-813 811.
Santa Maria, El Puerto de
Santa María,
tel: 956-813 111.
Sotogrande Marina,
tel: 956-790 000.

Granada
Marina del Este, La Herradura,
tel: 958-827 018.
Motril Marina, tel: 958-600 037.

Huelva
Puerto Deportivo de Ayamonte,
Ayamonte, tel: 959-321 694.
**Puerto Deportivo de Isla
Cristina**, Isla Cristina, tel: 959-
343 501.
Puerto Deportivo de Mazagón,
Palos de la Frontera, tel: 959-
376 237.
**Puerto Deportivo Marina Isla
Canela**, Isla Canela,
tel: 959-479 000;
www.islacanela.to

Málaga
Estepona Marina, tel: 952-801
800.
Fuengirola Marina, tel: 952-468
000.
La Caleta de Vélez Marina,
Torre del Mar,
tel: 952-511 390.
Puerto Cabopino, Marbella,
tel: 952-831 975.
Marbella Marina, tel:
952-775 700.
Marina Benalmádena, tel:
952-442 944.
Puerto Banús, Marbella, tel:
952-909 800.
Puerto de la Duquesa, Manilva,
tel: 952-890 100.
Málaga Marina,
tel: 952-228 636.

Seville
Club Náutico, Auda Tablada,
Seville, tel: 954-454 777.
Puerto Gelves, Gelves, tel:
955-760 728.

Scuba Diving

The rocky shoreline around much
of the coast offers plenty of
scope for **underwater exploring**.
Fishing with a spear-gun is
permitted only if you dive without
bottles. If you swim any distance
from the shore, you are required
to tow a marker buoy.

There are a number of scuba
clubs on the coast, offering
courses for beginners and
guidance for licensed visiting
divers. For details, contact the
**Federación Andaluza de
Actividades Subacuáticas**,
Playa de las Almadrabillas 10,
Almería, tel: 950-270 612.

The best areas for diving
include the following:
Almería: Cabo de Gata, Las
Negras, La Isleta, San José and
Morrón de los Genoveses, where
international underwater fishing
competitions have been held.
Cádiz: North of Tarifa, especially
for underwater fishing.
Granada: La Herradura and west
towards Málaga.
Málaga: from Nerja east towards
the Granada coast.

Skiing

There is skiing in the **Sierra
Nevada** 32 km (20 miles) from
Granada, the southernmost ski
slope in Europe. The slopes are
between 2,100 metres (7,000 ft)
and 3,390 metres (11,000 ft)
above sea level, with 45 ski runs
of varying difficulty and 21 lifts.
Facilities include equipment to
hire, instruction (with a special
school for children), first aid and
rescue service and emergency
clinic. The Sierra Nevada complex
offers a variety of accommodation
and *après ski* entertainment.
**General information (weather,
snow report, etc):** tel: 958-249
119; www.sierranevadaski.com

ABOVE: surfing with a twist.

Tennis

There are too many tennis clubs in the region to list them all, but the ones listed below have out-standing facilities, including tuition in some cases by ex-international champions:
Don Carlos Tennis Club, Hotel Don Carlos, Urb. Elviria s/n, Marbella, Málaga, tel: 952-831 739; www.marcotennis.com
El Casco Tennis Club, Urb. El Rosario s/n, Marbella, Málaga, tel: 952-837 651; www.elcasco.com
Hotel Puente Romano Tennis Club, Ctra N340, Marbella, tel: 952- 820 900; www.puenteromano.com
Lew Hoad's Tennis Ranch, Ctra Mijas–Fuengirola s/n, Málaga, tel: 952-474 858; www.tennis-spain.com
Los Monteros Tennis Club, Hotel Los Monteros, Ctra N340 s/n, Marbella, Málaga, tel: 952-771 700; www.monteros.com
Manolo Santana Raquets Club, Ctra de Istan km 2, Marbella, tel: 952-778 580; www.manolosantana.net

Watersports

Facilities for sailing, windsurfing, kitesurfing, scuba diving, snorkelling and waterskiing are available on the Atlantic and Mediterranean coasts. Many beaches have windsurfing and kitesurfing schools and equipment to hire. The best area is near **Tarifa**, Cádiz. The good winds attract surfers from all over Europe and various competitions are held throughout the year.

Spectator Sports

Soccer and **basketball** are Spain's most popular spectator sports. Andalucía's leading soccer teams are Betis and Sevilla (both of Seville) and Cádiz. Games usually start at 5pm on Sunday. Basketball attracts a fanatical following.

There is a **motor-racing** circuit in Jerez (Cádiz), with occasional car races, but the biggest event is the **Motorcycling Grand Prix**, on the first weekend in May (Circuito de Jerez, tel: 956-151 000; www.circuitodejerez.com).

Horse races are staged at Seville La Pineda hipodrome weekly during January–March; there are horse races on the beach in Sanlúcar de Barrameda (Cádiz), during August, a tradition dating back more than 150 years. Horse races are held throughout the year, with night races in summer at the Hipódromo Costa del Sol in Mijas-Costa (Urb. El Chaparral s/n, tel: 952-592 700; www.hipodromocostadelsol.com). The biggest events are held during the winter.

SPAS

Andalucía has a number of *balnearios* (spas) where the waters have medicinal properties. These are tranquil spots with doctors on hand to offer advice. Further information can be obtained from the **Asociación de Balnearios de Andalucia** (tel: 950-160 257).

Almería

San Nicolás, Alhama de Almería s/n, tel: 950-641 361. Open February–December. Recommended for digestive disorders, respiratory ailments, arthritis, sciatica, obesity, rheumatism, nerves.
Sierra de Alhamilla, Pechina s/n, tel: 950-317 413. Open all year. Recommended for arthritis, rheumatism, gout, bronchitis, asthma, digestive disorders, ulcers, gastritis and stress.

Cádiz

Fuente Amarga, Chiclana de la Frontera s/n, tel: 956-400 520. Open February–December. Recommended for rheumatism, arthritis, arthrosis, skin problems, alopecia, respiratory complaints and gynaecological problems.

Granada

Alhama de Granada, Ctra del Balneario (56 km/35 miles from Granada), tel: 958-350 011. Open April–November. Recommended for neuritis, rheumatism, sciatica, bronchitis, asthma, traumatism, obesity and gout.
Alicún de las Torres, Villanueva de las Torres (32 km/20 miles from Guadix), tel: 958-694 022. Open March–December. Recommended for respiratory problems, allergies, circulation, rheumatism, digestion, traumatism.
Graena, (8 km/5 miles from Guadix), tel: 958-670 681. Open March–December. Recommended for rheumatism, sciatica, bronchitis, allergies, stress, nervous disorders.
Lanjarón, Avenida de la Constitución s/n, tel: 958-770 137. Open March–December. Recommended for arthritis, rheumatism, lumbago, renal lithiasis, respiratory ailments, diabetes, insomnia, stress, kidney infections, cholesterol.

Jaén

San Andres, Canena (10 km/ 6 miles from Ubeda), tel: 953-799 701. Open all year. Recommended for digestive system, kidney and urinary disorders, respiratory system, rheumatism, traumatism, circulation, nervous system, gynaecological problems.

Málaga

Carratraca, Antonio Riobó 11 (50 km/30 miles from Málaga), tel: 952-458 071. Open 15 June–15 October. Recommended for rheumatism, circulation nervous system, skin problems and gynaecological ailments. **Fuente Amarga** (near the village of Tolox), tel: 952-487 091. Open 15 June–15 October. Recommended for respiratory system, bronchitis, asthma, pulmonary emphysema, renal lithiasis, pharyngitis and rhinitis.

CHILDREN'S ACTIVITIES

Spaniards love children and they are welcome virtually everywhere, including bars and restaurants. The local tourist office will supply a list of the attractions geared towards younger visitors. The major ones are listed here:

Almeria

Mini Hollywood, A7, km 464, tel: 950-365 236. Western theme park with daily Wild West show at noon and 5pm, plus an extra gunfight at 8pm from mid-June to mid-Sept.

Benalmádena

Sea Life, Benalmádena Port, tel: 952-560 159. An excellent aquarium with an educational "touch pool" for young children, who can handle crabs and starfish, and get a close-up view of baby sharks and rays. Open daily 10am–8pm.
Tivoli World, Ctra de Benalmádena, Arroyo de la Miel, tel: 952-442 848. The Costa del

Sol's biggest theme park with two dozen rides, including some geared towards tiny tots, as well as regular music concerts and flamenco shows. Open daily 10am–6pm.

Estepona

Selwo Safari Park, Ctra de Cádiz, Estepona, tel: 952-792 150. A magnificent wild animal park covering 100 hectares (250 acres) where you can see lions, elephants and a whole host of other animals their natural habitat. Open Oct–April 10am–5.30pm, May–mid-June 10am–6.30pm, mid-June–Sept 10am–8pm.

Fuengirola

Fuengirola Zoo, Calle Camilo José Cela, tel: 952-471 590. This small zoo is delightful, with animals kept uncaged in four different habitats. Open daily 10am–6pm.

Granada

Parque de las Ciencias, Avenida del Mediterránneo, tel: 958-131 900; www.parqueciencias.com. Excellent science park with numerous hands-on features and interactive experiences, plus an observatory and planetarium. Open Tues–Sat 10am–7pm, Sun 10am–3pm.

Mijas

Parque Aquático Mijas, Ctra N340, km 208, tel: 952-460 404. Water theme park. Open May–Sept.

Seville

Isla Mágica, Isla de Cartuja, tel: 955-03 7083; www.caac.es. A theme park on the former Expo site, with rides, a lake, giant screen cinema and the Torre Panoramica, providing spectacular views of the city. Open April–Sept, Tues–Fri 10am–9pm, Sat 11am–8pm, Sun 10am–3pm; Oct–Mar Tues–Fri 10am–8pm, Sat 11am–8pm, Sun 10am–3pm. Free entry on Tuesdays.

Tarifa

Whale Watching, Avenida de la Constitución 6, tel: 956-627 013. For whale- and dolphin-watching trips. Open all year round, depending on sea conditions.

Torremolinos

Ritmo a Caballo Equestrian Show, Centro de Equitación El Ranchito, Málaga, tel: 952-383 140. The Andalusians are arguably the most skilful riders in Europe and this weekly show is very professional. Call for exact timings.

BELOW: there's endless fun to be had at the beach.

A–Z

A HANDY SUMMARY OF PRACTICAL INFORMATION, ARRANGED ALPHABETICALLY

A dmission Charges

Most sights charge less (often half price) for students under 26 and senior citizens over 65, but it is necessary to show valid ID (a passport in the case of over-65s). There are also reductions for many joint sights, for example the Alcázaba and Castillo de Gibralfaro in Málaga.

Some museums, especially the various fine arts museums and archaeological museums, are free for EU citizens; it isn't always necessary to provide proof.

It is increasingly necessary to book tickets for Granada's Alhambra in advance, though you must still allow plenty of time to pick them up on arrival, as the queues can be very long. For more information on this, *see page 189.*

B udgeting for Your Trip

The introduction of the euro in 2002 resulted in a hike in prices in Spain. Nonetheless, you can still drink and dine out for a lot less than in the UK. Two people should budget using the rough guidelines below (though variables in meals and hotels can cause prices to rise considerably). Prices in Seville, Granada and on the Costa del Sol will be higher than in rural areas.
Double room per night in a three-star hotel: €80–100
Simple lunch: €20–30
Two-course dinner for two €30–50
Car hire per week: €180
Admission charges: up to €30 per day
Miscellaneous (drinks, tips etc): €20 per day.

Business Hours

Shops usually open 9.30am or 10am–1.30pm, opening again from 5–7.30pm or 8pm. **Department stores** and supermarkets open 10am–9pm or 10pm. Shops close on Sunday, although newsagents are open on Sunday mornings. In tourist areas, some stores open on Sunday in summer. **Government offices** are usually open to the public Mon–Fri 9am–1pm.
Banks open Mon–Fri 9am–2pm.
Museums and other tourist sights are often closed on Monday. Some also close for up to three hours at lunchtime.
Restaurants rarely open before 9pm for dinner, and most stop serving at 11.30pm. Lunch is normally around 1.30pm.

TRANSPORT

CLIMATE CHART

Málaga

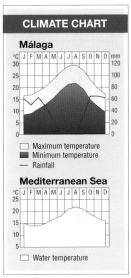

☐ Maximum temperature
■ Minimum temperature
— Rainfall

Mediterranean Sea

☐ Water temperature

 limate & Clothing

Andalucía's position at the southern edge of Europe gives it an excellent climate. Summers are hot and winters mild. However, there are considerable variations due to the size of the region, its mountainous character and the fact that it is bordered by both the Atlantic and Mediterranean. Summers can be extremely hot in the interior, with temperatures rising to 45°C (113°F) and higher in the provinces of Seville and Córdoba. Almería has an extremely arid, desert-like climate. Snow covers the Sierra Nevada from November to June, and frost is common in upland areas.

Weather in coastal areas is moderated by the sea and off-shore breezes so that neither extremes of heat nor cold are experienced, except for a few weeks at the height of summer. Strawberries ripen in Huelva and Málaga in early February, and tropical fruits can be grown along the Mediterranean without the aid of greenhouses. The levante wind

has considerable influence, often blowing hard for several days on the Cádiz coast and creating a persistent cloud over Gibraltar. June to October are mainly dry, but punctuated by occasional downpours. Heavy rain in the winter months is usually interspersed with brilliant sunshine.

The best seasons to tour the region are spring and autumn, when there are no climatic extremes.

What to wear

Light clothing is fine for much of the year on the coast, with perhaps a light sweater or jacket for the occasional cool evening. In winter take a heavy sweater or fleece and raincoat or umbrella.

Although Andalusians like to dress elegantly, they do not demand the same of visitors, and **informal dress** is acceptable almost everywhere, although avoid anything too garish or too scanty when visiting cathedrals and religious sites, and men should not go bare-chested anywhere but the beach or poolside.

More **formal clothing** (jacket and tie for men) is usual in casinos and more elegant dining spots.

Consulates

Seville

Australia
Federico Rubio 14
Tel: 954-220 971
United States
Paseo de las Delicias, 7
Tel: 954-231 885
Ireland
Plaza de Santa Cruz 6
Tel: 954-216 361

The Costa del Sol

Canada
Edificio Horizonte
Plaza de la Malagueta, 3
Málaga
Tel: 952-223 346
Great Britain
Mauricio Moro Pareto, 2
Málaga
Tel: 952-352 300

United States
Apartment 1c
Avenida Juan Goméz, 8
Fuengirola
Tel: 952-474 891.

Crime & Safety

Thefts from tourists and their cars have become common in recent years. Taking common sense precautions *(see below)* should prevent your holiday being spoiled in this way.

Cities, particularly Málaga and Seville, are black spots. Never leave anything of value in your car. Don't leave cash or valuables unattended while you are swimming. When staying overnight, take all your baggage into the hotel. If possible, park your car in a garage or a guarded car park.

When **driving into Seville**, do not leave anything of value within sight of other motorists, motorcylists or pedestrians. There have been many cases of thieves smashing the windows of cars stationary at traffic lights, seizing handbags and cameras and then speeding off on a motorcycle.

When **walking**, hold on tightly to all bags. Avoid badly-lit back

BELOW: the end of siesta

TRANSPORT

ACCOMMODATION

ACTIVITIES

A – Z

LANGUAGE

streets at night. Carry photo-copies of your passport and other documents and leave the originals in the hotel safe.

If you are confronted by thieves, do not resist, as they often carry knives. If robbed, remember that thieves usually want easily disposable cash and toss away the rest. Check the nearest gutters, rubbish containers and toilets for your belongings.

Police

Municipal police, who generally have limited powers and are mostly seen controlling traffic, wear blue uniforms and peaked caps. **National police** wear dark blue uniforms and caps. Both will assist you, but it is the national police who will take details of an offence and con-duct any investigation. In smaller towns and rural areas, **Civil Guards** – in olive-green uni-forms (but without the distinc-tive tricorn hat, which is only used for ceremonial purposes) – per-form these duties. Few policemen speak anything but Spanish, but many national police stations *(comisarías)* now have report forms in several European lan-guages to aid tourists.

Customs & Entry

Spanish customs officials are unlikely to hassle travellers unless they have reason to believe they are wrongdoers. They are particularly on the look-out for drug smugglers at such ports as Algeciras and Málaga.

EU nationals are not restricted in what they can import, but anybody moving prod-ucts in commercial quantities may require appropriate licences.

Non-EU nationals can import the following items duty-free: 200 cigarettes or 50 cigars or 250 grammes of tobacco products, 1 litre of alcohol over 20 percent proof or 2 litres up to 22 percent, and 2 litres of other wines, one-quarter litre of eau-de-cologne and 50 grammes of perfume.

D isabled Travellers

Spain is gradually making advances in improving facilities for disabled visitors.
Beaches: the official guide on Spanish beaches, with indication of suitability for the disabled is available on line at:
www.mma.es/costas/guia_playas
Train: RENFE usually provides wheelchairs at main city stations.

Parking: the UK's orange badge scheme is not recognised in Spain. However, holders of the EU document (blue, depicting a pho-tograph of the authorised person) will be entitled to the same park-ing provisions as local residents.

Wheelchair hire

The following organisations can assist with wheelchair hire.
Independent Living Spain
Mijas Costa
Tel: 952-493 419,
www.independentlivingspain.com.
Mobility Abroad
Benalmadena
Tel: 952-447 764
www.mobilityabroad.com
(also rents mobility scooters).

Specialist organisations

ECOM (Federation of Spanish Private Organisations for the Disabled)
Gran Vía de las Cortes Catalanas, 562 principal 2a
Barcelona.
Tel: 934-515 550
www.ecom.es
O.N.C.E. (Spanish Association for the Blind)
Paseo del Prado 24, Madrid
Tel. 915-894 600
www.once.es

E lectricity

The current in Spain is 225AC or 220V – the same as the UK and most of Europe but twice the mains voltage in the US. Ameri-cans bringing any 110V appli-ances must have a converter/transformer.

Spanish sockets take plugs with two large round pins, so bring a plug adaptor with any British appliances or buy one at the airport.

Emergencies

The nationwide emergency tele-phone number is 112. If you need an ambulance, call 061 *(see emergency numbers below)*. If you get stopped for a traffic vio-lation, fines are generally payable

BELOW: the Municipal Police is also known as the Policia Local.

on the spot. If you are subject to theft, report it to the local police immediately.

In the event of you being arrested, Article 17 of the Spanish constitution states that you must be informed of your rights and the grounds of your arrest in a manner that is understandable to you. You will also be entitled to the assistance of a lawyer during police interrogation and any judicial investigation. Within 72 hours of arrest, you must be brought before a judge or released.

National Police: 091
Local Police: 092
Emergencies (health and security): 112
Ambulance: 061

Entry Requirements

As requirements are subject to change, you should always check before leaving your home country. Visitors from **European Union** countries can enter and leave freely. However, they are still required to carry a passport or national identity card. If EU citizens stay six months or more in any calendar year, they are required to obtain a residence permit.

North Americans can stay for three months without a visa, after which time they can request an extension of stay (see below).

Visitors from **Australia** and **New Zealand** need a visa if staying more than three months. Note that in all cases, the three-month period counts from the time you first arrive in any of the Schengen States; i.e. if you spent six weeks in France first, that time is deducted from your three months in Spain.

South Africans, **Russians** and many other nationalities need a visa to visit Spain. Stays cannot be extended beyond the length of the visas, which must be obtained before arriving in Spain.

Extensions of stay

EU citizens wishing to stay in Spain longer than 90 days should apply for a resident's card. This is a lengthy bureaucratic process. Consult a Spanish consulate before you go or check at the local police station in Spain, where you will be required to show your passport, provide photos, and give evidence that you have the necessary funds to live without working in Spain.

United States citizens can stay for three months in a calendar year which can be extended to six months providing the request is made before the first three months expire. After six months you can apply for a *residencia*. This requires a visa which should have been requested prior to leaving the United States.

If you know before travelling that you will be staying longer than the permitted time, it can save trouble to apply for the necessary visa at a Spanish consulate in your home country.

Animal quarantine

You can import your cat or dog into Spain on presentation of the relevant health certificates, but check first whether you can take it freely back to your home country. Regulations require a health certificate and, depending on age of animal, proof of rabies vaccination.

G ay & Lesbian Travellers

Attitudes towards same sex relationships have relaxed considerably in recent years. All the major cities and resorts have lively gay scenes. The following websites include listings of gay bars, clubs, beaches and hotels and general information
www.orgullogay.org
www.guiagay.com
www.cogailes.org

Useful local organisations include **Colega** (www.colegaweb.net) has offices in Almería (tel: 950-276 540, Cádiz (tel: 956-226 262, Córdoba (tel: 957-492 779), Granda (tel: 958-263 853), Málaga (tel: 952-217 199) and Seville (tel: 954-501 377).

ABOVE: pets can be imported upon presentation of health certificates.

Information on the gay scene is available in *Spartacus España* and *Guia Gay Visada* publications (Spanish only).

H ealth & Medical Care

Common sense is the best preventative medicine. Don't overexpose yourself to the sun, which can be surprisingly fierce, don't drink too many iced drinks, and beware of excessive alcohol consumption. The last can produce devastating effects on your stomach, especially when eating food fried in olive oil with liberal doses of garlic and peppers. Take it easy until your body has become accustomed to changes in climate and diet. You are particularly warned to partake sparingly of cheap wine, as this is almost certain to give you a headache or worse, and is foolish in a country where superb wines can be enjoyed for just a little more.

Bottled water is the best bet for visitors. Tap water is safe to drink, but it tends to taste strongly of chlorine. Local stomachs are used to it, but those of newcomers may revolt to begin with.

TRANSPORT

ACCOMMODATION

ACTIVITIES

A - Z

LANGUAGE

ABOVE: forward planning.

Over-the-counter remedies are available at any *farmacia* (chemist), recognisable by the large green crosses outside.

Buying medicines

Farmácias (chemists) are well stocked and over-the-counter remedies are available at any *farmacia* recognisable by the large green cross outside. They all display lists of the duty chemists at night and on weekends. Be sure to bring any regular medicines that you need plus a letter from your doctor explaining any medical conditions, including generic names of medicines, if possible.

If you contract a stomach problem ask for *un antidiarreico*, the general term for antidiarrheal medicine. *Fortasec* is a well-known local brand.

Medical services

Private clinics offering a range of medical services – some open 24 hours a day – are located in most towns of any size. Emergency services are also provided by *ambulatorios*, national health clinics run by Spain's Seguridad Social (social security system).

Free medical attention is available if you are from EU countries, which have reciprocal arrangements with Spain. However, you must obtain a European Health Insurance Card (EHIC) in your home country prior to your departure. These are valid for five years and can be applied for on-line by logging onto www.dh.gov.uk/travellers. As Seguridad Social facilities are often over-stretched, visitors are also advised to take out private health insurance. Private health insurance is essential for non-EU visitors.

Dental treatment

Your EHIC does not cover private medical consultations or treatment, which includes virtually all dentists. If you need dental care urgently, check at the local *farmacia* or tourist office, or consult staff in your hotel, for advice on finding an English-speaking dentist. On the Costa del Sol, there are several, including the **English Dental Practice**, Edificio Don Marcelo, Avda Jesús Santos Rein, 10, Fuengirola, tel: 952-466 056.

I nsurance

The most comprehensive travel-insurance should cover trip cancellation, delay, medical expenses – naturally excluding any pre-existing medical condition – and loss of property (though you may want to check that loss of property isn't already covered by your household insurance). If EU visitors don't get medical insurance, which is strongly recommended, you must at least get the EHIC, which entitles EU members to reciprocal medical care (see Medical Services). Drivers must ensure they have at least third-party insurance

L ost Property

If you lose anything, report it immediately to the municipal police, who will issue a certificate for any insurance claim. Lost property offices *(Oficina de Objetos Perdidos)* are usually located in town halls *(ayuntamiento)* and railway stations *(estación de tren)*.

Lost passports should be reported to your nearest consulate *(see page 267)*. If you lose or have credit cards or travellers' cheques stolen go to the nearest bank, or phone the relevant emergency number.

Left Luggage

Most of the main bus and train stations have coin-operated lockers or left-luggage offices.

M aps

A useful touring map is found in the back of this book. Other good maps include **Michelin map 446**, on a scale of 1:400,000 (1 centimetre to 4 kilometres), is the clearest road map of Andalucía. **Guía Campsa** includes maps, as well as details of sights, hotels and restaurants. **Euro Tour**, 1:300,000, provides greater detail of the Costa del Sol and inland areas.

Hikers and horse-trekkers will find most useful the military maps, scale 1:50,000, produced by Spain's **Servicio Geográfico del Ejército**. A handy map of the Sierra Nevada, 1:50,000, is published by the **Federación Española de Montañismo**.

Media

Newspapers

National papers published in Madrid are available every morning. Dailies such as *El País*, *El Mundo* and *ABC* have special Andalusian editions printed in Seville. At least one local daily is published in each of Andalucía's provincial capitals. They can be very useful for finding out what events are scheduled locally and usually include emergency telephone numbers and transport information.

European newspapers are readily available on the Costa del Sol and in larger cities. Some UK dailies print editions in Spain and are distributed in the morning. Otherwise, foreign newspapers are available at midday or early afternoon.

A number of English-language publications serve the large number of expatriates living along the Mediterranean coast.

Several free newspapers come out weekly, with details of events in the expatriate community. They include *Sur in English*. The *Costa del Sol News* is a weekly newspaper sold on the newsstands.

Absolute Marbella and *Essential Marbella* are glossy monthlies devoted to the lifestyle of the rich and famous.

Television & radio

Andalucía is served by the two national state-run television channels, two Andalusian channels, several private networks and local television in many towns and villages. Satellites allow the beaming in of foreign programmes in English, Italian and other languages.

Most communities have their own FM radio stations in Spanish. Several radio stations on the Costa del Sol broadcast in English. The best is REM (Radio Europe Mediterraneo, FM 104.8), which is based in San Pedro de Alcantera .

Money

The currency of Spain is the euro, which comes in coins valued 1 euro, 2 euros, plus 50, 20, 10, 5, 2 and 1 cents. Bills are worth 5, 10, 20, 50, 100, 200 and 500 euros. Recent exchange rates are: €1 = £0.68; €1 = $1.2.

Although most major credit cards are known, the most widely used and accepted are Mastercard and Visa. Smaller establishments may be unwilling to take your Diner's or Amex card.

ATMs

ATMs (Automated Teller Machines) are often the most convenient way of obtaining money. Most banks have a hole-in-the-wall ATM with instructions in several languages. For both credit and debit cards you will need a PIN number in order to withdraw money. Most banks charge for using your card abroad.

Travellers' cheques

Travellers' cheques remain one of the safest ways of transporting your cash. Travel agencies and hotels will change currency as well as banks but it is worth checking rates – and commissions charged. You may often find that the savings banks *(cajas de ahorros)* offer a better deal than the big commercial banks. To get the most favourable rate, avoid changing small amounts at a time.

Banks have varied hours. Normal opening times are: Mon–Fri 9am–2pm and Sat 9am–1pm. During summer trading (June–September) banks do not open on Saturday. Some banks now stay open until 4pm on one or more days a week.

Important note: Unless you are importing very large sums of money, it is best to avoid transferring cash via banks. Many tourists have been left stranded for weeks, waiting for cash that inexplicably gets delayed in the pipeline. Even telexed cash can take days or weeks to arrive.

P hotography

With its wide variety of landscapes and people, Andalucía is highly photogenic. Some museums and monuments ban photography; others allow it for tourists, but not for professional photographers. Most Andalusians are very obliging if you wish to capture their image, but where possible ask permission and establish a relationship first. Nobody likes a camera thrust into their face by a stranger. **Gypsies** may be hostile and demand payment.

Professionals should have a list of all equipment ready to show customs. Film crews usually have to obtain permission to work in public places and sometimes pay a fee.

Postal Services

Post Offices Usual opening times for the *Correos* (post office) are from 9am–2pm, Mon–Fri and 9am–1pm, Sat. In larger cities, main post offices have longer business hours. More often than

BELOW: catching up on the news.

not, there are long queues at the stamp counters, but stamps can also be bought in *estancos* (they advertise themselves with a "Tabacos" sign in yellow and brown). Within Europe all letters go by air. *Aerogramas* (special airmail letters) are also available at post offices. The general information number for the postal service is 902-197 197.

You can receive mail at post offices if it is addressed to *Lista de Correos* (equivalent to Poste Restante), followed by the place name. Remember that Spaniards usually have two surnames, that of their father first with their mother's tagged on after it. This can lead to confusion with foreign names. Thus, if a letter is addressed, for example, to James Robertson Justice, it will probably be filed under "R" rather than "J".

Postboxes are bright yellow but you may also come across red postboxes; these are for express mail only.

BELOW: for home thoughts.

Public Holidays

There are a lot of public holidays. Apart from national holidays, every region and every community has its own celebrations, which usually fall on the most inconvenient day for a visitor. Remember also that if a holiday falls, for example, on a Thursday, Spaniards like to make a *puente* (bridge), meaning that they also take Friday off to create a long weekend. Many factories and offices, some restaurants and shops close during August when most of Spain, including the government, is on holiday. It is a month to be avoided if you intend to do much more than lie on a beach.

National holidays

January 1 New Year's Day (Año Nuevo)
January 6 Twelfth Night *(Día de los Reyes)*
February 28 Andalucía Day *(Día de Andalucía)*
Holy Thursday *(Jueves Santo)*, moveable feast, March or April.
Good Friday *(Viernes Santo)*, moveable feast, March or April.
May 1 Labour Day *(Fiesta del Trabajo)*
August 15 Assumption of the Virgin *(Fiesta de la Asunción)*
October 12 Columbus Day *(Día de la Hispanidad)*
November 1 All Saints' Day *(Todos los Santos)*
December 6 Constitution Day *(Día de la Constitución)*
December 8 Immaculate Conception *(Inmaculada Concepción)*
December 25 Christmas Day *(Navidad)*

Local holidays

Each town has two extra fiesta days when all businesses are closed. It is also likely you will encounter half-day opening during Semana Santa (Easter week), particularly in Seville and Málaga, and during the major fiestas, especially those of Córdoba, Jerez, Seville and Málaga.

Almería 25 August, 26 December.
Cádiz Monday after Carnival week, 7 October.
Córdoba 8 September, 24 October
Granada 2 January, 1 February, Corpus Christi
Huelva 3 August, 8 September
Jaén 11 June, 18 October.
Málaga 19 August, 8 September
Estepona 15 May, 16 July
Fuengirola 16 July, 7 October
Marbella 11 June, 19 October.
Mijas 8 September, 15 October.
Nerja 15 May, 24 June
Torremolinos 16 July, 29 September
Seville 30 May, Corpus Christi

R eligious services

In tourist areas, especially the Costa del Sol, there are churches and synagogues serving resident and visiting non-Catholics. There are also several mosques.

S tudent Travellers

Under-26s can obtain reduced rates on rail travel with the Inter-Rail card, which is valid for travel throughout Europe. The system divides Europe into five zones, Spain and Portugal representing one of those zones. For students holding an **International Student Identity Card** discounts are available on bus and rail travel and selected Iberia flights, accommodation, as well as entrance to museums, monuments and sports and cultural events.

Information can be obtained from **Inturjoven**, the Andalusian youth hostel network, at Calle Miño 24, Seville, tel: 902-510 000, www.inturjoven.com.

T elecommunications

Telex and fax facilities are available in main post offices. Telephone boxes *(cabinas)* take coins or phone cards, available from *estancos* and many newsstands. You cannot make reverse charge calls, or receive calls, from a *cabina*.

TRANSPORT

ACCOMMODATION

ACTIVITIES

A – Z

LANGUAGE

All Spanish phone numbers have nine digits.

In tourist areas in season you will find glass Portacabin structures housing small exchanges. These are handy for long-distance calls as instead of fumbling with change you pay the operator afterwards and have the added advantage of being able to pay by credit card (they are no more expensive than phone boxes). Bars also have telephones but make a surcharge. Avoid calling from hotels if at all possible, as they often treble the charge.

ABOVE: pay phones are plentiful and take coins or cards.

International calls

Dial 00, then the international code for the country you require, e.g. to Britain, 0044 + area code + number minus the initial zero; to the United States, 001 + area code + number.

Digital cell phones, European GSM standard, can be used if the "roam" feature is activated.

You can make a reversed charge call through the Spanish operator – 1009 – or by dialling the operator of your home country directly:

UK 900-99 00 44
Australia 900-99 00 61
Canada 900-990 015
Ireland 900-990 353
New Zealand 900-990 064
AT+T 900-990 011
MCI 900-990 014
Sprint 900-990 013

Useful numbers

Direct Enquires (Spanish only) 11818
International Enquiries 11825

Time Zone

Spain is on European Standard Time, which is one hour ahead of Greenwich Mean Time (UK) and six hours ahead of Eastern Standard Time (New York). The clocks go back one hour on the last Sunday in October and forward on the last Sunday of March.

Toilets

Public toilets can be found in cities and resorts and are clearly signposted and well-maintained. It may be more convenient, however, to use the *servicios* at a bar which is perfectly acceptable, even if you do not buy a drink. It's worth carrying some toilet paper with you, as many places don't provide it.

Tourist Information Offices

The official tourism site of the Junta de Andalucía is: www.andalucia.org.

For individual tourist offices see Useful Contacts below.

Useful Contacts

Algeciras

Tourist information Juan de la Cierva, s/n, tel: 965-572 636.
Bus stations Portillo (for Costa del Sol), Avenida Virgen del Carmen, 15, tel: 956-651 055; Comes (for Cádiz, Seville), San Bernado, s/n, tel 956-653 456.
Boats to North Africa Trasmediterranea, Recinto del Puerto, s/n, tel: 956-583 400, www.trasmediterranea.es.
Radio Taxis, tel: 956-654 343.
Post office José Antonio, s/n, tel: 956-588 317.

Almería

Tourist information Parque Nicolás Salmerón, s/n, tel: 950-274 355.
Airport, tel: 950-213 700.
Iberia Information, tel: 950-213 797.
Bus station Plaza de Barcelona, s/n, tel: 950-262 098.
Boats to Melilla Trasmediterranea, Parque Nicolas Salmerón, 19, tel: 950-236 155, www.trasmediterranea.es.
Post office Plaza San Juan Casinello, s/n, tel: 950-242 402.

Antequera

Tourist information Plaza de San Sebastián, 7, tel: 952-702 505.
Post Office Najera, 26, tel: 952-842 083.

Benalmádena-Costa

Tourist information Avenida Antonio Machado, 10, tel: 952-242 494.

Cádiz

Tourist information Plaza de San Juan de Dios, 11, tel: 956-241 001.
Bus station Plaza de la Hispanidad, 1, tel: 956-224 271. Los Amarillos, Avenida Ramón de Carranza, 31, tel: 956-285 852.
Teletaxi, tel: 956-286 969.
Post office Plaza de Topete, s/n, tel: 956-211 878.

ABOVE: sights and areas in cities are generally well signposted.

Córdoba

Tourist office Plaza de Juda Levi, Judería, s/n, tel: 957-200 522. Torrijos, 10 (Palacio de Congresos), tel: 957-471 235.
Bus station Plaza de las Tres Culturas, s/n, tel: 957-404 040.
Radio Taxi, tel: 957-272 374.
Post Office Cruz Conde, 15; tel: 957-478 102

El Puerto de Santa María

Tourist information Calle Luna, 22, tel: 956-542 413.
Ferry to Cádiz, summer service from San Ignacio Pier, Plaza de las Galeras Reales, s/n, tel: 956-542 475.

Estepona

Tourist information Avenida San Lorenzo, 1, tel: 952-800 913.
Bus station Avenida de España, s/n, tel: 952-800 249
Taxis, tel: 952-800 012.
Post office Calle Málaga, 6, tel: 952-800 537.

Fuengirola

Tourist information Avenida Jesús Santos Rein, 6 (near the train station), tel: 952-467 457.
Bus station Avenida Ramón y Cajal, s/n, tel: 952-475 066.
Trains to Málaga every 30 minutes.
Taxis, tel: 952-471 000.
Post office Plaza de los Chinoros, s/n, tel: 952-474 384.

Granada

Tourist office Corral del Carbón, s/n, tel: 958-221 022; also Plaza Mariana Pineda, 10, bajo, tel: 958-247 128.
Airport Tel: 958-245 200.
Iberia Plaza Isabel la Católica, 2, tel: 958-227 592.
Bus Station Avenida de los Andaluces, s/n, tel: 958-153 636
Radio Taxis, tel: 958-280 654.
Post office Puerta Real, s/n, tel: 958-224 835.

Huelva

Tourist office Avenida de Alemania, 12, tel: 959-257 403.
Bus station Doctor Rubio, 9, tel: 959-256 900.
Teletaxi, tel: 959-250 022.
Post office Avenida Tomás Domínguez, s/n, tel: 959-249 184.

Jaén

Tourist information Maestra, 13, tel: 953-190 455.
Bus station Jaén, Plaza Coca de la Piñera, s/n, tel: 953-250 106.

Jerez de la Frontera

Tourist information Plaza del Arenal, s/n, tel: 956-359 654.
Airport, tel: 956-150 000.
Bus station Cartuja, s/n, tel: 956-342 174.
Post office El Cerrón, 2, tel: 956-343 743.

Málaga

Tourist information Pasaje de Chinitas, 4, tel: 952-213 445; Paseo del Parque, s/n, tel: 952-604 410. Also at the airport, tel: 952-240 000.
Airport, tel: 952-048 804.
Iberia and flight information, tel: 952-136 166. City office, Molina Lario, 13, tel: 952-136 147.
British Airways (airport), tel: 902-111 333.
Bus station Paseo de los Tilos, s/n, tel: 952-350 061.
Radio Taxis, tel: 952-320 000.
Post Office Avenida de Andalucía, 1, tel: 952-348 431.

Marbella

Tourist information Glorieta de la Fontanilla, s/n, tel: 952-822. 818; Plaza de los Naranjos, 1, tel: 952-823 550.
Bus station Avenida del Trapiche, s/n, tel: 952-764 400.
Radio Taxis, tel: 952-774 488.
Post office Jacinto Benavente, 14, tel: 952-772 898.

Nerja

Tourist information Puerta del Mar, 4, Nerja, tel: 952-521 531.
Bus station Avenida Pescia, s/n, tel: 952-521 504.
Taxi rank, tel: 952-520 537.
Post office Almirante Ferrandiz, 6, tel: 952-521 749.

Ronda

Tourist information Plaza de España, 1, tel: 952-871 272.
Bus station Plaza Concepción, García Redondo, 2, tel: 952-871 992.
Post office Virgen de la Paz, s/n, tel: 952-872 557.

Seville

Tourist office Avenida de la Constitución, 21, tel: 954-221 404; Paseo de las Delicias, s/n, tel: 954-234 465. Also at airport, tel: 954-255 046.
Airport, tel: 954-449 000.
Iberia Avenida de la Buhaira, 8, tel: 954-988 208.
Buses Prado de San Sebastian station, Manuel Vazquez Sagastizabal, tel: 954-417 111; Plaza de

Armas station, Plaza de Armas, tel: 954-907 737.
Radio Taxis, tel: 954-675 555.
Teletaxi, tel: 954-622 222.
Post office Avenida de la Constitución, 32, tel: 954-216 476

Torre del Mar

Tourist information Avenida de Andalucía, 119, tel: 952-541 104.
Bus station Calle del Mar, s/n, tel: 952-540 936.

Torremolinos

Tourist information Plaza Blas Infante, s/n, tel: 952-379 511.
Bus station Calle Hoyo, s/n, tel: 952-382 419.
Taxis, tel: 952-389 600.
Post office Avenida Palma de Mallorca, s/n, tel: 952-384 518.

Vélez-Málaga

Bus station Avenida Vivar Tellez, s/n, tel: 952-503 162.
Taxi rank, tel: 952-500 088.
Post office Plaza San Roque, s/n, tel: 952-500 143.

W ebsites & the Internet

Internet cafés are common throughout the larger resorts on the Costa del Sol, as well as in the cities. Tourist offices will generally have a list of internet access points and in Seville's newest tourist office (on the corner of Sierpes, near Plaza Nueva) there are several machines which can be used for a half-hour period free of charge. At commercial outlets you can expect to pay approximately €3 for an hour's use.

Among the on-line information about Andalucía and Spain, the following sites are useful:
www.andalucia.org – official website of the Andalusian tourist office.
www.andalucia.com – private site devoted to information about Andalucía.
www.tourspain.es – home page for the Spanish tourist office. Includes a database of hotels.
www.okspain.org – put out by the Spanish tourist office in New York.
www.sispain.org – sponsored by the Spanish Embassy in Canada, one of the most complete sources of information about Spain.
www.parador.es – home page for the parador network.
www.renfe.es – home page of the Spanish national railway company.
www.iberia.com – official site for the Spanish national airline.

Weights & Measures

Spain has followed the **metric system** since 1971. To convert kilometres into miles divide by 1.6093; to convert metres into feet divide by 0.3048; to convert kilograms into pounds divide by 0.4536; to convert hectares into acres divide by 0.4047. To convert from imperial to metric multiply by the factor shown.

Some traditional Spanish weights and measures are still in use. These include: *fanega* (6,460 sq. metres or 1.59 acres); *arroba* (11.5 kg/25 lb); *quintal* (4 *arrobas* or 46 kg/101 lb). Farmers sell wine and olive oil by the *arroba*, referring to a wine container with a capacity of 15 to 16 litres.

What to Bring

Bring a sun hat, health insurance, first aid kit, sunglasses, anti-diarrhoea tablets, insect repellent (particularly if camping).

Pack a plug adaptor if you are bringing electrical appliances, such as an electric razor.

If you are bringing your own vehicle remember to bring car registration documents and valid insurance.

BELOW: you'll find internet cafés everywhere, even in small towns and villages.

TRANSPORT

ACCOMMODATION

ACTIVITIES

A – Z

LANGUAGE

LANGUAGE

UNDERSTANDING SPANISH

Spanish – like French, Italian, Portuguese – is a Romance language, derived from the Latin spoken by the Romans who conquered the Iberian peninsula more than 2000 years ago. The Moors who settled in the peninsula centuries later contributed a great number of new words *(see panel)*. Following the discovery of America, Spaniards took their language with them to the four corners of the globe. Today, Spanish is spoken by 250 million people in north, south and central America and parts of Africa.

In addition to Spanish, which is spoken throughout the country, some regions have a second language. Catalan (spoken in Catalonia), Valenciano (Valencia), Mallorquín (the Balearics) and Gallego (Galicia) are all Romance languages, unlike Euskera, the language of the Basques, which is notoriously complex and difficult – it is unrelated to any other European tongue. Its origins are unclear, but the most widely accepted theory is that this was an aboriginal Iberian language widely spoken on the Iberian Peninsula and best defended in the northern pocket of the Basque Country.

Unlike English, Spanish is a phonetic language: words are pronounced exactly as they are spelt, which is why it is some-what harder for Spaniards to learn English than vice versa (although Spanish distinguishes between the two genders, masculine and feminine, and the subjunctive verb form is an endless source of headaches for students). The English language is one of Britain's biggest exports to Spain. Spaniards spend millions on learning aids, language academies and sending their children to study English in the UK or Ireland, and are eager to practise their linguistic skills with foreign visitors. Even so, they will be flattered and delighted if you make the effort to communicate in Spanish. You should beware, however, of some misleading "false friends" (*see page 280*).

The Alphabet

Learning the pronunciation of the Spanish alphabet is a good idea. In particular learn how to spell out your own name. Spanish has a letter that doesn't exist in English, the ñ (pronounced "ny" as in "onion").

a = *ah*
b = *bay*
c = *thay* (strong th as in "thought")
d = *day*
e = *ay*
f = *effay*
g = *hay*
h = *ah-chay*
i = *ee*
j = *hotah*
k = *kah*
l = *ellay*
m = *emmay*
n = *ennay*
ñ = *enyay*
o = *oh*
p = *pay*
q = *koo*
r = *erray*
s = *essay*
t = *tay*
u = *oo*
v = *oobay*
w = *oobay doe-blay*
x = *ek-kiss*
y = *ee gree-ay-gah*,
z = *thay-tah*

Basic Rules

English is widely spoken in most tourist areas, but even if you speak no Spanish at all, it is worth trying to master a few simple words and phrases.

As a general rule, the accent falls on the second-to-last syllable, unless it is otherwise marked with an accent (´) or the word ends in D, L, R or Z.

Vowels in Spanish are always pronounced the same way. The double LL is pronounced like the y in "yes", the double RR is rolled, as in Scots. The H is silent in Spanish, whereas J (and G when it precedes an E or I) is pronounced like a guttural H (as if you were clearing your throat).

When addressing someone you are not familiar with, use the more formal "usted". The informal "tu" is reserved for relatives and friends.

Moorish Connections

The Moors arrived in Spain in 711, and occupied parts of the peninsula for the next eight centuries. They left behind hundreds of Arabic words, many related to farming and crops, as well as place names including those of towns (often identified by the prefix Al-, meaning "the" or Ben-, meaning "son of") and rivers (the prefix Guad- means "river").

Some of these Arabic words passed on to other languages, including French, and from there into English. Among those present in both English and Spanish are sugar (azúcar), coffee (café), apricot (albaricoque), saffron (azafrán), lemon (limón), cotton (algodón), alcohol (alcohol), karat (kilate), cipher (cifra), elixir (elixir), almanac (almanaque), zenith (cenit), and zero (cero).

Words & Phrases

Hello Hola
How are you? ¿Cómo está usted?
How much is it? ¿Cuánto es?
What is your name? ¿Cómo se llama usted?
My name is... Yo me llamo...
Do you speak English? ¿Habla inglés?
I am British/American Yo soy británico/norteamericano
I don't understand No comprendo
Please speak more slowly Hable más despacio, por favor
Can you help me? ¿Me puede ayudar?
I am looking for... Estoy buscando...
Where is...? ¿Dónde está...?

I'm sorry Lo siento
I don't know No lo se
No problem No hay problema
Have a good day Que tenga un buen día
That's it Ese es
Here it is Aquí está
There it is Allí está
Let's go Vámonos
See you tomorrow Hasta mañana
See you soon Hasta pronto
Show me the word in the book Muéstreme la palabra en el libro
At what time? ¿A qué hora?
When? ¿Cuándo?
What time is it? ¿Qué hora es?
yes sí
no no
please por favor
thank you (very much) (muchas) gracias
you're welcome de nada
excuse me perdóneme
OK bien
goodbye adiós
good evening/night buenas tardes/noches
here aquí
there allí
today hoy
yesterday ayer
tomorrow mañana (note: **mañana also means "morning")**
now ahora
later después
right away ahora mismo
this morning esta mañana
this afternoon esta tarde
this evening esta tarde
tonight esta noche

On Arrival

I want to get off at... Quiero bajarme en...
Is there a bus to the museum? ¿Hay un autobús al museo?
What street is this? ¿Qué calle es ésta?
Which line do I take for...? ¿Qué línea cojo para...?
How far is...? ¿A qué distancia está...?
airport aeropuerto
customs aduana
train station estación de tren
bus station estación de autobuses

metro station estación de metro
bus autobús
bus stop parada de autobús
platform apeadero
ticket billete
return ticket billete de ida y vuelta
hitch-hiking auto-stop
toilets servicios
This is the hotel address Ésta es la dirección del hotel
I'd like a (single/double) room Quiero una habitación (sencilla/doble)
... with shower con ducha
... with bath con baño
... with a view con vista
Does that include breakfast? ¿Incluye desayuno?
May I see the room? ¿Puedo ver la habitación?
washbasin lavabo
bed cama
key llave
elevator ascensor
air conditioning aire acondicionado

On the Road

Where is the spare wheel? ¿Dónde está la rueda de repuesto?
Where is the nearest garage? ¿Dónde está el taller más próximo?

EMERGENCIES

Help! ¡Socorro!
Stop! ¡Alto!
Call a doctor Llame a un médico
Call an ambulance Llame a una ambulancia
Call the police Llame a la policia
Call the fire brigade Llame a los bomberos
Where's the nearest telephone? ¿Dónde hay un teléfono?
Where's the nearest hospital? ¿Dónde está el hospital más próximo?
I am sick Estoy enfermo
I have lost my passport/purse He perdido mi pasaporte/bolso

TRANSPORT
ACCOMMODATION
ACTIVITIES
A – Z
LANGUAGE

Our car has broken down *Nuestro coche se ha averiado*
I want to have my car repaired *Quiero que reparen mi coche*
It's not your right of way *Usted no tiene prioridad*
I think I must have put diesel in my car by mistake *Me parece haber echado gasoil por error*
the road to... *la carretera a...*
left *izquierda*
right *derecha*
straight on *derecho*
far *lejos*
near *cerca*
opposite *frente a*
beside *al lado de*
car park *aparcamiento*
over there *allí*
at the end *al final*
on foot *a pie*
by car *en coche*
town map *mapa de la ciudad*
road map *mapa de carreteras*
street *calle*
square *plaza*
give way *ceda el paso*
exit *salida*
dead end *calle sin salida*
wrong way *dirección prohibida*
no parking *prohibido aparcar*
motorway *autovía*
toll highway *autopista*
toll *peaje*
speed limit *límite de velocidad*
petrol station *gasolinera*
petrol *gasolina*
unleaded *sin plomo*
diesel *gasoil*
water/oil *agua/aceite*
air *aire*
puncture *pinchazo*
bulb *bombilla*
wipers *limpia-parabrisas*

On the Telephone

How do I make an outside call? *¿Cómo hago una llamada exterior?*
What is the area code? *¿Cuál es el prefijo?*
I want to make an international (local) call *Quiero hacer una llamada internacional (local)*
I'd like an alarm call for 8 tomorrow morning *Quiero que me despierten a las ocho de la mañana*

Hello? *¿Dígame?*
Who's calling? *¿Quién llama?*
Hold on, please *Un momento, por favor*
I can't hear you *No le oigo*
Can you hear me? *¿Me oye?*
He/she is not here *No está aquí*
The line is busy *La línea está ocupada*
I must have dialled the wrong number *Debo haber marcado un número equivocado*

Shopping

Where is the nearest bank? *¿Dónde está el banco más próximo?*
I'd like to buy *Quiero comprar*
How much is it *¿Cuánto es?*
Do you accept credit cards? *¿Aceptan tarjeta?*
I'm just looking *Sólo estoy mirando*
Have you got...? *¿Tiene...?*
I'll take it *Me lo llevo*
I'll take this one/that one *Me llevo éste/ese*
What size is it? *¿Que talla es?*
Anything else? *¿Otra cosa?*
size (clothes) *talla*
small *pequeño*
large *grande*
cheap *barato*
expensive *caro*
enough *suficiente*
too much *demasiado*
a piece *una pieza*
each *cada una/la pieza/la unidad (eg. melones, 100 ptas la unidad)*
bill *la factura* (shop), *la cuenta* (restaurant)
bank *banco*
bookshop *librería*
chemist *farmacia*
hair-dressers *peluquería*
jewellers *joyería*
post office *correos*
shoe shop *zapatería*
department store *grandes almacenes*
fresh *fresco*
frozen *congelado*
organic *biológico*
flavour *sabor*
basket *cesta*
bag *bolsa*
bakery *panadería*

butcher's *carnicería*
cake shop *pastelería*
fishmonger's *pescadería*
grocery *verdulería*
tobacconist *estanco*
market *mercado*
supermarket *supermercado*
junk shop *tienda de segunda mano*

Sightseeing

mountain *montaña*
hill *colina*
valley *valle*
river *río*
lake *lago*
lookout *mirador*
city *ciudad*
small town, village *pueblo*
old town *casco antiguo*
monastery *monasterio*
convent *convento*
cathedral *catedral*
church *glesia*
palace *palacio*
hospital *hospital*
town hall *ayuntamiento*
nave *nave*
statue *estátua*
fountain *fuente*
staircase *escalera*
tower *torre*
castle *castillo*
Iberian *ibérico*
Phoenician *fenicio*
Roman *romano*
Moorish *árabe*
Romanesque *románico*
Gothic *gótico*
museum *museo*
art gallery *galería de arte*
exhibition *exposición*
tourist information office *oficina de turismo*
free *gratis*
open *abierto*
closed *cerrado*
every day *diario/todos los días*
all year *todo el año*
all day *todo el día*
swimming pool *piscina*
to book *reservar*

Dining Out

In Spanish, *el menú* is not the main menu, but a fixed menu offered each day at a lower price.

The main menu is *la carta.*
breakfast *desayuno*
lunch *almuerzo/comida*
dinner *cena*
meal *comida*
first course *primer plato*
main course *plato principal*
made to order *por encargo*
drink included *incluida bebida/ consumición*
wine list *carta de vinos*
the bill *la cuenta*
fork *tenedor*
knife *cuchillo*
spoon *cuchara*
plate *plato*
glass *vaso*
wine glass *copa*
napkin *servilleta*
ashtray *cenicero*
waiter, please! *camarero, por favor*

Menu Decoder

Snacks

pan **bread**
bollo **bun/roll**
mantequilla **butter**
mermelada **jam**
confitura **jam**
pimienta **pepper**
sal **salt**
azúcar **sugar**
huevos **eggs**
... cocidos **boiled, cooked ...**
... con beicon **with bacon**
... con jamón **with ham**
... fritos **fried**
... revueltos **scrambled**
yogúr **yoghurt**
tostada **toast**
sandwich **sandwich in square slices of bread**
bocadillo **filled bread roll**

Main Courses

Carne/Meat
buey **beef**
carne picada **ground meat**
cerdo **pork**
chivo **kid**
chorizo **sausage seasoned with paprika**
chuleta **chop**
cochinillo **suckling pig**
conejo **rabbit**
cordero **lamb**

costilla **rib**
entrecot **beef rib steak**
filete **steak**
abalí **wild boar**
jamón **ham**
jamón cocido **cooked ham**
jamón serrano **cured ham**
lomo **loin**
morcilla **black pudding**
pierna **leg**
riñones **kidneys**
sesos **brains**
salchichón **sausage**
solomillo **fillet steak**
ternera **veal or young beef**
lengua **tongue**
a la brasa **charcoal grilled**
al horno **roast**
a la plancha **grilled**
asado **roast**
bien hecho **well done**
en salsa **in sauce**
en su punto **medium**
estofado **stew**
frito **fried**
parrillada **mixed grill**
pinchito **skewer**
poco hecho **rare**
relleno **stuffed**

Fowl

codorniz **quail**
faisán **pheasant**
pavo **turkey**
pato **duck**
perdiz **partridge**
pintada **guinea fowl**
pollo **chicken**

Pescado/Fish

almeja **clam**
anchoas **anchovies**
anguila **eel**
atún **tuna**
bacalao **cod**
besugo **red bream**
bogavante **lobster**
boquerones **fresh anchovies**
caballa **mackerel**
calamar **squid**
cangrejo **crab**
caracola **sea snail**
cazón **dogfish**
centollo **spider crab**
chopito **baby cuttlefish**
cigala **Dublin Bay prawn/ scampi**
dorada **gilt head bream**

I am a vegetarian *Soy vegetariano/vegetariana*
I am on a diet *Estoy de régimen*
What do you recommend? *¿Qué recomienda?*
Do you have local specialities? *¿Hay especialidades locales?*
I'd like to order *Quiero pedir*
That is not what I ordered *Ésto no es lo que he pedido*
May I have more wine? *¿Más vino, por favor?*
Enjoy your meal *Buen provecho*

fritura **mixed fry**
gamba **shrimp/prawn**
jibia **cuttlefish**
langosta **spiny lobster**
langostino **large prawn**
lenguado **sole**
lubina **sea bass**
mariscada **mixed shellfish**
mariscos **shellfish**
mejillón **mussel**
merluza **hake**
mero **grouper**
ostión **Portuguese oyster**
ostra **oyster**
peregrina **scallop**
pescadilla **small hake**
pez espada **swordfish**
pijota **hake**
pulpo **octopus**
rape **monkfish**
rodaballo **turbot**
salmón **salmon**
salmonete **red mullet**
sardina **sardine**
trucha **trout**

Vegetables/Cereals/ Salads

ajo **garlic**
alcachofa **artichoke**
apio **celery**
arroz **rice**
berenjena **eggplant/ aubergine**
cebolla **onion**
champiñon **mushroom**
col **cabbage**
coliflor **cauliflower**
crudo **raw**
ensalada **salad**
espárrago **asparagus**

NUMBERS

0	cero
1	uno
2	dos
3	tres
4	cuatro
5	cinco
6	seis
7	siete
8	ocho
9	nueve
10	diez
11	once
12	doce
13	trece
14	catorce
15	quince
16	dieciseis
17	diecisiete
18	dieciocho
19	diecinueve
20	viente
21	veintiuno
30	treinta
40	cuarenta
50	cincuenta
60	sesenta
70	setenta
80	ochenta
90	noventa
100	cien
200	doscientos
500	quinientos
1,000	mil
10,000	diez mil
1,000,000	un millón

espinaca **spinach**
garbanzo **chick pea**
guisante **pea**
haba **broad bean**
habichuela **bean**
judía **green bean**
lechuga **lettuce**
lenteja **lentil**
maíz **corn/maize**
menestra **cooked mixed vegetables**
patata **potato**
pepino **cucumber**
pimiento **pepper**
puerro **leek**
rábano **radish**
seta **wild mushroom**
tomate **tomato**
verduras **vegetables**
zanahoria **carrot**

Fruit and Desserts

fruta **fruit**
aguacate **avocado**
albaricoque **apricot**
cereza **cherry**
ciruela **plum**
frambuesa **raspberry**
fresa **strawberry**
granada **pomegranate**
higo **fig**
limón **lemon**
mandarina **tangerine**
manzana **apple**
melocotón **peach**
melón **melon**
naranja **orange**
pasa **raisin**
pera **pear**
piña **pineapple**
plátano **banana**
pomelo **grapefruit**
sandía **watermelon**
postre **dessert**
tarta **cake**
pastel **pie**
helado **ice cream**
natilla **custard**
flan **caramel custard**
queso **cheese**

Liquid Refreshment

coffee café
... black solo
... with milk con leche
... decaffeinated descafeinado
sugar azúcar
tea té
milk leche
mineral water agua mineral
fizzy con gas
non-fizzy sin gas
juice (fresh) zumo (natural)
cold fresco/frío
hot caliente
beer cerveza
... bottled en botella
... on tap de barril
soft drink refresco
diet drink bebida "light"
with ice con hielo
wine vino
red wine vino tinto
white blanco
rosé rosado
dry seco
sweet dulce

house wine vino de la casa
sparkling wine vino espumoso
half litre medio litro
quarter litre cuarto de litro
cheers! salud

Days and Months

Days of the Week

Monday lunes
Tuesday martes
Wednesday miércoles
Thursday jueves
Friday viernes
Saturday sábado
Sunday domingo

Months

January enero
February febrero
March marzo
April abril
May mayo
June junio
July julio
August agosto
September septiembre
October octubre
November noviembre
December diciembre

Seasons

Spring primavera
Summer verano
Autumn otoño
Winter invierno

False Amigos

"False friends" are words that look like English words but mean something different. Such as:

Simpático **friendly**
Tópico **a cliché**
Actualmente **currently**
Sensible **sensitive**
Disgustado **angry**
Embarazada **pregnant**
Suplir **substitute**
Informal **unreliable (to describe a person)**
Rape **monkfish**
Billón **a million million**
Soportar **tolerate**

FURTHER READING

General Background

As I Walked Out One Midsummer Morning, by Laurie Lee (Penguin). The author's adventures as a young man crossing Spain on foot in the 1930s.

Handbook for Travellers in Spain, by Richard Ford. (Centaur Press, 1966).

Inside Andalucía, by David Baird (Santana). Entertaining yet profound – and brilliantly written.

South From Granada, by Gerald Brenan (Cambridge University Press, 1988). An account of the author's experiences living in an Andalusian village in the 1920s,.

Tales of the Alhambra, by Washington Irving (available in numerous editions). The 19th-century American author's account of Moorish legends is still enjoyable.

The Bible in Spain, by George Borrow. First published 1842. Eccentric, opinionated and entertaining.

The Face of Spain. Gerald Brenan's grim view of an impoverished post-war Spain.

The Road from Ronda, by Alastair Boyd. Vivid account of a horse-ride through the Serrania de Ronda.

Driving Over Lemons, by Chris Stewart (followed by a sequel: *A Parrot in the Pepper Tree*). Amusing autobiographical account of an Englishman living the good life in the Alpujarras (Granada).

Death in the Afternoon, by Ernest Hemingway (Cape). Hemingway's explanation of the bull-fight, although much maligned by purists, is still informative and gripping.

In Search of the Firedance, by James Woodall (Sinclair-Stevenson). Flamenco and its origins.

Or I'll Dress You in Mourning, by Larry Collins and Dominique Lapierre. Brilliant insights into Spain's post-Civil War hardships which moulded the Andalusian matador El Cordobés.

White Wall of Spain, by Allen Josephs (Iowa State University

FEEDBACK

We do our best to ensure the information in our books is as accurate and up-to-date as possible. The books are updated on a regular basis, using local contacts, who painstakingly add, amend and correct as required. However, some mistakes and omissions are inevitable and we are ultimately reliant on our readers to put us in the picture.
We would welcome your feedback on any details related to your experiences using the book "on the road". Maybe we recommended a hotel that you liked (or another that you didn't), as well as interesting new attractions, or facts and figures you have found out about the country itself. The more details you can give us (particularly with regard to addresses, e-mails and telephone numbers), the better. We will acknowledge all contributions, and we'll offer an Insight Guide to the best letters received.

Please write to us at:
Insight Guides
PO Box 7910
London SE1 1WE
United Kingdom
Or send e-mail to:
insight@apaguide.co.uk

Press). A thoughtful look at Andalusian folk culture.

Other Insight Guides

Europe is comprehensively covered by over 400 books published by Apa Publications. They come in a variety of series, each tailored to suit different needs.

Insight Guides, the main series of guides that Apa publishes, provide readers with a cultural background, plus comprehensive travel coverage linked to photography and maps. The series includes titles on Spain, Northern Spain, Mallorca and Ibiza.

Destinations in Insight's highly successful **City Guides** series include Barcelona and Madrid.

Apa Publications also publishes itinerary- based **Insight Pocket Guides**, written by local hosts. They come complete with a pull-out map. Titles include Barcelona, Valencia, Costa del Sol, Madrid, Costa Blanca and Bilbao and Northwest Spain.

Insight Compact Guides give you the facts about a destination in a very digestible form. Titles include Barcelona, Costa Brava, Gran Canaria, Mallorca and Tenerife

ART & PHOTO CREDITS

GENERAL INDEX

Southern Spain Wildlife Areas

0   25 km
0   25 miles